About the Author

Taner Akçam was born in the province of Kars-Ardahan in the northeast of Turkey and became interested in Turkish politics at an early age. He was very active in the student movement of the generation of 1968 and, as the editor-in-chief of a political journal, was arrested in 1976 and sentenced to ten years' imprisonment. He managed to escape one year later and fled to Germany.

He received his Ph.D. from Hanover University with a dissertation titled, *Turkish Nationalism and the Armenian Genocide: On the Background of the Military Tribunals in Istanbul Between 1919 and 1922*. He has since lectured and published extensively on this topic, with ten books and half a dozen articles in Turkish and German.

From 1988 to 2000, he held the position of Research Scientist in Sociology at the Hamburg Institute for Social Research. His scholarly interests focused on violence and torture in Turkey, a subject on which he has published a number of books and articles. He has also written extensively on Turkish national identity.

He has twice been Visiting Scholar at the Armenian Research Center, University of Michigan–Dearborn. He was Visiting Professor of Sociology at the University of Michigan–Ann Arbor, 2000–2001 and since then has been Visiting Professor of History at the University of Minnesota–Twin Cities.

From Empire to Republic

Turkish Nationalism and the Armenian Genocide

Taner Akçam

Zed Books

LONDON & NEW YORK

From Empire to Republic: Turkish Nationalism and the Armenian Genocide
was first published in 2004 by
Zed Books Ltd, 7 Cynthia Street, London N1 9JF, UK and
Room 400, 175 Fifth Avenue, New York, NY 10010, USA
www.zedbooks.co.uk

Cover design by Andrew Corbett
Designed and set in 10/12 pt Times New Roman
by Long House, Cumbria, UK
Printed and bound in Malta by Gutenberg Press

Distributed in the USA exclusively by Palgrave Macmillan, a division of
St Martin's Press, LLC, 175 Fifth Avenue, New York, NY 10010

A catalogue record for this book
is available from the British Library

US Cataloging-in-Publication Data
is available from the Library of Congress

ISBN   Hb 1 84277 526 X
       Pb 1 84277 527 8

Contents

To Jan Philipp Reemstma

Preface

I remember when, during the early 1980s, I was offered the opportunity to meet with the ASALA,[1] I became extremely angry. I recall even yelling at the hapless individual who had made the proposal: 'Don't you ever bring up this subject again, nor do I want to hear the name of that organization from your lips. It's an issue that's being put out there by some dark forces and I have nothing to say to this organization, which is an extension of these dark forces.' (The term 'dark forces' was commonly used to refer to foreign secret services and foreign powers.)

It was actually the typical reflexive response of a Turkish intellectual's struggle to deal with the issue, which was regarded as very complicated and troublesome. One preferred to keep oneself aloof from the issue, especially in light of 'the cooperation of Armenians with the imperialist powers.' I can see clearly today that the real problem lay neither with the type of organization ASALA was nor with the question of whether Armenians had 'made common cause with imperialist powers.' The real problem was that the subject referred to as the 'Armenian Problem' occupied such a perverse place in our mind. The subject was so foreign to our way of thinking and the way we viewed the world (our *Weltanschauung)* that to approach it seriously meant risking all of the concepts or models we had used to explain our world and ourselves. Our entrenched belief systems constituted an obstacle to understanding the subject. I refer to this as a 'fear of confronting' the issue.

It is fair to say that political parties and even individuals with diametrically opposed ideas nevertheless maintain a common mindset. They perceive the world and themselves with the same worldview. We can exemplify this mindset, which has such a fear of examining the Armenian Genocide, thus: 'The Ottoman Empire was the target of divisive maneuvers by the Western imperialists. Turks established their independent state by defending the last bit of territory they held in their power. The Armenians and Greeks were local collaborators with the imperialist forces in support of their expansionary aims and wanted to partition Anatolia.'

The common symbolic use of Mustafa Kemal Atatürk by disparate schools of thought and politics is an interesting example of the widespread sharing of this mindset in Turkey. Writing to his father in 1971, Deniz Gezmiş, one of the leaders of the radical youth movement of 1968,[2] stated in a letter: 'I'm grateful to you because you raised me with Kemalist principles...I've been hearing stories about the war for [Turkish] Independence since I was little...We're Turkey's second-generation independence warriors.' The generals who had Gezmiş executed for insurgency did so on the grounds that he had acted 'against the principles of Atatürk.' It is clearly not possible to find a place for the Armenian Genocide of 1915 within this atmosphere and frame of mind. Turks and Armenians have developed a historical account of events that is completely at odds with each other's.

The problem is not limited to the history of Turkish–Armenian relations. This trend is epidemic in almost all historiography of the end of the 19th and the beginning of the 20th centuries in the Balkans and the Middle East. This period, which has been defined as the transition from empire to nation-states, constituted a major transformation, with the breakup of the peoples who occupied these regions. I am referring not just to the breaking apart of peoples from one another, but also to a breaking away from one's own history. The histories of all the different cultures and religions occupying this large territory have been constructed more or less through this same nationalistic perspective. Nation-states developed different and separate histories in order each to create a common past, because territory is not enough to make a population homogeneous. In addition to the ethnic–cultural–religious, that is, objective, criteria for establishing nationhood, a nation needs a common memory. Collective memory and history are the building blocks of the 'imagined' nation and the ensuing real nation-state. History has to be written in a unique way to fit this aggregate of people, who will soon remember themselves as being one, both in happiness and distress. As stated boldly by Ernest Renan, 'a nation could only be formed by the distortion of its past. It is impossible to form a nation without distorting its past.'[3] 'The most common form of distortion is "forgetting."'[4]

Whenever one attempts to rewrite history based on this collective memory, it is almost a requirement that one should omit or redefine other nations. This means that one's own history must be put in a context where other nations emerge as alien or the 'other.' Consequently, common histories of nationalities that had lived together for centuries were deconstructed and these same nationalities became detached from one another. The new history embodied one set of remembrances in opposition to those of others. We can say that this itself poses a serious impediment to the solution of many contemporary problems. Furthermore, the prevalence of globalization today means that nations have less and less opportunity to live in isolation from one another.

The following question is in dire need of an answer. Instead of remembering this period as the demise of an empire and the emergence of separate nation-states, and instead of writing their respective histories as the histories of rival nation-states, is it possible to reread this period with a common historical perspective? Can we reread the history as one evolving between the Ottoman state and its citizens? It is obvious that Ottoman citizens of Armenian origin experienced this history far differently than Muslim citizens, but this should not be an obstacle for a new historical perspective. This book should be understood as a struggle for such an understanding and the product of a wish to read the transitional period from imperial state to nation-state as a history in which different nationalities comprised elements of a common history, rather than separate histories.

There is one other consideration that I would like to express with this book. Speaking openly about the Armenian Genocide in Turkish society, which means incorporating the Armenian Genocide into Turkish historical writing, has a direct impact on pushing Turkey towards becoming a truly democratic state. Unfortunately there is not yet enough awareness in Turkey of the positive and propelling effect that incorporating the narratives not only of Armenians but also of other ethnic–religious groups would have on democratization. Only nation-states that are at peace with their pasts and all their citizens can build futures based on democratic principles. Moreover, by eliminating the history of these various groups from its national narrative, Turkey has deprived itself of a rich and vibrant part of its own history.

The individual to whom I have dedicated this book, Jan Philipp Reemstma, is the Executive Director of the Hamburg Institute for Social Research. At a time when I had not yet received a doctorate, he accepted me into the institute and changed the direction of my life. He provided both emotional and material support for the research and work I did between 1988 and 2000. The more than ten books and numerous articles which I have managed to publish are the product of his encouragement and support. For these reasons he occupies a most important place in my life. I give immeasurable and heartfelt thanks to him.

In the publication of this book I had the support of several remarkable individuals. My special thanks go to the directors and staff of the Zoryan Institute. I would like to thank Greg Sarkissian, its president, who provided unstintingly the facilities and resources of the institute, and has encouraged me in my research. The deep belief that bringing the people of Armenia and

Turkey together is an indispensable element for the peace and prosperity of the region has drawn us very close together. I want to express special thanks to George Shirinian, the Director of the Zoryan Institute, whose tireless editing, challenging questions, and overseeing of the whole publication process helped make this book a reality. Vahakn Dadrian, its Director of Genocide Research, went over each page with a fine-tooth comb, making important critical analyses, despite undergoing heart surgery during the process. Müge Göçek gave me invaluable critical insight into how to put the ideas contained in this book within a general framework. I am also indebted to the many individuals who are not specifically named here, who provided important critical observations while I was preparing this book. Any shortcomings, however, are solely my responsibility.

Taner Akçam
Minneapolis
November 2003

NOTES

1. Armenian Secret Army for the Liberation of Armenia, an organization which was actively engaged in bombings and shootings, especially of Turkish diplomats abroad, aimed at bringing international attention to the recognition of the Armenian Genocide.
2. Gezmiş, who fought to topple the Turkish government by force, was executed for his involvement in armed struggle against the state.
3. Ernest Renan in Ulrich Schneckener, *Das Recht auf Selbstbestimmung, Ethno-nationale und internationale Politik* (Hamburg 1996), p. 26.
4. Ernest Renan quoted in Gary Smith, 'Arbeit am Vergessen.' In Gary Smith and Hinderk M. Emrich, eds, *Vom Nutzen des Vergessens* (Berlin, 1996), p. 15.

Introduction

One of the most significant features of Turkey's transition from Empire to Republic involved the development of two historical narratives that continue to shape the political attitudes of the Republic's elites. On the one hand, there is the story of the partition of the Empire among the Great Powers, which ended with its total collapse and disintegration. The process of partition created a feeling of struggling to survive against the West and caused very strong anti-Western sentiments among the Turkish ruling elite. On the other hand, there is the story of persecutions, massacres and, especially in the case of the Armenians, the annihilation of different ethnic and religious groups. This story was mostly justified by the Ottoman ruling elite as a response to the activities of its subjects which they believed contributed to a growing danger that the Empire could collapse and be partitioned. Today we can hardly find scholarly works that cover both stories as part of the same history. But without dealing with both aspects of this issue, we can never understand the history of the Ottoman Empire and especially today's problems in Turkey.

These two interrelated narratives have helped create a legacy that, whether consciously or subconsciously, is proving a formidable obstacle to the need for a national renewal through a process of democratization. Unless these two different aspects of modern Turkish history and their strong interrelationship are sufficiently understood and appreciated, one cannot grasp the ambiguities and contradictions besetting Turkish national and international politics. Turkey today still behaves according to the legacies of this double history: with great suspicion towards the West and towards the democratic reform demands of its civil society. The modalities of modern Turkish nationalism, in a sense, embody these fluctuations and variations in attitudes *vis-à-vis* the West, and Europe in particular. The fact is that these modalities cannot be entirely divorced from an acute national awareness that Europe was deeply involved in the processes that led both to

1

the demise and the partition of the Ottoman Empire, and also to the massacres and political annihilation of its subject peoples, which culminated in the genocidal fate of the Armenian subjects of the Empire. What follows is a brief review of the phases through which modern Turkey has been trying to cope with these problems.

Turkey is currently in the midst of a tumultuous transition affecting its social, political, economic and cultural structure. In describing the process as 'transitional,' we must define what it is that Turkey is changing from, and where it is headed. It is emerging from the legacy of its Ottoman past and is still on its way to becoming a normal, democratic nation-state by Western social and political standards. One of the most apparent reasons for this transition is the clear and compulsory demand by the European Union for political and economic structural reform. In economic terms, these reforms focus on establishing a standard free-market economy. In political terms, the reforms focus on establishing a democratic and parliamentary system in which a high premium is placed upon several types of freedom, notably freedom of thought, freedom of expression, and freedom of dissent.

The Turkish state remains under the influence and control of a civil–military bureaucratic elite, which has been institutionalized since the state's founding. One of the main conflicts within Turkey is between the duly elected body and the *de facto* body in power, namely the military–bureaucratic elite. In more general terms, the main conflict is between society and the state, which is controlled by this elite.

The Republic of Turkey was established in the early 1920s by the Ottoman military–bureaucratic elite. After the Second World War, this elite decided to share power with the democratically elected political parties, as a result of Turkey's decision to join the West. Since the 1950s, when civil society increased its demands for more liberalization, with each successive military coup—1960, 1971 and 1980—the elite has taken back more and more power under its control. The National Security Council (NSC) is the symbolic constitutional organ of this control and, since the military coup of 1980, has become entrenched as the real power within the state. The NSC is not only a consultative but also an executive body, with thousands of departments and employees. The NSC retains the right to supervise, inspect, and coordinate the activities of all ministries. Moreover, the NSC is constitutionally entitled to appoint the board members of major state institutions, including those concerned with education and the media. It is therefore no coincidence that the largest controversy in Turkey today and for the foreseeable future, regarding its relationship with the European Union, is the role of the NSC and its control of the state and civil society.

The elections in November 2002 marked an important turning point in the state–society relationship. It was the first time in Turkish history that a political party entirely outside the civil–military bureaucracy—Adalet ve Kalkınma Partisi, the Justice and Development Party (AKP)—had come to power. The prevailing misconception in the West is that the AKP is an Islamic fundamentalist party. This idea was initially promoted by the secular military–bureaucratic elite in Ankara to legitimize its authority. The establishment of an Islamic state, however, has never been on the AKP's political agenda. In many respects, the AKP is actually comparable to the Republican Party in the US, or the Christian Democrats in Europe, and its progression into power aims to merge Islam with a Western political structure. Such a successful merger would mark the first time that the divergent paths of Islam and modernity (and Western-style parliamentary democracy), which split in the nineteenth century, had been reconciled.

In a sense, this agenda is a breakthrough against the cliché in the West that an Islamic society has only two options: either to adopt secular authoritarianism, mostly under military control, or to convert into Islamic fundamentalism under the control of Islamic clergy. The AKP has not only refuted Samuel Huntington's famous thesis—which has become fashionable, especially after September 11—of a clash of civilizations, and demonstrated the compatibility between Islam and Western political norms, but it has also set the stage for Turkey's rapid transformation toward Western democratization. The future of this transformation depends on how the power struggle between the AKP and the military–bureaucratic elite plays out. The civil–military bureaucratic elite, which holds Ankara within its grip, will not likely voluntarily divest itself of power in favor of those who are democratically elected.

On this point, I cannot emphasize enough the importance of Western political policy towards Turkey. If Turkey's authoritarian state structure under the control of a civil–military bureaucratic elite has managed to maintain its existence through the years, it is because of external rather than internal factors. After World War Two, Turkey successfully entered into the Western European 'camp' and managed to maintain its authoritarian structure with little change, by virtue of the Cold War. Throughout its republican history, and particularly after the 1960s, the civil–military bureaucratic elite, with the aid of Western powers, has suppressed any steps taken towards democratization in Turkey. It is the supreme irony that the West, which holds democracy and human rights as its *raison d'être,* nevertheless has managed to become both a defender of Turkey's authoritarian–bureaucratic system and its primary support in destroying any moves made domestically towards democracy and human rights. The more cynical reader may feel that, when one considers all the authoritarian regimes the US has supported—for example, South Korea, Suharto in Indonesia, Pinochet in Chile, Mobutu in Zaïre, the Shah in Iran, Diem in South Vietnam, Somoza in Nicaragua—it is not a matter of irony. The military coups that have become a habit in Turkey, occurring roughly once a decade, and which have resulted in the repeated destruction of domestic democratic movements, could not have taken place without express agreement between Turkey's authoritarian-bureaucracy and the West. This alliance, which formed behind the principle of 'fighting against Communism,' continued without a hitch until the fall of the Soviet Union.

Today, Turkey faces a difficulty. With the end of the Soviet Union, one of the most important factors behind Western support for the Turkish Republic has effectively disappeared. The paradigm of Turkey being a bastion against the Soviet Union defined Turkey's place within the Western world from the beginning of the Cold War. With the new world order, Turkey must redefine its place within the region and the world.

The emergence of the Turkish state in 1923 was the product of four specific factors: the Great Powers' partition plans for Anatolia; Pan-Islamism and Turkic expansionism, independence movements of different ethnic groups within the Ottoman Empire, and the Bolshevik Revolution of 1917. These four factors determined not only the emergence of the Turkish Republic, but also all political boundaries in the Caucasus and the Middle East. These four factors also marked the end of the Eastern Question, which had dominated European diplomacy throughout the 19th and early 20th centuries. The 'question' was how the territory of the weakening Ottoman Empire was to be distributed among the Great Powers and various local nationalities. With the collapse of the Soviet Union, the Eastern Question returned to the forefront of political concerns in the region, and the situation is now exacerbated by American military and political intervention. Boundaries concerns and the future of nation-states that are now struggling to retrieve lands lost as a result of the conclusion of the Eastern Question in the early 1920s, are placed back into question.

The founding of Turkey in 1923 was an answer to the Great Powers' efforts to resolve the Eastern Question. The rapid decline of the Ottoman Empire throughout the 19th and early 20th centuries had forced Ottoman-Turkish rulers to decide on a strategy for rescuing the situation. Their decision was to expand the Empire towards the Turko-Muslim nations in the East. As a result of the defeat of the Ottoman Empire during the First World War, however, these expansionist efforts were abandoned.

Instead, the concept of a Muslim–Turkic Empire was replaced in the minds of the Turkish rulers by the idea of nation-states based on specific geographic boundaries. Misak-ı Milli, the National Pact that specifies the boundaries that surround today's Turkey, was based not on the ethno-cultural distinctions in the area, but purely on geographic considerations. The terminology of the National Pact was used to define and reclaim the remaining territories of the Ottoman Empire of 1918 that had not already been occupied by England or France. The proclamation of the Republic and the National Pact were fundamental breaks with the Ottoman Empire. This transformation from Empire to Republic emerged from pragmatic, *ad hoc* decision-making, without a fundamental analysis or serious understanding of previous expansionist policies. The debates in the emerging Turkish parliament during 1921–22 over the meaning of Misak-ı Milli, and the various speeches of Mustafa Kemal Atatürk, founder of Turkey, on Pan-Turkism and Pan-Islamism which reflect confusion over national boundaries and tension between the imperial tradition and the new nation-state, illustrate the *ad hoc* nature of this decision-making.

With the collapse of the Soviet Union, the idea of once again maintaining strong influence over the Turkic peoples from the Balkans to Central Asia surfaced on Turkey's agenda. Beginning in the early 1990s, a tendency has developed for Turkey to view its foreign policy from the perspective of a 19th century empire. The words of former prime minister Süleyman Demirel—'A Turkish world which will stretch from the Adriatic to Central Asia'—reflect the seriousness of these great-power fantasies. As a result, Turkish state policy has deviated from the principles of modern nation-statehood and citizenship based on universal rights, and rather has formulated its policies based on ethnic and religious kinship. The Muslim-Turkic majority in Turkey, the Turkomen in northern Iraq, the Cherkess and the Azeris in the Caucasus are the focus of these policies. The Turkish state now makes distinctions between citizens of Turkish descent and Turkish citizens of Armenian, Kurdish or other descent, categorizing the latter as ethnic aliens or external threats. This behavior clearly contradicts the founding principles of the Republic and the concept of a democratic nation-state.

The Ottoman-Turkish response to the Eastern Question was not only to pursue the goal of being a great power in the region. At the same time, this question created a strong fear of the demise of the Empire. With the decline of the Soviet Union, the fear has re-emerged that Turkey could once again become vulnerable to external influences, particularly to international decisions to partition Anatolia. Thus, Turkey views recent developments in the region as the legacy of the Eastern Question, which also partially explains Turkey's reaction to the US's policy towards Iraq in 2003.

Today, Turkey vacillates between the poles of being a great power and deep fear for its own existence. Its natural reaction has been to pull in its horns, to go into a defensive posture, and to treat every situation as a problem of vital security. The result of this posture is a desire to strengthen the authoritarian structures of the state. I deal with these issues and the consequences for Turkey in Chapter 1.

Because of the end of the Cold War, there is an international political struggle about the new world order. The impact of these concerns should be understood within the context of a particular pattern which emerged in the Middle East during the First and Second World Wars: the shifting of state boundaries, the unilateral redrawing of borders, and the emergence of new states. If we extrapolate on this pattern, we can foresee that the result for the Middle East after the Cold War will be the same. One significant characteristic on both sides of the conflict was the continuous support from the US and USSR of authoritarian regimes in the Middle East. Now, with the thawing of Cold War tensions, states in the Middle East that were once under the control of the USSR are now susceptible to US influence. It should not come as a surprise that the focus of this new period centers on Iraq and Syria, both of which were supported heavily by the USSR during the Cold War. It is foreseeable that this trend will also penetrate surrounding authoritarian states which were supported by the United States (for example, Egypt, Saudi Arabia and Turkey.) In a sense, these authoritarian regimes, originally supported but now criticized by the US, reflect a conflict of America with itself.

It is obvious that Turkey can no longer exist as part of the Cold War paradigm; it no longer has a part to play as the last bastion for the West against the Soviet Union. Turkey's place on the contemporary world stage requires radical changes in its internal structures, both socially and politically, as it moves toward being a standard Western democratic state. There is strong internal resistance to these changes in Turkey, however, by the military-bureaucratic elite. The basic reason for this resistance is the burden of Turkey's past. Turkey now responds to every development with its mindset of the 19th and early 20th centuries, the strongest component of which is very strong resentment of the West. This resentment manifests itself in a barrier against the eventual establishment of democratic and human rights. This idea is discussed further in Chapter 3.

This is a point that the United States and Europe do not seem to understand. They perceive Turkey simply as a partner in NATO and consequently expect it to go along with their political plans. They totally ignore this strong anti-Western sentiment, which was expressed during Turkey's transition from Empire to Republic. According to this mindset, the American military intervention in Iraq in March 2003 is comparable to Western desires in the 19th and early 20th centuries to partition the Ottoman Empire. It was perceived back then that the West was not going to be satisfied only with dividing the Empire; it was believed that the ultimate aim was to remove all traces of Turkish existence from Anatolia. It is in this context that the war in Iraq awakened memories of the First World War, and was perceived by Turkey as a direct threat to its existence.

It is possible to provide many examples of this mindset, which I refer to as an 'anti-West paranoia,' and is prevalent among Turkey's ruling elite. The statement given by the Turkish National Security Council general secretary, army commander Tuncer Kılıç, on April 15, 2003, before the Turkish Societies in Brussels, illustrates this mindset well.

> [Europe] won't open its doors to us. Since the conquest of Istanbul, the Euro-peans have viewed us as their foe ... a nation like the Turks, whose ancestors pushed their way up to the doors of Vienna, will never be welcome by them...Europe brought up the Armenian Question in the 1850s. After WWI, they turned the Armenians against us and created the foundation for dozens of horrific events that followed. The PKK [Kurdistan Workers' Party] is an organization that the EU has established. The EU is the reason 33,000 of our people were killed. The EU has secretly and openly supported terrorist organizations in Turkey. The EU is afraid that Turkey will rise up again to be a new Ottoman Empire.[1]

So does a book specially prepared in 2002 by the Turkish National Ministry of Education to be distributed to all schools in Turkey as part of a campaign to educate Turkish children about the problem of ethnic minorities in the region throughout history (that is, the Armenian Genocide), and especially the policy of the West towards Turkey. The main thesis of the book is that the West has always desired to divide and conquer Turkey, as it attempted to do in the early 20th century:

> The policy towards minorities and divisiveness, which Turkey's neighbors, along with the USA and France, Germany, Italy, Russia and Sweden, among other European nations, follow, and in fact are insisting on being enforced in Turkey today, brings to mind this question: What has changed in the world or in Turkey that makes the same countries force the same issues that they did on Turkish policy one hundred years ago?

The answer follows:

> These countries, which cannot tolerate a strong Turkey either in the short or long term, which seek out reasons or make up reasons to prevent this from happening ... these countries which have a monopoly on the world economies, don't want a strong Turkey. According to these countries, Turkey is a tree whose branches will be pruned whenever they grow long but whose roots will never be cut off because a Middle East without Turkey would lack stability. The same policies were followed when the Ottoman Empire was in its decline.[2]

It was within this context that the Bush administration's vocal policy in 2003 of liberating Iraq and democratizing the region in general was perceived as a threat to Turkey's existence. It is clear that as long as the US takes seriously its policy of democratizing Iraq and the region, it will come more and more into conflict with Turkey's authoritarian political structure. In this respect, Turkey's ability to effect a smooth political transition from authoritarianism to democracy is heavily contingent on the direction US foreign policy takes in the region.

If we regard the Bolshevik Revolution and the Ottoman Empire's defeat in the First World War as the external factors that determined the emergence of the Turkish Republic, the domestic factors were the ethno-religious conflicts in Anatolia and the ensuing wars and massacres in the Ottoman Empire. The Turkish Republic was born out of the destruction of Christian populations in Anatolia and the establishment of a homogeneous Muslim state. This subject is discussed in Chapter 4 on 'The Homogenizing and Ethnic Cleansing of Anatolia.'

The Armenian Genocide was the epitome of the policy of destruction and was declared a taboo subject immediately after the creation of the Republic. One important reason for this declaration was the connection between the Genocide and the foundation of the Republic. The Republic was founded to a significant degree by the members of the Committee of Union and Progress (CUP), which was responsible for the implementation of the wholesale deportation of and massacres against the Armenian population of Anatolia. The authority of the Ottoman civil–military elite continued, uninterrupted, into the period marking the establishment of the Turkish Republic. This elite perceived the Christian population of Anatolia, and especially the Armenians, as internal foes working for foreign imperialist interests and the destruction of the Ottoman Empire. It is therefore no surprise that in Turkey every reference to an open debate on the Republic's early history is suppressed and perceived as a continuation of a historical legacy of subversion. Individuals who call for an open debate are stigmatized as treasonous and enemies of the nation. In Chapter 7 on 'The Causes and Effects of Making Turkish History Taboo,' and Chapter 8 on 'The Genocide and Turkey,' I discuss the reasons for this policy of suppression of historical truth and its negative consequences for Turkey.

In Chapter 5 I provide some documentation on the Genocide itself. The tabooing of the Armenian Genocide not only impedes the process of democratization for Turkey, but also obstructs scholarly inquiry and debate. Scholarly activity has been locked into a cycle of verification or denial of what happened in history, as opposed to analyzing the socio-political and historical factors that allowed that history to unfold. We are lagging in the task of addressing the real question of why the Armenian Genocide occurred. There existed in 1915 a confluence of general factors—social, political, historical, and cultural—that combined in such a way as to make the implementation of genocide possible. These general factors must be viewed in conjunction with the specific factors, both political and psychological, that made the implementation of genocide seem desirable to those in power in 1915. In Chapters 2 and 3 I discuss aspects of Turkish national identity and the Armenian Genocide, and explore the general background factors to the Genocide, showing that it was not an aberration within the flow of Ottoman-Turkish history. The Armenian Genocide can best be understood within the framework of the transition period from Empire to Republic. I have argued that the emergence of Turkish nationalism in the years of the Empire's decline played an important role. One logical outcome of my approach is the recognition of a clear interconnection between the democratization of Turkey today and the need to address the Armenian Genocide. If Turkey is to develop from an authoritarian, bureaucratic state into a standard Western democracy, it must come to terms with history and take a critical approach towards the problems surrounding its national identity. For this to occur, Turkish society must take an active role in opening a debate on the Armenian Genocide as discussed in Chapter 9. The dominance of the denial syndrome must be overcome, and direct interaction between Turkish and Armenian societies must take place.

As I have described in Chapter 6 on the treaties of Sèvres and Lausanne, the history and issues surrounding the Armenian Genocide were dropped from the international agenda by the early 1920s. Securing their material interests was more important to the West than establishing human rights, or addressing the issue of crimes against humanity, which had been the rhetoric during the early stages of the First World War. Today, as we watch the US and Britain intervene in the Middle East, again under the banner of the 'liberation of oppressed people' in the region, we are grappling with the same problem as in the past.

Democracy in the Middle East has its challenges, owing to the mutual suspicions of the various ethnic groups in the region, which arose during the conflicts and massacres that occurred as part of the transition from Empire to nation-states. Each ethnic group today views the others from the perspective of that period. Without addressing the past problems between different groups, establishment of a secure and stable future would be very difficult in the region. The debate that took place on many sides in the region on the sending of Turkish troops into Iraq as a peacekeeping force is only one example of this reality. This issue too shows very clearly that any effort towards democratization in the region today must begin with a dialogue about history and, most important, the ensemble of events that transpired during the transition from Empire to Republic. Only such a process will complete Turkey's real transition from Empire to a normal Republic.

Chapter 1 will attempt to outline some of the obstacles facing contemporary Turkey in its efforts at transition from Empire to Republic. These include certain aspects of the imperial legacy of the Ottoman Empire, and particularly the pivotal role of some of the top leaders of the Young Turk Ittihadist regime in the forging of the Republic, and the determination of the chief architects of the Republic to dissociate themselves from that regime, which was doomed to remain identified with the Armenian Genocide. The basic problem was and remains today the continuation of the ruling elite from the Ottoman Empire to the Turkish Republic. This continuity is one of the biggest impediments to democratization.

NOTES

1. *Radikal*, April 26, 2003.
2. Yavuz Ercan, *Osmanlı Imparatorluğunda Bazı Sorunlar Ve Günümüze Yansımaları* (Some Issues from the Ottoman Empire and Their Reflection in the Present), National Ministry of Education, Directorship of Educational Policy, Ankara, 2002, pp. 71–72.

1

What Are Turkey's Fundamental Problems?
A Model for Understanding Turkey Today

For any Western society today, it is possible to give an answer to the question 'What are this country's fundamental problems' by focusing on several basic points. But if we were to pose a similar question in regard to Turkey, we would not know when to stop counting. Yet for all of Turkey's current problems, it is possible to speak of a main body of problems which we can describe as common to all.

Regarding Turkey, and especially since the collapse of the Soviet Union, we have struggled with the following fundamental problem, which has gained currency among sociologists: 'What is it that keeps a society together and/or leads to its collapse and dissolution?' Émile Durkheim's concept of 'anomie' would appear to have again gained importance. What Durkheim was trying to explain by this term was the condition wherein the relationship between the behavior of individuals (and groups) and social ties is severed. When the ties between the individual and society are severed it creates a situation wherein the society's very continuation is put into question. But the problematic aspect of the concept of anomie is that it presupposes the existence within societies of a normal condition, from which anomie represents a deviation. With regard to Turkey, however, our problem is our inability to define any single period, from the founding of the Republic until now, as a normal condition. Approaching past events in Turkey as a deviation from some sort of normal condition, which we would be able to accept as an ideal, is not a method that will aid us in understanding Turkey and its problems.

The roots of the problems with which Turkey grapples today stretch back to the establishment of the Republic of Turkey in the early 1920s. We can, without hesitation, formulate the problem thus: the roots of Turkey's current problems derive from its Ottoman inheritance. Such a formulation stresses the search for an answer to the question of what exactly that inheritance was, and this in turn opens the door to the debate on questions of continuity and discontinuity in the transition from Ottoman Empire to Turkish Republic. This question has not only been confined to academic debate in Turkey, but has also been the subject of heated polemics. Nevertheless, it is a question outside my field of interest here. I know that the questions which I will take up here can be explained within the framework of a 'continuity of mentality' which survived the empire-to-republic transition, and which fundamentally explains the behavioral worlds of both ruler and ruled in the Turkish Republic. But I would like to limit myself here to the period directly after the establishment of the Republic.

> From the ancient Greece of Aristotle and Plato until today, there is a venerable tradition of considering the factors which hold political collectives together and those which pave the way for their breakup. It claims that...for political collectives to be able to possess stability, there must be a clear agreement between the institutions which have an objective existence, and the subjective behavior of individuals toward these institutions.[1]

This means that the precondition for a stable political structure is an agreement between the institutions in society and the norms that form their basis, and between the norms and value judgments that order individuals' relationships with one another. This relationship can, in very general terms, be defined as 'political culture.' If the value judgments, norms, conscious and unconscious mental worlds and psychological makeup that determine the relationships between individuals and different groups in a society are not in harmony with its institutional world or its political culture, then there exists a serious systemic problem. This is the situation in Turkey.

The Fundamental Problem:
the Failure to Decide on a System

We can formulate Turkey's most basic problem in the following way. Turkish society has yet to answer the question of whether or not it lives or wishes to live within the same political borders. And if different segments of Turkish society do wish to live together as individuals and groups, they have not yet been able to achieve an understanding among themselves as to what foundations, what conditions to impose upon this political entity called the Turkish Republic. The questions of what shared sense of belonging should bind them together within the borders of the Republic, and on what consensus it should rest, remain unanswered. An overarching identity, one that would assist in conceptualizing their reasons for living together and tie both individuals and groups to one another, remains as yet unformed.

If this assertion appears too harsh, let me stress this point: the various collectives that live within Turkey appear to be still far from making a fundamental decision on whether or not it is actually necessary to live together, as a society, within the current political borders. In other words they, both as individuals and as groups, have not yet truly decided to live together. While there may indeed be certain signs that might hint at a decision having been taken in practice, they have not yet been identified as a social consensus, a 'social contract.' The people of Turkey have not formulated the necessary conditions for living together as one common society. In other words, they are at present casting about for these conditions. This can be observed in the daily political debates occurring in Turkey today. Almost every problem is characterized as being fundamental to the political system, and is thus debated as a problem concerned with the very foundations of that system. A good many features that in Western societies are accepted without question are still hotly debated in Turkey. When viewed from the outside, the picture that emerges is this: the Republic and the framework of a democratic state based on laws that are believed to hold the society together or at least appear to have been accepted by all of the country's political forces do not actually carry any meaning beyond being a platform that allows the political forces to carry on their struggles. Concepts like the democratic state based on laws and the Republic have not been internalized, either by society or by its political representatives.

In their current form, the Republic and the democratic state of laws are today nothing but a façade, to be used by the various political currents while searching for an alternative socio-political system as a means to further their own ends. These institutions, which must form the basis of coexistence for the entire society, do not currently provide a sound foundation, and instead are merely used by the various political forces, all of which regard one other as enemies to be excluded or eliminated. It is as if these groups and collectives, whether they describe themselves as political, ethno-cultural or religious, are all struggling for a different system, one outside of the existing democratic state based on laws.

For these groups, it is as if the Republic is equated with a transitional stage to be endured for the present. Tayyip Erdoğan succinctly summed up this sentiment when he was the mayor of Istanbul: 'Democracy is like a streetcar that will carry us to the final destination. When we get there, we'll get off.' Erdoğan, since February 2003 chairman of the Justice and Development Party (Adalet ve Kalkinma Partisi, or AKP), and since March 2003 President of Turkey, made this statement in the mid-1990s, when he was still a member of the Islamist Welfare Party (Refah Partisi, or RP).[2]

That the current political system is only a transitional device to be used for developing a new system is a belief found in all political currents and groups within Turkey. Viewed from the outside, it appears as if there is not a serious political group, except for the armed forces, that sincerely desires the continuation of the Republic. The armed forces act as the true owners of present-day Turkey. From the point of view of the large collective forces within society, today's Republic, and the democratic state based on laws by whose power it exists, are outside of society, existing somewhere else, like a strange, unfamiliar garment. There is a poor fit, an incompatibility between the state, with its existing structures, and society, with its social groups. What we are talking about here is alienation between the state and society. The relationship between state and society is in the manner of relations not between 'us,' but between 'us' and the 'other.' And perhaps the armed forces also act as they do because they are profoundly conscious that no one other than themselves has claimed ownership of the Republic in the true sense of the phrase.

It appears as if there is such a paradox at work. The moment the armed forces would withdraw their protective hand from the state the various groups in Turkey would strangle themselves as a society. All the groups would do everything in their power to eliminate the 'others,' whom they see as opposed to them, and to whom they have assigned no place in the new system they hope to establish. Whether we speak of the Turkish ultra-nationalists, or the Kurds, or the radical secularists who view the headscarf as a symbol of reaction, or the Islamists who seek to establish a social and political order on the basis of Islamic values, none would be able to tolerate the others' existence in the idealized societies that they hope to establish. Thus, the current situation in Turkey is comparable to that of Germany in the Weimar Republic of the 1920s. In that period, all of the then-current political movements aspired not to protect existing democratic institutions, but rather to use these institutions to destroy the system and to establish their own in its place. The ultimate success of the Nazis derived in large part from the general lack of interest displayed by other parts of society for democratic institutions. The gap between the mentality that prevailed in German society and the attitude of indifference toward democratic institutions brought the system to a collapse. In such a situation, the indifference of the German army, in particular with regard to the choice of either a democratic or an authoritarian regime, helped accelerate this process of collapse. A similar situation, I would assert, exists today in Turkey. Between the veneer of the Republic and a democratic, law-based state on one side, and the political currents' imaginings of an ideal future on the other, there exists a tear in the social fabric which has yet to be mended, a broad gap that remains unbridged. The fact that the system continues to function despite this mental divide is largely due to the armed forces' insistence that it do so.

It goes without saying that the existing institutions in Turkish society present an image that cannot easily be described as democratic. The existence on one hand of the basic principles of a law-based state, and, on the other, of seriously anti-democratic institutions, allows broad sections of society to perceive the system as one of repression. This perception is very keen among the Islamists, Alevis and Kurds, in particular, as well as among other groups who see themselves as bound by common linguistic, ethnic or religious characteristics and who feel that no measures have been taken in order to defend or preserve these characteristics. Not infrequently, these groups or their individual members have experienced oppression on account of these characteristics.

Furthermore, there is another, more important dimension than this. As the inheritors of the *Herrschaftsmentalität*, or 'ruling mentality' of the Ottomans, the current ruling elite possesses no such tradition of adapting itself to legal regulations, or of basing its governance on law. One reason for the widespread mistrust that exists in Turkey toward the legitimizing principles of the democratic law-based state is the fact that the ruling class itself does not comply with them. In other words, the rulers themselves lack the mindset to administer the country according to the obligations of the existing legal system. This can be illustrated with two examples: the Susurluk scandal and the prohibition on torture.

The Susurluk scandal was exposed by a car accident in that city in 1997. A mafia leader, a police chief, and a parliamentary deputy were all found dead together in the same car. It was thus revealed that the criminal element, the police and politicians had been working together for some time in the organization and running of death squads, heroin trafficking, extortion and murder. The death squads had been secretly formed to eliminate supporters of the Kurdish separatist organization, the PKK. This cooperation of criminals, the police, politicians and also the military expanded, with the aim of personal enrichment, into heroin trafficking and even the murder of Turkish businessmen who had no political involvement, simply in order to control their businesses, mostly hotels and casinos (useful for laundering drug money). When a commission of inquiry was established by parliament to investigate this situation, members of the military refused to testify. Even though the activities under investigation are completely illegal, the legal system has no power to proceed against the military. While the other elements in this criminal conspiracy did appear before the commission, there were no serious consequences for them.

Torture and the mistreatment of detainees have been outlawed in the legal system since 1854, and punishment is indicated for those committing such acts. Yet, we know that such sanctions are not carried out systematically. On the contrary, in open opposition to existing laws, those who carry out such deeds are generally rewarded. In other words, the ruling class considers it natural and normal not to comply with the rules that legitimize their own positions, and for whose proper operation they are responsible. The most important characteristic of the mindset of Turkey's ruling elite is its transformation of arbitrariness into accepted practice, if not a set of formal rules. This is the primary cause of Turkey's 'societal schizophrenia.'

Hypocritical Behavior: Societal Schizophrenia

What is meant here by societal schizophrenia is the enormous gap between the current *modus operandi* of the state structure in Turkey on one hand, and Turkish social reality on the other. Detachment between the state and the individual or collective groups is our present reality. A consequence of this detachment, over many years a strange mode of behavior has ordered the relations between the various individuals and groups, as well as those between these groups and the state. On one side there exists an order we might refer to as 'the everyday world of real life,' and on the other side there is the 'official world,' which is outside of the everyday world and in serious conflict with it.

On one hand, the legal system, with all its claims to order relations between individuals and between the state and its citizens, is fundamentally responsible for society's functioning. But on the other hand, neither the state itself nor citizens order their behavior according to the legal system, its values and institutions. There are, however, other value systems and models of behavior which everyone uses to order their relations. All of the internal social forces, including those that administer the state, are conscious of the fact that their own value systems are in conflict with those of the legal system, and that they are either secretly or openly different from it.

We may describe this as a product of the ruling tradition that harks back to the Ottomans. The inefficiency of the theocratic laws of the Ottoman state, which did not provide for all aspects of social life, created a situation whereby the ruling elite was required to exercise its discretion in the exercise of justice. This application of discretion led to abuses, and discretion became arbitrariness. Max Weber described the extraordinary insecurity in law as a basic characteristic of patrimonial Ottoman society.[3] In consequence of this Ottoman legacy, similarly a schizophrenic attitude of accepting the dichotomies between official state requirements and actual social norms developed among individuals and collectives within society. Over centuries, a culture of not speaking one's true opinion took root, particularly among the ruled classes. Individuals even have their official views and their private views with which to explain ideas. They express these different views, which are often diametrically opposed to one another, according to the time and the place. In official venues and in public, the ruled classes speak the official views in order to preserve their positions and not to create problems. As for their true opinions, they express these through their private views, which are only expressed in the private sphere. The true relations within the society may be determined by those things that are said off the record, when the microphone is turned off. The public sphere is like the stage of a theater upon which it is known that a good number of contradictory lies are spoken. Thus, there is no trust among groups in Turkish political culture.

One of the greatest obstacles standing in the way of the democratization process in Turkey is this widespread duality of thought and behavior, which fundamentally determines the behavior of the people of Turkey. It is as if the democratic institutions serve only to further the game that both the ruling elites and the broader social groups play with one another. Both the state and the groups and individuals within it know well that the relations of the former with society, as well as the latter's relations with one another, have not been fundamentally advanced by these institutions or by the cultural values which prevail within them. Outside of these democratic institutions, the relations between the state and society are ordered according to the 'real world' norms and rules that both sides know. It is for this reason that the cases of persons who are summoned to police stations and then 'disappear' do not cause undue alarm. The state neither forgoes its claim to be a law-based state, nor its right to 'lose' its own citizens at police stations. Reports of persons who 'commit suicide' after being taken into custody have become normalized, as have those claiming that Turkey is a democratic, law-based state.

The point I would like to emphasize here is not the oppressive character of the state institutions. Nor is it the reality that the state itself tramples those very same legal norms that it puts in place in order to regulate public life. Instead, what I want to stress is the cultural norms that have been created as a result of this dissonance between simultaneously paying lip service to and disregarding the law, and by the manner of relations between illegality and dependence on the law. One of the most significant manifestations of these cultural norms is that the problem of democratization of the legal institutions in Turkey, which should be the foundation for the regulation of state–society relations, has never really received the attention it deserves from either the state or society. As a result of Turkey seeking membership in the European Union, especially since 2003, there has been an important change in this attitude. This is, no doubt, at least partially due to the fact that EU membership would necessitate the fundamental reordering of state–society and interpersonal relations. What is important for both state and society is the question of how they can exploit democratic institutions in order to achieve the relations that the various groups themselves deem important, and the degree of societal reordering that they themselves desire. The result, then, is the emergence of a political culture that belittles democratic norms and institutions, and even rejects them.

The existence of this way of thinking produces 'dual behavioral norms' on both the micro and the macro levels. The whitewashing of illegal actions has become a rule to live by in Turkey. Government ministers struggle to cloak their behavior and actions with the appearance of legitimacy and conformity with legal norms, but this simply encourages a deep sense of mistrust and widespread suspicion within society, because all are aware that everyone is behaving in accordance with this same understanding of legality. As a result, suspicion of others—a sort of art of suspecting the hidden or real intentions of others, of stripping off the masks of others and exposing them—is now deeply entrenched at all levels of Turkish life. The publication in 2000 of certain videotaped sermons of Fethullah Gülen, who had been considered a respectable religious figure, is a fine example of this.

Gülen had essentially been depicted as tied to the state, and respectful of the basic principles of the Republic. He was known as a partisan of secularism, and was seen as aligning himself with the state in its struggle against political Islam. But in the videotapes that appeared, he himself claims that his behavior was actually *takiye*, 'dissimulation', and he actually mentions that one's true aims must be kept secret until they are able to pass into important state institutions and offices.

In this sense we can speak of a widespread schizophrenia in Turkish society. Before us we see a society in which everyone, from individuals to collective actors, feels the need to hide their own true thoughts and intentions, and to mold their behavior according to at least two very different norms. As a result, the relations between individuals, collective groups and the state are enmeshed in an atmosphere poisoned by deep, mutual suspicions. The very serious problem remains, then, of how persons and groups can live together within a world wherein the main features of the prevalent mindset are suspicion and distrust. Behind the lengthy debates on whether or not Tayyip Erdoğan and his AKP are convincingly pro-Republic lies the problem of trust, which arises from these suspicions.

A Civil–Political Culture of Impropriety

Another result of the gap between state and society is that the 'we' connection has not been established between state and society. The ruling elite controlling the state sees itself as outside of society, as a foreign element. This is, essentially, the Ottoman state tradition. The state derives authority not from society, but from itself. It is a self-contained entity; the state has a nation, not the opposite. As for the nation, it is like a piece of private property, with which the state can do as it pleases. This situation is achieved through the state's control of some 60 percent of the country's economy. The National Security Council (Milli Güvenlik Kurulu, MGK), which is the supreme, constitutionally authorized power running the state, publishes and distributes brochures at certain intervals on the subject of the fundamental philosophy of the state. These brochures are more important than the Constitution itself, and their texts clearly express the idea that 'the state has a nation.' At the end of the 1980s it was revealed in the Turkish press that the MGK possessed a special 'National Policy Document' ('Milli Siyaset Belgesi') authorizing its actions, policies and publications, and that this document was reviewed and amended on occasion when there was a need to do so. It was understood that there existed a 'Secret Constitution' of which no one was aware. 'Secret Constitution' is perhaps a bit of an overstatement, because this document had neither been submitted to the public for approval, nor discussed and approved in parliament. This concept was mentioned a second time some ten years later, this time by the then prime minister, Mesut Yılmaz. Yılmaz, while on the way to Rhodes for a state visit, told reporters that the 'National Policy Document' had been brought up to date in the National Security Council. The Ankara bureau of *Hürriyet* acted upon the prime minister's report and, after getting hold of the document, published it. No state functionary either confirmed or denied any of the document's articles as published, though ultimately the existence of the document was confirmed indirectly when a case was opened against the newspaper for publishing it.[4]

The 'state has a nation' mindset is likewise reflected in the political order. The political parties, which act as representatives of social forces, accept the fact that there exists another state, outside of themselves. They know that coming to power, that is, winning an election and forming a government, is not the same as being in control of the state. The state has a different owner, one outside of the overt political system, one that has never been under the control or supervision of the parties.[5] The effect of this is that, because the parties know the state does not derive its legitimacy from them, or from the people they represent, they do not view themselves as the real bodies to deal with the important problems of the state. It is accepted that the problems of the state, which are not 'theirs,' lie outside of their area, meaning society's responsibility. The state and those who believe themselves to be its true owners also see it this way.

The absence of an 'us' connection between the state and society limits the duties of the political parties to forming elected governments. But the government does not equate to sovereignty within the state, and the parties both know and accept this fact. For this reason, what matters most to them is to gain access to the State Treasury, the wealthiest entity in the country, in order to distribute its funds among spouses, family and friends, on the one hand, and party members, on the other. This mentality finds its most succinct expression in the Turkish saying 'The riches of the state are an ocean; it is a fool who does not drink from it.'[6] Thus the political parties serve as enrichment companies.

This is actually a common characteristic of every nation-building process. Patronage and getting fed at the public expense can be observed in almost all fledgling states. What was written about Greece in the middle of the 19th century can be read as Turkey's political reality today. 'Elsewhere, parties come into existence because people disagree with each other, each wanting different things. In Greece, the exact opposite occurs: what causes parties to come into existence and compete with each other is the admirable accord with which all seek the same things: to be fed at public expense' (Emmanouil Roidis, 1875).[7] As a rule, the parties interpret fundamental and serious political problems as questions of national security and thus, instead of expending their energies trying to solve them, refer them to the armed forces.

Not a single Turkish political party possesses any serious political program or formulated strategy concerned with either the internal or the external problems facing the country. In their programs, one encounters but few sentences devoted to fundamental problems, and even these have not been penned out of any need to do so. Because Turkey's political parties possess such a political mindset, they are in no position to carry out the necessary social reforms; they do not even consider them.[8]

The parties have grown so distant from important political problems and the steps needed to solve them that one frequently encounters a situation wherein a member of the government, a minister, will make some absurd statement, such as 'I condemn this action,' in response to an action by the security forces. Their mentality is such that they are not even aware that they themselves are the ministers, the persons with the fundamental responsibility for the government's actions. Recent developments on such issues as Cyprus and the European Joint Security Agreement have been in a direction exactly opposite to that given by the government, as if a hidden hand had decided to direct affairs.

The political parties' divvying up of state resources among their own supporters can be understood as an institutionalization of theft and impropriety. This is one of the reasons for the armed forces' abiding mistrust of civilian politicians. It is indeed an odd situation: civilian politicians, by appearing unqualified, are dismissed from being involved in essential state problems, and this alienation of the politicians, in turn, gives birth to an institutionalization of theft and impropriety. Although it is known that the solution to the problem lies both in state matters being left under parliamentary supervision and in the prevalence of a greater transparency in the affairs of state, not a single substantial step has been taken in this direction. For example, Turkey remains one of the few countries where questions about the military's expenses cannot be asked, and where the Assembly has no supervisory function over how the military budget is formulated and how it is allocated.[9]

The Reasons for This State of Affairs Must Be Sought in the Republic's Formative Years

In order to understand the reasons for this situation in Turkey today, it is necessary to look at the conditions under which the Republic was founded. The internal and external conditions that allowed the emergence of the Turkish Republic are also the causes for the basic problems that the country faces today.

Let me make clear that the dividing here of internal and external factors is solely a question of procedure. Among the external conditions we can list the following:

(a) The Great Powers' plans for the partitioning of the Ottoman Empire among themselves;
(b) the First World War; and
(c) The October 1917 Russian Revolution.

As for internal factors, the main ones are:

(a) The Pan-Turkic and Pan-Islamic policies embarked upon in an attempt to forestall the collapse of the Empire; and
(b) The struggles waged by various peoples within the Ottoman Empire (Arabs, Armenians, Kurds, etcetera) whose aims ranged from autonomy to independence.

The borders of the Turkish nation-state were defined as a result of these five factors. During the First World War there were two dominating and mutually hostile political directions. One was the Great Powers' desire to divide up the Ottoman Empire, the other the Ottomans' ambition to create a homogeneous state on the basis of either ethnicity or religion, through a Pan-Turkic and Pan-Islamic expansionist policy. For their parts, the various ethnic and religious groups within the Empire eventually wanted to take advantage of the power vacuums created by these conflicts and to establish their own national states. As a result of the Ottoman military defeat in the First World War, the Pan-ist dreams were shattered. All that remained were the Great Powers' plans for partition. But the truth was that, together with the dreams of the Pan-ists, those internal elements, or ethnic groups, had been obliterated.

This picture describes, in a basic way, the prevailing official ideology today in Turkey. According to it, the Republic of Turkey was formed as a result of a life-and-death struggle waged 'against seven states.' The Republic, then, is a product of the 'war of rejuvenation.' As a result, a defining aspect of the identity of the Republic is the belief that Turkey was surrounded by enemies who sought to partition the country. Among these enemies, the entire West (and Europe, in particular) was arrayed beside those countries that border Turkey. This persistent fear of division or partition can be termed 'Sèvres Syndrome'—referring to the Treaty of Sèvres, 1920, which apportioned today's Turkey among Britain, France, Greece, Kurds and Armenians—and this psychosis of fear retains its vitality today.

We can also add that this psychosis of fear is not limited to the period in which the Republic was established. Rather it is based on historical experiences, and is very powerful for that reason. Between the years 1878 and 1918, the Ottoman Empire lost 75 per cent of its territory and 85 per cent of its population. This period was marked by a series of secessions, lost wars, massacres, etcetera. The Republic found a way to escape this trauma by drawing a sharp line between itself and its Ottoman past, and by viewing its own establishment as a creation *ex nihilo*, a project built from the ground up. A significant aspect of this radical break with the past has been the erasing of collective memory. The ensuing emptiness of memory, like a blank page, was filled with the foundational ideology of the new Turkish state.

After the defeat in the First World War and the establishment of a new Republic, expansionist policies were abandoned. The understanding of the nation, as defined by the Commitee of Union and Progress (the Young Turks movement that ruled the Ottoman Empire in its last decade of existence, 1908–18), which was based on a sense of ethno-religious brotherhood, was discarded. A cultural understanding of the nation that would include all Turkish-speaking Muslims was abandoned in favor of a political concept of the nation, whose location and borders would now be defined by the geographic borders of the state. But this transformation was not the result of a coherent or consistent rejection of the previous model, one that had been realized after prolonged thought. Instead, it was the result of a pragmatic choice. It had to be accepted as a manifestation of the situation in which Mustafa Kemal made his pronouncements on the subjects of Pan-Islamism and Pan-Turkism. Kemal claimed he was opposed to neither Pan-Islamism nor Pan-Turkism in principle, but the Turks simply lacked the strength to realize such goals at present; and they should not try to bite off more than they could chew, and thereby succeed only in acquiring for themselves new enemies.[10]

This pragamatic view is the reason why, even today, insufficient attention is paid to the fact that the preference for the Republic over the Empire was essentially a political decision, not an emotional one. There is still a constant oscillation in Turkish understanding of the nation between the idea of a nation that is basically defined by its political borders and the idea of Turkey being a great power that is defined by the qualities of ethnicity, culture and religion.

The internal conditions that allowed for the creation of the Republic were determined by the internal wars that were fought in Anatolia. This process, which I will call the 'first wave of nationalization,' developed on the basis of religious clashes.[11] As a result of these clashes, which reached their apex with the Armenian Genocide, the Christian population of Anatolia was either annihilated or expelled from Anatolia. The Turkish Republic was then established as a state of all Muslims, free of all ethnic or cultural senses of belonging. But in its early years, there was a desire to form the state in accordance with an understanding of the political nation, which was described as a 'National Pact and national sovereignty.' This was in direct contradiction to the Union and Progress Party's idea of an empire that had been founded on and whose main unifying element was ethnic-religious-cultural brotherhood.

Here I must emphasize a crucial factor which determined the transitional process from Ottoman Empire to Turkish Republic: this transition was basically realized without any similar, accompanying transformation within the country's ruling elite. I do not say this simply because the cadres who founded the Republic were by and large the same Unionist cadres who had run the Empire in its last period of existence. The Republic was essentially founded under the leadership of the Ottoman army, and of its officer corps, in particular. The army was the foundational pillar that established the Republic, and subsequently it was a factor which, to a significant extent, determined the behavioral norms of the political elite. The prevailing norms were and are still not democratic and liberal values, but rather martial values of heroism, authority, discipline, and other, similar military codes of behavior. Herein lies the reason that no serious critique, which a civilian republic requires, can be made.

The Republic Was Founded on Taboos

As a result of the internal and external factors I listed above, there was an attempt to establish a national state on the French model. It was desired by the founder of the Turkish Republic that a new nation should be created, one which would be determined by the political borders of the state. The fundamental logic behind such an entity is well summed up in the famous saying of the Italian minister and president Massimo d'Azelglio in 1861: 'We have created Italy, now let us find [i.e., create] the Italians.' Therefore, a series of reform movements was quickly undertaken in an attempt to create the individuals to match the state. It is especially appropriate to explain the period between 1925 and 1940 along these lines.

For reasons that I cannot go into in detail here, this attempt naturally ran up against its own limitations, for no national state can be founded on a pillar of citizenship that is only abstractly defined. The logic of the national state requires an unavoidable homogenization. The national state must rest upon the unity or totality of feeling of persons who have decided to live together 'no matter what.' A shared cultural foundation that can attain this must be established. The Republic indeed did this. The remaining non-Muslims were defined as 'the other.' Turkish cultural identity, then, became the cement with which to build this homogenization.

The efforts at homogenization that were directed inward ran up against the walls of their own society's reality. The new rulers, whose behavior was based on the mentality of the Ottoman ruling tradition and who, as we have noted, were heavily imbued with military values, discovered that the society that was 'outside' themselves formed a serious problem for the state that they had idealized. In addition to the foreign threat, which found expression in the aforementioned Sèvres Syndrome, and which forms the founding ideology of the Republic, a new threat, the 'internal threat,' was discovered. In connection with this 'threat philosophy,' the rulers began to act to create taboos in designated areas of social life. These taboos also formed foundational principles for the Republic and became state dogmas.

The taboos are as follows:

(1) Turkish society has no classes. We are a classless, unified society.
(2) There are no ethnic-cultural differences. All citizens are Turks.
(3) Turkey is a secular state. Islam and Islamic culture have been declared enemies.
(4) No massacre whatsoever was carried out and directed at the Armenians.
(5) The armed forces are the guardians of these taboos, and the role of the armed forces within the state is a taboo subject.

These points are the pillars upon which the Republic stands. Every action contrary to these principles has been prohibited by the Constitution and criminal laws, and all groups who would defend alternative views have been declared enemies. Relevant articles in this regard have been inserted into the Turkish Penal Code: Articles 141 and 142 forbid mention of a class struggle; Article 163 forbids religious propaganda; Article 125 forbids pro-

Kurdish propaganda. There is no single article mentioning the Armenian Genocide, but this is because there is no existing social group or circle that would challenge this taboo. The armed forces are the guardians of these taboo topics, and their duty of guarding and protecting the state are off limits to inquiry.

In short, the Turkish state was established on the foundation of a national psychosis forged in the struggle and preservation of its existence against internal and external enemies. This psychosis continues to the present. The National Policy Documents, or Red Books, of the National Security Council are rewritten according to the perceived dangers posed at the specific period, and they give direction to the manner in which the state will direct its efforts against these threats. The nature of the state's ideology is about protecting the integrity of the country and nation against enemies. The first task of every new government is to reclassify the enemies of the Republic according to the degree of danger that they currently pose. The descriptions in government propaganda of the dangers are first and foremost a product of this tradition.

Given this situation, we can conclude that the Turkish state was formed in opposition to its own social reality. The ethnic, confessional and cultural differences of Turkish society find their places in the foundational philosophy of the Republic as problematic or threatening elements. In other words, the state–society opposition that was inherited from the Ottomans was given a new twist by the Republic according to the conditions of its own establishment.

Reading the History of the Republic as the History of Revolts against Taboos

The history of the Republic can be seen as the history of continuous revolts undertaken by social groups whose existence had not been acknowledged by the state. These groups attempted to do away with the oppressive laws imposed on them and to force the state to accept the fact of their identity and existence. We can view the prohibitions enacted up to the 1940s, a period that can still be considered formative, as responses to attempts by these taboo groups to gain reform. The Kurdish revolt in the province of Dersim (present-day Tunceli province) in 1938 can, in this sense, perhaps be considered the last revolt. The first reappearance of serious opposition to the taboos, which had until then seemed to have been accepted by the various parties, began in the second half of the 1960s.

First, the leftists revolted. They argued for the existence of classes and the class struggle, and against the state doctrine that asserted that Turkey is one unified society. They found themselves confronted by articles 141 and

142 of the Penal Code. Later on, the Kurds and the Islamists revolted. The armed forces, who are the 'guardians and protectors' of the state, responded to each of these revolts with a military coup. A brief history of the military coups of 1960, 1971, 1980 and 1997 could be summed up as the history of the suppression of those taboo groups that proclaim their existence.

Although these revolts originated for different reasons, they had two striking characteristics in common:

First, given the Republic's denial of their existence and the active repression it imposed, the taboo groups viewed the Republic as their enemy. Each one of these groups aimed, in its own way, to overthrow and destroy the state, having concluded that the existing state and the prevailing political currents were incapable of reform. They therefore formulated alternative state models, which proposed different social and political structures for the country. The models proposed, however, were limited to those that would solve only their own particular problems, and not necessarily those of society as a whole. And within these models for the salvation of the state, each taboo group identified the other taboo groups as problems. Because each group had refused, during its own revolts, to take any other group's interests into account, each group saw the existence of the others as a danger to itself. Each political movement that represents some taboo area longs for power solely for itself. The Socialist State, the Islamic State, and the Kurdish State were conceived as being established in place of the current Republic after its 'inevitable' collapse. That these blueprints were not very precise, and that often they were not even expressed openly was not very important. Rather, the philosophy of destroying the existing structure was always more important than any philosophy of what positive alternative might replace the collapsing edifice.

The leftists wished to destroy the existing state and erect a socialist state in its place, but there were the other social forces represented by the bourgeoisie and the Islamists, who would need to be eliminated as well. Similar schemata could be drawn up for the Islamist and Kurdish movements. Even if one group did not see the others as dangers to be removed, they still had no program to address the demands of the others. In other words, all pursued a homogeneous, authoritarian or totalitarian option. An important result was that none of these taboo groups took the existing democratic institutions and laws within society seriously, instead seeing them merely as devices to be temporarily employed to attain their own objectives. The leftists attacked the democratic atmosphere of the 1960s as a 'Philippine-type democracy.' The Islamic movement frequently echoed the statements of Tayyip Erdoğan and Fethullah Gülen quoted earlier. The PKK pushed for the Kurdish state model, which provided no allowance for dissenting ideas. (The number of persons from PKK ranks executed by the PKK is estimated at over 3,000 from 1990 to 2000.)

The second characteristic that all the taboo groups had in common was that each saw the other groups' plans for a political society as a threat to its own existence—and not without reason. Thus each one of these groups sided with the armed forces, either directly or indirectly, in its struggle against the revolts by the other taboo groups. As a result, the various groups categorized each other as the enemy, and this perception prevails to the present. It is no exaggeration to say that the leftist factions view the Islamist movement as a serious threat to their own existence, and the latter, in turn, views the Kurdish movement likewise. These groups' suspicions and doubts about one another are what fundamentally determine their behavior toward each other.

The Situation: Stalemate

The revolts and military struggles that have appeared since the 1970s have produced three important and interconnected results.

First, all of the taboo groups have lost their struggles with the state. They have been crushed in the true sense of the word. Not only have they failed in their efforts to destroy the state, but the very ideas that they offered as an alternative model to the state have been defeated as well. But one result has been achieved: almost all of these taboos, which we spoke of as having determined the foundation of the Republic, have been broken. It has now been accepted by all—the armed forces included—that Turkey is a class-based society, that the country's cultural life has in large measure been determined by Islamic culture, and that there does indeed exist a Kurdish people. But this has simultaneously delivered a blow to state dogmas and caused a collapse of the ideological pillars upon which the state rests. The result is a situation of stalemate.

Second, the three societal groups that were made taboo have undergone (and continue to undergo) internal transformation. These groups have abandoned their revolutionary strategies and totalitarian ideals, and in connection with this, they have begun to examine and reevaluate democratic institutions and laws in a different manner than in the past. These institutions have begun to emerge, in their view, as something more than a democratic means to revolutionary ends. Each one of these groups, in fact, appears to have adopted the democratization of the existing state structure as its goal. Democratic institutions are now interpreted as indispensable elements, not for the necessary destruction of the state, but instead for its renewal. If we were to describe this situation a bit flippantly, we might well say that these groups have had democracy and tolerance for human rights hammered into them by the state. Each group, upon its own defeat, has discovered human rights and democracy, and they are now working to secure for themselves the place they feel they deserve in the state administration, in which they see themselves as parties and partners. We can explain this as a process, at the end of which the state will be a product of consensus between various social forces in society.

Third, perhaps the most evident characteristic of this stalemate is that the political-cultural atmosphere is essentially based on a foundation of suspicion. The various parties' basic opinions of one another are founded on doubt and suspicion. It would not be wrong to assert that Turkey's fundamental political and psychological problems at this moment are doubt or mistrust, and the continual question of credibility. Each party enters the fray with the proclamation 'I've changed!'—even if not always voicing it loudly. The one who has been most vocal in this regard, it should be pointed out, is Abdullah Öcalan, the captured leader of the PKK. The general rule is that all others tend to view such appeals with an attitude of 'We've all heard that before.' A profound mistrust prevails in the political arena: everyone suspects a lack of truly democratic values on the part of others, and no vow or promise can convince them to think otherwise.

The military, guardian of the state and the Republic from these internal threats, also accepts the formerly taboo groups' testimonies of 'true democratic conversion' with more than a little suspicion. As a consequence, the army offers a transitional model, in which control is left in their hands. In this sense, we can say that Turkey is experiencing a process of democratization supervised from above, and the limits of that democratization are set by the military. For this reason, the democratization program that is emerging as a part of the process of joining the European Union could be described as a model of authoritarian democracy. This program is consistent with that traditional ideological pillar of the Republic which defines society as a problem.

In the process of democratization we observe the emergence of two types of civil society organizations. On the one hand, there are grassroots movements that have developed and favor a civil democratic society; on the other hand, there are those supported by the state and military, which favor the status quo. Naturally, the forces that exercise power will not, of their own volition, give up their positions of power. Thus, there is tension between civil society and the military as to the boundaries of democratization.

Generally speaking, there are domestic and external factors that have fostered the process of democratization. The domestic factor is that the formerly taboo groups are changing their approach from one of undermining the state to one of exerting pressure on the state for reforms. The external factor comes in the form of pressure from the European Union and the US, which seek democracy in Turkey as a precondition for Turkey to take its place in the new world order. Even economic aid from the World Bank and International Monetary Fund is conditioned on political reform. Due in large part to this external pressure, Turkey's ruling elite has in fact already undertaken certain reforms, even if accompanied by much foot-dragging. In this sense, it would not be incorrect to say that the ruling elites now find themselves between a rock and a hard place.

The process of change generated within the taboo groups also has its problematic aspect. The taboo groups under discussion do not yet believe that their opponents (the other taboo groups) have truly democratized themselves, and this failure to unite around a shared democratic consensus is the primary reason for the non-development of a multicultural, democratic alternative in which all groups could find a place. Nevertheless, change has now encompassed each of these taboo groups from within. The splitting of the religious Virtue Party (*Fazilet Partisi*) after it had been banned by Turkey's Constitutional Court is a meaningful indicator in this direction. It was the debates that took place within the party before the court's ruling that caused the reformed party to emerge as two separate entities. The older, more conservative faction coalesced around Recai Kutan as the Felicity Party (*Saadet Partisi*) while the younger faction regrouped as the AKP under Tayyip Erdoğan. This situation now reflects the emergence of two different streams of renewal within Turkey's Islamic movement. Both of these streams appear to be abandoning the Islamic state model. The advocates of the Islamic state model had never clearly defined their vision, and the tendencies within the present-day Islamic movement are beginning to give some serious consideration to possible options that would allow them to live together with the other taboo groups. Similar tendencies have long since begun among the other taboo groups.

This wave of change has become so powerful that the traditional political parties, which were established on the principle of consuming the political and economic benefits of the state, have now entered a serious crisis. The Motherland (*Anavatan Partisi,* ANAP), the Nationalist Action Party (*Milliyetci Hareket Partisi,* MHP, also known as the National Movement), and the Democratic Left (*Demokratik Sol Partisi,* DSP) parties are all on the verge of disappearing.[12]

The state has, by its present *modus operandi*, undermined and destroyed its function as a unifier and solidifier of its citizens and social groups. The result is to strengthen the position of the military by giving them a perpetual role in the political arena (if not always in the form of a *coup d'état*). They are the country's only unifying force. Despite the winds of reform that are blowing today, any sort of unity of society and state would still be hard to achieve without the army. The current status of the army must be realistically factored into any equation for democratization.

During the process of integration into the European Union, the diverse social forces within Turkey have begun to voice their own alternative plans for a democratic society more forcefully, and the search for two separate democratic systems is beginning to appear. On one side, the protective and conservative forces of the Republic and the state (namely. the military and bureaucracy) will opt for an authoritarian democracy in which they themselves would in large measure continue to exercise control; on the other side, there is the choice of a pluralistic, civil democracy informed by liberal values, and which wants to reduce the role of the military in state power.

The Rebirth of the 'Eastern Question'

Turkey's current crisis derives from the fact that the country is now at a crossroads, and from its need to redefine itself. Yet perhaps there are external factors that are at least as relevant as these, if not more so. The founding paradigm of the Republic has been destroyed, and Turkey is now confronted with the problem of redefining itself.

The most important external factor is the breakup of the Soviet Union, and the new perspectives that have emerged in Turkey as a result. The whole network of problems and issues arising from this event can be termed a 'rebirth of the Eastern Question.' The collapse of the Soviet Union—whose existence had profoundly affected the formation of the national state and the process of defining its borders, as well as having put an end to the Eastern Question—has upset all of the region's social, economic and political balances. The peoples and countries who believe they were treated unjustly during the previous partition have now begun to reassert their former demands, as well as to put forward new ones. The Eastern Question has been revived on the basis of the question of redrawing the borders of the region's new states, for example, in relation to the ethnic conflicts in the Caucasus and the Middle East. The 2003 war in Iraq will only serve to accelerate this process.

The reordering is important for Turkey in two ways. On one hand, with the renewed demands by some states or ethnic groups for further territory, the old fear in regard to national borders has been revived. On the other, the repressive state apparatus that had long forced the abandonment of any Pan-Islamic or Pan-Turkic expansionist strategy has now been removed. There has been a recreation of the material conditions that may cause a change from the understanding of a nation-state as a republic, which was the most practical option at the time the Republic was established. Today there is an evident conflict between the structure of the republican state and the revived longing to be a powerful player in the region. In the end, Turkey will have to make a conscious choice: it will either have to content itself with the Republic and the present borders of the state and continue to move forward on the path toward democratization, or its dreams of a resurrected Empire will be revived—if not in the former manner of Pan-Islamic or Pan-Turkic expansionism, then in seeking out ways to unite with other Turkic-Muslims and to extend the existing borders. The current developments around Cyprus and northern Iraq can be seen as a examples. The second option continues to be favored among Turkish elites, either as a hidden or an expressed desire. The ruling elites—and first and foremost among them, the military, who up to now have avoided making the reforms that would be eventually necessary for entry into the European Union—have frequently expressed demands along these lines through the far-right MHP. Indeed, claims that Turkey needs to face east and to form an alliance with powerful states that will emerge in the East in order to confront the West have begun to be voiced with increasing frequency. The policies toward Armenia and Azerbaijan in particular can be seen as open displays of this aspiration. The country's policies toward the Caucasus, which are based on ethnic and cultural brotherhood with the Azeris and other Muslim groups, either ignore Armenia or consider it an enemy. This demonstrates clearly that the Unionist tradition, best personified by Enver Paşa's failed Pan-Turkish dreams, continues to be robust. The persistence of such ideas is reflected in the oft-repeated phrase 'The Turkish world stretches from the Adriatic to Central Asia.' Although such talk, which was often employed by former president Süleyman Demirel, has not really gelled into a concrete political alternative, it is nevertheless understood to stem from a deeply held desire among Turkish elites.

Until now Turkey has either been unaware of the problems of the new period, or it has responded reflexively. We can foresee, nevertheless, that any reorganization based on great-power fantasies will fail, especially if democratization is rejected as its central tenet.

Just as much as the fall of the Soviet Union, the September 11, 2001 attacks on the United States raised the issue of whether Turkey needed to re-define itself. The ruling elites have been inclined to view September 11 and its aftermath as counter to the country's traditional strategy of *Westbindung*, or Western orientation, which has so frequently been asserted as a necessary condition for Turkey's further democratization. According to this argument, the military–strategic alliance that can be formed in the region along the Israel–Turkey axis would increase Turkey's power, both in the Eastern Mediterranean and in Central Asia. This is seen as an alternative strategic choice to what many consider an excessive dependence on the West, and would require that Turkey refashion itself along these lines. What is being discussed here, then, is a powerful merging of the old dreams of Empire with a continuation of the present authoritarian socio-political construct.

But I do not wish to raise military or strategic questions here, such as Turkey's heightened geopolitical importance within the context of the new world order, or in connection with the struggle against terrorism. Rather, I want to emphasize the fact that, along with this new wave of change, the regimes and borders of the Middle East are likely to undergo some adjustments.

The current borders of the Middle East were largely drawn after the world wars. The First World War and the Russian Revolution were both factors in determining these borders. After the Second World War a new reordering accompanied the establishment of the state of Israel, and with it the foundations were laid for new problems. And now another period—that of the Cold War—has come to an end. In the present period it is anticipated that the Middle East, as the most important source of the world's problems, will be restructured. We can see two different elements in the restructuring of this region. One is the establishment of new nation-states, such as the Palestinians and the Kurds, which have not established their own states. The other is the erosion of authoritarian regimes in the Middle East following the March 2003 war in Iraq, such as those of Syria, Egypt and Saudi Arabia. This turmoil requires Turkey to redefine itself and its role in the region. Either it will react according to its traditional fears, seeing its existence threatened, especially with the reopening of the border question, and will oppose every change in the region vehemently—this would entail a hardening of the authoritarian bureaucratic state tradition—or Turkey will redefine itself through a democratization process and can then play a leading role in the democratization of the region. The Turkish reaction against the US-led war in Iraq is an example of this authoritarian approach. This approach now leads Turkey to seek alliances with Syria and Iran against every change towards democratization in the region. However, it is inconceivable that Turkey will overcome the problems that face the region so long as it fails to bring about democratization and liberalization within its own borders, and to overcome its authoritarian–bureaucratic state tradition.

The Western Connection:
The Crucial Condition for Democratization

One of Turkey's most significant problems is that the internal dynamics that would lead to democratization are, in fact, very weak, for a number of historical reasons which I shall touch on only briefly here. The state–society conflict has not produced a strengthening of democratic values. For this reason, membership in the European Union with its Western orientation carries a special importance in regard to the country's prospects for democratization. The foreign connection has always been significant in Turkey, and has even played a sort of catalytic role in whatever progress toward democratization has been made up to now.

If we begin with the *Tanzimat* reforms of 1839, the various reform initiatives that have been introduced by the Ottoman–Turkish rulers from then until today did not derive from deeply held belief in such reforms. Rather, the rulers were more or less forced to introduce them as a result of external pressures that resulted from the process of developing relations with Europe. It is fair to say that behind every great wave of reforms there lay pressure from foreign politics. The democratic institutions that have taken root in Turkey up to now have been introduced by an unwilling, or at least unenthusiastic, ruling elite, and as a result of the country's foreign ties. This is why Turkey's ruling elites do not feel themselves obliged to adhere to the existing democratic legal institutions, and this, in turn, is the reason for the appearance of a gap between these institutions and the political culture of the elites.

I would now like to explain this situation further through a comparison of Germany and Turkey.

Comparison between Germany and Turkey

The nation (and nation-state) building processes of Turkey and Germany share many characteristics. The process of establishing a national state was determined in both countries by the tension resulting from the difficult choice of whether or not to be a state confined to one region, with clearly defined borders, or an empire. If we leave for now the transformations in Germany since the Second World War, we can see that there are striking parallels between the two countries' prevailing political cultures. I am referring here to their collective behavioral norms, the characteristics of their ruling ideologies and their mindsets. Just as the fact of Germany's central location—in Central Europe—played an influential role in the formation of the country's behavioral norms, ideology and mentality, the same must be said for Turkey. It must be clarified, however, that I am not viewing this sense of being in the middle as a geographic category. The deeply held sense of being in the middle, of being surrounded by nations or states, or environs that constitute a threat to one's existence, determines one's psychological makeup in the most fundamental way.

It is even possible to list certain characteristics of the political culture resulting from such a worldview. In short, we are talking about a neurotic pattern of behavior which is highly susceptible to being incited against the national state. This behavior pattern manifests itself as a dissatisfaction with the situation in which the person, or in this case, country, finds themself. The national identities belonging to both of these states were formed at a time when different maximalist nationalist aims were being confirmed, and simultaneously, as a political collapse was being experienced. The disillusionment that resulted from the failure to realize these ambitions formed an important part of the national identities of both countries. The German state ideal, which was defined in utopian and maximalist terms, was confronted by a series of disappointments and blows to the dream of a Greater Germany which had, from 1849 until the Versailles Treaty of 1919, been continually held up as the goal. The logical conclusion was that other states or peoples who were rash enough to try and realize the ideal state would need to be destroyed. This process was no different for the Ottoman-Turkish elites. The great ideals, which were formed at a time of imperial collapse and in the depths of this collapse, met with immense disappointment, as every campaign in the Ottomans' drive towards the east resulted in defeat; carried to their logical conclusion within the country, these ideals led to the Genocide and expulsion of the Christian population of Anatolia.

It is possible to list other characteristics of the political culture resulting from the sense of being in the middle.

(1) A positive dependency on modes of military behavior and their relations which pervade civilian life to the point that the country does not hesitate to define itself as a military nation, as a nation of soldiers.[13]

(2) The authoritarian tradition of government, wherein power is not truly found in the parliament or in political parties, but is rather in the hands of a military bureaucratic elite, infused with a powerful culture of discipline.

(3) The close interface of the social and economic imbalances that have been experienced as a result of rapid modernization, and the insecurities created by a political system that has been unable to keep pace with this social and economic development.

(4) The near-hysterical dependency on and idealization of massive modernization and technological development, on one hand, and suspicions and doubts about it on the other.

(5) Persistent anti-parliamentarian, anti-Western, anti-liberal attitudes which have a long-standing tradition in both societies.

(6) The great longing for internal unity and wholeness, the search for political harmony, and the doubts about class differences and social pluralism, and, in the absence of a collective *Überpersonalität*, or over-arching and defining social character, the search for a strong man who, it is believed, would be able to bring together and unite society.

These shared characteristics, which currently prevail in Turkey, and which once did in Germany, have left profound traces in both societies. With regard to Turkey, a few more things should be added:

(1) The transition from an Empire straddling three continents to a small Republic squeezed into Anatolia remains an issue that has not yet been fully digested by Turkish society.

(2) An enormous strain caused by the burden of Turkey's 'glorious' past. This results in a deeply rooted belief that, essentially, the Turks do not deserve the current situation in which they find themselves and need to strive for something higher.

(3) The ensuing inferiority complex which all this has brought on has produced extreme sensitivity on these issues.

(4) There is an utter inability to accept that nothing currently remains of Turkey's past importance and influence in international affairs, and ideas, obsessive to the extent of paranoia, relating to a belief that everyone (and Europe, in particular) is constantly picking on them.

(5) There is a profound conviction that Turkey is surrounded by powers who have no objective other than desiring its disappearance and the partitioning of the country.

(6) Insecurity and fear for Turkey's borders have been brought on by the more-than-century-long, grievous collapse and partition of the Ottoman Empire.

(7) There is a belief that behind every demand for democracy within the country lies an international plot aimed at partition.

(8) All attitudes to Turkey that are felt to be utterly undeserved are assessed as humiliations; being ever conscious of its past greatness, Turkey has great difficulty enduring such slights.

With regard to the subject at hand, these characteristics can only be understood in one way: as cultural values that form an imposing obstacle to societal democratization. However much Germany's current democratization is indebted to its Western connection or integration into the West after the Second World War, a similar situation exists for Turkey. In Germany today, the right-wing ultranationalists criticize integration into the West at every turn, emphasizing the special characteristics peculiar to Germany. While they put forward theses proclaiming Germany's *Sonderweg* (special path), similar tendencies can be seen in Turkey today as well.

Because of Turkey's authoritarian and military culture, and its historical heritage, the ruling elite in Ankara possesses a traditionally anti-Western attitude. These elites are not very enthusiastic about the European Union, or overly desirous to join it. Given their 'druthers', they would ultimately prefer not to enter into the process of membership, or at least to delay it. If a few steps are indeed being taken toward greater integration into Europe today, the fact is that they are being taken largely because of pressure from foreign powers' demands arising from the country's civil society. If today in the West there is the belief that Turkey's ruling elites have a serious longing for the European Union, I must say that this is mistaken. The current rulers, just like those of the 19th century, are being slowly forced to enter upon a process against their wills—and with much foot-dragging— and they are doing so largely because this is their last chance. For them, the goal is not rapid democratization, but rather the slowing down of the process. To put it simply, there are dozens of Milosevics or Saddams among the military–bureaucratic elite in Turkey, and other countries, who believe that by suppressing different ethnic-national groups within their nation-state and establishing authoritarian regimes they can be very strong powers in their region. They also think that they can underpin their policy with the notion of 'sovereign right' and sell this idea as 'anti-imperialism.' Turkey's Milosevics and Saddams have never done this very openly and always defended these ideas as an element of 'independence.' The only difference between them and the real Milosevic and Saddam is the significant one that, due to the important geo-strategic position Turkey occupies, they are not subject to removal through some special operation. Just as significant, this allows them the ability to maneuver at important historical junctures, such as the one in which we now find ourselves. (Milosevic and Saddam have the common characteristic that both of them interpreted the end of Cold War era in the same way.)

The strong ties that have been established with Europe are a factor that will strengthen those sectors who do desire democracy and greater civil freedoms in Turkey. Every initiative that distances Turkey from Europe can only create a situation which strengthens those elements who do not want the questions of democracy and liberalization in Turkey placed on the nation's agenda. What may be needed is a will to push forward the country's democratization against all odds. Integration into Europe is an indispensable condition for democratization in Turkey.

As we know, such integration presupposes a clear sense of belonging, cultural values and a collective will to make ultimate choices involving national interests. In this respect, Turkey's political culture, which developed during the period of transition from Empire to Republic, especially its dealing with nationality problems, seems an important factor in relation to the development of civil democratic values. The propensity to resort often to violent methods, including massacre, as a preferred method of conflict resolution still seems to be a problem. In Chapter 2, I will make an attempt to understand the emergence of this political culture and how it became one of the important elements of Turkish national identity. It is a quest for Turkish national identity. The emergence of this Turkish national identity was one of the important reasons for the occurrence of Genocide and today is one of the important obstacles on the way to integration with Europe. What we are observing here is a strong parallel between past and present. The existence of the same mindset that caused the Armenian Genocide seems today a major hindrance to solving the Kurdish question, and, therefore, to membership in the European Union.

NOTES

1. Gesine Schwan, *Politik und Schuld, die zerstörische Macht des Schweigens* (Frankfurt a.M., 1999), p. 164.
2. Other statements by Erdoğan include his reference to democracy as 'the means, not the way (*Amaç değil, araç*) and the proclamation 'Allah be praised, I'm a Shari'a advocate' (*Elhamdülillah Şeriâtçıyım*). He also recited a poem by the Turkish nationalist theoretician Ziya Gökalp to a crowd, a poem in which the poet likens the domes of mosques to helmets, their minarets to spears. One columnist described Erdoğan's utterances as remaining in his memory like naked photographs of a famous movie star that were taken before the star became famous. This was because both Erdoğan and his new AKP appear to have since abandoned the view which sees the Republic and democracy as temporary platforms to be exploited for the eventual attainment of another political system (in this case, an Islam-based social and political order). They now declare themselves as conservative democrats within a normal Western democratic system. The views that the AKP and Erdoğan have since expressed as criticisms of their own pasts have two aspects worth mentioning. The first is that there appears to be a serious attempt among the Islamist factions to abandon their old confrontational and triumphalist behavior, and to seek out a consensus within the current social order. It is precisely this type of self-criticism that has produced the new type of statement. The second is that they show how fluid and open to change Turkey's current political order is: the Erdoğan phenomenon is an important demonstration of just how unpredictable the system is. The fact that some of its main political actors are currently moderating their views, views that could be considered radical, highlights another of Turkey's fundamental problems. That is that these actors, just like Erdoğan and his AKP, are confronted with the problem of doubt and trust among the general populace as well.
3. Wolfgang Schluchter, *Max Webers Sicht des Islam.* (Frankfurt: Suhrkamp Verlag, 1987), pp. 58ff. See also Taner Akçam, *Siyasi Kültürümüzde Zulüm ve İşkence* (Istanbul: Iletişim, 1991), pp. 35–59.
4. Ertuğrul Özkök, 'Milli eylem stratejisi belgesi,' *Hürriyet*, June 24, 1999.
5. At the beginning of every year in Turkey, the government publishes a circular in which the authority and the duties of the National Security Council is recounted. Such a circular was published in the newspaper *Radikal* on June 23, 2000. According to this article, the NSC possesses secret directives and has the duty of supervising and reviewing all manner of activities within the provincial administrations as well as among government ministers. Turkey, then, is a country under the rule of law, but which is nonetheless governed by secret directives.
6. *Devletin mali deniz, yemiyen domuz.*
7. Richard Clogg, *A Concise History of Greece* (Cambridge University Press, 2002), p. 59.
8. The reader may be incredulous and find these statements harsh. But a recent example can

be given as evidence. At the 2003 party congresses of two of the most powerful center-left (the CHP—Republican People's Party—Turkish social democrats) and center-right parties (the ANAP—Motherland Party), not a word was said about either the Kurdish question or the problem of Cyprus—arguably the two most important problems faced by Turkey at present. Other such subjects were similarly ignored. It was no different at the first congress of the governing AKP in September 2003.

9. Ahmet Insel, *Radikal*, December 2, 2001.

10. Kazım Öztürk, *Atatürk'ün TBMM Açık ve Gizli Oturumlarındaki Konuşmaları*, Vol. I (Ankara 1992), pp. 66–9.

11. For more detailed information on this subject, see Chapter 4.

12. In the November 2002 elections, of the four main center parties of the previous 15 years—the DSP, DYP, ANAP and the CHP—the first three failed to gain the 10 percent of the vote required for parliamentary representation. The same fate befell the far-right Nationalist Action Party, or MHP, which before the election had held the largest parliamentary representation of all the parties. The overall impression was that Turkish voters had voiced their dissatisfaction with the status quo by punishing the four parties, none of which came even close to clearing the 10 percent bar.

13. There is an old adage in Turkish, told with numerous variations, but all of which refer to the Turks as a 'nation of soldiers.'

2

A Theoretical Approach
to Understanding Turkish National Identity

One of the most problematic aspects of Ottoman-Turkish history is the series of social and political ruptures experienced during the 19th century. It is fair to claim that the most characteristic feature of the period of passage from the multinational Ottoman Empire to the national Turkish state was these ruptures. It thus follows that the question of historical continuity would be a significant one in Turkish history. For the Ottomans, one consequence of the traumatic events experienced in this period was a shaken confidence in their own physical security, in their society itself, and a loss of self-worth. They began to doubt the values they had held up to that point. Research on the issue of ruptures in the social fabric has shown that when social disruptions, military defeats, and decline in power are experienced as massive internal traumas, as they were here, a disturbed sense of history and identity are likely to emerge. Such a process is liable to have serious consequences for national identity formation, with national identity often forming around the three main components of wounded national pride, loss of self-worth and a sense of insecurity.

Constraints of time and space prevent me from examining here the full spectrum of problems created by wounded national pride. However it can be fairly asserted that there is widespread belief in Turkey that there exists a cabal of enemies, internal and external, bent on Turkey's destruction. This belief has reached the level of paranoia in many cases, and has produced an imbalance in the national mood, which fluctuates wildly between an exaggerated self-importance, derived from being the descendants of a 'great empire,' on one hand, and a chronic lack of national self-confidence and an inferiority complex on the other. Just as with individuals, this hurtling on a national level between delusions of greatness and feelings of impotence and haplessness prevents nations from devising realistic responses to the problems they face. Theirs is a fictional world, one immersed in fantasies. In such a world, the past is generally defined in accordance with some desirable, idealized future. In order to reach this ideal, however, the resort to violence is often inescapable.

The main problem derives from the fact that social collectives, like individuals, find it difficult to integrate negative experiences or past traumas into their life stories, or their self-perceptions. We are often confronted with this problem today in Turkey. The history of Turkey—especially around the turn of the 20th century—has been a history of traumas. These traumas were not merely limited to those large-scale outbreaks of lethal violence that have been described as 'massacre,' 'genocide' and 'expulsion.' From the perspective of the Turks, this period is largely perceived as one of military defeats, territorial losses, national humiliations at the hands of foreign powers, and by nagging fear arising from perceived threats to their national existence. The traumas were so profound as to cause Turkish society to try and forget them, but they have left their scars on the national psyche just the same.

One of the most negative manifestations of wounded national pride, which in the Turkish case is a product of this immense shock and trauma, has been a nationwide difficulty in accepting civilized norms of behavior, and a consequent propensity to resort to violence. The reason for this is simple: for civil behavioral norms to prevail, it is essential that individual human instincts and drives be placed under societal control. If we accept that the suppression of natural drives and self-control by individuals are the price to be paid for civilization, it is essential that a system of rewards for this sacrifice be established. In other words, compliance with civil behavioral norms for an individual is akin to an act of self-sacrifice because it results in suppression of the realization of certain basic instincts. This forbearance, or sacrifice, can only work if there is a corresponding reward for engaging in it. Herein lies one of the psychological functions of national pride. If the national identity which translates to self-love (an idea that I will deal with in greater detail below) is a balanced and firmly established one, it will be perceived by group members as a reward for their forbearance. However, if this identity is somehow wounded or damaged, if it moves recklessly from one extreme self-image to another, it no longer becomes possible to reward compliance with civil behavioral norms, and the resort to violence is thus facilitated.

The only way that wounded national pride can be treated is for the person—or, in this case, the nation—to integrate the past into his or her life story; to successfully bring it to the point that it can be openly discussed. In this essay I will apply a theoretical approach in order to understand Turkish nationalism and integrate the Armenian Genocide into Turkey's life story.

The Difficulty in Comprehending Acts of Genocide

The basic aim of this chapter is to develop a 'perpetrator approach.' The questions I wish to answer are: what were the moods, the mentality and the motives that produced the Armenian Genocide and why has the subject become so taboo in Turkey? I will try to understand the perpetrator and will first focus on some theoretical problems related to the perpetrator approach.

The most important problem in attempting to understand such savage acts as Genocide is the difficulty in maintaining sufficient distance from the research topic. This problem can be said to have two different dimensions: the first we may term the 'moral' dimension; the second is the direct relationship of the subject to the issue of national identity. In other words, the extent to which the researcher belongs to a clearly defined national group is a factor that in large measure determines his ability to remain free of subjective judgments, as is the overall attitude with which he views the subject. Both dimensions may ultimately hinder the researcher from maintaining sufficient professional distance from the subject matter, and thus may render any impartial comprehension of the issue impossible.

Let us start with the second dimension. It is easy to come up with stereo-typical national characteristics for nations other than our own. We may be quick to refer to someone as, say, a 'typical German' or a 'typical English-man.' But when the subject is the national group to which we ourselves belong, we are not as quick to speak. In order to describe the characteristics of our own group it is necessary to make a special effort to put some distance between ourselves and the subject. The difficulty derives from the inability to make a distinction between individual and national identity, a distinction which is made in theory, but cannot be made in practice so easily.

One of the most important characteristics of national identity is the emotional connection. Norbert Elias defines this as the 'like/love' relation-ship. But he claims that the 'love of nation is never something which one experiences toward a nation to which one refers as "them."' This love is something we experience towards the group we refer to as 'we,' in other words self-love. This means national identity is an integral part of individual identity. So we can assert that there is no 'I' identity, and that there is no 'we' identity, alone. In fact, the 'I/we' balance within identity is in constant flux. However, the 'I and We' identities are never derived from separate places.[1]

It is for this reason that the image that one retains of one's nation is at the same time a self-image. The individual and the nation do not occupy two separate spaces. It is in fact this coupling of the two concepts that makes individuals of the same nation identify with one another, and which makes it difficult to put distance between oneself and the crimes committed by one's nation, especially those against another nation. This is comparable on an individual level to the ease with which one may discuss the transgressions of others as opposed to those that one may have committed oneself. What we should strive for is the ability to observe our own nation at arm's length. This requires a very special kind of effort, and we can argue that the social sciences can provide to individuals and groups the tools needed to acquire this distance.

Let us turn now to the first, moral dimension. The difficulty associated with the moral dimension is this: the contempt for violent acts like Genocide, arising as it does from moral contempt commonly felt towards the perpetrators, results in their being declared 'inhuman.' This revulsion toward these actions in turn discourages us from trying to understand the underlying motives of the individuals who have performed them. This often leads to the use of terms that put distance between ourselves and such actions as well as their perpetrators, and thus prevent any identification with the 'bad guys.' This wall of morality that we place between ourselves and the action/actors may help to assuage our consciences, but it does nothing to help us to understand, and thereby to pass informed judgment on the phenomenon. In the final analysis, the issue concerns the manner in which the past is recalled and integrated into the present. Theodor Adorno suggests two possible approaches to the subject of the past. The first is to 'simply remain stuck in the pattern of blaming,' while the alternative is to 'marshal the strength to withstand the horror and attempt ourselves to comprehend the incomprehensible.'[2]

It is also important to understand that certain problems are created when we assume we ourselves have transcended our moralizing and are approaching a phenomenon with scientific objectivity. For starters, the scientific terminology, which can be described as the 'vocabulary of inhumanity,' also hinders us from distancing ourselves from the language of activists, because it objectifies events. Second, the very effort to understand an event leads one to seek out rational explanations, which often results in making excuses, seeking out and finding mitigating circumstances, or searching for signs of innocence in the perpetrators. As Walter Benjamin correctly stated, the effort to recreate historical events, which starts with asking the question 'How did it happen?' very often results in adopting an attitude very close to that of the 'winners,' and for this reason it always remains insufficient for the adoption of a moral stance.[3] What is important here is the difficulty of constructing a scientific language that also manages to contain a moral stance.

What must be done, then, is to find a scientific language that would also enable us to construct moral categories regarding such events. 'Objective and 'cold bureaucratic language' (Jürgen Habermas) may make it possible to place the necessary distance between ourselves and an event which, due to its savage and horrific character, carries the danger of otherwise rendering it impossible to come to terms with.'[4] But at the same time, cold objectivity may not provide a sense of moral outrage.

The Perspectives of 'Victim' and "Perpetrator'

Despite all the attempts there have been at explanation, it would be more useful to mention the existence of real contradictions between moral attitude and cold objectivity, and thereby to eliminate any thought of uniting these two extremes with wordplay or theoretical maneuvers. Instead of searching for theoretical formulas that would bypass this contradiction, we must devise an approach that will incorporate the contradiction within its theoretical structure.

In order to overcome this problem, Dan Diner suggests avoiding the adoption of a unitary or singular perspective in understanding a phenomenon like genocide. Instead of a single perspective, dual perspectives based separately on perpetrators and victims have been a fruitful source of discourse.[5] The most important feature separating these two perspectives is the different elements that are taken as the terms in which genocide and other similar historical events are analyzed. The victim perspective has as its central focus those things or actions that were done to the victims. In this perspective the experienced event (in this case, genocide) is removed from the general historical process and is closely examined from a singular perspective, its effect on the victim. One could perhaps say that the victim is given a privileged position. A byproduct of the moral attitude taken in this perspective—an important feature of this approach—is to disregard objective analysis, to lay the emphasis on feelings. The result is a desire not to want to understand events on a cool, rational basis. I am not arguing here that the victim perspective cannot claim objectivity. We know that there is no objectivity that goes beyond our normative positions. What I am saying is simply that 'not to want to understand' is an important moral stand that we cannot easily exclude from the analysis. Shouting out against such cruel acts is very important and must be included in the analysis. The victim perspective enables us to include this aspect of the problem.

Another important point of difference between the victim and perpetrator perspectives is in the degree of emphasis they place upon historical continuity. While the victim perspective concerns itself with the rupture in the historical process, taking as its focus the annihilative aspects of an event, the perpetrator perspective tries to situate the event within a historical process. In regard to mass slaughters, there is another important reason for developing a long-range, historical perspective: to deny a place to those who prefer to treat phenomena like genocide as exceptional events, as aberrations that are unlikely to recur, and which should be treated as isolated accidents of history.

By adopting the perpetrator perspective, it will be possible to conceive of genocide as an explainable product of a specific historical–cultural process. Of course, what is being asserted here is not that events like genocides are the inevitable product of a specific cultural background. The existence of very special conditions and the merging of these conditions with an existing cultural background are what make collective actions of annihilation such as genocide possible. The important factor is how the merging of cultural backgrounds and the particular conditions takes place. By this means we will be able to better understand both what those special conditions are and how to define them. We will also be better able to answer the question of whether or not those factors that determine the requisite cultural background for such actions are present in Turkish society today. In this way, we can oppose those who claim that genocide is a unique deviation not to be repeated in history, an explanation which lulls societies into carelessness rather than provokes them to diligence in monitoring the warning signs of such an occurrence. This approach enables us to take the position that we are face to face with violent eruptions every day and strives to create the kinds of mechanisms which will prevent their recurrence.

Genocide as a Product of National Identity

The studies carried out so far on the Armenian Genocide have, for reasons that are obvious, been done mostly from a victim perspective. I will attempt to approach the subject from the side of the perpetrator, something that has not been tried because of both a prevailing, even overwhelming attitude of denial of the Genocide from that side, as well as the transformation of the events into a sort of taboo subject among the Turks. If our purpose is to analyze a barbarity perpetrated on a collective level, to understand it, and to prevent its recurrence, focusing our attention on the victim group will not bring us any closer to an answer. The fundamental focus should be placed on the perpetrator group, and the effort should be made to reveal the conscious and subconscious mechanisms at work within this group. It is here, in the functioning of these mechanisms, that we may discover how the perpetrator is created.

In light of the existing theoretical questions that I have described, the first thing that should be said on the subject, in order to understand the Armenian Genocide from the perspective of the perpetrators, is that

Turkish national identity plays a central role in understanding the characteristics of the Armenian Genocide and the conditions under which it emerged. In order to clarify this approach I will use Norbert Elias's *Studien über die Deutschen* (Studies on the Germans) to illustrate how this identity should be defined; how its fundamental characteristics should be classified; and how the factors that shaped it can most intelligently be understood.[6]

Studien über die Deutschen is considered a successful response to the debates surrounding the Jewish Holocaust, particularly to those questions emerging within the 'rupture' versus 'continuity' debate. Elias examines historical phenomena over a long-term historical continuum (something he insists upon doing, and which separates him from other social scientists). He examines and evaluates the process by which German national identity developed, as well as its fundamental character, over a 150 to 200-year period. His purpose is to be able to answer the question, 'Which elements of long-term developments within Germany and of the thing known as German national character facilitated the rise of National Socialism?'[7] In other words, his book was an attempt to locate Hitler's regime and the Jewish Holocaust within the context of German history. I am asking the same question in trying to understand the Armenian Genocide.[8]

Because of the broad areas covered by works on the Jewish Holocaust, they are very difficult to sort out and classify. If we were to attempt to classify them according to three different categories, we could speak of a philosophical/historical, a political/ideological, and a moral dimension. In each dimension it is possible to speak of different poles. The studies done within the philosophical/historical dimension can be located between two main poles. The first is known as the 'linearity' argument, whose advocates wish to shed light upon the Holocaust by analyzing it through the characteristics of early German tribes through the Protestant Reformation and beyond. The other pole tends to approach the problem by viewing the Holocaust as an incident or accidental historical event within the general procession of German history.[9] In addition, there is the debate between the 'intentionalist' theory, which argues that the decision to carry out the Holocaust had been made already from the outset, and those opposing theories that claim there was never such a concrete idea—and even that no such overarching decision may have ever been taken. Rather, they claim, it was the course of events that gave birth to the Holocaust. Those debates that fall under the category of the moral dimension revolve around the question of whether or not such actions can be rationally understood.[10]

All of the research and argument surrounding the Jewish Holocaust share a single problem and difficulty: situating this event within the context of German history. This, in fact, was one of the main questions of the 'Historians' Controversy' (*Historikersstreit*) that erupted in Germany in the mid-1980s. The tension was between those who viewed the Jewish Holocaust as a unique event in history and those who situated it within the context of the historical period in which it occurred.[11] Elias's success lies in having established a theoretical relationship between the continuity of certain characteristics of Germany's history and its national identity on the one hand, and the specific conditions that allowed for the Jewish Holocaust; in other words, between continuity and rupture.

Understanding Turkish National Identity

The Long-range Perspective

One of Elias's initial points of departure is the thesis that the real effects of important social events begin to be felt only one hundred years or more after their occurrence. 'Each time they are viewed anew with great surprise, so that certain patterns of thinking, of feeling and of behaving reappear in the same society after [having been absent for] many generations, by adapting themselves in a remarkable fashion to new conditions.' For this reason he states that, in order to be able to understand human history, we need models that can explain history within century-long increments.[12] For if we wish to speak of social transformations, we need to be aware that they are completed only after passing through stages of development that are often several generations in length.[13]

Certainly, the idea of developing a historical perspective which encompasses lengthy processes was not unique to Elias. One of the fundamental points separating the 19th century thinkers–in particular, August Comte and Karl Marx—from the social scientists of the 20th century, is the former's creation of theoretical models that attempt to understand social events within the framework of lengthy processes. In the preface to his book *Der Prozess der Zivilisation* (The Process of Civilization) and in many other of his articles and books Elias mentions this fact, while speaking in laudatory terms of the direction taken by Comte and Marx, whom he considers the 'fathers' of sociology.[14] Likewise, he sees his own work as a continuation of the work that Marx and Comte began but were unable to complete because of the excessive imposition of their own subjective anxieties onto their analysis of historical development. Elias is quick to point out, however, that his approach is not an attempt to 'fill in the missing components.' In his acceptance speech for the Adorno Prize, Elias claimed that he was simply the bearer of a torch which was lit before him and which will be borne by others after.[15]

The most distinctive aspect of Elias's analysis of the long-range historical process is ultimately his rejection of explanations of historical processes that rely upon a single-causality relationship. He stresses the distinct differences between various historical periods. On this subject Elias has employed different methods of classification in his various works. For example, in his article 'Über sich selbst' [About one's self]. Elias speaks of four processes: a) the development of means of production; b) the development of means and instruments of violence; c) the development of self-control of the individual; and d) the development of the means of orientation (knowledge).[16] These different dimensions overlap with one another and mutually and reciprocally affect one another. Yet each one has its own internal developmental dynamic. The development of one does not necessarily result in the decline of the other, nor does it translate into the natural completion or conclusion of another.

In another of Elias's works we see the following classifications: a) social differentiation (usually—but never entirely—limited to the area of the economic division of labor); b) the development of increasingly large integrated units and the integration of larger and smaller units; c) changes in the yardsticks of social behavior which determine how permissible and non-permissible are defined—which can be understood as the steady civilizing of the human personality-construct; d) the development of means for human self-orientation (knowledge) and e) the steady accumulation of capital. In total, five levels are identified.[17] None of these dimensions is a prerequisite for any other, nor does any act as the catalyst or instigator for the others. Therefore to understand the Armenian Genocide it is essential to take a perspective of at least a hundred years, back to the beginning of the dissolution of the Ottoman Empire.

The Role of Psychology in the Development of Social Processes
If we were to select the distinguishing aspect of Elias's analysis of long-range processes, it would have to be his direct use of psychology to understand the processes of social transformation: the use of the relationship between the Freudian concepts of super ego, ego and id, which he explains with such phrases as 'the individual's exercise of self-control,' and 'the transformation of external pressure to internal pressure' to under-stand social processes of change. The important point here is his rejection of the concept, so dominant in sociology, of constructing models according to an individual–society dichotomy, whereby the individual and the society are seen as irreconcilable poles of interpretation. We are all familiar with the debate as to whether the individual or society is the 'correct' point of focus, or over which is abstract and which is real. With his concept of 'figuration,' Elias moves beyond this oppositional approach. He discusses humans not as individuals but in the plurality.

The starting point for Elias's analysis of social processes is the relationship that is established between societal transformation and the evolution of human psychology. He speaks of the existence of a mental construct within both individuals and communities, which shows change as dependent upon the evolution of social relations. In *Über den Prozess der Zivilisation* Elias admits that this issue occupies a central position in his works:

> In the course of all my labors, I have attempted to show that the structures deriving from psychological functions and the behavioral standards specific to each period are closely related to the structures created by social functions, the transformation of these functions and the changes in human relationships.[18]

In order to understand how this mental construct in humans actually functions, there is a need for long-range models of analysis.

> Whether to aid in the comprehension of the mental construct of the individual, or to better understand historical development over a number of generations, it is necessary to take under observation a succession of generations much longer than is today possible.[19]

In essence, long-range psychological analysis is the fundamental point distinguishing Elias's work from that of other social scientists who use psychology to analyze historical events.

This is the dimension that is directly concerned with the Armenian Genocide. During the 19th century, there were rapid changes in the social structure of the Ottoman Empire. These rapid changes caused a certain change in the mental attitude of people who responded to these changes. The culmination of these changes and changing attitudes had a direct bearing on the Armenian Genocide of 1915.

Defining National Identity as a Mode of Behavior

National character develops within a close relationship with each nation's process of nation-state building. With this approach, national identity is defined as 'a way of behaving' or mental state and actually takes shape within the process of nation-state building. By reason of this direct relationship between national identity and the national state, the question of which ethnic, religious or language groups the national identity comprises is a secondary one. What is important is the formation of a common mindset, and for this to manifest itself in shared modes of behavior.

These theoretical premises serve as the starting point of my analysis of how the mentality that was formed during the process of Ottoman collapse and the formation of the Turkish national state influenced the manner in which Turkey responds to contemporary problems. When the subject is the Kurds, the situation is very easy to observe. Not only the rulers, but ordinary citizens also display reactions that closely resemble those of their predecessors in Turkish history. Here I would like to draw a parallel between the discussions regarding the non-Muslim population of the Ottoman Empire, who were defined as the 'other' during the late 19th and early 20th centuries, and the current discourse surrounding the Kurds.

The standard claims heard daily in discussions in Turkey are that the real motive behind Kurdish demands for greater democracy is the partition of land and ultimately Kurdish secession from Turkey; that the West is consciously attempting to resurrect the 1920 Treaty of Sèvres by playing the 'Kurdish card';[20] that the Turkish nation is surrounded by hostile enemies who wish to topple and partition it; and so on. All of these views date from a century ago. To a large degree these feelings are a reflection of the mindset of that period.

Eighty years ago, those who 'forged relationships with our enemies' and tried to 'divide the nation' were the non-Muslims. The use of violence was a 'natural' response against those elements harboring such aims. In 1991 and 1992, the Turkish armed forces fired upon the city of Cizre in eastern Anatolia. The civilian population fled for their lives into the mountains. A tiny newspaper article on the incident caught my attention. In it, an elderly Kurdish man from the city asked the following question when being inter- viewed: 'Are we Armenians that you do this to us?' Although such senti- ments are not always expressed openly, they are a reflection of subconscious mental processes at work, of a mentality that allows for such automatic, spontaneous reactions. What I hope to achieve is to bring these processes, this mentality out into the open; to have them acknowledged openly.

The Five Main Elements
for Understanding Turkish National Identity

I present the development of the Turkish national state as a fabric in which five different processes are interwoven. Four of these are drawn from Elias's analysis of German national identity. I will explain these processes by way of a comparative analysis. What is important is not to ascertain the points of similarity and difference in the histories of these two peoples, but to broaden our perspective for understanding the subject at hand.

National Identity and Location: 'The Middle Position'

Elias defines Germany's middle position as one of the decisive factors in the formation of German national identity. But the expression 'middle position' is being used here not merely to denote a geographical location. Rather, it defines the feeling created by the nature of Germany's relations with the other nations in its region.

The process of German nation-state building has been deeply influenced by its position of having been in the middle of three ethno-linguistic national blocs.

The Latinized and Slavic groups continually felt themselves threatened by the more heavily populated German state. At the same time, the representatives of the newly-formed German state felt themselves threatened in turn by those groups on their borders. Each side exploited every opportunity to expand their territory without regard for any other considerations. From the perspective of the centrally-located German state, the need for states to acquire territory in such a manner would mean the constant threat of its border areas being lopped off to form independent states.[21]

One aspect of the mental state produced by being in the middle is the perception of the states on one's borders as threats to one's existence. There is a belief that one is surrounded by enemies bent on one's destruction. It would be no exaggeration to characterize Turkey's relationship with its neighbors today as similar. Turkish national identity already contains an aspect of siege mentality and sees Anatolia as the last refuge against the hostile environment surrounding it and the bloodletting that it has experienced on its borders. It was this siege mentality and perception of Anatolia as the last refuge that played an important role in Turkey's policies towards the Armenians that were different from those taken toward other nationalities, and their culmination in genocide.

Problems Arising from the Loss of Superiority

The second significant factor in the formation of the Turkish national mindset was the Ottomans' loss of their previous hegemony within the international hierarchy of states. Just as in relations between individuals, claims Elias, the issue of status is the most important of those factors motivating and influencing individuals on the level of inter-state relations. Differences in status, the tensions related to these differences and the fear of loss of status can be seen not just in modern societies but throughout history, and they are the source of a great many problems.[22]

States that have fallen from positions of great power often find their new, lowered status difficult to digest.

> Down to our day it has been a proven fact in human history that the members of states or other units of social organization that have lost their position of superiority—or their claims thereto—during the final days of their wars have usually had difficulty in reconciling themselves with the new situation, and most importantly, in overcoming the sense of loss to their own self-esteem. A lengthy period—sometimes an entire century—must often pass before this can be accomplished. And perhaps they never will succeed [in overcoming this].[23]

The situation most likely to come about as a result is that the members of society perceive this loss as a form of humiliation. Rather than accept the reality of a new, reduced status, they prefer to behave as if nothing has changed. Fantasies are created—often completely at odds with their new reality. Demonstrations of power are held, wars are even waged in order to prove to the world that nothing has changed. Along with the change in the state's place in the world hierarchy, members of society often experience an observable state of depression. This depression manifests itself as a profound sorrow over the loss of greatness. The prevailing sentiment among such a group will be 'the desire to struggle against fate and to turn the clock back by a resort to violence.'[24]

Traces of this situation can be seen in two important cultures of behavior. The first is the culture of drinking to forget, wherein the individual tries to drown his/her pain in alcohol. The second is the culture of bellicosity. The relative weakness of a state, and the great ease with which other states can make military incursions across its borders, leads to militaristic behavior within that society and a heightened level of bellicosity. A poignant expression of this mental state was related by the Hungarian orientalist Arminius Vambéry when recounting his discussions in London with Namik Kemal and Ziya Paşa, prominent members of the Young Turks group, which was an early opponent of the Ottoman regime:

> The discourse during the day…was somnolent. But when the glasses of anisette (*raki*) were brought out at night, the air became livelier. The esteemed gentlemen's eyes would begin to sparkle…the pain and longing they felt at the decline of the once-powerful Ottoman State, a state which, in their opinion, could once again return to its previous strength, would grow sharper in tone and more forceful. The reverence and admiration that they felt towards the successes of their warlike forefathers and the deep regard in which they held the heroes of Islam, whose names they recounted…appeared perfectly natural to me.[25]

This mental condition is one of the main causes of violence in societies. Elias explains it thus: 'When a person's own state is weak relative to other states, it creates special, extraordinary conditions. Psychologically, such persons become crushed by feelings of self-doubt. They become consumed with doubt over all their values; they feel themselves humiliated and that their honor has been toyed with. They yearn to take revenge on those who have created these conditions.'[26] To say that many wars have begun as a result of this condition would not be incorrect.

> [O]nly in rare cases when others are growing stronger and they are growing weaker do powerful social formations submit peacefully to a narrowing of their power, to a lowering of their social status and, with it, to a change in their self-image, their we-ideal, their identity…Like wild animals, powerful nations or other powerful social formations are at their most dangerous when they feel concerned—when they have the feeling that the balance of power is going against them, that the power resources of potential rivals and enemies are becoming greater than theirs, that their values are threatened and their

superiority slipping away. Under past and present conditions of human social life, developments of this kind are one of the most typical and frequent situations in which people are driven to use of violence; they are one of the situations which lead to war.

Instability and Late Nationalization in the Process of Nation-State Formation

One of the most important factors in the development of German national identity is that, in comparison with France and England, the German state followed a particularly unstable path during its formative stages. Compared to these other countries German history is full of many more twists, turns and breaks in continuity, which in turn created barriers to the development of national self-confidence and security. It could be said that the fact that London maintained its identity as a capital city for over a thousand years is a sign of stability in England's development of its statehood, culture and civilization. One can observe the same linear progression and continuity in regard to France. But as for Berlin, it was not until the late 18th and 19th centuries that it became the major German city and capital city that we know today. The meaning of this break in historical continuity was an inability to establish strong cultural traditions that could find their symbolic reflection in an urban center.

Even Istanbul served as a capital city for the Ottomans for centuries. The historical process of the late 18th and 19th centuries, however, created a strong sense of insecurity in the Ottomans. Due to the multiethnic character of the Empire, the Ottoman ruling elite was unable to offer a stable national identity to replace this insecurity. Turkish nationalism, as a political movement, arrived only in the 20th century. This late arrival of the national identity created chronic self-doubt and constant vacillation between exaggerated praise of one's value on the one hand, and suffering from an inferiority complex on the other.

Military-Bureaucratic Caste and National Values

Elias claims that, to a great extent, 'military models' determined German national identity. This was the result of a conflict whose roots lay in the tensions between the German feudal classes and the bourgeoisie. From our standpoint, what is important is that two main tendencies were present within the developing German bourgeoisie: a liberal/idealist current and a conservative/nationalist current. Both shared the political goal of a united Germany, but in the end German unity did not come about by way of the bourgeoisie; it was won on the field of battle by the Prussian, feudal class of Junkers. The German military victory in 1871 over France was simultaneously a victory of the German aristocracy over the bourgeoisie. It consolidated the power of the German military and aristocracy, and a large part of the German bourgeoisie subsequently fell into line with the military state and adopted its values and behavioral norms. The fact that a culture took root in Germany that gave birth to Hitler, a culture in which violence was seen as a means of solving political problems, can be understood in light of this background.

It is also possible to understand the processes of Turkish modernization and formation of national identity through the framework of this model. In Turkey the main problem was how to save the declining Empire, or state, from collapse. The Ottoman bourgeoisie, which had been created by modernization, essentially consisted of members of the non-Muslim population. Due to the fact that the centrifugal forces of nationalism received support from the Western powers, the liberal and decentralized model for future Ottoman administrations that had been developed by these non-Muslim groups was transformed from a model for salvation into one of dissolution. The Ottoman military and bureaucratic elites became the main vehicle of Turkish national identity and, later, of the development of the state. As a result, militarist values were decisive in the development within Turkish culture of an inclination to solve problems through violence.

The Longing for Unity and the Search for a Leader Who Could Achieve It
The fifth element of the development of Turkish national identity is the sentiment of longing for unity resulting from the nature of the process of nation-state formation, and the concomitant search for a leader who can fulfill this longing. In the German case, the geographically dispersed and politically fractured nature of the polities in which the Germans lived made it impossible to defend their territories as a single region. What's more, the area under imperial sovereignty and ruled by the first Holy Roman Emperors, and which was the starting point for the first German national state, was vast. A direct result of this lack of a single center of power was a long history of protracted wars between the different German feudal entities over these broad tracts of land, and a very weak and delayed process of centralization relative to its neighbors. The perception of being dispersed had a fundamental role in forming the Germans' understanding of both themselves and the nations around them.

As a result of this historical dispersion, the Germans came to believe that they were a collective that 'could not manage to stop fighting amongst themselves.' The longing therefore developed, almost a national yearning, for a strong leader who could put an end to their internal strife and bring about national unity and togetherness. Since it did not seem possible of their own accord to live together in peace, perhaps a strong, centralized administration could bring about such unity.

One important result of this desire for a strong leader and administration was a continued lack of confidence in the country's parliamentary system, because such a system can only take root in societies in which problems are considered a natural part of life, in which they are solved through debate and discourse, and the ability to arrive at a consensus is considered a talent. In contrast, the Germans, as a result of their centuries-long experience, had come to view conflicts and disputes between different social groups and struggle among different parties as a negative phenomenon. In their view these were precisely what destroyed unity and togetherness. The longing for external control or pressure—in other words, for a powerful leader—was great indeed.

Based on the arguments set forth above, Elias attempted to explain the emergence of Hitler and his rise to power, as part of a greater effort to place Hitler within the purview of general German history. From his perspective, Hitler is a bearer of the fundamental characteristics of German national identity. The existence of these general traits shows that the phenomenon of Nazism was not a deviation from the general lines of German history. On the contrary, Nazism is seen as having been entirely within the realm of the possible. Nevertheless, it would be incorrect to present the Holocaust as a natural result of these general traits which make up the German national character. What led to the Jewish Holocaust was the combination of these characteristics with other factors in a special type of nexus. Elias posits that there were, at that time, certain specific socio-pathological elements, which, when combined with the general factors already in place, led to Genocide. Likewise, specific socio-pathological factors played as great a role as did certain fundamental characteristics of Turkish national identity in the decisions leading to the Armenian Genocide. I define these special factors as the 'desperate fear of annihilation.'

'Annihilation Psychosis' and the Decision for Genocide

In both the German and Turkish experiences, it can be said that we are confronted with a particular scenario: one in which the perception of being threatened from across one's borders due to the situation of being in the middle, and of having tumbled from a position of high status among nations to one of humiliation produced a condition wherein both countries found themselves unable to accept the existing socio-political situation. The imbalance between a former position of strength and a present one of weakness results in more than just an inferiority complex and anger: it transforms into a reactive impulse in the form of an excessive focus on past greatness and strength. Feelings of longing for former greatness grow increasingly strong, to the point that it becomes impossible to acknowledge that the 'glorious past' has passed into history. Instead, it is re-created as an ideal to be realized.[28]

The immensity of the abyss between a state's former grandeur and its current debased and devalued condition does more than just increase the desire for the glorious past. It brings with it a desire to wreak vengeance upon those who have brought about this situation. When this desire merges with a prevalence of militaristic values and behavioral norms, what emerges are 'rescue strategies' which promise to restore the former greatness through wars and other acts of violence. We can argue that this mindset was the principal reason for the Ottoman decision to enter into the First World War.[29] The war seemed a last hope, though, as it turned out, it was a final exit.

When the hoped-for victory led instead to defeat, the situation took on a more dramatic character. There was a direct relationship between the speed with which the regime and Empire began to crumble and the heavy-handedness of the means employed to block this.

> As their power, their sense of security and their hope faded on the road to defeat, and as they felt themselves increasingly to be fighting with their backs against a wall in their struggle for power, the standards of behavior that had been their source of pride grew increasingly crude; in fact, they began to ignore and even destroy them.[30]

The situation became perceived as a 'do or die' struggle for the existence for the nation. As feelings of sinking, of being besieged by enemies and of utter hopelessness reached the chronic level, the conviction became sharper that the only way to save oneself from this situation was through an absolute intolerance and complete disregard of others and their needs. If the process of decline fails to follow a gradual, linear course, and if hopes of emerging from the condition in which the nation finds itself fluctuate greatly, the result is even more severe. The nation that feels itself to be in free fall is more likely not to accept that it has hit rock bottom, and the further off the prospect of achieving a glorious future becomes, the more likely that nation is blindly to hitch its hopes to that prospect's realization. In short,

> The stronger the downward tendency toward decline, the greater the coarseness of means used to stop this progression…Having their backs against the wall turns the fierce defenders of civilization into its greatest destroyers. They quickly become barbarians.[31]

I believe that this was the Ottoman mindset before and during the First World War. For that reason, it appears to me no coincidence that the decision behind the Armenian Genocide was made during the fierce battles of the Gallipoli campaign, when the Ottoman Empire's very existence seemed to balance between life and death. The hopeless situation into which Ottomans had fallen produced a willingness to rely on extraordinary acts of cruelty.

In summary, as in the case of Germany, Turkish national identity was imprinted by the long experience of military defeats and the resulting losses of power. This process, which occurred over a long period of time, had the cumulative effect of producing a national identity replete with wounded honor and self-doubt. A nostalgic national ideal emerged that held forth the vision of a glorious past as a future goal. This condition, in turn, facilitated the emergence of particularly pernicious tendencies in thought and behavior. When repeated defeats made this ideal impossible to attain, recourse to the most barbaric methods became inevitable.

The conclusion and warning that may be extracted from all this is that the mindset that emerges as a result of a series of past defeats, can, under similar circumstances, resurface in the future. There is no inherent obstacle to its re-emergence. Elias stresses this point.

> A great number of events that have occurred in our time have shown us the conditions of today's societies [that] can produce certain untoward tendencies in 20th-century thought and behavior, of which National Socialism is perhaps the clearest example, and that these conditions may well appear in other places as well.[32]

That being the case, it makes more sense to examine the societal conditions that give rise to massacres and genocide than to assuage one's conscience and take comfort in the thought that the actions of the Nazis or the crimes of the Ottoman Unionist (*İttihatçı*) leaders will never be repeated in the same way or manner.

The fact is, methods such as 'specially constructed concentration camps, forced starvation, deaths in gas chambers or by firing squads, along with the subjecting of an entire population group to a highly organized and planned scientific annihilation,' all of which reached their apex in the Nazi example, have not lost their relevance for humanity.[33] A simple glance at what has transpired in Rwanda, Bosnia-Herzegovina, Kosovo, and Chechnya over the past decade, I believe, makes any further defense of this point unnecessary. These examples show that there are certain patterns in the occurrence of genocide. In numerous scholarly works, scholars try to develop models of these patterns, which can be subsumed as psychological and cultural bases of genocide.[34]

No theoretical explanation can fully and adequately account for the organization of mass murder. Emerging crises and a set of singular opportunities attending these crises facilitate the successful organization of mass murder. In Chapter 3, an attempt is made to interconnect the peculiar characteristics in the formation of Turkish national identity with the targeting of the Armenians for wholesale annihilation. Ideological developments, lethal doctrines depicting the victim group not only as an internal foe in the midst of a war for existence but also as dehumanized and utterly degraded creatures, are part of a comprehensive framework through which the perpetrator group sees itself saved by the elimination of the targeted victim group. Chapter 3 examines this type of targeting in a broad context of international relations and conflicts in which Turkish images of European disdain towards Turkey, and awareness of designs for the eventual partition of Ottoman Turkey, are seen as key determinants in the formative episodes of Turkish national identity, along with a strong dose of anti-Christian animus.

NOTES

1. Norbert Elias, *Studien über die Deutschen* (Frankfurt 1990), pp.196–7; and Elias, *Die Gesellschaft der Individuellen* (Frankfurt 1987), pp. 246ff.
2. Theodor W. Adorno, 'Was bedeutet: Aufarbeitung der Vergangenheit,' *Gesammelte Schriften*, vol. 10.2 (Frankfurt 1977), p. 569.
3. Walter Benjamin quoted in Jan Philipp Reemtsma, 'Vergangenheit als Prolog,' *Mittelweg* 36, August/September 1992.
4. Immanuel Geiss, 'Massaker in der Weltgeschichte, Ein Versuch über Grenzen der Menschlichkeit,' in: Uwe Backes/Eckard Jesse/Rainer Zitelmann, eds, *Die Schatten der Vergangenheit, Impulse zur Historisierung des Nationalsozialismus* (Frankfurt 1990), p. 111.
5. Dan Diner, 'Die Wahl der Perspektive. Bedarf es einer besonderen Historik des Nationalsozialismus?', in W. Schneider, ed., '*Vernichtungspolitik': Eine Debatte über den Zusammenhang von Sozialpolitik und Genozid im nationalsozialistischen Deutschland* (Hamburg 1991), pp. 65–75.
6. Since in *Studien über die Deutschen* Elias modifies many of the views he advanced in his previous work *Über den Prozeß der Zivilisation* (The Process of Civilization), the former is considered by many to be a tacit self-criticism. Elias's concept of civilization remains a point of controversy and argument. The earlier work has been criticized for the manner in which civilization is presented as an 'optimistic progression,' in which mass barbarities like massacres and genocide are evaluated as 'partial and temporary deviations from the process of civilization.' *Studien über die Deutschen* appears to be a response to those criticisms.
7. Elias, *Studien über die Deutschen*, p. 412.
8. This will be explored in greater detail in Chapter 3.
9. For further information see Ian Kershaw, *Der NS Staat, Geschichtsinterpretationen und Kontroversen im Überblick* (Hamburg 1994).
10. For further information see Wolfgang Schneider (ed.), '*Vernichtungspolitik': Eine Debatte über den Zusammenhang von Sozialpolitik und Genozid im nationalsozialistischen Deutschland* (Hamburg 1991).
11. For a documentation of 'Historikerstreit', see Der Verlag (ed.), '*Historikerstreit', Die Dokumentation der Kontroverse um die Einzigartigkeit der nationalsozialistischen Judenvernichtung*, Serie Piper, vol. 816 (München, Zurich 1987).
12. Elias, *Studien über die Deutschen*, pp. 8 and 165.

13. Elias, *Was ist Soziologie* (Munich 1981), p. 18.

14. Elias, 'Zur Grundlage einer Theorie sozialer Prozesse,' *Zeitschrift für Soziologie*, vol. 6, no. 2, 1977, p. 127.

15. Norbert Elias and Wolf Lepenies, *Zwei Reden anläßlich der Verleihung des Theodor W. Adorno-Preises* (Frankfurt 1977).

16. Elias, *Über sich selbst*, Frankfurt 1990, p. 157.

17. Elias, *Über den Prozeß der Zivilisation*, vol. 2, 1997, pp. 140–5.

18. *Ibid*, p. 452.

19. *Ibid*.

20. According to the Sèvres Treaty of 1920, Anatolia was to have been divided between the Kurdish, Armenian, Greek and Turkish populations. Among these groups, the Turks were to be given a limited territory in central Anatolia, while the Kurds were to be given autonomy in southeastern Anatolia, with the conditions for a future independent state of their own being left open.

21. Elias, *Studien über die Deutschen*, p. 9.

22. Elias,'Soziologie und Psychiatrie', in Hans Ulrich Wehler (ed.), *Soziologie und Psychologie* (Stuttgart, Berlin, Köln, Mainz 1972), p. 13.

23. Elias, *Studien über die Deutschen*, p. 10.

24. Elias, *Engagement und Distanzierung, Arbeiten zur Wissensoziologie,* Frankfurt 1983, p. 134.

25. Cited in Niyazi Berkes, *Türkiye'de Çağdaşlaşma* (Istanbul 1978), pp. 596–7.

26. Elias, *Studien über die Deutschen*, p. 13.

27. *Ibid*, p. 467.

28. *Ibid*, p. 447.

29. Taner Akçam, *İnsan Hakları ve Ermeni Sorunu, İttihat ve Terakkiden Kurtuluş Savaşına* (Ankara 1999), pp. 191–215.

30. Elias, *Studien über die Deutschen*, p. 463.

31. *Ibid*, p. 464.

32. *Ibid*, p. 395.

33. *Ibid*.

34. Erwin Staub's extensive psychological research can be given here as an example for developing such a general framework. He also emphasizes the danger of past greatness combined with present weakness as an important cultural aspect of genocide. See Erwin Staub, *The Roots of Evil: The Origin of Genocide and Other Group Violence* (Cambridge University Press, 1992), pp. 51–67.

3

Some Aspects of Turkish National Identity and the Armenian Genocide

One of the main factors that led to the Armenian Genocide is to be found in the mental conditions and characteristics of Turkish national identity.[1] This unique national character was decisive in the creation of the Turkish Republic on the ashes of the Ottoman Empire, and it has also played a major role in making the Armenian Question a taboo issue within Turkish society. The reason for the Turks' deafening silence (at best) or categorical denial (at worst) of the Armenian Genocide is that Turkish national identity has made the subject utterly unapproachable. This study of Turkish national identity, then, essentially attempts to grapple with such restricted areas of Turkish history and identity.

This is no easy feat. To understand the difficulty the topic poses, we can examine Turkish works dealing with the formation of Turkish national identity and the formation of the Turkish national state. In nearly all of these works, the Armenian Genocide is either passed over entirely or is cursorily mentioned—as an exodus (perhaps forced) or other movement of population. For example, even in the 1988 work *Sosyalism ve Toplumsal Mücadeleler Ansiklopedisi* (The Encyclopedia of Socialism and Social Struggles), which was published by a leftist press and is filled with articles by well-known and prominent Turkish socialists and social critics, there is no reference to the Armenian Question. It would be no exaggeration to say that the prevalent mood in Turkey is the desire to forget the issue entirely.

Works on the Armenian Question published in Turkey are bizarre. These works are mostly written by official state functionaries or persons of a nationalist or Islamist bent. The main focus in these works is always the Armenians themselves as the culpable party, and their 'lies' or their 'ingratitude.' The works are characterized by an extremely belligerent tone toward the Armenians. Phrases such as 'the 'Armenian question' which closely threatens our very homeland and nation'[2] and 'Armenian ingratitude'[3] are frequently encountered. In general, these works claim that it was not the Armenians who were slaughtered, but rather the Turks. One, for instance, claims that 'The number of Turks killed by the Armenians during the First World War is greater than the number of Armenians who were allegedly killed.'[4] For this reason, books on the subject are often given titles such as 'Armenian Cruelty,'[5] and some even speak of a million Muslims having been killed by the Armenians.[6]

In the majority of such works a blatantly racist language is employed against the Armenians. It is interesting that the writers do not directly present these racist conclusions as their own views. Other writers are continually shown as the source of these judgments, and the authors hide behind passages taken from these other works. In the works of the Turkish Historical Society (*Türk Tarih Kurumu*), which have the character of 'official' history, such racist depictions are encountered especially often. A few examples will convey the tone of these publications.

> Sir Mark Sykes provides some noteworthy information concerning the true nature and intentions of the Armenians. According to this individual, the Armenians are base persons and inculcate hatred of other persons. Although even the Jews have their good sides, the Armenians have none...[7]

In another work, we read the following:

> Basically, the Armenian leaders were 'worthless individuals,' just as British Foreign Secretary Lord Curzon had also characterized them...According to the American High Commissioner Colonel Haskell, who was responsible for American aid in Yerevan, 'the Armenians were thieving, lying, utterly debased ...persons.[8]

Again, from another work by the same author:

> Lieutenant Dickson, the assistant to the British Consul, would also criticize... 'the Armenians: The Armenian who is under citizenship, so far as I've seen, is an unsympathetic person, who is without values or conscience and base in his behavior'...Furthermore, Dickson stressed the following: 'The Armenian, who is downtrodden, who cowers like a dog...and is the lowliest form of existence...'[9]

Quotations such as these can be found in a large number of works.

Among more critically thinking, leftist and socialist authors I cannot think of a single work that directly deals with the question of the Armenian Genocide. These writers, who publish works in great numbers on the Otto-man system and the establishment of the Turkish Republic, have not as a rule broached the issue of the Armenian massacres. This page of history is effectively a non-event.

The approach of those groups who take up the subject only to prove that no massacres ever took place, or to attack the Armenians, can be understood to a certain degree. What is more difficult to understand is the silence of critical thinkers and their circles. Neither legal difficulties nor state pressure are adequate to explain this phenomenon. There is no law in the penal code against writing about the Armenian Genocide. The same critical thinkers who fail to address the Armenian Genocide did not hesitate to write about the Kurdish Question, which was a crime. In my opinion, this silence is voluntary, because whenever the subject is broached, the thought structure that Turkish scholars use to explain the world and Turkey crashes. Researchers must confront a number of unpleasant questions that they find daunting to answer using the prevailing patterns of thought. Thus, they prefer not to open a wound which they believe to be closed since 1916.

Turkish National Identity and Some of its Characteristics

In the following discussion of the relationship between the emergence of Turkish national identity and its character on one side, and the Armenian Genocide, on the other, one of the first questions we must answer is the question of what it is we mean by national identity. I am obliged to make certain qualifications. First of all, I do not intend to take up the question of national identity as one of a general cultural identity. Instead, by this concept I mean some of a nation's characteristics and behavior which have been formed during the establishment of the national state. These characteristics reflect a shared state of mind that encompasses the entire nation, and which can explain why shared modes of behavior were able to arise in certain situations. What is under discussion, then, is not fixed, unchanging qualities. Rather,

> the national character of a people is not fixed for all time as unchanging biological properties. The national character is very tightly bound to the process whereby every people establish their own national state.[10]

Therefore, what will be examined here as national identity is mutable qualities, which were formed during the establishment of the Turkish national state. Second, my understanding of the concept of 'nation' is highly political. I state a direct relationship between national identity and the national state, and I assign a central role to shared history and the national state in defining national identity. The shared experiences of the past leave similar traces in the memories of those who experienced these things together. A commonality of historical experience creates symbols that reinforce the beliefs of both the group and the individual. Shared memories and constructed symbols concerning the past, as well as understandings that have been imposed on these, all come to expression in the defining of certain shared goals, and allow for the formation of a network of shared communication within that society. Thus, what I mean here is a secondary question, in which national identity encompasses all manner of ethnic, linguistic and religious groups.

It is now possible to list those fundamental characteristics—although without any claim at comprehensiveness—which I feel have determined national identity in the process of establishing the Turkish nation-state. I believe that, in light of these characteristics of national identity, we will be able to comprehend the Armenian Genocide as the result of a certain national mindset and certain conditions.

'Delayed' Turkish National Identity and the Aggressiveness Resulting from the Anxiety about Closing the Gap

Turkish nationalism or, in more general terms, Turkish national identity, appeared on the historical stage very late. Certain anecdotes are often repeated which clearly highlight this lateness. Toward the end of the 19th century, when certain members of the Young Turks who were located in Paris were asked what nation they belonged to, they would at first reply, 'We are Muslims,' and only after it was explained that Islam was a religion would they reply, 'We are Ottomans.' They would then be reminded that this was not a nation either, but it was utterly inconceivable for these youths to say that they were Turks.[11] The crowds that poured out into the streets of Istanbul and Salonica to praise the restoration of the constitutional regime in 1908 were serenaded by the French national anthem while celebrating the new order, since there was no Ottoman anthem.[12]

Serious consideration of the national identity of Turkish-speaking Muslims in the Ottoman Empire only began at the outset of the 20th century. In a work he published in 1898, the Hungarian orientalist Arminius Vambéry wrote that 'among the Turks of Istanbul, I never encountered a single person who seriously engaged himself with the question of Turkish nationalism or the Turkish languages.'[13] Ziya Gökalp, who has been seen as the ideological father of Turkish nationalism, claims to have begun to develop an interest in ancient Turkish history in 1896, after reading the writings of Léon Cahun about the Turks. 'The first book that I purchased when I arrived in Istanbul was Léon Cahun's history of the Turks. It was as if this book had been written in order to encourage me to labor over the ideal of Turkism.'[14] At this time, and even in the first years of the 20th century, nothing relating to the history of the Turks was taught in Ottoman schools. Even in 1911,

...two thirds of the pages of the basic books that were taught in Turkish middle school institutions and that dealt with modern history were devoted to French history, and the rest was devoted to the history of the other European states. Almost nothing at all was said about Turkey or the Turks.[15]

Until the Revolution of 1908, the doors of the Islamic religious schools (*medrese*) were closed to the Turkish language. The history that was taught there was Ottoman–Islamic history, which began with the life of the Prophet.

The natural result of this late coming to the idea of nationalism was an anxiety about closing the gap, so much so that it took the form of a belligerence toward other national groups. It would not be too much of an exaggeration to claim that Turkish nationalism possessed an aggressive character similar to a number of other delayed nationalisms. The reasons for this delayed nationalism are the following.

(1) The most important reason is Islam. In contrast to other Islamic countries, among the Ottomans, Islamic identity developed in tandem with the lapse of any sense of Turkishness. The effect of Islam upon the Turks was so profound that, even though the Turkic peoples did retain their languages after entering the Islamic fold, in not a single Turkic state was the official language a Turkic one. On the contrary, up to the end of the 12th century, all of the Turkic states used Arabic as their state language.[16]

All of the specialists in this subject have mentioned the negative effect that Islam has had upon the formation of Turkish national identity.[17] According to Vambéry, Islam 'in its tendency to 'de-nationalize,' has never been more successful than among the Ottoman Turks.'[18] We find a similar assessment in Lewis: 'Among the different peoples who embraced Islam none went farther in sinking their separate identity in the Islamic community than the Turks.'[19]—so much so that 'all the pre-Islamic Turkish past was forgotten...Even the very name Turk, and the entity it connotes, are in a sense Islamic.'[20]

In their own works, the Turkists drew attention to this negative aspect of Islam:

> From the eighth century until now, 'Arab and Persian culture' have obliterated Turkish culture and Turkish thought, as well as Turkish history. Falling under the religious and cultural oppression of the 'Arab world' has resulted in the loss of Turkish identity.[21]

Mustafa Kemal's view on this subject was nearly identical:

> We are a nation that has come very late to and acted very negligently in the implementation of nationalist ideas...Our nation has paid an especially bitter price for having arrived without knowing nationalism. We have [now] understood that our error was that we have forgotten ourselves...[22]

(2) The fact that the Ottomans possessed a vast Empire had an effect on their own historical consciousness. Terms such as 'homeland' (*vatan*) and 'nation' (*millet*) were foreign to them. For this reason the Ottoman rulers never fully understood the nationalism that developed in the West. Even in situations wherein it could be argued that they did understand it, they tended to perceive it as the actions of 'civilian hooligans.' The attitude with which they viewed the French Revolution is a prime example of this. In the minds of the Ottoman leaders, the revolution was 'the blaze of sedition and disorder' (*fitne ve fesat ateşi*). Ali Efendi, one of the chief secretaries during the reign of Selim III, prepared a rather lengthy report on the French Revolution, in which he described its leaders as 'a few loathsome persons who have formed an alliance...instigators...persons with corrupt aims.'[23] Even after the passing of nearly a century, Cevdet Paşa, who includes this report in his famous history *Tarih-i Cevdet,* concurs with Ali Efendi's assessment, calling the revolutionary leaders 'lowly characters' and 'hooligans' and claiming that the revolution was a 'debasement of the word itself (*sözün ayağa düşmesi*) and the affair was in the hands of hooligans.'[24]

We can say—if we set aside these assessments, which today strike us as odd—that the Ottoman leaders remained bound to an understanding of universalism that had arisen as a result of their being the rulers of a multi-national state. This can also be observed when the present-day term for homeland (*vatan*) is examined. 'Until the 19th century, this concept...had been used only in a very narrow sense, indicating place of birth or residence, and commanding some sentimental loyalty.'[25] In the middle of the 19th century, Cevdet Paşa claimed that the word *vatan* never had any other meaning for a Turkish soldier than simply the village square.[26] Even as late as the end of the century the term continued to be used in this sense. For example, Sultan Abdulhamid II said that 'the *vatan* is the place where people have gathered together.'[27] 'I cannot understand why someone would be willing to die for it. It is not a good thing for so many persons to slaughter one another for the sake of the *vatan*.'[28]

There was basically one other reason behind this cautious distance from nationalism and the lack of desire to understand it. This was that the Ottoman leaders knew that developments in this area would mean the dissolution of the Empire. Already in 1862, Ali Paşa, Grand Vizier and a leading figure in the Tanzimat era, informed the French foreign ministry that inciting the Balkans with such ideas would mean 'chaos and eternal' war. He added: 'if all of the national demands in Turkey are freely recognized, think for a moment what will be...One portion will require a whole century and rivers of blood in order to create a stable situation.'[29] An interesting example in this context is the manner in which the Ottoman leaders viewed the Bulgarian national uprisings. The Ottoman leaders, who made no mention whatsoever of the national character of the revolts, assessed them rather as the product of 'Russian incitement' or of minorities who had for years possessed clear opportunities, but who did not know their value. The utter absence among the correspondence and documents of the time of any evaluation that the disturbances were an uprising with a national character is truly fascinating.[30]

Turkist writers frequently asserted that the multinational, cosmopolitan character of the Ottoman state had negatively affected the development of Turkish national identity. The Ottomans 'had not withdrawn from making efforts to dissolve and eliminate all of their ties to their nation or their roots, their consciousness of self-identity, their customs and ideals. The state was, in a very brief time, removed from its status as a Turkish state.'[31] For this reason, the Turkists (particularly in the Republican period) spoke of the Ottomans as 'those who desire to destroy the Turkish race.'[32]

(3) The multinational character of the Ottoman state forced the ruling national group into a strange dilemma. Because the main goal had been the preservation of the multinational state, the members of the ruling nation could not openly claim their own national identities. They always defended their integrationist ideology, which gathered all of the nationalities within their embrace, as 'official' state ideology. Thus up to 1912–13 they were unable to say publicly that they were Turkists, even though that was indeed the case, preferring instead to continually hide behind the ideology of Ottomanism. In his memoir Halil Menteşe, the President of the Ottoman Chamber of Deputies for much of the Young Turk period, claims that, because the Turks were obliged to unite various communities within the country, they did not dare announce in parliament that they were Turks.[33] Upon losing a great segment of its non-Muslim minority population in the Balkan Wars (1912–13), the Committee of Union and Progress, which until then had been unable to make Turkism a necessary component of its rule, now 'pulled out all the stops.' 'It was as if the current of Turkism within the CUP emerged from the clouds of war. The Turks, who could not have said 'I exist' before the Balkan War, now were able to say it freely.'[34] Thus, the Unionists embarked on a Turkification policy, with anxious haste from having started so late.

An important aspect of these policies was a marked hostility toward other nations, both because these powers were the parties who desired to topple and partition the Empire, and because the Unionists had long found themselves forced to watch in silence while these others had freely come to embrace their own national identities. The various Turkist associations and societies which sprang up like mushrooms, one after the other, especially after 1912, were formed with clear and concise programs. As one of their leaders put it, 'The newly awakened Turkish world, which longs for 'Great

Turan,' has raised up the four pillars of the edifice of the Sultanate that shall wear the golden crown of Turan: The Turkish Knowledge Society (*Türk Bilgi Derneği*), the Turkish Homeland (*Türk Yurdu*), Turkish Hearth (*Türk Ocağı*) and Turkish Strength (*Türk Gücü*) Societies!'[35]

Among those organizations established with the goal of accelerating the Turkification process, the Turkish Strength Society wrote in its program that its members had made their goal the 'protecting of the Turkish race from collapse;' it did not refrain from using the most racist and belligerent language. This is clear in the society's mission statement:

> The Turkish Strength [Society] is the straight and strong stream which springs forth and flows outward from Karakurum, and floods the whole world with its raging torrents. It is the unbroken sword. It will resurrect and reinvigorate the power of the Turk, which in its time left no stronghold standing, but which is today fallen and dispersed. It will cause the Turk to proudly raise his broad and pure countenance anew. It will cause his sharp, undaunted eye to shine again, his broad chest to thrust outward in pride. It shall be the custodian of the Association, the guardian of the Hearth (*Ocak*), the defender of the Homeland, the raider of Turan!
>
> The iron embrace of the Turk shall surround the world; the world will again tremble in fear before this embrace.'[36]

(4) In fact, Turkism was not a strongly promoted preference, above all because the term 'Turk' had long been used within the Ottoman Empire as a pejorative. Even travelers had remarked that this word was used in Ottoman lands as a curse word. In Ottoman newspapers of the late 19th century, mention is made 'of youths who are ashamed of being Turks.'[37] Additionally, the main aim was to save the crumbling Empire, to prevent its partition. Turkism was therefore the worst of the various existing options, because it excluded both Christians and non-Turkish Muslims. However, the vast Turkish population of the Empire did think of itself as Muslim, and the Ottoman rulers hoped up to the very last moment for some sort of unity around an Ottoman–Islamic axis. Thus, although Turkism was not preferred, when the other collective identities such as Ottomanism and Islamism proved themselves incapable of reviving the Empire, Turkism emerged as the inevitable alternative.

(5) One of the more significant results of this delayed national consciousness was the predominance of racist ideas within the national identity. At first an understanding of the nation relied on 18th century European concepts of popular sovereignty, parliament and political aspiration, an understanding clearly compatible with social democratization. But by the second half of the 19th century, this understanding of the nation had largely given way to theories of social-Darwinism and to the new hybrids that grew out of the integration of these theories into conceptions of the nation. These

race-based Darwinian theories of the nation formed the intellectual raw material for Turkish nationalism. By means of such theories, Turkish thinkers labored to prove that the race of the Turks, debased and despised, was actually a superior race. The first Turkist thinkers, for example, mention with admiration the influence of the early French theorist of race, Arthur de Gobineau.[38] Tekin Alp (also known as Moise Cohen) relates that the journal *Genç Kalemler* (Young Pens), which began publication in Salonica in 1891, was greatly influenced by the writings of de Gobineau.[39] All of the theoreticians of Turkism, without exception, observed frequently that the 'German' understanding of nation and culture, which they saw based on unchanging elements like race and innate characteristics, represented a model for them to emulate. 'This culture [German culture], and its edifice, which was based upon such concepts as race, *Volk*, and history, well-suited the condition of Turkishness, which was struggling to form its own historical and national identity.'[40] The nationalist Gökalp claimed that it was imperative for the Turks to be influenced by the supporters of German unity. If the Turks continued down the path that the Germans had followed, they would then be able to achieve political unity. According to Gökalp:

> The Germans have passed through three stages that can be termed 'cultural unity,' 'economic unity,' and 'political unity.' With cultural unity, [the first step] was taken toward 'National Union'...After cultural unity followed the ideal of economic unity...Now it is necessary for the Turkish Unionists to follow the same path also.[41]

With this perspective, Gökalp helped to lay the theoretical foundations for a belligerent nationalism, claiming that 'the political borders' of the Turkish homeland 'would spread as far as their languages and cultures.'[42]

Turkish National Identity: A Reaction to Continual Humiliation

Turkish national identity arose as a natural reaction to continual humiliation. In the words of one Turkish writer,

> While the Turks possessed a feeling of superiority [i.e., before the 19th century], they did not know they were Turks...The Turks began to understand that they were Turks only when they were totally engulfed with feelings of inferiority...
> Turkism means helplessness for the Turks...It is a forlorn and inescapable flight from a sense of inferiority.[43]

This feeling of inferiority is a characteristic both of domestic history and of foreign relations, and has been continually highlighted as a central theme both in domestic and foreign politics.

In Ottoman history, being a Turk has been understood to be the same as being humiliated. As one example, let us examine the statements of the late-17th century Ottoman court historian Naima Mustafa Efendi about the Turks, which appear in his history of the same name (*Tarih-i Naima*). Naima refers to the Turks as 'brainless' or 'dull-witted' *(idraksiz Türkler)*, 'ugly in appearance' (*çirkin suratlı Türk*), 'deceitful' (*hilekar Türk*) and 'large and sheepdog-shaped' (*çoban köpeği şeklinde bir Türk-ü sü-türk*).[44] Clearly, the Ottomans themselves did not appreciate being referred to as Turks, particularly not by Westerners. The orientalist Vambéry relates an experience he once had in Istanbul:

> ...upon inquiring among learned Turks as to their interest in the matter of their racial and cultural relationship to the Turks of Central Asia, these learned souls felt as if they had been insulted, because it was claimed that they were somehow related to this nomadic people. In their eyes, 'Turk' was a term used only for the lowly levels of society, particularly for villagers.[45]

Veled Çelebi, one of the important figures among the Turkists, was scorned not just by his social circle, but even by his family during the time that he labored to develop the Turkish language. The work that Çelebi did was innocent in the extreme, changing the Arabic spelling of a few words and bringing them closer in line with the Turkish language. But even this was sufficient for him to be ostracized and cursed. In his foreword to a 1941 reissue of a work he had originally translated in 1897, Çelebi wrote:

> ...at that time it was a great sacrifice to make this revolution. Because of my love and ardor for my nation, my language and its grammar, some of my own community and family were furious at me; they criticized me viciously, saying 'Instead of humbly continuing to follow the pure path of great persons of exalted lineage, is it proper for this underling to rush headlong and adopt such improperly novel habits, or even to write a piece in a manner so contrary to everyone else and in opposition to the previous rules [of orthography]?' And they imparted to everyone in the council at which we were present a pearl of wisdom from the eternal and noble forefathers and, considering this poor soul a decadent type, they cast him out from among them.[46]

The widespread hostility toward the 'Turks' was, in a general sense, due to the following causes.

(a) The *devşirme* identity of the Ottoman bureaucracy. The Empire's central administrative arm was formed for several centuries by the forcible levy, or *devşirme*, of Christian children, who were then converted to Islam and educated to be the Empire's bureaucratic and military elite. This group always looked poorly upon Turkish tribesmen and humiliated them. Some officials even explained the decline of the Empire by the 'seepage of Turks' into administrative structures.[47]

(b) The defeat by Timur (Tamerlane). In the period before the momentous Battle of Ankara in 1402, the Turkish beys of Anatolia betrayed the Ottoman cause and went over to Timur's side, thereby paving the way for Sultan Beyazid's defeat and the temporary collapse of the Empire. 'Exploiting the House of Osman's inferiority complex and the bitter feelings born out of this defeat at Timur's hands...the *devşirme* leaders strove to exacerbate the feelings of mistrust...and rancor against the Anatolian Turks.'[48]

(c) Arab–Islamic science. This was one of the main reasons for anti-Turkish hostility and scorn for things Turkish in Ottoman society. In Ottoman *medreses*, the foundation of the educational curriculum was comprised of works of Arab–Islamic origin, which denigrated the Turks. In the Arab–Islamic world, and particularly in the koranic commentaries, Turks were imagined to be a herd of monsters, hostile to humankind, a race that visited disaster upon humanity. In all of these works, certain *hadith*s, ('traditions of the Prophet') that described the Turks negatively were included. The contents were attributed to Muhammad himself: 'The Day of Judgment shall not arrive before war is waged against the Turks, who are beady-eyed, red-faced, flat-nosed, and whose visages resemble shields made of thick leather.'[49] These and other similar denigrating descriptions can be found in nearly all of the fundamental Islamic works. Here are but two examples: the land of the Turks 'is the source of unbelief and sedition'; the Turks are creatures who 'have nails like claws, tusks and molars similar to those of wild animals, they have teeth that resemble those of dogs, chins that resemble those of camels, their entire bodies are covered with bristles, and when they eat something, their teeth are heard clicking together like the sound made by mules and mares.'[50]

d). The Alevi-Türkmen revolts. These occurred at various times throughout Ottoman history, and were often socio-economically motivated rebellions by Anatolian villagers, and even more so by nomadic groups, against the central administration of the Empire. Whether the rebels in large part consisted of Türkmen tribes or were of a religious character, they served to push the Ottoman rulers into a more generally hostile attitude toward the Alevi Türkmen.

This denigrating and hostile view of the Turks, which emerged as a by-product of Ottoman history, was sharpened by foreign relations. In both the Middle Ages and more recent history many foreign works depicted the Turks as barbaric, violence-prone creatures. For example, Esther Kafé, who has pored over European works of the Renaissance period, says that in many of these works, legends abound about the Turks, who are described as 'boorish, lustful, and beast-like persons' and 'unchaste, rotten and disgusting dogs'...who only open their moldy mouths in order to shout at and attack the very holy Christian religion.'[51]

This description of the Turk as barbaric, violence-prone, and animal-like continued into the modern era. In the theories of well-known historians and theoreticians of civilization such as Oswald Spengler, Nikolai Danilevski and Arnold Toynbee, as well as in the works of many other writers, this opinion is encountered again and again. For Danilevski, for instance, the Turks were 'the most negative factor in history.' For his part, the famous French historian Ernest Renan saw the Turks as 'a coarse and boorish people, devoid of intelligence.'[52] In the letters of Voltaire, who has won a place in the hearts of many as a champion of liberty, there are numerous references to the Turks as 'these bullies' and 'these pillaging people.'[53] In a letter to the Russian Czarina, Catherine II, who was then at war with the Turks, Voltaire says that he 'wanted to help her, at least by killing a few Turks,' and reports his sorrow at being unable to do so.[54]

In travel accounts, in particular, this anti-Turkish attitude is expressed in the most casual manner. One can find in such works countless passages about the Turks as a violence-prone nation, as having obliterated civilization and culture in Europe, and about the absolute necessity of driving them out of the continent. Here are but a few examples: 'ignorant and bullying Turks…';[55] 'With every step he took on the Balkan Peninsula, the Turk trampled underfoot the products of thousands of years of culture';[56] 'Wherever the Turk sees a tree, he cuts it down'; 'The Turks have destroyed cultures in every place, and have not preserved those things that they have taken into their possession. They were not a people of culture in any sense of the word, and they also failed to build upon the cultural foundation of the places they occupied.'[57] Thus, most authors concluded, it was necessary to save Christians from the clutches of these barbarians: 'We must hasten to the assistance of our Christian brethren…Let us cast the Turks out of Europe.'[58] It was also proposed to solve the problem of the Turks by immediately conquering and dividing up the Ottoman Empire: 'The solution to the Eastern Question is nothing other than the elimination of the Turks.'[59] 'It is the destruction of the Turkish holdings that they call the Eastern Question…'[60]

What is significant here is not the continual denigration and contempt of the Turks, but the Turkish consciousness of being disparaged. The Ottoman Turkish officials and learned men were well aware of the negative judgments of them in the West, and this awareness was a factor that in large measure determined their behavior. Thus, it should not be surprising that the first Turkist thinkers devoted a great portion of their labors to proving that each of the accusations directed against the Turks by westerners were false and slanderous. While stating the aim of his book *Türk Tarihi* (Turkish History), Necip Asım expressed the hope that he would be able to recount the triumphs of the Turks with the aim of disproving the baseless claims of persons not ashamed of ridiculing this great and felicitous nation.[61] Both in the newspapers (for instance, in *İkdam*, which appeared for the first time in 1893 with the motto 'The Turkish Newspaper') and history books of the period, ample place is given to laudatory views of the Turks. In these writings the Turks are praised for their cleanliness, their honesty and their superiority, and it is claimed that 'human virtues...like patience, courage and civility are traits of the noble Turkish nation.'[62]

In Europe during this period, positive writings about the Turks and the Ottomans began to be sought, and brochures and books were published and disseminated. Among them were both translations and local publications, which collected those passages that praised the Turks and showed them in a positive light, such as those found in *İkdam*. The 1898 work *Türklerin Ulûm ve Fününa Hizmetleri* (The Contributions of the Turks to the Sciences and the Arts) by Bursalı Mehmet Tahir is but one of many examples. In the book's introduction the author writes the following:

> My aim is not to write a broad history of the Turks. Rather, by writing briefly in the form of an index about the historical situation of our writers who have grown up among this people and have left behind valuable works in the scientific and technological fields, my aim is to disprove the senseless ideas of our writers who suppose that each one of the Turks is simply a coarse warrior from a marauding race.[63]

These attempts continued into the first part of the 20th century. In the journals published by the Young Turks, some writers stated their goal as 'the elimination of the negative aspects of the Turkish image in the eyes of the Europeans.' The *Türk Gazetesi*, for instance, which was published in Egypt, claimed that 'the Turks have earned Europe's hatred even though they don't deserve it in the least,' and published numerous pieces aimed at erasing this negative image.[64]

Erasing the West's negative image of the Turk turned out to be one of the major endeavors of the leaders of the Turkish War for Independence,[65] because throughout both the First World War and the War for Independence the Western powers exploited the image of Turkish 'barbarism' and 'savagery' as a propaganda tool in their struggles against the Turks. Some Entente propaganda even claimed that the First World War itself had basically been waged against the Turks. In a bulletin dated January 10, 1917, for instance, which was issued with the goal of encouraging American participation in the war, the authors describe the Allied war aims thus:

> The Entente states are conscious that they have not fought for selfish aims. Above all...they are fighting in order to preserve truth and humanity. The war aims of the Entente principally and necessarily include...the rescue of fallen

peoples from the bloody tyranny of the Turks and the eviction from Europe of the Ottoman Empire, which is totally foreign to European civilization.[66]

British Prime Minister David Lloyd George always mentioned the Turks in a tone of disdain and loathing. In November 1914 he characterized them as 'a cancer on humanity, a wound that has worked its way into the flesh of the earth that it has misruled.' He characterized a potential Turkish victory as 'the torch of pillage, cruelty and murder…that would be carried from Asia to Europe.' Toward the end of the war, in a speech delivered on June 29, 1917, Lloyd George said that the Turks had turned Mesopotamia, the ancient cradle of civilization, into a wasteland, and Armenia into a grave-yard, adding that the areas of this cradle of civilization 'shall not be left to the incendiary and destructive brutality of the Turks.'[67]

It would thus be no exaggeration to claim that the reaction to this denigration and ostracizing was an important motif during the Turkish War for Independence. Even as the first preparations were being made in Ankara in 1919, Mustafa Kemal gave a speech on the nature of the independence struggle that sounded like a reply to Lloyd George's accusations:

> Because our nation as a whole was devoid of natural ability, it has entered into places which were gardens and has reduced them to ruins. By means of the first accusation, tyranny is attributed to [our] nation; by the second, its natural abilities are placed into question…Both of them are pure calumny.[68]

The intent of the speech was to present the War for Independence as counter-proof against these baseless accusations. Kemal's assertion, that it was necessary to fight in order to prove to the Europeans that the Turks were not barbarians, was not at all a new idea. It had also been held by some of the leadership of the CUP. Upon the Italian invasion of Tripoli (Libya) in 1911, in order to convince the members of the CUP central committee to resist the occupation, Enver Paşa said, 'We must act in such a fashion that it will demonstrate to civilized Europe that we are not barbarians but are persons deserving to be treated with respect.' The Turks, he said, should then wage war, wherein 'we shall either emerge victorious, or, if we perish, we shall do so with our honor intact.'[69]

The existence in the West of the type of prejudice described above against the Turks has had an important result in establishing as an *idée fixe* in the minds of many Turks the perception that they have been made the whipping boy of history, because of which the whole world is against them, and a great injustice has been committed against them. Feelings of being the focus of universal and undeserved contempt have worked their way into and embedded themselves in the Turkish marrow. Like an overly sensitive person who feels misunderstood no matter what he does, it has become a

Turkish national characteristic to react negatively in almost all relations with foreign powers. Even in the daily Turkish press one often finds exclamations such as 'They don't understand us,' 'They willfully don't want to understand us,' and 'They all just want to see our bad side.' This touchiness amounts to a societal paranoia. It is as if a powerful syndrome of being misunderstood and the psychology of isolation determine all forms of behavior.

> Even though the Turks performed the earliest and greatest services to world civilization through their language, science and arts, there have been efforts— behind which lie a variety of purposes—to forget all of these civilized contributions and to unjustly show them as idle and insignificant in the view of history.[70]

These words were actually spoken at the opening speech of Turkey's first History Conference in 1932.

The Nation Destined to Rule: The Turks

For a nation that has been this denigrated and is conscious of the fact, the first order of business is naturally to work to prove that the opposite of the accusations against it is true. There is no need here to assess the fantastic theories concocted, especially in the republican period, in reaction to the constant denigration: theories of the racial superiority of the Turks and of their role as the founders of all the world's civilizations and languages. From our perspective, what is significant is the taking root of a belief that the Turks are superior to other nations and peoples, and thereby have the right to rule them. The Turkish founding of world empires and rule over other nations were frequently repeated as demonstrations of this superiority and of the uniqueness of Turkish history.

In the debates among the Ottoman opposition movement of the late 19th century and later among the Young Turks, Turkish domination within the Ottoman Empire was regarded as perfectly natural, and any discussion on that point was seen as simply unnecessary. The existence of the other nations within the Empire would only be recognized on the condition that they accepted the principle of Turkish domination. Even in the period before Turkism existed, and ideas such as Ottomanism and Islamism still did not predominate, those who promoted these ideas reiterated in no uncertain terms that what they meant by these ideas was, essentially, a continuation of Turkish domination. Thus, it should come as no surprise that those persons who made the first attempts at formulating a Turkish nationalist ideology in language and literature were the same persons who had earlier promoted Ottomanism or Islamism. Ahmet Rasim, who was involved in the debates of the period, made an important observation: 'In those days, meaning after 1278 (1861), when [the newspaper] *Tasvîr-i Efkâr* began to be published, the obvious answer to the question of who constituted of the Ottoman nation was Turks.'[71]

This point is of great significance in the nationalism debate. The answer to the question of when Turkish nationalism actually began is an aspect of this debate: to what extent can the absence of a political Turkish nationalism in the early period of attempts to simplify the Ottoman language (which began after 1839) be interpreted as a lack of developed nationalist ideas? If the advocates of language simplification clearly understood from their attempts the dominance of the Turkish language, should their work not be considered an aspect of Turkish nationalism as well? Some scholars of Turkish nationalism have seen the efforts at language reform during the Tanzimat period as the starting point for Turkist thought. Even so, these reformers can in no way be considered Turkists in their political sensibilities.

A crucial error committed by some who would locate Turkish nationalism's advent in this period is their consideration that Ottomanism and Turkish nationalism are one and the same. While this position must be rejected, a connecting thread runs between the two that must not be overlooked. Even in periods in which Turkism had not yet developed as a political ideology, the cosmopolitan ideologies that were developed in order to bind together the multinational Ottoman Empire were themselves understood as the continued domination of the ruling group, and this group was understood to be the Turks. Yusuf Akçura, for instance, in his work *Yeni Türk Devletinin Öncüleri* (The Pioneers of the New Turkish State), examines the first attempts at Turkism, and explains that the early pioneers like İbrahim Şinasi, Namık Kemal, Ahmed Vefik, Mustafa Celâleddin and Suleyman Paşa were not Turkists in the political sense, but advocated the politics of Ottoman nationalism or Islamic unity. But, Akçura assures us, these persons understood the policies they advocated as Turkish domination far more than as an equality of all the component nations within the Empire. Even the Ottoman ruling class, which politically speaking was miles from any notions like Turkish nationalism, thought that it would only be possible to hold together the various peoples living in the Empire under Turkish domination. For his part, Ali Paşa, 'having observed the conflicting interests and aspirations of the various nationalities within the Empire, commented on the particular role of the Turks as the unifying element in the Empire.'[72]

Many more examples can be given that show that the idea of Ottomanism must have been understood as continued domination by the Turks.[73] One of the more important reasons for this attitude is that the Turks had, by virtue of Islam, always found themselves in a position of dominance as 'the

Ruling Nation' (*Millet-i Hakime*). It is often argued that Islam is a religion of tolerance. Nevertheless, 'this toleration was predicated on the assumption that the tolerated communities were separate and inferior, and were moreover clearly marked as such. This was because 'the Muslim superiority over the infidels had...roots both in tradition and morality,'[74] and abandoning their position of dominance was therefore inconceivable.

Namık Kemal argued that 'we can reach an understanding if the Christians desire our domination. It is very natural, because since we have not allowed them into the government, they could not possess the right to complain about it.'[75] And Kemal established this idea on a clearly racial basis: 'Because there is both a swirl of populations and abilities within the Ottoman collective, the Turks, who possess excellence and virtues and qualities such as 'breadth of comprehension' (*vus'at-ı havsala*), 'sobriety' (*itidal-i dem*), 'patience and calm-headedness' (*tahammül ve sükûnet*), take pride of place.'[76] Similar ideas are found in the writings of Ali Suavi, a leading member of the Young Ottomans, who explained why the Turks needed to be rulers with the theory that 'the Turkish race is superior to and older than all other races on account of its military, civil and political roles.'[77] Şinasi, who can be considered one of the first secularist Ottoman intellectuals, even adopted and defended the principle of the Ruling Nation. He claimed that the fact that this principle was not being sufficiently defended was one of the main reasons for his publishing the daily *Tercüman-ı Ahval*.[78]

The attitude of the Committee of Union and Progress on this subject turned out to be no different. Ahmet Rıza, the European-educated positivist who played a central role in the movement's theoretical debates before the Revolution, states that by Ottomanism he too meant the continuation of Turkish domination;' he placed at the center of his policies the Turkish nation's establishment of its domination over the other communities. Ahmet Rıza's Ottomanism was that of someone proud to be a Turk.[79] In 1908, when the official state ideology was still Ottomanism, in a debate with some Greeks the Unionist journalist and publicist Hüseyin Cahit Yalçın openly defended the idea of Turkish domination: 'Say what you will,' Cahit stated, 'the dominant nation in the country is and shall remain the Turks.'[80]

One of the most important demonstrations of the shared understanding of the theoreticians and politicians of the period that Ottomanism meant Turkish domination was the massive response to the article '*Üç Tarz-ı Siyaset*' ('Three Types of Policy') written by Yusuf Akçura in 1904. In this Akçura essentially argues that Ottomanism would not maintain the unity of the Empire; therefore it should give way to Turkism. Many of the responses to the article said in effect: 'For us, the Turk cannot be separated from Islam, nor Islam from the Turk, neither the Turk and Islam from Ottomanism, nor Ottomanism from the Turk and Islam. The singularity cannot be divided into three.'[81] The prevailing mood of that period understood Islamism, Ottomanism and Turkism not as separate concepts, but rather as one and the same. Mizancı Murat, one of the earliest leaders of the Young Turk exiles in Paris in the late 19th century, subtitled the newspaper he published 'the Turkish Newspaper,' and frequently referred to himself as both a Muslim and an Ottoman. When a reader called this approach a contradiction in terms, Murat reaffirmed his previous position of adhering to all three appellations, 'which to those who hold them are not contradictory.'[82]

Even during the First World War, when the dual currents of Turkism and Ottomanism diverged from one another, plenty of writers continued to defend the latter. They continued to criticize the Turkists, claiming that Ottomanism meant Turkish domination. 'If Ottomanism becomes stronger, most Turks will draw the greatest advantage from it...Is it not Turkishness that represents the spirit of the Ottomans?'[83] In short, even in periods when Turkism had not fully developed as a political ideology, the Turks considered themselves the dominant nation and argued the need to promote acceptance of this dominance by the Empire's other nationalities.

Turkish National Identity Developed against a Fear of Extinction

Turkish national identity emerged and developed against a background of fear of nonexistence or obliteration. The Ottomans passed their last century which was, in the words of one Turkish historian, 'the Empire's longest century,'[84] amid the constant fear that if not today, then tomorrow they would disappear politically, or be partitioned. The problem known as the Eastern Question that engaged European diplomacy for nearly the entire 19th century was actually no more than the question of how to divide the ailing Empire between the imperialist powers. The Ottoman Empire was the 'sick man' of Europe, and the patient was only able to survive as long as it did because the Great Powers were unable to reach an agreement among themselves over its division.

It was a condition well known both to the Empire's rulers and to their opponents that the fate of the Ottoman state lay not in its own hands, but in those of certain foreign powers. The belief that the Empire's days were numbered was so widespread that Western statesmen did not even feel the need to mince words when communicating with their Ottoman counterparts. In 1895 the British prime minister, Lord Salisbury, wrote the following to Grand Vizier Said Paşa:

Every day the opinion grows that the Ottoman state will not endure. The only reason for its continuation is England's misunderstanding with Russia. If this understanding is reached, the Ottoman state will come to an end.[85]

An air of anticipation pervaded Ottoman ruling circles about the judgment to be given in regard to their fate. 'The ruling class and even the intellectuals were in a profound moral crisis.'[86] Among these groups Ibn Khaldun's theory of history was considered utterly valid—and many may even have found a certain amount of comfort in its inevitability. According to Zeki Velidi Togan,

> The ideas of Ibn Khaldun concerning the state and politics, and the fate of nations had a great effect upon the ideas of Ottoman statesmen during the period of decline. His views, which recognized the same degree of mortality in states as in individuals and showed it as 'inevitable and destined' to occur, were the reason that a certain pessimism took hold among us.[87]

All that could be done, they thought, was simply to prolong the dying process.

Cevdet Paşa, who translated Ibn Khaldun into Ottoman Turkish, expressed this openly:

> Just as among all people there is an age of development and growth, an age of learning and knowing and an age of decline, so among every state are found three stages like this. Just as all persons behave in accordance with their age in regard to preserving their health, because it too resembles a person, it is also necessary for the ruling Council of State to be mindful that their actions are appropriate in every situation and át every stage.[88]

The sense of helplessness and the psychosis of awaiting collapse among the Empire's ruling circles affected developing Turkish nationalism in a variety of ways. By far the most visible was the monumental effort and concern expended in order to prevent the collapse and halt the decline. The 'sick man' thesis was accepted, but the assumption that nothing could be done to prevent his demise was not. Among the Young Turk cadres, in particular, the prevailing mood of panic stemming from fear of decline and annihilation was one of the most significant factors in determining their actions. It was likewise this panic that acted to spur these groups to carry out the 1908 revolution.

On June 8–9 of that year, English and Russian leaders met for a conference at Reval. In the accounts in both Russian and Western sources concerning the protocols of the conference there is not a shred of evidence that what was discussed was the question of the Ottoman Empire and its partitioning.[89] But what is interesting here is that this meeting was 'interpreted in Turkey…in a way that [suggested that] a definitive decision had been reached between England and Russia over the partition of Turkey.'[90] The fear of foreign intervention and partition, and the belief that the Ottoman Empire only remained standing because of the inability of its two eternal enemies (England and Russia) to reach an understanding were so powerful that any sort of *rapprochement* between those two states was bound to create a panic. The Reval conference 'had the role of signaling the Young Turks in Rumelia to begin the revolution.'[91] What pushed Enver and Niyazi to take to the hills was the belief that with Reval, the decline and partition was about to become unstoppable. Subsequently, as a group the Young Turks believed that with the 1908 revolution they had halted the collapse and partition and saved the sick man. Enver Paşa, when he declared the return of liberty before the government house in the Macedonian town of Köprülü on July 23, sounded like he was giving a reply to Reval: 'We have cured the sick man!'[92]

But the process of collapse did not come to an end with the declaration of the constitutional regime in July 1908. On the contrary, it accelerated, and the situation gave birth to a continuous existence/nonexistence complex among Ottoman-Turkish intellectuals. Turkish national identity, then, may be said to have developed in parallel with the fear for its own future, its own existence. The fear of elimination was the midwife of Turkish national identity, which was formed in tandem with the consciousness of its own relative weakness and helplessness.

One of the results of such a state of mind was contemplation of the reasons for this evil state of affairs, as well as the individuals and groups responsible. If the national minorities were revealed to be responsible for Ottoman weakness and for bringing the Empire to the edge of elimination, there would be no need to strain oneself further. A direct relationship was perceived between the process of Ottoman decline and the increase of nationalist and democratic demands by the other nationalities and ethnic groups in the Empire; these democratic demands were increasingly perceived as threats directed at the Ottomans' very existence. Those Turks concerned with Ottoman-Turkish national identity saw the Christian minorities as chiefly responsible for the decline and collapse. It is therefore very important to examine more closely the process whereby the tension between Turkish national identity and the Christian minorities was formed.

Turkish National Identity and Christian Enmity

Under the influence of the ideals of the French Revolution, one after another the Balkan Christian minorities within the Ottoman Empire fought for their political independence and ultimately succeeded in splitting off from the Empire. But these independence movements were perceived by the ruling nation as treacherous acts directed against it. This perception was, in fact, an important determinant in shaping the main characteristics of the process of imperial decline. Although the enlightened secular ideas behind the French Revolution had indeed influenced the Christian minorities, in a very short period the independence movements took on the character of a religious struggle—so much so that the revolts generally moved from being national independence struggles against the Ottoman state into a series of massacres and counter-massacres between various religious and national groups. In these actions—especially in the Balkans, the masking of social and class divisions by religious divisions played a significant role. In the Bulgarian provinces, for instance, the large land-owners had generally been Muslims.

The revolts opened the way for the imperialist powers to interfere in the Ottoman Empire's internal affairs, and almost every national or religious group would ultimately receive patronage and support from one of the Great Powers. That several of these minority groups gained privileges not held by the Muslim population through the assistance of the imperialist states and through the Capitulations,[93] together with the unceasing demands by these imperialist states for new privileges for their protégés exacerbated tensions and fostered a profound hatred toward the Christian population of the Empire.

Although these feelings of hatred had been there before the Tanzimat Period (1839–76), they reached a peak with the Reform Decree (*Islahat Fermanı*), which declared the principle of general equality of all Ottoman subjects. 'The declaration, through the reforms, of the equality of the *dhimmis*,[94] or protected religious minorities, with the Muslim population was an affront to the religious sensibilities of the latter.'[95] Cevdet Paşa later wrote about the day on which the decree was announced, that

> according to the terms of this Rescript, Muslim and non-Muslim subjects would now have to be equal in the eyes of the law. This [declaration] profoundly affected the Muslim population…a good many of whom began to say that 'this was a day for weeping and mourning.'[96]

The Muslims saw it as an insult that they were now to be considered equal to those religious groups who were inferior to them. Furthermore, according to Cevdet, the perception was that 'we have lost our sacred rights, which our forefathers won with their blood. That the people who are accustomed to rule are now losing their right…is the perception not just of the ignorant, uninformed masses, but of the men of state, as well.'[97]

The main problem was that the Muslims, who up until that point had denigrated but tolerated Christians, now began to lose their position of dominance in Ottoman society. As we have seen, one of the main reasons for this loss of status was the ability of the imperialist powers to secure a number of economic and political concessions for themselves and for the Christian minorities under their protection. Over time these privileges grew to such dimensions that the Ottoman state even lost the right to inspect and monitor some of its own Christian citizens. Foreign embassies and consulates became new loci of power within the Empire. In many areas the consuls 'tended…to conduct themselves like little lords.'[98] Firing Ottoman officials who did not work with them was not a problem.

> From Governors (*vali*) and Lieutenant Governors (*mutasarrıf*) on down, anyone who did not get along with the local consul, meaning if he did not sacrifice his own duties and rights in order to serve the consul's interests, with just one letter from the consul to the embassy Dragoman, such persons would be dismissed from their duties.[99]

As a result of the hated Capitulations, the consuls were able to help Ottoman Christians to take advantage of the privileges that had been obtained for their own citizens. Not content to simply hand out declarations of consular protection, they would even give Ottoman Christians passports as if they were fellow citizens. It was often sufficient merely to write a letter of request to its consulate in order to receive the citizenship of a foreign power. Those who took advantage of these privileges could no longer be tried in Ottoman courts; they were exempt from Ottoman taxes, and also received significant tax exemption when trading within the Empire. All of these factors allowed for the formation of a very wealthy class of Ottoman Christians—or ex-Ottoman Christians, as the case may be. Whether or not this group formed its own minority within the Christian population of the Empire was not very important, because the external hostility that developed was directed at all Christians.

The social philosophy of life of the Muslim and Turkish population played a significant role in the loss of dominance. One can compare the attitude of the Muslim majority toward the Christian population in the Ottoman Empire with the attitudes that developed in Europe toward the Jews. For the Muslim-Turkish population of the Empire, the ideal social role was to serve in either the state bureaucracy or the army. In the words of historian Zafer Toprak:

> For centuries, the Ottoman Muslims had girded themselves with swords, conquered the country and ruled the state. Throughout their entire existence, commerce and crafts were denigrated, and the fundamental concern of every Ottoman Muslim was the desire to be a *kapıkulu*, or 'slave of the Porte,' or to become a 'servant of the state.'[100]

For this reason, busying oneself with commerce and money were not looked on favorably. 'Trade, crafts and guild matters were looked upon with scorn, or at least distaste; not a single young man in Istanbul saw such occupations as suitable [careers] for himself.'[101] Thus, the Trade School (*Ticaret Mektebi*) that opened in Istanbul in 1882 was soon forced to close its doors again due to a lack of students. The careers that were looked upon unfavorably by the Muslim population were taken up by the Christian minorities, who had little other choice, so long as the possibility of achieving high position in the bureaucracy and army remained closed to them. The Muslims did not want equality with the Christians because they felt the latter undeserving of the highest social positions that had been their private domain. We may sum this up with the words of Yusuf Akçura, who wrote that

Muslims, and especially the Ottoman Turks, did not want to mingle and socialize with the Christians. Because their 600-year domination would legally come to an end, and thereby they would fall to a level of equality with the *raya* (protected subject peoples), whom they have grown accustomed to seeing as under their domination. The earliest and most tangible result of this was that it would be necessary to take the *raya* into the bureaucracy and the army, over which the Turks had, until then, a monopoly. Expressed differently, it would be necessary to enter into a field of endeavor which was considered by aristocrats as comparatively less difficult and honorable, to embark upon industry and commerce: two areas to which they were not accustomed and which they held in contempt.[102]

But there are other reasons for the development of anti-Christian hostility that must be considered. The Christian population did not perform military service and thus remained largely untouched by the wars that wore away at the Muslim population. As a result,

although the Ottoman Christians may have wanted equality in theory, they preferred in practice to pay taxes and so gain exemption from five years of military service and possible death, and to devote their time to trade or agriculture.[103]

If we add to this picture that the Christians 'took advantage of the absence of the Muslims who had gone into the army, to take control of agricultural lands and commerce,'[104] it becomes easy to understand why the seeds of hatred toward the Christians grew. The attainment by hitherto second-class citizens of privileges through the protection of the foreign powers and the consequent improvement of their economic lot, as well as their exemption experiencing all of the burden and bitterness of the wars that were endured solely by the Muslim population—all of these greatly helped to fan the flames of hatred against them. Toward the end of the nineteenth century, this hatred and enmity found open expression in many of the Ottoman dailies:

They [the Turks] are ordered killed on Crete, they have been slaughtered on Samos, massacred in Rumelia, cut into pieces in Yemen, mowed down in Hawran, and strangled in Basra. But it's not the Greeks, the Bulgars, the Vlachs, the Jews, the Arabs or the Armenians...who are sent there, is it? Let them sit in their houses, in their yurts, in their tents! Let them put all their energies into their work and grow rich! Let them marry and multiply! It wouldn't have been right to upset them, to trouble their lofty souls, to tire their delicate bodies. If it were otherwise, how could we have warmed them to the idea of Ottomanism? We had to please them so that they would beg and plead to remain Ottomans.[105]

Beyond this, it was certainly true that the impoverished Muslim population in certain regions was in much worse shape than their Christian neighbors in a number of ways. Unlike the Christians, when local Muslims were subjected to oppression there was neither a foreign consulate where they could seek redress, nor a foreign state that would stand behind them. This situation was noted by a number of foreign diplomats and travelers. The British diplomat Sir Henry Bulwer, who served in Istanbul during the 1860s, made the following assessment:

Under the maladministration here, the Turks, who inhabit the lower classes, truly endure more bitterness than the Christians in the countryside. This is because while the Turks have no protectors whatsoever from their own oppressors, the Christians are at least protected to a certain degree by the officials of the foreign powers.[106]

A report written by an Englishman in Izmir 'emphasized that the Turkish villager is under far greater pressure than the Christian villager.'[107] A similar report was sent from Trabzon by the German consul there:

If...legal injustices were to be discussed, the situation of the Turks is more difficult than that of the Christians, because, while the latter benefits from the influence of the various consulates, like the Greek or Russian, there is no place from which the former knows he may receive legal assistance.[108]

As a final example, a consular report from Bursa for the years 1873–74 stated that 'among the slaves of the Porte, a differentiation must always be made between Muslims and non-Muslims. The former are protected by the state. But if the Muslim is without sustenance, even greater terror is wreaked upon him.'[109]

Regardless of how accurate such statements may be, it is certainly true that the Ottomans *felt* them deeply to be true. Both the Young Ottomans and the Young Turks movement (CUP) used this resentment to promote anti-Christian hostility, in the name of claiming possession of the ownerless Muslim population of the Empire. As stated above, they made acceptance of Turkish superiority and domination the condition for other peoples within the Empire to live together.

A predictable result of this jealousy-tinged hostility directed at the Christian minority was an intolerance of their demands for democracy. It would not be an exaggeration to say that there was no difference between the state and the opposition parties in their approach to this matter. This is clear in the personality of Midhat Paşa, an Ottoman statesman of the reformer mold, and a person to whom the internal Muslim opposition attached great hopes. A good number of intellectuals in our day have also made him into a prime symbol of Turkish 'enlightenment' movements. But when one looks at Midhat Paşa's attitude toward the democratic demands of the non-Muslim communities, a very different picture emerges.

In Bulgaria, Midhat Paşa became known as the 'Bulgar executioner' (*Bulgar celladı*) for his actions during the Bulgarian uprising of 1876.[110] He imposed such terror on the Bulgarian villagers and executed so many of them that the official historian Lütfi Efendi even mentions this as 'hacking [them] to pieces,' and accuses Midhat Paşa of having caused the strengthening of the Bulgarian independence movement by his 'grim slaughter' of the rebels.[111]

Midhat Paşa's harsh attitude toward the minority peoples appears to have been a continuation of the attitude held by the Young Ottomans. Despite the fact that the latter sometimes 'argued that all of the peoples of the Empire should have equal treatment, that all should equally love and defend the Empire, that it was impossible to separate them,'[112] they generally nurtured a hostility toward the Christian population due to the latter's special privileges and their revolts against the state. Thus, the Young Ottomans spoke of the national uprisings in the most negative light and only mentioned the Muslims killed. They attacked the two principal directors of the Tanzimat, Ali and Fuad Paşas, whom they declared to be enemies, largely on account of the Grand Viziers' conciliatory attitude toward the foreign powers and the native Christians. Matters even went so far on this issue that at one point a *fetva*, or religious opinion, was printed in the newspaper *Hürriyet* permitting the killing of Ali Paşa for backing the Christians.[113]

Another Young Ottoman, Ziya Paşa, referred to the Montenegrans who fought for their independence as 'bandits.' Ali Suavi and Namık Kemal vehemently protested the handing over to Serbia of one of the Turkish fortresses located there. They came out against releasing the rebels captured during the Crete uprising. They rejected retreat in the face of the pressure imposed by the European states, and the granting of independence to several Balkan nations as a result of this pressure.[114]

Their ideological successors, the Young Turks, looked no more favorably upon the non-Muslim minorities. In the Young Turks' view, the latter represented a potential threat that would or could split the Empire. In his memoirs, İbrahim Temo relates that he was deeply hurt by Ahmet Rıza's rejection of his proposals regarding the minorities, being 'unable to convince Rıza that he would never be able to instill a sense of national devotion into the minorities if he was not prepared to make certain concessions at the same time.'[115] Rıza believed that according them certain special rights or privileges would open the door to separatism and partition, and he stated that 'autonomy is treason; it meant separation...Our Christian compatriots shall be Ottomanized citizens.'[116] Thus, although in their publications the Young Turks acknowledged that injustices had been done to the religious minorities, they perpetually hurled invective at the political and military struggles carried on by these groups. This criticism, which blamed these struggles as being the reason for interference by other countries in the internal affairs of the Empire, reached its high point in 1902 with an article on the aims of the various national organizations in *Meşveret*. It claimed that 'the Armenian and Macedonian revolutionary committees have always admitted that the revolts in Turkey are only carried out so as to draw the attention of Europe and achieve its intervention.'[117] In such a situation, it would be impossible to remain silent in the face of their actions, whose intent was to 'divide' or 'destroy the homeland.'[118] Thus, if any understandings were reached in certain periods with the minority organizations, if any decisions were taken for joint action, the basis of such unity would be 'enmity and wrath.'[119] Any such understanding could not endure for long, and would after a short period give way to hostile relations.

In short, this was an Islamic prejudice,[120] which could not accept either being on a level of equality with Christians or the latter achieving a superior position. Traces of such attitudes can be found even today, and they were clearly seen in some of the literature of the late 19th century. In nearly all of the 'Tanzimat novels, Greek, Armenian and Jewish subjects generally appear as flighty women, quack doctors and businessmen, or as minor service personnel, such as waiters, coachmen or menservants.'[121] The Muslim Turkish population, however, appear in these novels as if they are taking their revenge on the non-Muslims for having their social status taken from them.

And it is no different in many present-day works. As we know from the plentiful literature of leftist and communist circles in Europe, in which they explain European anti-Semitism as a belief originating in the fact that Jews symbolized the class of the bourgeoisie, or, more simply, of money, so we observe that in Turkey similar views have emerged in regard to the Christian minorities. In the vast majority of theoretical treatises we encounter 'proof' of 'Turkey having been colonized by an internal process and having become dependent on imperialism.' The Christian minorities appear as a branch of imperialism, which has been nourished and transformed into a comprador class, (that is, a bourgeoisie cooperating with foreign interests) by the Capitulations. The capital-holding class becomes synonymous with the Christian minorities.

Of the hundreds of examples that can be found in the literature of the Left, we will limit ourselves to two. The Turkish historian Doğan Avcıoğlu, who claims that the goal of the Ottoman rulers 'was to make the Ottoman Christians into the most beloved subjects,' claims that 'the ones who took on the role of local middlemen for Western capitalism were the Greek and Armenian intermediaries,' and that those imperialist interests could thus be seen behind the idea raised by the Ottoman administration of recognizing the general equality of the Christians.[122]

Similar ideas are advanced by those who claim that all of the non-Muslims were basically capitalists: 'In Istanbul, the Greeks lived with a luxury and comfort that far overshadowed that of the Turks.' Despite this reality, it is said, much effort was expended by the imperialist powers to portray these wealthy capitalists as oppressed communities with the aim of 'creating the possibility of interfering in the internal affairs of the Ottoman state, and simultaneously strengthening the situation of the non-Muslim Ottoman citizens.'[123] Effort is thereby made to denigrate the members of a religious or ethnic group, by equating them with an economic class. By equating 'Christian' and 'bourgeois', whereby Christians are identified as collaborators of imperialism, these authors attempt to imbue anti-Christian ideas with class content. A natural result of this is to view the principle of general equality with suspicion, and to perceive imperialist intrigues behind it.

In brief, the Ottoman Christian peoples were seen by the Empire's Muslim Turkish population not merely as defeatists intent on dividing up or partitioning the Ottoman realm, but as a force yearning to be in a position of dominance and power themselves. And the Muslims had certainly not abandoned their steadily weakening position out of pacifism. In the words of Norbert Elias:

> ...if the others become strong while the powerful social formations are growing weaker, the latter would accept—in certain very limited situations—the weakening of their own powers and the decline of their social status, and, thereby, the transformation of the image of themselves...[but] if they perceive that the means of power of their potential rivals and enemies has grown greater than their own, that their values are being threatened and that their superiority has disappeared...they become as dangerous as wild animals. Such a series of developments in the conditions of both people living together, both in the past and at present, is an extremely normal and common situation which compels people toward the use of violence. It is one of the conditions in which these wars appear.[124]

The Ottoman Muslims experienced the process of a continual loss of dominance *vis-à-vis* the Christians in a similar way. So affected was their honor by the loss of power 'before the Bulgarian milkmen, Serbian swineherds and Greek tavern owners, over whom they had lorded for the last 500 years,'[125] that it was even openly declared that much blood would flow before they would give up power peacefully. Ziya Paşa complained that, in the actual implementation of the principle of equality, the Christians had by far overtaken the Muslims; he considered this situation intolerable for the Muslims:

> Although up to now the nation of Islam has endured it calmly and in silence, a day will come when the matter will be unbearable and unendurable, and it will reach levels at which Islamic honor and zeal can no longer stand it. Muslims will [eventually] reach their limit, and [then] they will take matters into their own hands (*gemi azıyaalacak*).[126]

Ali Suavi takes this threat one step further, claiming that 'apart from the fact that Muslims could not bear a subject nation (that is, the Christians) being superior to them, they could never accept being ruled by them. They will be ready to risk everything and shed blood [in order to prevent] that.'[127] And indeed, such was the case. Throughout the entire nineteenth century, one sees Muslim attacks and revolts directed against Christians, attributable to the anger caused by their loss of power. The events in Lebanon in 1844, in Mecca in 1855, in Jedda and Syria in 1858 are but a few of the revolts of this nature.

One of the reasons for the Serbian uprisings was also that the Muslims could not accept the loss of their position of dominance. The treaties of Akkerman (1826) and Edirne (1828) foresaw that Turkish villagers in Serbia would sell their lands and leave Serbia. But a good many Turkish villagers would not leave their lands. Furthermore, they were in no way willing to accept 'that, having suddenly left the position of being lords of Serbia, they had now arrived at a state wherein they were equal to them (the Serbs) in some cases, subject to them in others.'[128]

> In the face of this, the Serbs began to come to the consciousness that they had slowly become a nation through the concessions they had won. That they continued to be treated in the same manner as before, they found equally impossible to digest…This transformation that took place in the psychologies of both the Turks and the Serbs was the reason for the violent clashes and bloody struggles between them.[129]

The advent of another loss of Muslim dominance—this time *vis-à-vis* the Armenian population—played a significant role in the series of massacres of the Armenians. Anti-Armenian sentiment is asserted in some works to have been the natural and understandable result of this Muslim irritation.

'The Muslims in the province of Van thought little of the Armenians there, whom they had ruled for hundreds of years, and could not stomach, at least over that generation, the thought of the Armenians ruling and commanding them.'[130]

Turkish National Identity: Caught Between the Glory of the Past and the Humiliation of the Present

The movements of the Christian minorities were at first limited to democratic demands that reflected social goals. A gradual hardening of Istanbul's attitude resulted in the establishment of independent states—to the extent the minorities were able to receive assistance from the foreign powers. Thus, every demand for democracy by one of these national groups during this period became perceived as yet another step toward the partitioning of the Empire. The fact that the Christian communities who revolted lived in the border regions of the Empire and that the Empire progressively lost territories from the border regions were primary factors determining the policies of Ottoman and Turkish statesmen toward their national minorities.

One characteristic that Norbert Elias has said helped to determine the process of German national state formation can also be discerned in the formation of the Turkish national state.

> The Germans' process of state formation was profoundly influenced by their status as one of three ethnic population blocs. The Latinized and Slavic blocs felt themselves continually threatened by the populous German state. At the same time, the representatives of the German state also felt themselves permanently threatened from different sides. Each side availed itself of every opportunity that appeared in order to expand at all costs. From the German state's perspective, the need of these states to acquire more land in this way was understood to mean the continual carving off of border regions and the formation of new states.[131]

That this crumbling at the edges was not the result of military defeats at the hands of the rebels was a crucial determinant in the formation of Turkish national identity. As a rule, the revolting national groups were crushed. But even in situations where the uprisings were suppressed, the Ottomans often turned out to be the losers, due to the pressure applied by the foreign powers, and they found themselves forced to grant political concessions to those they had militarily crushed. To be forced to acknowledge themselves as defeated, even after wars in which they emerged victorious, violated the honor of the Ottoman-Turkish rulers. Moreover, in peaceful periods as well, the Western powers never hesitated to interfere in ways that would humiliate the Ottomans.

Numerous instances of these humiliations and helpless situations could be cited. One example can be found in the reply given on October 7, 1913 by Grand Vizier Said Halim Paşa to the French ambassador Bompard, who was pressing for reforms to be carried out in the Armenian provinces. Said Halim Paşa, weeping like a child, addressed Bompard thus:

> ...we are counseled to attain the assistance of foreigners in order to run this country, after which if we appeal to some state to bring us some officers of the gendarmerie we are told that they should not be given...Programs are devised without our involvement and even if we offer our opinions they are ignored ...who would lower himself to examine the reform proposals that we have sent?[132]

The humiliations and insults became so grave that they became a topic of open discussion between the Western powers and the Ottoman leaders. Ottoman officials were continually proposing that solutions that had been insisted upon by the West should be formulated in a way 'that will not injure Turkish self-esteem.' In the official documents given to the Western ambassadors on December 16, 1913, one finds expressions such as 'on the condition of preserving appearances before Ottoman public opinion.'[133] For the Ottomans, the 19th and 20th centuries were not simply a period of military defeats, more important, they were a period of belittlement and wounded pride.

There is another dimension which is not often touched upon. In relation to the Armenian Genocide, the raw materials for the belligerent tendencies found in the intellectual and emotional construct that is Turkish national identity are in large measure to be found in this feeling of belittlement and humiliation. A society that finds itself continually humiliated by a more powerful adversary will certainly foster feelings of hatred and enmity against this enemy. The Turks, who could not openly oppose the Western powers that had put them in this situation, cast about for weaker groups upon whom they could vent the hatred and spite that they needed to release. These turned out to be none other than the Christian minorities.

Another major reason that humiliated and belittled nations develop such belligerence is that they strain under the burden of their glorious pasts. Such was the case with the Ottomans. The vast gap between owning an Empire that spanned three continents on one hand and their subsequent, debased state on the other was truly awesome. And above all, this glorious past was not so distant. This made it all the more difficult to accept the condition of decline into which they had fallen.

> It is a truth that has been proved in human history up to now, that the members of states or other social units that lose their claim to a superior position during the last days of a war long feel the need, sometimes for an entire century, to

reconcile themselves with the changed circumstances and, more important, to be able to rid themselves of their feelings of devaluation regarding their own worth.[134]

In Ottoman Turkish history we can see that coming to terms with this fallen condition has not come easily. One of the principal reasons is the freshness of the memory of the glorious past. This is most easily observed in the evolution of Ottoman Turkish society's relations with the West. We may liken this situation to someone's incurable desire for revenge against those who have forcibly taken from them a place that belongs to them, and their inability to accept the changed circumstance. Thus, it would be largely accurate to claim that what dominated the Ottomans' feelings of admiration toward the West were jealousy and an incurable hatred, far more than love.

Until the start of the 19th century, the Ottomans had been the ones belittling and humiliating the West. 'Until the reign of Selim III (1789–1807), the attitude of looking down on the Christian states of Europe predominated among Ottoman statesmen. To conclude political agreements with any of these states under conditions of equality was considered to be in opposition to religious beliefs.'[135] This belittlement was so great at first that 'the Turks even considered it debasing to learn a foreign language.'[136]

When, as a result of continual military defeats, they found themselves obliged to borrow new technological inventions from the West, this was utterly unacceptable for the Ottomans. To do so would have been tantamount to open acknowledgement of Western superiority. In this early period, one finds frequent expressions along the lines of 'it is not proper for the people of Islam to imitate the infidels.' [137] As time passed their writings which looked down on the West began to undergo a transformation: gradually, an undisguised sense of both admiration and despair toward the West began to take hold of Ottoman rulers and intellectuals.

According to many historians, the point at which the Ottomans acknowledged that the West was their equal was the Reform Rescript (*Islahat Fermanı*) of 1856 and the Treaty of Paris signed in its wake. Others, however, claim that this notion had already begun to emerge as early as the reign of Selim III.[138] Regardless of when this process was completed, it remained difficult. It took a great deal of time before it could be admitted out loud that the West was superior. Furthermore, this idea has continually imposed itself on Turkish collective memory. The phenomenon has been experienced under the influence of a state of mind dominated by an inferiority complex, rooted in the sense of being at the bottom.

In the 19th century, when Western superiority emerged in a very clear manner, even the Ottomans began to look upon the West with respect, even admiration;

but not with love. And why should they love the West? During this period the West had continually defeated the Ottomans on the field of battle; they belittled them during diplomatic encounters...Admiration for the West was the very frequent topic of conversation in Turkey, and it was often criticized. But it never entered their consciousness that this admiration was not mixed with love.[139]

While the superiority of the West was eventually admitted, nevertheless, everything that came from there, and especially its culture, was looked on with the greatest suspicion. This initial division has been preserved down to our day. The science and technology of the West were good, but its morals were corrupt. What prevailed among them was rot and decadence, and all that should be taken from them, therefore, was their scientific and technical know-how. From their wild and disgusting culture, however, Turks would have to protect themselves. One Young Turks' newspaper article summed it up concisely:

> In order to advance our civilization we shall try to obtain scientific and industrial progress from Europe. We do not want their street dances, amorality, and satanic afflictions, such as callousness toward people who are starving to death, or to view fairness and tenderness of heart as outlandish notions.[140]

What was being experienced was essentially a type of culture shock. One Turkish statesman, who had been sent to Europe in the 19th century to expand his view and knowledge of the continent, explained this state of shock, brought on by his encounter with the new and alien culture, in a letter to the Sultan written in Paris:

> The shadow of infidelity has darkened every corner in the Land of the Franks (*Frengistan*), our Mehmet Dede Efendi [a sheikh from the Mevlevi order who accompanied the Ottoman statesman] was indeed not mad. We are passing the time with great difficulty, reading the Koran and having conversations on this topic...May God save [and deliver] us safely and speedily from here.[141]

That a civilization so rotten and morally corrupt could be superior and defeat them...this was a situation not easily accepted.

The first result of this mental state was, naturally, a longing for the past. A return to the Golden Age was made into the ideal and transformed into a sacred aim. By constantly evoking the past and how superior the Ottomans had been to the West, minds were soon directed toward seeking out ways in which to re-create this former glory. Until the Turkish War for Independence, nearly all Ottoman Turkish opposition movements were obsessed with the thought of being the children of a great and glorious Empire, and with the idea of reestablishing it anew.

One can find many examples of this yearning to recreate past glories in the works of both the Young Ottomans and the Young Turks. Of the numerous and lengthy conversations he had in London with prominent

Young Ottomans like Namık Kemal and Ziya Paşa, the Hungarian orientalist Arminius Vambéry relates the following:

The mood at the daily discussions was tame, even sleepy, but it would liven up toward evening when the bottles of raki would increase the excitement. The gentlemen's eyes would sparkle...The tone would rise and grow stronger with the bitterness and loss that they felt for the decline of the Ottoman state, which had once been so powerful and would then grow to assume its former power in their thoughts. The admiration that they felt for the successes of their warrior ancestors, the profound respect that they felt toward the religious heroes of Islam, both seemed to me as natural as the allegiance that they nourished, despite everything, for the Ottoman royal house.[142]

In a period of continual military defeat and territorial losses, each time they fell into a state of powerlessness or weakness, the longing for the bygone days of magnificence and splendor increased all the more. During the First Balkan War, for instance, when it was feared that Istanbul itself might be lost, efforts commenced to celebrate the city's conquest by the Turks. Among the various subjects for ceremonies and for discussion in the newspapers, the Turks were constantly reminded that they were the descendants of Mehmed the Conqueror and Suleiman the Magnificent, and that they were the equals of their heroic ancestors. Tekin Alp, in describing one of the demonstrations, said 'it was as if Istanbul had been conquered anew.'[143] Consolation for the present state of powerlessness and hopelessness were being sought in the greatness of the past.

We cannot truthfully claim that Turkey has fully emerged from this mindset. Along with the inferiority complex due to Western superiority in many fields, a mood of anger or sadness along the lines of 'Ah, didn't we have it all' can still be said to prevail among many of the country's citizens. One Turkish historian has compared this mood to that of the children of the *paşas* who saw their fathers being ejected from their positions of power during the Second Constitutional Period:

After the mansions...the elegant carriages and the comforts provided by a small army of servants, 'melted away like a candle from sorrow,' as they say today; sometimes we resemble a child of the palace, who diverts himself with sentences beginning with 'Ah...once, way back when...' This complex has found itself a significant place in some of our historical literature, and more importantly, in the people's consciousness. The adorning of the Ottoman centuries with gold, the emphasizing of their bravery and virtue, the capturing of wisps of inspiration, during the Janissary Band (*Mehtaran Bölüğü*) concerts at Rumeli Hisar, from the majestic reed pipes of our ancestors who made Europe tremble, the lamentation and regret directed at neighboring countries who oppose Turkey, saying 'Oh my, just look at the ingratitude of our former provinces!' Let's admit: it is a mentality that makes us feel good.[144]

In short, the humiliations, condescension and denigration experienced by a nation and its leaders, who for centuries had been used to ruling and looking down on others, shook them and profoundly disrupted their mental and spiritual world. One manner of response often observed in nations that have fallen from a place of dominance to a state of near annihilation or of being the whipping boy of others is the desire to take revenge on those believed responsible for this situation.

> The weakness of one's own state in comparison with other states creates, among other things, special, extraordinary conditions for persons affected by this weakness. Such persons are psychologically oppressed by feelings of insecurity, they are plagued by doubts about their own worth, feel themselves debased and humiliated, and feel the strong desire to avenge themselves on those who have brought about this state of affairs.[145]

These observations by Elias, a sociologist, are confirmed by Bernard Lewis, the eminent historian of Turkey.

> We have seen that a similar process was at work among the Ottomans. Military defeat and political humiliation had indeed shaken the torpid and complacent trust of the Turks in their own invincible and immutable superiority, but the ancient contempt for the barbarian infidel, where it yielded, often gave place to rancour rather than emulation.[146]

Indeed, Turkishness and Turkism were advocated as the way to restore the Ottomans' wounded pride before the 'Bulgarian dairymen, Serbian swineherds and Greek tavern owners' whom they had lorded over for five hundred years. Turkish nationalists then warmed to the desire to take revenge for the situation in which they found themselves, and to take it against the non-Muslim minorities who were the reason for their humiliation, oppression and denigration at the hands of the West. When the opportunity arose, they seized it, and did not hesitate to carry out massacres in places and against groups who lacked the protection of foreign powers.

The Desire to Avenge Massacres and Territorial Losses

Turkish national identity developed in tandem with a desire for revenge, which was created by military defeats, the massacre of Muslims in many places, and the loss of Ottoman territories. The history of the uprisings of the 19th century is not simply the history of the massacre of Christian groups, who revolted for legitimate demands such as equality and social justice. At the same time, 'it includes the subjection of the indigenous Muslim population to large-scale massacres.'[147] From the middle of the 19th century, large-scale migrations into Anatolia were undertaken by Muslim populations attempting to flee these massacres. Both the migrations and the massacres of Muslim Turks left deep marks on Turkish identity. In the aftermath of the Crimean War alone, approximately one million Muslims emigrated into Anatolia and Rumelia between 1855 and 1866.[148] As a result of the Serbian, Cretan and other uprisings, hundreds of thousands left hearth and home in order to save their lives, and arrived in Anatolia 'in a destitute and dispersed state.'[149] The migrations during the 1877–78 Russo-Ottoman War, in particular, and the massacres that were experienced on the way reached truly dramatic proportions. Later still came the migrations that followed in the wake of the massacres during the 1912 Balkan War.

The refugees, who had surmounted a myriad of obstacles merely to reach their destination, struggled to keep alive the memory of their experiences through the associations and publications they founded in the new regions in which they were settled—often by the government's conscious choice. All the while, they never abandoned the idea of avenging themselves for their dispersal. A poem published by an association founded by Balkan refugees in Istanbul after the 1912 war well reflects this mood. The poem, entitled 'May it be an earring,' concludes with the couplet, 'Oh, Muslim, don't distract yourself [from your purpose]! / Do not let your heart lose its desire for revenge.'[150] Another publication was titled 'Bulgarian Atrocities, the Banner of Revenge.' These examples shed light on the mood of the refugees and help to explain how these persons, despite being helpless masses saved from massacre themselves, could soon afterwards become the willing executioners of other, non-Muslim communities of Anatolia—the Armenians, above all. We can better understand the dimensions of the refugee problem and its effects if we recall that, between the years 1878 and 1904, some 850,000 Muslim refugees were settled in the areas in which the Armenians had previously been the majority.[151]

The territorial losses of the Ottoman Empire occupy a place in Turkish national identity every bit as important as the murders of Muslim Turks, and the hunger-, poverty- and disease-filled migrations. The loss of the Balkans, in particular, remains a vivid tragedy in memory. The massacres and the mass migrations to escape them are likewise important because they are national reminders of the lands that were lost at that time. Mustafa Kemal Atatürk expressed this sense poignantly in 1931: 'The refugees are a national reminder of our lost country.'[152]

Because of historical memory, the desire has persisted to recover these lost lands, intimately connected with a desire to take revenge on those who took them in the first place. This desire has paved the way for a militaristic and belligerent mindset to develop. Beginning during the era of Abdülhamid II, we see the prevalence of a militaristic, *revanchiste* spirit in the education given at the Ottoman military schools. Şevket Süreyya

Aydemir describes the military education and the mood it inspired in its students:

> War would certainly break out one day, and during this war, these young officers would take revenge for the defeat suffered in the war of 1878. An accounting would have to be made for the Greco-Ottoman War of 1897, which, despite our victory, concluded with adverse results for us. We can track the mood of the schools in the recollections of that generation.[153]

But this mood was not confined to the military schools. Belligerent, chauvinistic and militaristic ideas had embraced the entire society.

A good example is the situation in Istanbul in 1912 when it became clear that a war was likely to break out in the Balkans. Large demonstrations were held, both by the government and by the opposition parties. University students poured out onto the streets. Speeches were given that reminded the Ottoman Muslims that they were 'the heroic descendants of their glorious ancestors who had made the world tremble with their warlike nature.' Poems were recited saying: 'We are the Ottomans who instilled dread in the world / We were the ones who would suddenly set the world aflame / …when we were angered.' Calls for war were echoed in the newspapers: 'To say Ottoman is to say soldier / Long live the army! Long live war!' And the lost territories absolutely had to be reclaimed: 'The natural border of the Ottoman state is the Danube. We shall seize our national border. March, Ottomans! To the Danube!'[154]

But the Balkan War only resulted in a new wave of trauma. Another defeat, another massacre of Muslims, more refugees and more lost territories…The bitterness of the loss of Macedonia, which had been the birthplace of most of the leaders of the Committee of Union and Progress, was indescribable. The Unionist publisher and journalist Hüseyin Cahit [Yalçın] wrote: 'Being cast out of Rumelia…I still cannot forget the bitterness that this phrase produced in my heart at the time.' Such things were 'utterly incomprehensible.'[155] The profound effect of the territorial losses can be seen in the 1914 speech opening the Chamber of Deputies by its president, Halil Menteşe:

> Other nations do not forget those portions of their homeland that they lose in war, rather they always keep their memory alive before the succeeding generations. Along with these the reasons for the disaster shall always live on. In this manner, they protect the future against the same disastrous results occurring again for the same reasons. From this exalted seat, I call on the nation: Do not forget! I call on it: Do not forget beloved Salonica, verdant Manastir, Kossovo, Scutari, Jannina; all of beautiful Rumelia.

He was answered from the Chamber by cries of 'We shall not forget.'[156]

Until the republican period, the thought of recouping portions of their lost territories—the eternal goal of the Ottoman Turkish cadres—was something of an *idée fixe*, especially among the Unionist leaders. Read, for instance, in the memoirs of Hüsamettin Ertürk, this utterance by Enver Paşa:

> How can a person forget those fields, those meadows, over which the blood of the ancestors has flowed? To abandon them, along with our mosques, our tombs, our dervish lodges, our bridges and our fortresses, over whose squares Turkish raiders let their horses run, to the children of yesterday, and then, after 400 years, to be cast out of Rumelia and to move to Anatolia: this is something that cannot be borne. I would be prepared to gladly give the remaining years of my life in order to take revenge on the Bulgarians, the Greeks and the Montenegrans.[157]

Ertürk says that when Enver spoke these things, he became excited: his face turned a bright red and his eyes flashed like lightning.

The Unionists would ultimately go to great lengths in order to regain the Balkans. For them, to take back these lands that had been taken as a result of one crusade was a matter of honor. Again, Enver:

> Everywhere there appear traces of the misery created by this latest Crusade. If I could recount to you all of the horrors done by the enemy, even those done right here in sight of Istanbul, you would understand what has happened to the poor Muslims that are far away. But our anger is strengthened: revenge, revenge, revenge...There is no other word.[158]

The same mood prevailed in the Ottoman press immediately after the Balkan defeat. Poems about lost territories were printed, containing phrases such as 'sighs and laments,' and 'still unfulfilled' (*Sana Doymadan*) and with titles like 'Enmity.' 'Oh, my well-known father, who sleeps restfully in the grave / Your children's name today is Conquering Vengeance (*Sâdi İntikam*).'[159] The bitterness of a defeat that had not been accepted held an entire society. Even the children were brimming over with feelings of vengeance:

> It was the desperate, fiery year in which the Balkan War ended. We children were also immersed in the bitterness of a defeat that we had not digested any better than the adults, who had learned to forcibly bow their heads in respect.[160]

In his work *Lausanne*, Cemil Bilsel claims that one of the reasons for entering the First World War was this feeling of not wanting to forget these lost territories, and of revenge:

> The Balkan peoples had turned Rumelia into a Turkish slaughterhouse...The Turks hadn't forgotten this bitterness. They relived the narratives of the loss of Rumelia. Reciting these narratives, to students in the schools, to children at home, and to soldiers in their barracks, they awakened a national spirit, a

national grudge. They instilled a mood of demanding to one day see an accounting for the insults and cruelties inflicted upon the Turks. On maps, Rumelia was shown colored in black. The entire army was encouraged to take revenge for their sullied honor. The soldier would go to lessons every day with the song 'Turkish honor was sullied in 1328 (1912), ah. Ah, ah, ah, revenge!' The soldier returning to his village would plant the seeds there by singing this song. On the day that the Great War broke out, every Turk in whose heart burned the fire of revenge for the bitter pain of the Balkan disaster sensed that the day had come in which he would have the opportunity to redeem his lost honor.[161]

As was previously described, this feeling of vengeance, formed among Ottoman Turkish officials as a result of continual territorial losses, was largely directed at the non-Muslim minorities, the 'servants of yesterday,' who lived on these lands. And during the First World War this revenge, which could not have been taken against the Bulgarians or the Greeks, was instead taken out against the 'ungrateful' Armenians, who, by 'collaborating with the imperialists, struck us from behind.' The other peoples existing within the Empire, such as the Arabs, also received their share of this vengeance. The memoir of Sergeant Selahettin well reflects the Turkish attitude toward the Arabs.

> Baghdad has fallen. The Ottoman Army was in the grip of panic and making preparations to leave the city...Army Corps Commander Kazım Karabekir Paşa was there. At that period the people assembled in the square upon the order of Bekir Sami. Bekir Sami sprayed fire into the crowd with the machine gun in his hand. Karabekir Paşa asked: 'Bekir Sami, what are you doing? What transgression has this people [committed]?' The reply he received from Bekir Sami Bey was, 'I am settling the account of four hundred years of Ottoman History.'[162]

The West's Double Standard and the Tactics of the Christian Minorities

The fact that in Europe news of the massacres was limited only to those against the minorities, and tended to be exaggerated and one-sided, and that almost no discussion took place regarding massacres directed against Turks and Muslims, left deep marks upon the Turkish national identity. As a rule, it was indeed true that European public opinion was above all concerned about those things done to the Christians. Moreover, on some occasions the noisily proclaimed massacres of Christians consisted of fabricated reports.

A recollection of Murad Efendi, an Ottoman state official of German origin who was stationed in Bosnia in 1858, sheds some light on this issue:

> The German newspapers, which I had done without since leaving Istanbul, arrived for me from Ragusa (Dubrovnik). I was astonished to read detailed reports of events that were said to have occurred very close to where we were. I

read the detailed account of a massacre that had happened in the village through which I had only yesterday passed. [I was especially astonished] since, as it was now the incubation period for poultry, not a single chicken had been slaughtered for a week...Here, for the first time, I began to form an opinion about the gossip mill in which sensational stories were prepared and by which public opinion was formed.[163]

One reason for the appearance of this type of exaggerated and gossipy report before the public was the desire on the part of both local independence organizations and of the states that had already gained their independence for Western intervention. As a result of ample propaganda about 'the massacre of Christians,' the Western powers were to be forced to intervene. In this manner, either new territories would be plucked from the Ottoman Empire or, at the very least, new rights or privileges would be won for the minority groups within the Empire. The widespread distribution of this type of 'massacre' story by Greece, carried out with the intent of expanding her rule to the Aegean islands, is particularly noteworthy. In his memoirs, a German general recounts one of these tales of massacre:

> The efforts of the foreign consuls and the Italian captain Ruggieri to placate the extremists remained fruitless. However, the massacre of Christians, so much discussed and which was claimed to have occurred on the streets of Kanca on February 4, was pared down to the level of Turkish soldiers having fired from the windows and rooftops...a simple Turkish soldier had died, and not even a single Greek corpse could be found to confirm the so-called 'massacre of Christians.' The order had come from Athens [to the local rabble rousers] to provoke the Turks with violent actions, and to make impossible any and every new movement toward reform that might delay Crete's [eventual] annexation to Greece.[164]

The West's interest only in the massacres of Christians and media exaggerations about events contributed to the development of a deep belief among the Turks that no one cared about injustices done against Muslims or Turks. One of the results of this belief was the Turks' tendency to view themselves as the real victims of history. *They* were the ones who had really suffered evil and injustice, but this fact had been utterly ignored, because it was not in line with the interests of the West. They saw themselves as the whipping boy of history, always being portrayed as the guilty party. The reason for this was that the West had cast an eye on Turkish lands, and had the intention of partitioning or annihilating the Ottoman Turks.

> In addition to pursuing a foreign policy that treats us as its loathed stepchild, the Concert of Europe, setting its sights upon our possessions like a treacherous guardian without a conscience, has divided our country into spheres of influence for when they partition it in the future, and within these spheres they have interfered in the natural functioning of our sovereign rights.[165]

What was being complained of was that, for the sake of its own interests, the West followed a moral double standard and behaved in a biased manner. The West's tendency to side with the Christians in their actions was perceived by Muslims as a great injustice. Perceptions such as 'if a Christian got a nosebleed, all of Europe would be up in arms, but if thousands of Muslims were killed, they would stand watching,' became central to Muslim national identity. In almost every work in Turkish on the Christian uprisings, the sense predominates that a great injustice was done to the Turks. A few examples may suffice:

> To consider a slight oppression or crime against them [the Christians] as the gravest of sins, while the barbarities performed by the enemy [the Christians] were counted as a promise of justice for the sake of the common good: this is the mindset that prevails among those who today make war in Europe.[166]

> Like the European imperialists, President Wilson and the USA use two [separate] yardsticks: when it concerns Christian oppression of Turks and Muslims, nothing is accepted; but when it's Turkish or Muslim oppression against Christians, simply the accusation is sufficient for all hell to break loose.[167]

One may well ask, why did Great Britain and France, who claimed to be the champions of law, justice and democracy, allow these injustices?[168]

But the perception of the West's double standard was not limited to those injustices done to Turkey. More important for many Turks has been the Christian minorities, who are seen as those chiefly responsible for the behavior of the Western powers toward the Ottoman Empire.

> All of the Christian communities played the game of carrying out bloody butcheries and thereby provoking the Ottoman army and Muslim population to suppress them with even bloodier assaults. Afterward, they would undertake [propaganda] campaigns of 'Let's rescue those poor, oppressed Christians' among European public opinion…For example, in the first months of the Greek Revolt (1821) they cold-bloodedly butchered some twenty to thirty thousand Turks, the majority of whom were women and children, and then published a painful cry in Europe, claiming that the Turks were angrily falling upon them and killing them.[169]

Furthermore, these propaganda methods proved to be successful, and continued to be so throughout the 19th and on into the 20th centuries. In the years 1913–14 'the Greek Government labored to and ultimately succeeded in raising the ire of the European public, which never batted an eyelash when Muslims were encountering oppression, but which was immediately aroused when Christians were harmed in the slightest way.'[170] The same picture appears during the Bulgarian uprising of 1876:

> The event found immediate response in Europe in the form of a great uproar. Naturally, no mention was made of the Turks who had been killed, or that the

first attacks had originated with the Bulgarians. While the innocent Christians had stood silently by, the fanatical Turks passed to the offensive and annihilated them.[171]

It is frequently mentioned that the Armenians resorted to similar methods. Reports to this effect are gleefully cited by Turkish authors. In one report, the British ambassador, Sir P. Currie, writes that 'the primary goal [of the Armenian] Revolutionaries is to provoke quarrels and disorder and, by attracting the foreign representatives of humanity to their cause, to thereby open the way for the [European] States to intervene in the name of humanity.'[172] The Ottoman Sultan Abdülhamid II made similar remarks:

> The apparent goal of the Armenians is to provoke the Turks and then, when they forcefully come to suppress them, they will, by claiming that they have suffered oppression, draw upon themselves the sympathies of Europe, and above all, of England.[173]

The founder and first president of Robert College, Dr Cyrus Hamlin, also reported such tactics when quoting the words of an Armenian revolutionary in an American newspaper article:

> …The Hunchaks' [the major Armenian revolutionary organization at the time] armed bands will look for the opportunity to kill Turks and Kurds and to raze their villages. The Muslims, becoming wildly enraged at this, will then revolt and go out and attack defenseless Armenians and kill them with such great savagery that Russia will be compelled to occupy the country in the name of humanity and Christian civilization.[174]

The goal here is not to debate the character of these actions by the Christian groups, or even the accuracy of the descriptions. Rather, the reason for providing such detailed accounts is to highlight a belief that found resonance within Ottoman and, later, Turkish circles: the massacres directed at the Christian minorities were ultimately caused by the Christian minorities themselves.[175] According to this ingrained belief, this 'was the traditional way of plucking off [territories] from the Ottoman Empire.'[176] What's more, it was said, all of the Christian minorities acted according to these methods of 'armed actions, revolts, and shouting 'massacre' as soon as either the government or the Muslim population reacted against these… [and] getting the larger states to react.'[177]

In short, the perception was that there were no massacres, only a Muslim population provoked by its Christian neighbors. All of the actions undertaken were organized by the minorities, who demanded that the West intervene. This mindset has produced the very important result of either providing a logical explanation for the mass killings of minorities, or even allowing them to be perceived as justified. When Mustafa Kemal Atatürk claimed that 'what happened to the Christian elements who reside in our country was the result of the separatist policies which they wildly followed, using their...special privileges for evil,'[178] it was as if he spoke for the whole nation. Explaining or even justifying the Armenian massacres with this logic is a widespread phenomenon in Turkey.

> The Armenians...attempted a genocide of the Turks during the First World War; then they raised hell when the Turks resisted in order to defend themselves... Yet, that's how it is. It means that when a Turk was killed, nobody raised an eyebrow, but when a Turk killed someone, they raised a ruckus.[179]

The hardening of the belief that an injustice has been done to the Turks by those who never mention the massacres against them has had significant consequences. The Turks now accuse the Christians of falsification and Westerners of using charges against the Turks as an excuse to intervene in the Turks' internal affairs. Turks continually invoke the 'evil' aims of others in order to deflect any honest discussion of the oppressive actions taken against the minorities. This is an aspect of Turkish national identity that has remained unchanged and vital down to our day.

Turkish National Identity and the Perception of Humiliation in Relation to Human Rights and Democracy

The Western powers exploited every opportunity they had to interfere in Ottoman internal affairs. The oppressive measures taken against the Christian population gave them plenty of pretexts. 'It was well known that every state that wanted to snatch something or other from the Ottoman state would resort to propaganda about Christianity and the Christian nations being subjected to 'cruelties.''[180] For this purpose slogans such as 'rights of humanity,' 'democracy,' and 'reform' were employed most often when intervening in the Ottomans' internal affairs. But by voicing these slogans only during oppressive actions against the Christian minorities, without displaying the same sensitivity in regard to the massacre of Turks, the Western powers caused these slogans to be looked upon with deep suspicion, both among Ottoman rulers and among the opposition.

The common opinion of historians of Ottoman and Turkish history is that the West only employed such slogans in order to advance its own imperialist interests. One diplomat who was stationed for years in the Russian embassy in Istanbul described this tension:

> The interventions made by the Western powers in the Ottoman Empire were generally evaluated from standpoints entirely contrary. The Turks and their attorneys claimed that the sole purpose of the interventions was to serve the selfish interests of the states making them. Likewise, İsmet Paşa, the chief

Turkish delegate at the Lausanne Conference, attempted through a long discussion on this matter to prove that the protection of the Christian minorities was nothing but an excuse gladly used by the [Western] powers to interfere in Turkish internal affairs.

As for the others, they argued that the actions of the Powers in Turkey were an intervention made in the name of humanity, a humanist intervention, so to speak.[181]

Ottoman Turkish leaders cannot be considered unjustified in their complaints about the West's use of such slogans as 'human rights' and 'democracy' for the purpose of advancing their own colonialist aims. There are, after all, numerous examples of ardent opposition—and even of attempts to block Ottoman reform efforts of this sort by the Western states, who simultaneously and constantly accused the Ottomans of oppressing their Christian subjects and failing to carry out reforms. It has even been argued that this was one of the causes of the 1877–78 Russo-Ottoman War. It has been reported that, after the declaration of the Constitutional Government in 1876, the Russian ambassador told the Ottoman leaders that 'Russia shall pay you dearly for the shame of remaining the only state without a constitution or parliament.'[182]

More than three decades later, when the Second Constitutional Period was declared in 1908, Britain adopted a similar attitude, fearing that a robust constitutional regime might rejuvenate the ailing Ottoman Empire and thereby influence the Muslim populations in the British colonies. In a message to the British embassy in Istanbul, Foreign Secretary Sir Edward Grey wrote the following:

> Turkey has truly established a constitutional administration and if they can breathe life into it and reinforce it, it might progress to a degree, the outcome of which none of us would have been able to foresee…Up to now, everywhere in which we have Muslim subjects we have been able to say to them that there have been merciless despots in the countries ruled by the ministers of their religion (the Caliphs). Therefore, our absolutism is compassionate (*şevkatlı*).
>
> …But now, if parliamentary life were to begin and affairs were to be put in order in Turkey, the demand for a constitutional regime in Egypt would be strengthened, and our power to act against this would be greatly reduced.[183]

For this reason, the Western powers, being fully aware that the power vacuum created by such attempts to rebuild the Ottoman regime presented an opportunity, preferred to occupy Ottoman territories in place of supporting attempts at reform within the Empire. One example of this was Britain's seizure of Cyprus and Egypt on the pretext of protecting them from Russia after the Ottoman defeat of 1878. But perhaps the best example of the attitude of European states actually to Ottoman reforms and democratizing tendencies was the stance they took after the 1908 revolution. Taking advantage of the power vacuum within the new revolutionary regime, 'Austria seized the opportunity to proclaim the annexation of Bosnia and Herzegovina; Bulgaria declared her independence; Crete announced her union with Greece. The precedents had been set which were to be followed by Italy, in her attack on Ottoman Tripolitania in September 1911, and by the Balkan States, in their combined attack on Turkey in October 1912.'[184]

The entire Ottoman state was seen as free for the taking. Austria was so brazen as to send representatives into Anatolia in 1913 with the aim of 'studying whether or not these areas were places worth occupying.'[185] The Germans had since 1883 been preparing detailed plans for the German colonies that were likely to be established in Anatolia and Rumelia.[186] The West's attempts to present their actions as humanitarian interventions only caused Ottoman Turkish political circles, both in power and in opposition, to equate all Western talk about democracy and human rights with imperialism and colonialism. Thus, the Ottomans rejected these ideas and became outrightly hostile toward them.

During the years in which Ottoman-Turkish national identity was being formed, it was repeated in numerous press organs that 'the claims of humanity and civilization of Europe, which has acted as the spokesperson for human rights, are simply not credible. Europe's humanitarianism and justice consist of pure hypocrisy (*yakârlık*).'[187] It was generally believed that behind the humanitarianism of the West lay the idea of partitioning and dividing up the Empire.

This perception was well expressed in an article in the Unionist *Genç Kalemler* (Young Pens) journal, the publication in which Turkish nationalism had its first public expression. The article, entitled 'Homeland! One and only homeland,' was penned with the intention of warning the Muslim Turkish community against 'secret international aims.' The author of the piece claimed that he 'would oppose the idea of "internationalism" and the fanciful notion of 'humanity,' and prove just what horrible and destructive wounds (*rahne*) these were for the homeland.' The goal, for which the Europeans took to arms was simply 'to swallow us.' But 'it is demanded that the nationalist idea and patriotism be exercised' against these games of 'the Europeans, who have crushed the peoples of the East, carried out civilized robberies that were far removed from their alleged 'compassion' and 'mercy' that had trampled humanity underfoot in the East, and desired to enslave and curse all persons different from them.' Anything other than a patriotic response would mean being 'imprisoned, annihilated and erased from history.'[188]

As already noted, the fact that the efforts to eliminate the Ottomans were made in the name of natural rights and universal humanity helped to create a national mindset that was hostile to these concepts. On this point there is an interesting parallel with German national identity, which was formed in reaction to the French occupation.

The conservative-nationalist sectors of the middle classes in other countries often attempted to fuse humanist and moralist ideals with nationalist ones. The comparable sectors of the German middle classes rejected this compromise. Often with an air of triumph, they turned against the humanist and moral ideas of the rising middle classes as ideals whose falsehood had been unmasked.[189]

It was precisely for this reason that the German liberal thinker Friedrich Naumann understood the Turks' reaction to all reform proposals that emanated from the West, and that he remarked that they were of the same mindset as the Germans, who, due to their occupation by Napoleon, had also reacted negatively to the ideas of the Enlightenment.[190]

But what is significant here is not just the reaction of clear opposition to the West's slogans of 'human rights,' 'democracy' and the like. In the political regimes that later came to power in the country, these concepts were treated with great suspicion, and concepts such as human rights and democracy were associated with policies that would open the way for separatism and partition. In the years since, Turkey has not moved far from this outlook.

Spiritual Unity and Integrity against the Foreign and Internal Enemy

The perception of having to contend with a broad coalition arrayed against the Ottoman Empire, which was intent on its partition and destruction, the sense that they were members of a declining empire, that their homeland was slipping away from them and that it needed to be saved established itself as an *idée fixe* in the minds of Turks. 'Sedition was rampant, Crete was gone, Tripoli was about to go, Turkey was going, Islam was going...'[191] 'I looked at the map this week. Most of [the Empire's territories] is gone and only a small bit remains. It, too, shall go soon.'[192]

The situation was one of extreme panic. It was as if the Empire itself was dissipating like the sand in an hourglass. In discussions in the Ottoman Chamber of Deputies that took place in 1911, a dramatic picture was painted. An Arab deputy announced that 'a retreat has been made from Rumelia. Bosnia-Herzegovina has been abandoned, Eastern Rumelia was forcibly evacuated. Mighty Egypt has seen military occupation... Gentlemen, the Province of Tripoli (*Trablusgarp*) is going out from our hands...The Arab people is crying blood-filled tears.' Another deputy, calling out from his seat, said, 'It's not just [the Arabs], all Ottomans, and even all of Islam is crying blood-filled tears.'[193]

The panic over partition and collapse, which developed from the assumption that the homeland was slipping from their fingers, resulted in the Ottoman Turkish opposition groups—in particular, the Young Turks—making the salvation of the state and the prevention of further decline and collapse their central concern. As a Turkish constitutional scholar has stated, 'the solution to the problem of 'how to save this state' became the fundamental question that occupied Ottoman Turkish intellectuals. Their objective and their greatest concern, the beginning and end of their thoughts, was to save the state.'[194]

Nor was this concern limited to intellectuals. How to stem the tide of decline and partition became the most important question to engage the intellectual life of Ottoman society, including both the rulers and the ruled. In 1878, the Ottoman newspaper *Tercüman-ı Ahval* conducted a survey of its readers, asking, what were the problems with which the Ottomans were most concerned? The most frequent answer was, 'How is it possible to preserve the life of the Exalted State with all its remaining territories?'[195]

The panic produced the idea that unity would inevitably prevent collapse and partition. Ottoman Turkish intellectuals began to believe that it was their task to create the shared moral values and mentality that could hold the various peoples within the Empire's borders together in unity and accord: the goals of unity, brotherhood and shared moral values represented a fundamental threat to every force working to disperse the Empire. As these thinkers saw it, the Ottomans faced a common threat and they would have to replace the notions of personal liberty and individualism (*ferdi şahsiyet*) with the guarding of independence and defense of the nation.[196] The group would have to be emphasized in place of the individual.

To say 'we' meant to say 'one.'
You and I shall subject ourselves to 'it...'
There is no 'you,' or 'I'—only 'we.'[197]

Emphasis on the individual and his rights was incorrect, because 'there were no rights, only duties.'[198]

The Empire's condition of being in a continuous, if slow, process of dismemberment helped to create the belief that it was surrounded by forces that desired its annihilation. Kamil Paşa, the Grand Vizier in numerous governments during the reign of Abdülhamid II, expressed this fear in a letter penned in 1911:

> While [the Ottoman State] stands alone, exposed to the ambitions and attacks of the other states, .. the end of this path is, may Allah prevent it, partition.[199]

This situation, as was previously mentioned, facilitated the formation of a serious anxiety psychosis within the Ottoman Turkish individual: each felt surrounded by enemies wanting to annihilate, to obliterate them. The press of the day was full of articles on this subject. Resolutions were frequently passed at the Committee of Union and Progress's party congresses. At the 1912 congress, for instance, one resolution announced that 'despite being surrounded with internal and external enemies, [we are] confident that truth shall prevail.'[200] In his speech at the 1916 congress, Talat Paşa stated that 'everyone is our enemy.'[201]

In short, the ruling members of an Empire that was continually losing territories, that stood on the verge of collapse, perceived the national and democratic demands of their Christian subjects through the psychoses of isolation, fear and annihilation, and adopted an approach to them that was in line with these feelings. That is, they approached these national demands with the understanding that they would have to conduct a 'war for survival'; their actions to suppress such demands and their advocates possessed a level of brutality appropriate to this understanding.

Before concluding our discussion of the factors involved in shaping Turkish national identity, it is necessary to consider one more important question. To what extent were the feelings, anxieties and concerns that we have described here the products of an objective reality? The Ottoman Turks perceived themselves to be surrounded by foreign powers that wished to carve up the Empire; they felt themselves to be constantly humiliated and insulted; they saw themselves as being the perpetual victims of injustice, as the stepchildren of history; they saw Europe as always willing to intervene in order to protect the Ottoman Christian population, while massacres of Muslims would go practically unnoticed. Were these perceptions solidly grounded in reality? Were they merely exaggerations, fabrications and illusions? Where was the dividing line between reality and fantasy? Additionally, because these questions have been ignored, because of a failing to differentiate between fantasy and reality, has not a state of paranoia developed and spread throughout society?

Some of the perceptions mentioned above certainly have a basis in clear historical realities. However, even these have been exaggerated to the point that they have formed a sort of societal paranoia, and have been turned into excuses for the aggressiveness of Turkish nationalists toward other groups. In particular, the effects of this paranoia are manifested in the sharp reaction shown to any event that touches on the issue of the country's territorial integrity, sometimes even leading to demonstrations of extreme violence.

One way to escape from this societal paranoia is via an ability to openly discuss and discover the impulses and motives that have driven Turks to action in the past. What were the impulses that motivated their behavior, including displays of barbarism such as the Armenian Genocide and other massacres? What is being suggested is that the distinction between reality and fantasy in Turkish history is not the main point. If fantasies are believed to be real, then they can have the same effect as if they were real. The distinction loses its importance. The question I want to ask is, even if these facts all reflect reality, can they be used as a justification for such great barbarity as the Armenian Genocide?

Here we can cite the Turkish historian Yusuf Hikmet Bayur on the subject of the Armenian Genocide, because it is representative of a general view within Turkey. In his monumental ten-volume work *The History of the Turkish Revolution*, Bayur continually asks, 'Who started it?'

> Because…it's one thing to say that the Turks killed the Armenians spontaneously, and another to say that, when the Armenians revolted, the Turks, who were locked in a life-or-death struggle, used excessive force and killed a good many people.[202]

In his works, Bayur has criticized the massacre of the Armenians as 'excessively harsh' behavior, and labored to show that it was the work of Talat Paşa alone. But the logic of his argumentation is something like 'Yes, we killed, but not without provocation; there was always a good reason.' In all Turkish works concerning the Armenian massacres, one can detect this tone even among those authors taking the most moderate line. We can summarize this logic as, 'If something happened, there must be a reason for it; nobody does something without reason.' It is as if there are *reasonable* Genocides. According to this logic, victims have earned their suffering by their action or character;[203] they deserve what was inflicted on them.[204]

As a result, what is deemed important is not whether or not one behaves barbarically, but rather whether or not one is justified in doing so. It thus becomes apparent that, through such logic, barbarism is excused. Disposition toward justification and rationalization is a very common response, one which we can observe in every Genocide or act of human destructiveness.[205] What is significant in our case is how the Turks, as a society, have related to the tendency for violence that has developed for one reason or another. Do they—or will they—welcome it and excuse it on account of its being justified? If not, will they seriously consider its causes with the intent of reducing, preventing and eliminating their own potential for violence?

The logic that, for one reason or another, excuses or justifies barbarism not only has laid the groundwork for large-scale massacres, but also heralds future ones. What I have attempted to do here is to first of all define this type of mental state, and to explore the causes that allow it to develop. In part, the task of bringing these subconscious processes to the conscious mind is necessary for preventing the barbarisms that this mental state allows. Now let us look closely at the Armenian Genocide in light of this foundation, and at the question of what conditions produced it.

We could no doubt expand on those elements that I have explored as characteristic of Turkish national identity. But, more important, we need to understand that these characteristics played a crucial determining role in the events surrounding the Armenian Genocide. Turkish national identity, which appeared and developed within the conditions and mindset I sketched in broad lines above, was prone to view the last remaining Christian minority group within its control as responsible for all the 'negative' developments. The Armenians, as the last large Christian group left in the Empire, ultimately paid the price for the other Christian communities that had, one after the other, broken off from it.

It is necessary to add that the Armenian Genocide was not a product solely of these characteristics. Genocide was a product of these characteristics combined with a number of other factors, such as World War One and the great losses experienced in that war. I have tried in my book *İnsan Hakları ve Ermeni Sorunu* (1999) to elaborate on these special factors. My point here is that these specific factors only had an impact within the continuum of the Turkish national attitude toward the Christian minorities in the Ottoman Empire.

NOTES

1. This chapter is a slightly modified version of the first chapter of my 1991 book *Türk Ulusal Kimliği ve Ermeni Sorunu* (Turkish National Identity and the Armenian Question) (Istanbul). At the time of its publication, this book was the first critical work published in Turkey on the issue of the 'Armenian Question'. While relatively few other works on the issue have appeared since then, the book has gone through more than five printings up to now.
2. Süleyman Kocabaş, *Ermeni Meselesi Nedir Ne Değildir* (Istanbul, 1987), p. 9.
3. Emekli Tümgeneral İhsan Sakarya, *Belgelerle Ermeni Sorunu* (Ankara, 1984), p. 160.
4. *Ibid.*, p. 475.
5. Selahattin Turgay Daloğlu, *Ermeni Zulmü 1915–1918* (Istanbul, 1983).
6. Azmi Süslü, *Ermeniler ve 1915 Tehcir Olayı* (Van, 1990).
7. Enver Ziya Karal, *Osmanlı Tarihi*, vol. VIII (Ankara, 1988), p. 145.
8. Salâhi Sonyel, *Türk Kurtuluş Savaşı ve Dış Politika*, vol. II (Ankara, 1986), p. 36.
9. Salâhi Sonyel, 'İngiliz Belgelerine Göre Adana'da Vuku Bulan Türk-Ermeni Olayları (Temmuz 1908–Aralık 1909),' *Belletin* 51, no. 201 (December, 1987): 1245, 1247.
10. Norbert Elias, *Studien Uber die Deutschen* (Frankfurt a.M., 1990), p. 8.
11. Çetin Yetkin, *Türk Halk Hareketleri ve Devrimleri Tarihi* (Istanbul, 1984), pp. 344–45.
12. Tarık Zafer Tunaya, *Türkiye'de Siyasal Partiler, vol. III: İttihat ve Terakki* (Istanbul, 1989), p. 22.
13. Quoted in François Georgeon, *Türk Milliyetçiliğinin Kökenleri: Yusuf Akçora (1876–1935)* (Ankara, 1986), p. 14.
14. Ziya Gökalp,*Türkçülüğün Esasları* (updated into modern Turkish) (Istanbul, 1978), pp. 10–11.

108   FROM EMPIRE TO REPUBLIC

15. Georgeon, p. 84.

16. Ağah Sırrı Levent, *Türk Dilinde Gelişme ve Sadeleşme Evreleri* (Ankara, 1960), p. 6.

17. It should be added that there do exist writers who understand the relationship between Islam and Turkism (*Türkçülük*) differently. Charles Warren Hostler, for instance, argues in his work *Türken und Sowjets* (Berlin, 1960) that the theory that the Turks destroyed their national identities through Islam is incorrect. On the contrary, they were able to preserve their identities under the broader, overarching identity of Islam. Similar views were put forward in the works of Tekin Alp. In both *Türk Ruhu* (Istanbul, 1944) and *Türkismus und Pantürkismus* (Weimar, 1915), the writer claims that those among the Turks who accepted Islam thereby preserved their Turkishness, whereas those Turks, like the Bulgars and Magyars, who adopted other religions became entirely assimilated. It is necessary to discuss these claims separately. Suffice it here to say that what the aforementioned authors have meant by preserving their identity is the preservation of a good number of Turkic languages, or that the Turks who accepted Islam became the rulers of the states, but it is incorrect to interpret these phenomena as a preservation of some consciousness of 'Turkishness.'

18. Quoted in Gotthard Jäschke, *Die Turanismus der Jungtürken, Zur Osmanischen Außenpolitik im Weltkriege* (Leipzig, 1941), p. 3.

19. Bernard Lewis, *The Emergence of Modern Turkey,* 2nd edn, Oxford, 1967, p. 329.

20. *Ibid.*, p. 8.

21. Ali Kemal Meram, *Türkçülük ve Türkçülük Mücadeleleri Tarihi* (Istanbul, 1969), p. 70.

22. Quoted in M. Goloğlu, *Milli Mücadele Tarihi, vol. V: Türkiye Cumhuriyeti 1923* (Ankara, 1971), p. 177.

23. Quoted in Ahmet Rasim, *Osmanlı İmparatorluğu'nun Reform Çabaları İçinde Batış Evreleri* (Istanbul, 1987), p. 81.

24. Quoted in Yalçın Küçük, *Aydın Üzerine Tezler*, vol. II (Istanbul, 1985), p. 257.

25. David Kushner, *The Rise of Turkish Nationalism 1876–1908* (London, 1977), p. 50.

26. A. Cevdet Paşa, *Maruzat* (Istanbul, 1980), p. 114.

27. We already see in this period that a separate understanding of *vatan* was—although still novel–beginning to be developed by the Turkists in connection with Anatolia. We will revisit this trend later in this chapter.

28. Enver Ziya Karal, *Osmanlı Tarihi*, vol. VIII (Ankara, 1996), p. 260.

29. Orhan Koloğlu, *Abdülhamit Gerçeği* (Istanbul, 1987), p. 383.

30. Fikret Adanir, 'Die osmanische Geschichtschreibung zur Gründung des bulgarischen Staates,' *Südosteuropa Mitteilungen* 29, no. 2 (1989).

31. Meram, p. 46.

32. *Ibid.*, p. 65.

33. *Osmanlı Mebusan Meclisi Reisi Halil Menteşe'nin Anıları* (Istanbul, 1986), p. 13.

34. Tunaya, p. 310.

35. Words spoken by the Responsible Delegate (*Murahhas-ı Mes'ul*) of the Turkish Strength Society, Kuzcuoğlu Tahsin Bey, and quoted in Zafer Toprak, 'II. Meşrutiyet Döneminde Paramiliter Gençlik Örgütleri', *Tanzimat'tan Cumhuriyet'e Türkiye Ansiklopedesi*, vol. II (Istanbul, 1985), p. 532.

36. *Ibid.*, pp. 531, 533. The words Hearth, Homeland, etcetera allude to the various Turkish youth associations mentioned in the previous passage.

37. Kushner cites an article entitled 'Our Young People' (*Gençlerimiz*) in an 1875 edition of the Ottoman daily *Basiret*.

38. Hilmi Ziya Ülken, *Türkiye'de Çağdaş Düşünce Tarihi* (Istanbul, 1979), p. 81. The mid-19th century French diplomat De Gobineau was perhaps the first thinker to present a social theory of race that was both overarching and workable. In his main work, *Essay on*

the Inequality of the Races (1853) and others, de Gobineau cited racial purity as the central determinant in the survival and prosperity of civilization. His racial theories made almost no impression at the time, and it was only four decades later, and then not in his native France but in Germany, that they came to prominence when they were adopted by a number of Pan-German and 'Volkish' groups. For more on de Gobineau and the development of racial theory in Germany, see George L. Mosse, *The Crisis of German Ideology* (New York, 1964), pp. 91–2.

39. Tekin Alp, *Türkismus und Pantürkismus*, p. 7.
40. François Georgeon, p. 84. German influence on the Turkish nationalists was great, and is a matter for research in its own right. In almost every field, German experts were invited into the country and a good number of economic and political associations were placed under their administration. For instance, the Founding Declaration of the Turkish Strength Society, which was founded, as we mentioned earlier, in 1913, was full of praise for German nationalism. The association was in fact established under the influence of the German *Pfadfinder* organization. The chairman of the youth associations that were established as a continuation of this, von Hoff, served in the Ottoman army with the rank of Colonel. Toprak, 'II. Meşrutiyet Döneminde Paramiliter Gençlik Örgütleri,' p. 535.
41. Zafer Toprak, *Turkiye'de 'Milli İktisat' (1908–1918)* (Ankara, 1982), p. 28.
42. Quoted in Tunaya, p. 320.
43. Küçük, p. 23.
44. Quoted in Yetkin, p. 4.
45. Quoted in Jäschke, pp. 2–3.
46. Quoted in Ali Kemal Meram, p. 63.
47. The official who was most well-known for such views was Koçi Bey. See *Koçi Bey Risalesi* (Istanbul, 1972).
48. Muzaffer Özdağ, 'Osmanlı Tarih ve Edebiyatında Türk Düşmanlığı,' *Tarih ve Toplum,* 65 (May 1989), p. 270.
49. İlhan Arsen, *Arap Milliyetçiliği ve Türkler* (Istanbul, 1987), p. 37. This work examines in detail all mention of the Turks in Islamic sources.
50. *Ibid.*, pp. 32, 38.
51. Esther Kafé, 'Rönesans Dönemi Avrupa Gezi Yazılarında Türk Miti ve Bunun Çöküşü,' *Tarih İncelemeleri Dergisi, II* (1984), p. 203. [Originally published as: 'Le mythe turc et son decline dans les relations de voyage des Européens de la Renaissance,' *Oriens,* XXI–XXII (1971).
52. Doğan Avcıoğlu, *Türklerin Tarihi*, vol. I (Istanbul, 1979), p. 9.
53. Kafé, p. 221.
54. Taner Timur, *Osmanlı Kimliği* (Istanbul, 1986), p. 146.
55. Karl Kassner, *Bulgarien, Land und Volk* (Leipzig, 1918), p. 16.
56. Gustav Rasch, *Die Türken in Europa* (Prague, 1873), p. viii.
57. Waldemar Frey, *Kût-El-Amâra, Kriegsfahrten und Erinnerungsbilder aus dem Orient* (Berlin, 1932), pp. 96–7.
58. Karl Braun Wiesbaden, *Eine türkische Reise* (Stuttgart, 1876), p. 341.
59. Phillip Franz Bresnitz, *Die Christenverfolgungen in der Türkei unter dem Sultan Abdul Hamid* (Berlin and Leipzig, 1896), p. 1.
60. Thilo von Trotha, *Zur historischen Entwicklung der Balkanfrage* (Berlin, 1897), p. 1.
61. Kushner, p. 47.
62. *Ibid.*, p. 48.
63. Quoted in Yusuf Akçura[oğlu], *Türkçülük* (Istanbul, 1990), p. 100, from Akçuraoğlu's writings of the year 1928. These writings were also published in book form by the Turkish Ministry of Culture (*Yeni Devletin Öncüleri: 1928 yılı yazıları* (Ankara, 1981)), where

the cited passage is given in somewhat different form, the content, however, is the same.
64. Georgeon, p. 36.
65. The armistice in October 1918 which sealed the Ottoman defeat opened a new phase in Turkish history. A Turkish nationalist resistance movement formed in Anatolia under the leadership of Mustafa Kemal Atatürk against the partition plans of the Great Powers, which ended in the establishment of the Republic of Turkey. It is generally accepted that the period of resistance lasted from 1919 to 1923.
66. Doğan Avcıoğlu, *Milli Kurtuluş Tarihi 1838'den 1995'e*, vol. I (Istanbul, 1981), p. 34.
67. *Ibid.*, pp. 35–6.
68. Yusuf Hikmet Bayur, *Türk İnkilap Tarihi,* vol. II, part IV (Ankara, 1983), pp. 329–30.
69. Şevket Süreyya Aydemir, *Makedonya'dan Ortaasya'ya Enver Paşa*, vol. II: 1908–1914 (Istanbul, 1981), p. 228.
70. Yalçın Küçük, p. 112.
71. Yusuf Akçura, *Yeni Türk Devletlerinin Öncüleri*, p. 29.
72. David Kushner, p. 5.
73. For a more detailed discussion concerning how this subject was understood at the time, see Mümtaz'er Türköne, *Siyasi İdeoloji Olarak İslamcılığın Doğuşu* (Istanbul, 1991), p. 245ff.
74. Bernard Lewis, p. 107.
75. M. C. Kuntay, 'Namık Kemal', *Devrinin İnsanları ve Olayları Arasında*, vol. I. (Ankara: Milli Eğitim Bakanlığı, 1949), p. 186.
76. Enver Ziya Karal, *Osmanlı Tarihi,* vol. VII, p. 296.
77. *Ibid.*, p. 293.
78. Lewis, pp. 147–8.
79. E. E. Ramsaur, *The Young Turks: Prelude to the Revolution of 1908* (Princeton, 1957), p. 92.
80. Sina Akşin, *Jön Türkler ve İttihat ve Terakki* (Istanbul, 1987), p. 169.
81. Yusuf Akçura, *Üç Tarz-ı Siyaset* (Ankara, 1987), p. 37. In this edition, which was published with a Foreword by Enver Ziya Karal, the replies of Ali Kemal and Ahmet Ferit Tek to Akçura's article are also included. The aforementioned quotation was taken from Ali Kemal's reply.
82. Mizancı Murat, 'Mazeret', *Mizan* 19 (February 24, 1887), Quoted in Kushner, p. 26.
83. İsmail Kara, 'Bir Milliyetçilik Tartışması,' *Tarih ve Toplum* 28 (June 1986), p. 57.
84. İlber Ortaylı, *İmparatorluğun En Uzun Yüzyılı* (Istanbul, 1983).
85. İhsan Sakarya, p. 67.
86. Niyazi Berkes, *Türkiye'de Çağdaşlaşma* (Istanbul, 1978), p. 325.
87. [Zeki] Velidi Togan, *Tarih'ten Usül.* Quoted in Yalçın Küçük, *Aydın Üzerine Tezler,* vol. II, p. 80.
88. *Tarih-i Cevdet*, vol. I, p. 36.
89. Aydemir, *Makedonya'dan Ortaasya'ya Enver Paşa, vol. I: 1860–1908*, p. 514.
90. *Ibid.*, p. 67.
91. Aydemir, *Makedonya'dan Ortaasya'ya Enver Paşa, vol. I: 1860–1908*, p. 552.
92. *Ibid.*, p. 552.
93. After their capture of Constantinople in 1453, the Ottoman sultans began, in their dealings with the states and kingdoms of Europe, to grant European merchants a variety of legal and commercial privileges and exemptions, which became known as 'Capitulations.' According to such understandings, a subject of a state granted such privileges could not be tried in Ottoman courts, his residence could not be entered and searched, and he was given a number of significant economic and commercial advantages when conducting trade within the Empire.

94. The word *dhimmi* is the standard English transliteration, although modern Turkish spells it *zimmi*.

95. Gülnihâl Bozkurt, *Alman-İngiliz Belgelerinin ve Siyasi Gelişmelerin ışığı altında Gayrimüslim Osmanlı Vatandaşlarının Hukuki Durumu (1839–1914)* (Ankara, 1989), p. 60.

96. Cevdet Paşa, 'Tezâkir,' *Tezâkir*, vol. 10 (Ankara, 1986), pp. 67–8.

97. Bozkurt, pp. 60–1.

98. Roderic H. Davison, *Reform in the Ottoman Empire 1856–76* (Princeton, 1963), p. 72.

99. İhsan Sungu, *Tanzimat ve Yeni Osmanlılar, vol. I: Tanzimat* (Istanbul, 1941), p. 791.

100. Zafer Toprak, *Türkiye'de Milli İktisat (1908–1918)*, p. 49.

101. Ali Birinci, *Hürriyet ve İtilaf Fırkası* (Istanbul, 1990), p. 19.

102. Akçura, *Üç Tarz-ı Siyaset*, p. 28.

103. Davison, p. 94.

104. Great Britain, Parliamentary Papers, 1861, vol. 67; Accounts and Papers, vol. 34, no. 8: '...condition of Christians in Turkey,' quoted in Davison, p. 113 n. 47.

105. Bekir Sıtkı Baykal, *Şark Buhranı ve Sabah Gazetesi* (Ankara, 1948), quoted in Yetkin, p. 303.

106. James Baker, *Die Türken in Europa* (Stuttgart, 1879), p. 167.

107. İlber Ortaylı, *Tanzimattan Cumhuriyete Yerel Yönetim Geleneği* (Istanbul, 1985), p. 72.

108. Baker, p. 373.

109. Zentrales Staatsarchiv Potsdam, Auswärtiges Amt, I-C, 52364, Bursa, Bd. 1.

110. Dr Alois Hajek, *Bulgarien unter der Türkenherrschaft* (Berlin and Leipzig, 1925), p. 294.

111. 'He compared Midhat Paşa's lightning-fast butchery to trimming back a vineyard because, just as the roots of the vines are strengthened when the vineyards are pruned, these actions of his produced the final result that appeared later, by decisively reinvigorating the nationalist sentiments of the Bulgarians.' Cited in Enver Ziya Karal, *Osmanlı Tarihi*, vol. VII, p. 95.

112. Davison, p. 222.

113. Türköne, p. 83.

114. Yuriy Aşatoviç Petrosyan, *Sovyet Gözüyle Jön Türkler* (Ankara 1974), pp. 132–3.

115. İbrahim Temo, *İttihad ve Terakki Cemiyetinin Teşekkülü* (Medjidia, Romania, 1939), pp. 182–6. Cited in Ramsaur, p. 92.

116. Quoted in Ramsaur, p. 93.

117. Orhan Koloğlu, *Abdülhamit Gerçeği*, pp. 335–36.

118. İbrahim Temo'nun, *İttihad ve Terakki Anıları* (Istanbul, 1987), p. 148.

119. Petrosyan, p. 267.

120. It could be argued that the term 'Islamic prejudice' is not entirely accurate, because exclusion and denigration generally refer to cultural characteristics, which are claimed to be innate and unchanging and reflect a certain structure and relation in society. However, the social boundary was crossable. The person being denigrated possesses the possibility of escaping the target group, by becoming a Muslim.

121. Taner Timur, *Osmanlı-Türk Romanında Tarih, Toplum ve Kimlik* (Istanbul, 1991), p. 41.

122. Doğan Avcıoğlu, *Türkiye'nin Düzeni*, vol. I (Ankara, 1987), p. 122.

123. Yetkin, p. 265.

124. Elias, p. 467.

125. Hüseyin Tuncer, *Türk Yurdu Üzerine Bir İnceleme* (Ankara, 1990), p. 47, citing an article by Yusuf Akçura from the 3rd volume of *Türk Yurdu* (1929). The fact that Akçura, who was considered a moderate and liberal nationalist, would say such things is an important demonstration that the loss of domination over the Christian minorities had in no way been countenanced.

126. Quoted in Türköne, p. 70.

127. *Ibid.*
128. Enver Ziya Karal, *Osmanlı Tarihi,* vol. VI, p. 70.
129. *Ibid.*
130. Salâhi Sonyel, 'İngiliz Belgelerine Göre Adana'da Vuku Bulan', p. 1247.
131. Elias, p. 9.
132. Yusuf Hikmet Bayur, *Türk İnkilabı Tarihi,* vol. II, part III (Ankara, 1983), pp. 148–9.
133. *Ibid.,* p. 164.
134. Elias, p. 10.
135. E. Z. Karal, *Osmanlı Tarihi,* vol. V, p. 73.
136. *Ibid.,* p. 9.
137. Şükrü Hanioğlu, *Osmanlı İttihat ve Terakki Cemiyeti ve Jön Türklük (1889–1902)* (Istanbul, 1985), p. 13.
138. Yalçın Küçük, *Aydınların üzerine Tezler* gives the year 1856 for the changes, while Tarik Zafer Tunaya *Türkiye'nin Siyasi Hayatunda Batılılaşma Hareketleri* (Istanbul, 1960), pp. 23–4 and Ahmet Mumcu, *Osmanlı Devletinde Siyaseten Katl* (Ankara, 1985), p. 13, place the turning point during the reign of Selim III.
139. Timur, p. 13.
140. Hanioğlu, *The Young Turks in Opposition* (Oxford, 1995), p. 14.
141. Enver Ziya Karal, 'Gülhane Hattı Hümayununda Batının Etkisi', *Belleten,* no. 112 (October, 1964), p. 112.
142. Berkes, *Türkiye'de Çağdaşlaşma,* pp. 596–7.
143. Tekin Alp, *Türkismus und Pantürkismus,* p. 18.
144. A. Turan Alkan, 'Osmanlı Tarihi: Bir 'İnanç Alanı!' *Türkiye Günlüğü,* no. 11 (Summer 1990), pp. 7–8.
145. Elias, *op. cit.,* p. 13.
146. Lewis, *op. cit.,* p. 127.
147. Stanford Shaw, 'Osmanlı İmparatorluğunda Azınlıklar Sorunu,' *Tanzimattan Cumhuriyete Türkiye Ansiklopedisi,* vol. IV (Istanbul, 1985), p. 1004.
148. Davison, p. 151, footnote 32.
149. Karal, *Osmanlı Tarihi,* vol. VII, p. 277.
150. 'Ey Müslüman kendini hiç avutma! / Yüreğini öç almadan soğutma.' Quoted in *Tarih ve Toplum,* no. 87 (March, 1991).
151. Artem Ohandjanian, *Das Verschwiegene Völkermord* (Vienna, 1989), p. 36. The Ottomans did not possess a central department for the resettlement of immigrants until the 1910s. Dilution of the density of the Christian population in certain regions was an important issue, but how planned these attempts were is a point of debate.
152. Bilal Şimşir, *Rumeli'den Türk Göçleri, Belgeler,* vol. I (Ankara, 1970), cover.
153. Şevket Süreyya Aydemir, *Makedonya'dan Ortaasya'ya Enver Paşa,* vol. II (Istanbul, 1981), p. 296.
154. Celal Bayar, *Ben de Yazdım,* vol. III (Istanbul, 1966), pp. 808ff. This section contains an excellent picture of the pre-war mood.
155. Quoted in Tunaya, *Türkiye'de Siyasal Partiler,* vol. III, p. 462.
156. Quoted in *ibid.,* p. 465.
157. Hüsamettin Ertürk (editor Samih Nafız Tansu), *İki Devrin Perde Arkası* (Istanbul, 1964), p. 121.
158. Şükrü Hanioğlu, *Kendi Mektuplarında Enver Paşa* (Istanbul, 1989), cited in Orhan Koloğlu, 'Enver Paşa Efsanesi'nde Alman Katkısı (1908–1913),' *Tarih ve Toplum,* no. 78 (June, 1990), p. 22.
159. Celal Bayar, *Ben de Yazdım,* vol. IV (Istanbul 1966), p. 1082.
160. Ahmet Hamdi Tanpınar, *Sahnenin Dışındakiler* (Istanbul, 1973), p. 54.

161. Cemil Bilsel, *Lozan*. Quoted in Sina Akşin, *Jön Türkler ve İttihat ve Terakki* (Istanbul, 1987), pp. 270–1.
162. İlhan Selçuk, ed., *Yüzbaşı Selahettin'in Romanı, I. Kitap* (Istanbul, 1973), pp. 286–7.
163. Murad Efendi, *Türkische Skizzen*, vol. I (Leipzig, 1877), p. 153.
164. Generalmajor Ritter von Steinitz. ed., *Zwei Jahrzehnte im Nahen Orient, Aufzeichnungen des Generals der Kavallerie Baron Wlademir Giesl* (Berlin, 1927), pp. 83–4.
165. 'İttihat ve Terakki 1916 Kongre Raporu,' *Tarih ve Toplum*, no. 33 (June 1986), p. 135.
166. 'Dr Reşit Bey ve Hatıraları,' *Yakın Tarihimiz*, vol. III, p. 334. The author was the governor of Diyarbakir. He is referring here to events between the end of the 19th and the early 20th century, and especially the First World War and its aftermath.
167. Doğan Avcıoğlu, *Milli Kurtuluş Tarihi*, vol. I (Istanbul, 1981), p. 342. This passage relates to Wilson's reaction to the massacre of Muslims by the Greeks in and around Smyrna (today's İzmir) in 1919. Avcıoğlu is known as a leftist in Turkey and not a chauvinist. It is very illuminating to see how pervasive the attitude is.
168. Süleyman Kocabaş, *Ermeni Meselesi Nedir Ne Değildir*, p. 112.
169. Orhan Koloğlu, *Abdülhamit Gerçeği*, p. 91.
170. Bayur, *Türk İnkilabı Tarihi*, vol. II, part III, p. 252.
171. Orhan Koloğlu, *Abdülhamit Gerçeği*, p. 119.
172. Doğan Avcıoğlu, *Milli Kurtuluş Tarihi*, vol. III, p. 1084
173. *Ibid.*, p. 1089–90.
174. *Ibid.*, p. 1084. The article appeared on December 23, 1893 in the *Boston Congregationalist Journal.*
175. Robert Melson summarizes this issue under the rubric of 'the provocation thesis.' For his analysis on this topic, see, Robert Melson, *Revolution and Genocide* (Chicago and London 1996), pp. 152–9.
176. Sina Akşin, *İstanbul Hükümetleri ve Milli Mücadele* (Istanbul, 1983), p. 241.
177. *Ibid.*
178. From a conversation between Kemal and the notables of Ankara, made upon his first arrival there, Quoted in Doğan Avcıoğlu, *Milli Kurtuluğ Tarihi*, vol. III, p. 1053.
179. Ergin Muharrem, *Türkiye'nin Bugünkü Meseleleri* (Istanbul, 1975), p. 68.
180. Bayur, *Türk İnkilabı Tarihi*, vol. II, part III, p. 123.
181. André Mandelstam, *Das armenische Problem im Lichte des Völker und Menschensrechte* (Berlin, 1931), pp. 8–9.
182. İlber Ortaylı, *Uluslararası Mithat Paşa Semineri, Bildiriler ve Tartışmalar [Edirne, 8–10 Mayıs, 1984]* (Ankara, 1986), p. 53.
183. Quoted in Doğan Avcıoğlu, *31 Mart'ta Yabancı Parmağı* (Ankara, 1969), pp. 35–6.
184. Lewis, p. 214.
185. Bayur, *Türk İnkilabı Tarihi*, vol. II, part III, p. 94.
186. Detailed information about these settlement plans are found in Wilhelm van Kampen, *Studien zur Deutschen Türkeipolitik in der Zeit Wilhelms II* (Kiel, 1968).
187. Quoted from a Unionist journal in Şerif Mardin, *Jön Türkler ve Siyasi Fikirleri* (Istanbul, 1983), p. 117.
188. The article was written after the Italian attack on Tripoli (August 4, 1911). Although it was signed by the journal's staff, it is known to have been penned by Ömer Seyfettin. Reprinted in *Tarih ve Toplum*, no. 70 (October, 1989), pp. 43–50.
189. Elias, p. 173.
190. Van Kampen, p. 123.
191. Hanioğlu, *Bir Siyasal Örgüt Olarak Osmanlı İttihad ve Terakki Cemiyeti ve Jön Türklük* (Istanbul, 1985), p. 620.
192. *Ibid.*, p. 633.

193. Celal Bayar, *Ben de Yazdım*, vol. II (Istanbul 1966), p. 461.
194. Şerif Mardin, *Jön Türkler ve Siyasi Fikirleri*, p. 14.
195. Orhan Koloğlu, *Abdülhamit Gerçeği*, p. 340.
196. Tarık Zafer Tunaya, *Türkiye'nin Siyasi Hayatınde Batılılaşma Hareketleri*, pp. 89–90.
197. Ziya Gökalp, quoted in Ahmet Bedevi Kuran, *Osmanlı İmparatorluğu'nda ve Türkiye Cumhuriyeti'nde İnkilap Hareketleri* (Istanbul, 1959), pp. 608–9.
198. Ziya Gökalp, quoted in Bayur, *Türk İnkilabı Tarihi*, vol. II, part IV (Ankara, 1983), p. 352.
199. Şevket Süreyya Aydemir, *Makedonya'dan Ortaasya'ya Enver Paşa*, vol. *II: 1908–1914*, pp. 271–2.
200. Tarik Zafer Tunaya, *Turkiye'de Siyasal Partiler*, vol. III, p. 233.
201. *Tarih ve Toplum*, vol. VI, no. 2, p. 135.
202. Bayur, *Türk İnkilabı Tarihi*, vol. III, part III (Ankara, 1983), p. 35.
203. For more information see Erwin Staub, *The Roots of Evil: The Origin of Genocide and Other Group Violence*, Press Syndicate of the University of Cambridge, 1992, pp. 79–88.
204 Erwin Staub, *The Psychology of Good and Evil: Why Children, Adults, and Groups Help and Harm Others*, Cambridge University Press, 2003, pp. 49, 405.
205 For more information on that issue see Staub, pp. 122–4; Roy F. Baumeister, *Evil: Inside Human Cruelty and Violence*, New York 1996, pp 186–90.

4

The Homogenizing and
Ethnic Cleansing of Anatolia

As we have seen, examination of the evolving phases in the formation of Turkish national identity indicates that the lethal strains of that identity are intimately connected with a pervasive apprehension about the future survival of the Ottoman Empire in the history of which these processes of national identity formation are anchored. This chapter will examine a particular feature of that empire that evidently gave rise to and continued to fuel these apprehensions, namely, a heterogeneous social-political system comprising a host of nationalities with centrifugal propensities.[1] In other words, there remained an abiding cleavage between 'the ruling nation,' that is, Muslim Turks, who were totally identified with the Islamic theocracy upon which the Ottoman Empire was predicated, on the one hand, and the Christian nationalities, that is, the ruled ones, on the other. That cleavage was increasingly perceived as a potential threat to the Empire and with it to the Turks, its undisputed custodians. In brief, this chapter will expound the initial stages of the Turkification of the Empire, which was affected by attacks on its very heterogeneous structure, thereby ushering in a relentless process of ethnic cleansing that eventually, through the exigencies and opportunities of the First World War, culminated in the Armenian Genocide.

Perhaps the most interesting dimension of Turkish history concerns the general problem of nation building, or more specifically, its ethnic dimension. One striking characteristic of Turkish nation-state formation is the numerous parallels we can draw between its early and its contemporary periods. For that reason, every discussion of Turkish history leaves the impression that we are discussing the present. Generally speaking, there is a strong relationship between the past and the present in Turkish history. This is true not only regarding the nation-state formation process; it is also true regarding the collective identities, that is, self-perceptions, that were formed in the past and which continue to evolve today. In one of his articles on the problem of identity, Fernand Braudel says that one of the important aspects of identity is to create 'harmony between the past and the present.'[2] When we grapple with problems concerning the past and collective identities, such as ethnicity and nation, we have to deal with parallels between the past and present in Turkey.

I would first like to clarify one problem I have with the term 'history,' lest it foster unintended associations. Norbert Elias pointed out the negative side of the concept of history: the term 'history' is generally applied to past or completed events, and this creates the false impression that the influence of the past upon the present is usually rather limited. In fact, the effect of the past upon the present is difficult to overestimate, and even determines in large measure our present-day behavior.

> Clear patterns of thought, feeling and behavior will reappear after several generations in the same society, adapting themselves to new conditions in a striking manner, and each time they appear, they are met with great surprise and astonishment... In truth, the effects of events within society are, generally speaking, only made manifest a hundred years later.[3]

I would not go so far as to claim that when we speak of the past, it is as if we are speaking of the present. The reason for this is not, however, the problem of whether or not this type of general relationship can be established between the past and the present. I would like to go beyond this, and assert that what is being experienced in Turkey at present is actually a second nation-building process, one which, with regard to its basic characteristics, resembles the Turkish experiences at the beginning of the 20th century. It is as if this second wave of nation building is attempting to complete those things that the first wave left unfinished.

In this sense, I believe that any discussion of history in Turkey carries a dimension that could be understood in the exact same manner as speaking of the present. I will attempt to shed light on this first wave of nation building.[4] But I would first like to present some general points with regard to both waves of nation building, and to draw attention to the continuity between them. My study here can be described as having a 'macro' perspective. Additionally, I would like to show in exactly which context I will examine the first nation-building process.[5]

On the Process of Nation Building

The first wave of nation building in the Ottoman Empire began in the 19th century, and was accompanied—after 1908, in particular—by massive levels of violence. The current Turkish state is the product of this first wave of nation building in Anatolia, and in this sense, it appears to have been founded upon it. Despite all of the nationalist characteristics, this first wave of nation building was actually experienced as fundamentally deriving from religious sources. Despite all of the problems and unequal relations between the Muslim communities of Anatolia—and here we mean mostly Kurds and Turks—these communities were largely in harmony with one another and together they drove the non-Muslim population out of Anatolia. We must be clear that the organizers of this first wave of nation building, after 1908 and especially after 1913, were aware of their Turkishness and acted as Turkish nationalists. However, it is very difficult to assert that this was the case for the broad masses. They understood themselves mostly as Muslims and acted according to that understanding, especially against the non-Muslim population of Anatolia. Their ethnicities, beyond their religious identity, were not very important. This is what we are experiencing in the current phase.

The Second Wave of Nation Building

Whereas the first wave of nation building saw the expulsion of non-Muslims from Anatolia, the second wave of nation building is engaging the remaining Muslim populations. The primary characteristic of this second process is that simply being Muslim is now not enough to hold these groups in a harmonious relationship. Both sides have embraced an identity that goes beyond simply being Muslim.

The question that needs to be taken up is why this second wave of nation forming, which has gained speed particularly since the 1980s, began. While it has occured partly as a result of great changes in the international arena, through the development of new nationalisms (as well as the reemergence of old ones) that appeared upon the collapse of the Soviet system, it seems that internal factors are even more important. Whatever the explanations there is no doubt that all of these various factors have had a mutually exacerbating effect.

What is taking place at present in Turkey can be described as the natural stages of the processes of modernization and nation-state formation. In both the first and second waves of nation building, it is the Turks who have dominated. The Turkish majority is now experiencing the second process of nation building along two separate dimensions. The first dimension is an internal one (among the Turks themselves), as a separation of their religious identity from their ethnic identity. Throughout the 20th century, the Turks always defined themselves in national and religious terms, despite some limited attempts to do otherwise in the late 1920s and early 1930s, which were unsuccessful in any case.[6] What we are experiencing now is a decrease in self-identification as being both Turk and Muslim, to the point that such a self-identification is disappearing entirely. The natural result of this development has been that a significant section of the Turkish population has begun to identify (or re-identify) with their respective cultural identities, such as 'secular', 'Alevi', and the like; being a Muslim has been demoted to the characteristic of a cultural or political subidentity among the Turks.

The second dimension of the second process of nation building was experienced as a separation of the Turks from the other Muslim groups of different ethnic origins. Different ethnic groups, who had previously been united under the banner of Islam, gradually started to define themselves on the basis of their own ethnic or cultural—not religious—particularities. This is most obvious in the division between Turks and Kurds. It should be added that other Islamic ethnic groups (Laz, Circassians, etcetera) have been experiencing a similar process. These ethnic identities are being reconceptualized in cultural or political terms and are thereby made into the most important element for separating or defining the borders of collective groups.

Generally with modernization religion loses its quality as a politically or culturally unifying element. Within this process, religion is thrust into a civil society framework as more of a cultural particularity. The Turks are experiencing this phenomenon today. The main reason that the modernization process is so difficult and painful is that, during its initial stages, Turkish modernization was experienced in a manner that was not reconciled with religion. I believe this is a point which in large degree distinguishes Turkish modernization from the process as it was experienced in the West. One can argue that the process in the West was the same in essence. No doubt modernization was also a struggle between religious and secular forces in the West, and today's reconciliation between religion and modernization is a very late product of this process. It is fair to assert that, for all of its internal conflicts, Western modernization succeeded in great measure in reconciling itself with Christian culture and tradition, and was even based upon it. The difference in the Turkish case is that the modernization process went through a struggle not only between religious and secular forces: it was also experienced as something contrary to, and often openly in conflict with, Islamic culture. Two significant reasons for this present themselves.

The first is that Turkish modernization was experienced as a change of civilizations. In comparison with the West we can say that Western modernization was experienced as a change within the same civilization, and so reconciliation was not difficult. In the Turkish case, however, it was experienced as a change from Islamic civilization to Western civilization. The fundamental conception behind Turkish modernization was that its philosophy and its institutions were borrowed from another civilization, although the approach may have been to change, imitate or modify them into something new.

The second reason was that Islamic thought and practice, as they were institutionalized, were opposed both to the principles of citizenship independent of any religious identity or allegiance and to universal equality—two fundamental ideas in the political order accompanying modernization. Thus, in its formative period, all of the efforts of Young Ottoman thinkers like Namık Kemal, Ziya Paşa and others to reconcile Islam with modernity proved ineffective. Indeed, when the new Turkish state was ultimately reborn out of the Ottoman ashes, its founder saw no other way, in order to establish the principle of equality, than to opt for a head-on struggle and even a radical break with Islamic tradition.

Religion and Nation Forming

What is significant and interesting here is that, despite all of the claims by the early founders of the Republic that they were making a clean break with religion, which had been the major dividing line during the first wave of nation building, Islam largely preserved its status as a unifying supra-identity, and has thereby continued to exist not only within Turkish *society*, but also in the *state structure* as well. The founders of the new state were well aware of the powerful unifying aspect of religion. Despite the new regime's secular appearance, religion both remained one of the pillars of the Turkish Republic, and preserved its character as a supra-identity that could hold together all of the sectors of society.

On one hand, Turkishness could not be completely separated from religion and defined in purely ethnic terms. Primarily on account of the existence of the Kurdish nation and other ethnic groups, there were attempts, especially on the level of official state identity, to define Islamic identity and Turkishness as one and the same. The ideology known as the 'Turkish-Islamic Synthesis,' was proclaimed—in some periods openly—as the official identity of the Turkish state and society. Particularly in the policies pursued against the non-Muslim communities of Anatolia, it was painfully clear that the deciding identity was not fundamentally ethnic, but religious. The best-known example of this situation is that, in the population exchange with Greece in 1923 and after, the communities who were subject to deportation were determined on the basis of their religious, not ethnic identities. For example, ethnic Greeks in Greece who spoke Greek but were Muslim were exchanged with ethnic Turks in Turkey who spoke Turkish but were Christian. It is for this reason that I am asserting that the first wave of nation building, which reached a turning point with the establishment of the Turkish Republic, failed to sever fundamentally its relationship with religion.

What the Turks are currently experiencing can be described as a process of detaching themselves from the religious identity they have up until now accepted as a unifying supra-identity. Today, the Turks are in the process of social dissolution. The Alevi/Sunni and secular/anti-secular disputes are manifestations of this, and the result of this process of nation building is the emergence of various secondary or sub-identities. What I am asserting is that, in Turkish society, religion is ceasing to be an overall unifying identity. This development is actually the collapse of the special unifying character of religious identity. In this process of decline, religion has become the political identity of a subgroup within society. This is being viewed in the West with alarm as the rise of Islamic fundamentalism in Turkey, but incorrectly so.

Despite the rise of political religious movements within the country, to conclude that this marks an increase in Islamic fundamentalism is inappropriate. Religion is gradually being transformed into a political identity of a subsection of society. The strengthening of the Islamic move-ment should be understood as the destruction of that quality of being a unifying supra-identity that religion has played in Turkish society up to the present. For the first time in Turkey, people have begun to put a distance between politics and religion. Islam is collapsing as a defining basis for collective identity, and is being relegated to the cultural–civil sphere. For this reason, we may say that we are now in the process of 'true' Turkification.

I believe that as a part of this process, political Islam, which has been gaining strength since its appearance, and its political representatives[7] are a product of the second wave of nation building. Contrary to the prevailing belief in the West, these parties do not actually represent a desire for a fundamentalist government, as has been widely claimed, especially by the military in Turkey. On the contrary, the mission of these Islamic movements is the reconciliation of modernization with religious–cultural tradition.

The separation of Turkish modernization from its religious–cultural foundations, which began in the 19th and early 20th centuries, as a result of a massive civilization change, is coming slowly to an end. We can define this as a process of closing the gap between religion and modernization. The main tendency, especially of the Justice and Development Party (AKP), is the reconciling of modernization with the religious–cultural foundations of society and improving on them. The efforts of the AKP can only be understood as setting religion in its proper place in the civil/social order. This accounts for the success of this party in the election of 2002. From a long-term perspective we can say that the Turkish modernization process, which went awry in the 19th century, is now getting back on a normal path.

In order to understand the increasing influence of the so-called religious movement in Turkey, we have to understand another basic characteristic of Turkish secularism. The founder of the Turkish Republic initiated a secularization program on three different levels. The first was that of relations between the state and religion. Separation of state from religion was the basic aim of this program. The second aspect of this program was public restrictions on daily religious life, and the third, to reform religion itself. Apart from the first point, it is possible to say that this program resulted in failure. And despite all claims of secularism, even the first point, separation of state from religion, has remained rather problematic. Contrary to popular belief, the Turkish state is not based on a strict separation from religion. Religion is a matter of the state, and there is a Ministry of Religious Affairs. There is now strong opposition to this situation.

The Alevis and the secularist social forces, as well as a significant current within the Islamic movement, want to remove the last vestiges of the state's attempts to organize itself on a religious basis. This is the basis of the dispute about the Ministry of Religious Affairs (*Diyanet İşleri Bakanlığı*), which is the largest government ministry in Turkey. The forces mentioned above have advocated the abandonment of any sort of official organizing of state religion and instead want to place the state at equal distance from all religions. In this sense, it can be said that the first dimension of the secularization program is successfully under way. On the contrary, the radical Kemalist secularization program failed on two other dimensions. In the area of public restrictions on daily religious life, many groups are now organizing themselves and openly opposing these restrictions. For example, the Alevis are now explicitly using this name in their associations, even though to do so is prohibited by law. The current debate over the meaning of the wearing of the headscarf (*tesettür*) in public is another good example.

Regarding internal religious reforms, all attempts have failed. At the end of 1920s, it was planned to install bench seats in the mosques; the playing of Western classical music in the mosques was introduced; and the call to prayer was issued in the Turkish language rather than Arabic. The use of Turkish during prayer has engendered a prolonged debate, which resurfaces every few years. In the end, all such measures have been rejected by society—a sign of people's refusal to accept state interference in religious affairs.

To sum up, the main characteristic of the second wave of nation building is the removal of religion as a supra-identity of the Turks, with other ethnic-cultural characteristics becoming more important.

The Second Wave of Nation Forming
and the Kurdish Question

As I mentioned above, the second characteristic of Turkey's current nation-building process is the increasing distinction between various ethnic groups. The Kurdish question is the prime example of this. Because the Kurds have come to resist openly the injustices to which they have been subjected, they have embraced their particular ethnic characteristics. This helps to distinguish them from a purely Islamic identity, which gave them a shared background with the Turks. This distinction becomes clear when one notes that all of the other sub-identities that have emerged within Turkish society, whether they refer to themselves as secular, religious, Alevi or other, have reconciled with one another in opposition to the national demands of the Kurds. While during the first nation-building process the Muslim communities succeeded in adopting a shared, religion-based attitude toward the non-Muslim communities, in a similar fashion today the different ethnic groups within Turkish society have managed to unite around a shared approach toward the Kurds. In a sense, the Kurds today have replaced the non-Muslim communities of the 19th and early 20th centuries as both a source and a target of intergroup or intercommunal conflict.

If the current nation-building process has not yet emerged as a direct conflict between Kurds and Turks, as we have seen in Yugoslavia and other countries, it is because of the unifying effect of Islam.[8] Because of the place Islam has occupied in its own process of nation forming, the Kurdish national movement has kept its own religious tradition. In regard to the connection they have established with religion, the Kurds of today are reminiscent of the Turks in the 1920s. An example of this is the creation of mosques for 'Kurdish Islam' by the allegedly communist Kurdish Workers Party (PKK).

In each of these two levels of nation building (first, the separation of the Turks from their own internal religious bonds, and, second, coalescence around national identities that were defined between the Turks and Kurds in overwhelmingly non-religious terms), each ethnic group claimed to possess different characteristics setting it apart from the others. The Alevis, the Kurds, the secularists, the Islamists—in short, all of these groups— embrace their own unique particularities, and desire to forward these identities as a political program. I believe that this is nothing less than a sort of social dissolution. In this respect, we find ourselves confronted with a situation different from that of the first wave of nation building. In the first wave, society divided itself along religious lines. Religion was recognized as the fundamental border between the various collective groups, as

Muslims and non-Muslims. But today, in the second wave, we can see that the distancing from religion has been a determinant in the redrawing of borders among the various ethnic groups.

One of the results of this distancing from religion is an ethnification process comparable to the first wave. A new process of forcible homogenization may therefore be experienced. In a society that is divided, every ethnic group can see the existence of those who are different from itself as the main threat to its own existence, and would opt for political solutions that would define its own collective identity as the dominant element. In this regard there could be a serious resemblance with, even repetition of the first wave. The first wave of nation building basically came about as a homogenizing experience and put an end to the diversity that had characterized relations between Muslims and non-Muslims in Anatolia.

In Turkey there is one argument which all groups use freely. Great pride is taken in the fact that Turkey is now a country which is 90 percent Muslim. But the simple question of how this 90 percent homogeneity was obtained is never addressed. In fact, it was achieved through the expulsion—often violent—of the non-Muslim communities from Anatolia. What today's ethnic groups do not realize is that Anatolia may now be entering a second process of ethnic conflict which could end up with another cleansing. Both a Turkey politically divided as well as a Turkey proud of being 90 percent Turkish remain as possible results of this process. Certainly what I am saying is only a hypothesis. Turkey has neither fully entered such a process, nor is this inevitable. But what I want to emphasize is that, if Turkey has not yet entered this process, it is largely the dynamics of foreign affairs that have prevented this. It must be admitted, though, that the structure of this process certainly allows for ethnic conflict and civil war. If the foreign powers had wished, they could have easily brought Turkey to a condition like that of the former Yugoslavia. One other obstacle to such a process is that Turkish society has still not expended great effort in seeking democratic alternatives that would unite it in all its various elements. In this regard, the prospect of membership of the European Union remains an extremely important, positive alternative preempting the worst scenarios.

I believe that the problems faced by both waves of nation building are identical. Essentially, it is the question of whether or not a shared sense of identity and feeling of belonging, one superior to the various sub-identities, can be created that will bind together society's different ethnic, religious and cultural sub-groups. Ethnic cleansing and homogenization, which in the past, were experienced along religious lines, appeared as the only alternative after it had become clear that the policy of Ottomanism—of imbuing the Empire's inhabitants with a supra-communal identity to ensure their loyalty to the Ottoman state—had failed. Ottomanism failed because, although it claimed to promote a cosmopolitan ideal, it was actually understood as continued Turkish-Muslim domination, and was indeed used in this way. Today as well, the various supra-identities that are put forward by the state are but manifestations of Sunni-Turkish domination. In both periods, the political programs promoting a supra-identity have not aimed at *implementing* the principle of universal equality between the various groups within society.

In one sense, we can say that the situation today is better than in the past. We at least know that the possibilities bestowed upon Turkey by its international position and its national historical inheritance are much greater than in the past. The civil and democratic alternatives, wherein the spheres of life of all of the different sub-identities are institutionally guaranteed, still stand before Turkey as yet another possible avenue in this process.

A Common Characteristic
of Both Nation-forming Processes

One of the primary characteristics of the Turkish modernization process, however, poses a serious obstacle to the various types of non-nation-based alternatives, that is, alternatives that go beyond the nation-state and nationalism. This characteristic can be described as an alienation of the intellectual currents and systems, (namely, Islamist, leftist, Kurdish and state) from the idea of accepting individual rights and liberties. In fact, liberalism is still a swearword among these political movements. As opposed to the Western modernization process, intellectual and political movements based on the individual, on his or her rights and liberties, have not taken root within the process of Turkish modernization. Where they have appeared, they have been all but wiped out. Modernization has developed in the context of ideological trends and currents of thought that have been based on collective identity, and the question of what this should be. Two basic political and intellectual movements, which emerged as a response to this question, had little room for the individual and his rights; for both of them it was necessary to create a collective 'we' and 'the other.' This phenomenon continues to a large extent today. This is a significant element in hindering the development of democratic alternatives.

During the nation-building process of the late 19th century, the borders of collective identity were formed in response to Western attempts to partition the Ottoman Empire. The main question was how to save a state that was undergoing collapse. The fundamental question in this regard was what were to be the main characteristics of the collective needed for the survival of the state. To answer this vital question two main political movements emerged in the middle of the 19th century and are still current today. One movement formed along the lines of 'progressive/reformers,' the other, 'reactionary/traditionalists.' These are known popularly in Turkey today as the 'barracks' and the 'mosque,' respectively. But despite all of the serious differences between these two movements (and the debate was indeed experienced as a clash of civilizations on the question of whether Islamic or Western civilization would win), the sides do appear to have united on one point: recognition of some shared, homogenous elements which separated the 'us' from the 'them.' Individual rights and liberalism generally were rejected throughout this entire process by these opposing sides because they perceived these rights as damaging to the collective. The common characteristic of both movements was that they both developed only authoritarian alternatives, which aimed at internal homogenization.

We can observe how powerful similar tendencies have been during the second, current wave of nation building. The main problem of the collective sub-identities that have come about is that, in differentiating themselves from each other, their homogenous, collective characteristics are brought to the surface. The political options being advanced by such groups are incapable of going beyond political models in which their own sub-identities are central. Thus, in regard to the sub-identities which seek individual rights and liberties, we can say that they do not appear important. Just as this situation has raised the danger that society will be divided along the lines of the collective sub-identities, it also leaves the door open to new authoritarian alternatives, through the assertion that they can prevent such a division. When the situation is looked at from this point of view, we can assert that the main currents which have formed themselves into political alternatives have preferred highly authoritarian alternatives over libertarian ones, and that they resemble one another.

It is certainly true that civil alternatives do exist that focus on individual rights and liberties. For these civil alternatives to succeed, it is essential that belonging to an ethnic group or subgroup not be the basis of the political programs being developed. The ability for individuals to live together in a society must be based on a common shared identity, which cannot be based only on an ethnic or subgroup identity. There need to be civil–democratic norms which have at their center individuals and their rights and liberties, which give meaning to belonging together. (The multi-ethnic Swiss system, which is governed by a cantonal arrangement, is typical in this respect.)

The greatest problem here is that there does not exist, in either the social or political spheres, a powerful advocate of these values. My point here is that what was lacking in the Turkish modernization process is a bourgeois class as found in Western cases of modernization. The question of why the

Turkish modernization process has not brought forth a bourgeoisie has been and remains even today a separate topic for debate. The best-known fundamental reason is the continuation of the Ottoman ruling elite into the republican period. The military-bureaucratic elite has been the primary transmitter of modernization. Ottoman modernization was accompanied not by a broadening of the ruling class, but by its narrowing. In this process, wherein the state more or less modernized and centralized itself, the bourgeoisie that existed was largely expelled or wiped out because it had been largely non-Muslim in makeup. The absence of a bourgeoisie within the process of Turkish modernization is the reason that the present-day military–bureaucratic elite continues to wield its influence over the state.

The question of which alternative will come to dominate in Turkey during the modernization process does not appear simply dependent on preferences within the country itself. One must also take into consideration the important role that international relations will play. It might even be claimed that, with regard to the various sub-identities within Turkey, the country's international connections and the importance given to Turkey by the great powers are what prevents the current conflicts between the sides from becoming too sharp. When viewed from this angle, Turkey's rapid integration into the European Union must be seen as a critical factor in increasing the odds that a democratic alternative will be brought to realization. It would not be too great an exaggeration to describe the process of democratization currently under way in Turkey as being promoted from outside of the country. In this sense, there is indeed a close parallel between current events and the reforms of the mid-19th century.

Indeed, such great parallels appear between the events then and now that any discussion of history, in this sense at least, is a discussion of current events. Beyond purely academic interest, I find it most informative, for this reason, to look at a cross-section of the initial efforts toward the Turkification of Anatolia at the beginning of the 20th century. It is not well understood that the first great planned leap toward the homogenization of Anatolia on ethnic–national lines was a disaster not only for the people of the region at the time; it has also left deep scars that have influenced and even formed Turkey's present national identity. What Turkey is currently undergoing is like a rerun of the events of the turn of the 20th century. Thus, if the previous process of ethnic homogenization is understood, it will help us to understand better both the current process and the dangers that this ethnification can pose today. I believe that historical consciousness possesses a special importance for the strengthening of non-nationalist alternatives.

How Did Anatolia Become Homogenized?

The Union and Progress (*İttihad ve Terakki*) movement, which became a driving force in the exercise of political power in the Ottoman Empire in 1908, wanted to create a centralized, modern state. The fundamental condition for this, however, was the principle of citizenship on the basis of universal equality. Yet, the Ottoman *millet* system was basically the opposite of this. Society was divided up into a number of religious communities. Each community was endowed with special rights. The concept of citizen had not taken root in the fullest sense.[9] The important functions of the state, such as tax collection, courts, etcetera, were largely carried out by the communities themselves. The state dealt not with individuals, but with these communities (and tribes).

What the Committee of Union and Progress wanted to do was to create, out of a society that was divided into special compartments, a modern state which bound all its individual members to one another around a shared identity that was to be based on the principle of universal equality. Among the plans that had been considered were the linkage of the various regions that did not provide soldiers or pay taxes to a central point, and the implementation of a central educational program in order to create a shared sense of unity.[10] It was necessary to gather the different religious–national groups of the Empire under one roof, for a 'union of peoples' (*İttihad-ı Anasır*) to be created.

The greatest problem was the question of what would be the shared moral values and cultural identity between the Empire's disparate communities, and how they were to be created. In the words of Yusuf Akçura, one of the principal founders of Turkish nationalism, 'What could be the point of connection between a Christian Serb who plows the fields on the Kosovo Plain and a Muslim Arab who leads a nomadic existence in the desert of Najd?' Or, 'What sort of harmony is imagined by the union of these elements?' In other words, was this worth fighting for? These questions arose because 'the historical tradition of those different elements making up the Ottoman subjects, their religion, relations, hopes and dreams, thought patterns, means of subsistence and levels of civilization were so very different from one another, that even conceiving of this unity as "harmonious" came across as strange.' This would not work, because not one of the sides who were to be brought together would agree to such a thing.

I ask: can a single Muslim be found who would sacrifice even an iota of his religiously defined personality (*şahsiyet-i muayyene-i diniye*) for the sake of a union of peoples?...Likewise, the Greeks and Bulgars have their own communal features that are today manifest, and their own special form of civilization that is a part of the civilization of Christian Europe. Do they want to diverge even a little bit from that communal character, that form of civilization? The two civilizations, the two life philosophies which view life and the world very differently from one another, collide within the vast Ottoman domains. Is harmony between them at all possible?[11]

Even from the outset, it appeared as if the effort was being made for an unattainable goal.

Ottomanism for the 'Union of Peoples'

With the 1908 Revolution, the Unionists advocated a policy of 'union of peoples,' and opted for an extremely classical approach in solving the problem of how to create a shared cultural identity to be imposed upon the modern state. The principle of universal citizenship, which viewed everyone as equal, was combined with a cultural identity that could be defined as Ottomanism, and which would be formed around the values of the dominant Muslim Turkish society. For this purpose, the unionists implemented the necessary policy of assimilation. There was a contradiction, however, in the element of violence that was introduced during the same period. It is fair to state that, up to 1913, when the CUP took sole hold of the reins of power, their policies were fundamentally formed around this pillar. The Ottomanization program was most concretely manifested in the field of education. In the newspaper *Osmanlı* (*The Ottoman*), one of the movement's press organs in the early years, numerous articles appeared saying that a shared culture that would unite all the Ottomans was inevitable, that a situation wherein each religious community came to possess its own culture would necessarily lead to a breakup of the Empire, that in order to create a shared culture a shared language would need to be created, and that it would have to be Turkish.[12] The Committee's 1908 program contains explicit articles on this subject: 'mixed state schools are to be opened to each community. Turkish-language instruction will be mandatory in primary education. Primary education at the state schools is to be free.'[13] Entering the bureaucracy was to be possible only after graduation from one of the higher-level state schools. In this fashion, it was hoped, non-Turks would be bound to the central state apparatuses at least on the basis of the Turkish language.

Extensive efforts were made, particularly after the so-called 'Counter-revolution' of 1909, to promote the goal of establishing a centralized state. This, it was thought, would help to forestall separatist movements. At the CUP congress of 1909, 'after reiterating that the Ottomans were obliged to look upon their interests as common to all, it was announced that legal means would be used against those who, by asserting ethnic and religious differences, or by any other means wished to promote separatism or to sow discord.'[14] In line with this aim, the Law of Associations was decreed on August 16, 1909, which contained the following passages:

> It is forbidden to form political associations which are based on an unlawful basis contrary to legal precepts and common decency, or whose aim is the disturbance of the public order and the integrity of the state, the altering of the present form of government, or the sowing of political division between the various Ottoman communities (Article 3). It is forbidden to form political associations based on national or other communal particularity, or whose names contain references thereto (*kavmiyet ve cinsiyet esas ve unvanıyla*) (Article 4).[15]

By such decrees the establishment of political associations and unions bearing the names of various nationalities was forbidden. The prohibition was quickly followed by the closing down of the Greek, Bulgar and other minority clubs and associations in Rumelia.[16]

Through the amendment of certain relevant articles of this law, it was made into an article of the Constitution on August 21, 1909. 'Ottoman citizens possess the right to come together and form associations, subject to the special Law of Associations. It is forbidden to form associations which serve the goals of disturbing the political integrity and sovereignty of the Ottoman state, changing its legal system or form of government, acting against the legal precepts of its Constitution or sowing division among the Ottoman peoples, or which are in opposition to public morality and decency.'[17] The aim of such efforts was to preserve the union of peoples. Other laws, too, were enacted during this period with the purpose of holding together multinational Ottoman society, such as the law regarding the conscription of non-Muslims into the military.[18]

But the policies aimed at achieving this union of peoples, which are implemented in the name of Ottomanism, were actually efforts to culturally homogenize Ottoman society around an Islamic-Turkish identity, and they were correctly perceived as such by the Empire's non-Muslim elements. They thus met with great resistance—even open rebellion—on their part. In such a situation, repressive centralizing policies were inevitable. But it was not only the Christian population that was subjected to suppression: non-Turkish Muslim communities, whether Arab, Albanian or other, were also subjected to similar measures. Efforts were made to force other Muslim communities to learn and accept Turkish as their common language. The inevitable result was rebellion. The Albanian revolt which broke out in 1910 was in this sense an important turning point. Education actually became one of the main causes of the revolt.[19] The revolt by the Muslim Albanians was a warning sign that the unity policies would not work.[20]

In the summer of 1910, the disillusioned CUP leaders met and accepted the fact that the program which they had undertaken to unite the Empire's various nationalities was now bankrupt. What they had learned in this brief period was that

> [t]he spread of nationalism among the subject peoples of the Empire,... ended forever the 'Ottomanist' dream of the free, equal, and peaceful association of peoples in a common loyalty to the dynastic sovereign of a multi-national, multi-denominational empire.'[21]

The level to which nationalism had grown among the various Ottoman nationalities was such that 'in the face of such a deep enmity between the various nationalities and between Christian and Muslim, there remained no possibility of either uniting or reconciling the Empire's various groups to create some sort of Ottoman unity.'[22]

The Idea of a Homogeneous National State in Place of the 'Union of Peoples'

On July 27, 1910, the second anniversary of the Young Turk Revolution, the CUP organ *Tanin* carried a sort of state of the union address by the CUP to the nation at large. It gave a general assessment of the policies of the previous two years and officially declared their policy of Ottomanism to be bankrupt. Furthermore, the CUP

> confessed that its measures to bring about the union of the different communities had failed, owing to the excessive zeal it had shown in the first two years of constitutional rule. It now recognized the opposition of the ethnic communities to Ottomanism, and would therefore leave them alone. The Committee [that is, the CUP] would continue to pursue the cause of unity in a different way, namely, by concentrating all its energy on the material and educational development of the Empire, hoping thereby to unite all the elements through a community of interests.[23]

We can find more detailed information as to what that new way was to be from a meeting which was reported to have been held the following month. At a meeting in Salonica, the Unionist leader Talat, who had embarked upon a tour of Macedonia in the company of finance minister Cavit with the aim of correcting some of the CUP's mistakes and shoring up the resulting low morale among their supporters, gave some interesting explanations for the failure of the Ottomanist policies, as well as some hints as to what new directions the CUP could be expected to take. The acting British consul in Manastir (Bitolj) relates Talat's words thus:

> You are aware that by the terms of the Constitution equality of Musselman and Ghiaur was affirmed but you one and all know and feel that this is an unrealizable ideal. The sheriat, our whole past history and the sentiments of hundreds of thousands of Musselmans and even the sentiments of the Ghiaurs

themselves, who stubbornly resist every attempt to Ottomanize them, present an impenetrable barrier to the establishment of real equality. We have made unsuccessful attempts to convert the Ghiaur into a loyal Osmanli and all such efforts must inevitably fail.[24]

A few days later, in comments written by the British ambassador to the Porte, Gerald Lowther related the following:

That the Committee have given up any idea of Ottomanizing all the non-Turkish elements by sympathetic and Constitutional ways has long been manifest. To them, Ottoman evidently means Turk and their present policy of Ottomanization is one of pounding the non-Turkish elements in a Turkish mortar.[25]

The French consul in Salonica also provided some details regarding the meeting. According to his account, among the Unionists there were those who saw as impossible the peaceful cohabitation of the various nations, and said that 'only military force' could solve the problem. The divisions of opinion that arose regarding the Macedonian question and the Bulgars of Edirne were between 'expulsion' and 'massacre.' The forced expulsion of the Christian population of the region into Anatolia and the resettlement of Muslims in their place was proposed, and, if this did not solve the problem, it was suggested, they should be killed.[26] The Unionist leaders leaned toward the use of force in a situation wherein '[the efforts] by Turkey to peacefully achieve unity, by fostering the patriotism of the Turks as [they] wished, have met with failure.'[27]

The information provided by Austrian, French and British sources on this meeting is very similar.[28] It appears that, from this time on, the idea prevailed of binding and uniting the other national communities to the Empire by force, or in the words of Y. H. Bayur, 'The tendency to see issues [of national unity and such] as simply problems to be solved by military force (*ordu ile görmek düşüncesi*) gradually became stronger and took root.'[29] To give some sense of the degree of shift in their views, at the 1909 Congress, the CUP's delegate for Istanbul, who advocated laying the foundations for a more nationalist policy, had not even been given permission to speak.[30] One important reason for the rapid transformation was that the policy of Ottomanism, which in practice was understood as meaning Turkification of the other communities, had paved the way for revolts against the central government, and it was thus quickly perceived to have failed.

At the 1911 Congress, another general assessment of the situation was made. The policies that had been pursued up to that point were evaluated, as well as those that were to be pursued in the future. How would the policy of a union of peoples be achieved? And how was the concept of Ottomanism, with which this was to be brought about, to be understood? Some answers can be found in the details of the report read at the congress. The report stated that 'in regard to the Committee for Union and Progress, there are two different types of Ottomanism. The first is political, and is composed of individuals possessing legal rights. The second is social, and it is composed of communities which lack legal rights, but possess social institutions.'[31] The CUP defined its own position as falling somewhere between these two poles. The CUP was sharply opposed to those who understood Ottomanism as 'a (federative) state formed out of a fusing of forces possessing political rights and the various communities,' and equally opposed to those who argued that Ottomanism was only composed of individuals, and that, for the sake of the unity of the Empire, the communities and associations in which these individuals were found would have to be assimilated into the Ottoman totality.'[32]

What should be implicitly understood from the concept of 'Ottoman' is defined here in entirely unambiguous terms. According to the CUP, Ottomanism was nothing other than preservation of the unity of all of the component peoples of the Empire around the three pillars of Islam, Turkishness and the Caliphate.

> If one refers to the Articles of the Constitution that we mentioned, it will be seen that it preserves and confirms all of the rights of the Ottomanness, of the territorial integrity of the homeland and national unity, the religion of Islam, the Turkish language, Islamic jurisprudence and Islamic custom, the Holy Caliphate, the Sultan and Imperial household as well as the Office of the Sheikh ul-Islam.[33]

The CUP thus declared its fundamental goal to be that Ottomanism, defined as the domination of Islam, would continue to prevail within the Empire:

> In our minds, the goal of the Committee of Union and Progress [should be] the implementation of the principles of the Constitutional Regime and the establishment of a united and progressive Ottomanism. Just as the Islamic peoples have acquired the right to rule on account of their majority within the national ruling body (*hakimiyet-imilliye*) established by the Constitutional Regime, as they also possess an historic sovereignty due to their conquests, defense of the homeland and relation to the Caliphate, the Committee of Union and Progress considers Islam as the support (*mabihil-kıvam*) of Ottomanism and attributes its [continued] existence to [Islam]'s moral force.[34]

At the congress it was said that the CUP had up to that time struggled to bring about a policy which recognized the possibility of organizing the minority communities as social or cultural units (with 'characteristics such as language, religion and literature'), but this had failed. The self-criticism of 1910 was reiterated:

The required level of activity has neither been seen nor displayed in regard to the most important points of [the party's] line of action, [which were] stated as respecting the languages and nationalities of the various peoples [of the Empire], reinforcing the historical bonds which tie these elements to one another, not viewing a single one of the component nationalities as separate [from the others], not being deceived by any temporary appearances, and never forgetting the goal of unity.[35]

A number of researchers have viewed this congress as the point at which 'a doctrine and program based on the Ottomanist union of peoples was transformed into one tending toward nationalism and Turkism.'[36] Of relevance to this, some observers at the congress reported that the question of systematically organizing Pan-Islamic activity toward the Caucasus and Central Asia was debated in detail. The Austrian consul in Salonica reported the following in regard to Pan-Islamist policies: 'The ability to organize these policies in the Caucasus (where there are 8 sub-committees present), Iran, China, India (72 committees active) and others was explored in detail, and it was determined that many more possibilities needed to be acquired for this propaganda.'[37] From other sources we learn that, from this date on, a great number of agents were sent into the Caucasus and Central Asia. British consuls from the places in question sent detailed reports concerning the agents sent to Central Asia and their activities.[38]

One more point should be added here in regard to the Congress: in a number of foreign sources it was reported that the decision was adopted here to suppress all ideas opposed to Turkism, and even that the decision for the Armenian Genocide was taken here.[39] Nevertheless, we possess no other information at this time that could confirm the veracity of this information.

What the Central Committee report shows us, however, is that the Unionists simply used Ottomanism as a screen for their policy of Turkifying the country around the axis of Islam. The writings on Turkism by the party leaders, who were at the same time openly advocating Ottomanism, are a clear reflection of this situation. For example, Ziya Gökalp, who was a Central Committee member from 1910 on, wrote several articles in 1911 stating that he 'support[ed] the Ottomanism movement...as do a good number of CUP members.'[40] But at the same time, he directed the Salonica-based Turkist newspaper *Genç Kalemler* (The Young Pens).[41] Finding the conceptualization of Turkism in the language and in literature to be insufficient, Gökalp called for the appearance of 'Turkism along with all its ideals, its entire program.'[42] With this goal in mind he published his poem 'Turan' and labored to bestow a political content on the idea of Turkism. Through his writings, Gökalp was the person who, in his words, 'gave a theoretical support to the Turkist movement.'[43] He is a significant figure for having simultaneously defended Ottomanism and shown where the CUP's main problem lay.

In similar vein, in a piece titled 'Whatever Happened to Turkishness' (*Türklüğün başına gelenler*), Gökalp openly discusses this contradiction and engages in a certain amount of self-criticism. He admits with surprising sincerity that neither the Tanzimat leaders nor the CUP had been sincere in their promises to grant the various groups their national rights:

> The proponents of the Tanzimat desired to draw a deceptive veil over the face of Turkishness...Not one of the [Ottoman] communities believed this lie. When, after the [proclamation of the] second Constitutional Regime [in 1908], greater importance was given to this chimera (*göz boyacılığı*) the minority communities began to raise a ruckus, saying 'You want to Turkify us!' In truth, this Ottomanization policy was nothing but the secret advent of Turkification.[44]

Turkism Replaces Ottomanism

Here we should make a fundamental observation on the subject of the CUP's relationship to ideologies. During the period of the collapse of the Ottoman Empire, the question of how it could be saved brought forth various ideas and intellectual movements, such as Ottomanism, Islamism, Westernism and Turkism. Despite all of the differences between them, it is possible to assert that, on one topic at least, these currents tended to agree: at the core of all of these ideologies, their proponents more or less openly explained, was an expectation of the continuation of Turkish domination of the other nations. The fundamental reason for this was the concept of the 'Ruling Nation' (*Millet-i Hakime*). The Turks, who had identified themselves with Islam, saw themselves as superior to the other peoples—if not necessarily in a purely, Turkish national sense—and thus saw themselves as the natural rulers of the others. Thus, all of the ideologies that attempted to save the Empire took the continued dominance of the Turks as their starting point.

Even though politically speaking the state's rulers were far from espousing ideas such as Turkish nationalism, they nevertheless thought it possible to bring together the various nations within the Empire under Turkish rule and defended this idea. For example, Ali Paşa, Grand Vizier and a leading reformer during the Tanzimat period, 'having observed the conflicting interests and aspirations of the various nationalities in the Empire, commented on the particular role of the Turks as the unifying element in the Empire.'[45] Nor were the attitudes of the first Ottoman opposition movements any different. Namık Kemal, one of the prominent personalities of the Young Ottoman movement, had this to say: 'If the Christians desire our [continued] dominance, we shall come to an understanding; naturally, they would not have the right to complain, if we have not taken them into the government.'[46] Kemal also provided a racial basis for these ideas, asserting that

> in regard to both the confusion of populations and abilities within the Ottoman community, pride of place is occupied by the Turks, who possess excellent virtues and qualities, such as vast intelligence (*vüsat-ı havsala*), sang-froid (*itidal-i dem*), tolerance and calm (*tahammül ve sükunet*).[47]

Similar ideas were expressed by another prominent member of this group, Ali Suavi. Suavi argued that it was necessary for the Turks to rule, arguing that 'in regard to their military, civilizing and political roles, the Turkish race was superior and more ancient than all the other races.'[48] Even Şinasi, who can be called one of Turkey's first secular intellectuals, came to adopt the principle of Ruling Nation concept and defend it.[49]

The Union and Progress movement basically took over this legacy. In all of the CUP's press organs one encounters numerous pieces mentioning the 'primary group' (*unsuru asli*), or claiming that, in multinational constructs such as the Ottoman Empire, the domination of one nation should be seen as normal.[50] One example concerns the Unionist publicist Hüseyin Cahit Yalçın, who wrote an article entitled 'Ruling Nation' in November 1908, when Ottomanism was still the official ideology of the government, and which he penned in response to certain articles appearing in the Greek newspapers. Cahit wrote that Ottomanism did not mean that 'the country should be the country of the Greeks, or of the Armenians, or of the Bulgars...No, this country will be the country of the Turks...The Turks conquered this country...whatever is said, the ruling nation in the country is and will remain the Turks.'[51]

The CUP never felt itself bound to a single ideology. The Unionists determined their approach according to practical needs, and easily jumped from one ideology to another when necessary. For this reason, those among the CUP ranks who asserted the necessity of openly choosing an intellectual or ideological direction had little influence, and their views even provoked reaction from others. A good example of this is the reaction to Yusuf Akçura, who, in the article '*Üç Tarz-ı Siyaset*' (Three Types of Policy') that he wrote in 1904, openly advocated a policy of Turkism. Akçura defined Ottomanism, Turkishness and Islamism as three totally different policies developed for the rescue of the Ottoman Empire. In the responses to Akçura, we can observe the perfunctory attitude towards ideologies of the CUP: 'for us [Turks], it is impossible to separate Turk[-ishness] from Islam, nor Islam from Turkishness, nor Turkishness and Islam from Ottomanism, nor Ottomanism from Turkishness and Islam. This unity cannot be divided into three.'[52]

Even during the First World War, when the Turkist and Ottomanist currents separated from one another, those authors who defended Ottomanism continued to criticize the Turkists, saying that Ottomanism in any case meant Turkish domination: 'If Ottomanism becomes strong, most Turks will leave it...Does not Turkishness form the spirit of Ottomanism?'[53] In short, cosmopolitan ideologies such as Ottomanism and Islamism, which were developed in order to hold the Ottoman state together, carried at their base the nationalism of the dominant nation, and were understood and advocated as a form of continued Turkish domination.

Another point that should be mentioned is that, in light of the pragmatic attitude that was adopted toward these ideologies, changes in the regime's political stance were not always declared as open ideological preferences. For instance, even in July 1913, when Turkism as an ideology had already begun to dominate the political attitudes of ruling circles, the Unionist Party adopted the decision to promote an Islamist policy, due to the problems that had emerged in the Arab provinces. But in the words of Mehmet Cavit, the Unionist Finance Minister, 'the decision to pursue an Islamic policy' was 'not written,' but a decision taken 'in the minds of the rulers.'[54] Similar statements can be found in the memoirs of the Republic's third president, Celâl Bayar, who for years had served as CUP party secretary in various provincial organizations. According to Bayar, 'there was no change in the CUP's basic internal regulations (tüzük). This new nationalist current could not be officially accepted or announced. But those occupying the forward ranks of the committee began to accept Ziya Gökalp's suggestions as a new ideal (mefkûre).'[55]

These statements of Cavit and Celâl Bayar are significant for showing us the political culture that prevailed among the rulers of the Ottoman state. It is worth quoting here the words of Hüseyin Kazim, an Islamist thinker, who at one time served as a member of the CUP Central Committee: 'The policies followed within the Ottoman state since the Tanzimat were not the product of a revolution in thought or accumulation of ideas...Behind a chosen policy or administrative method, an ideology suitable to it was developed, and shortly after that, accepted as correct.'[56]

Just as the Unionists jumped from one ideology to another in accordance with the circumstances, their approach to those very ideologies was functional in the extreme, and in this sense their approach was far from doctrinaire. First came the political exigency, afterward the ideology, which would in any case be chosen in accordance and could be changed where necessary. Thus, the CUP's drift toward Turkism should be understood as the result of necessity much more than of doctrinaire preference. The Turkism of the CUP was the result of a political reckoning, and one of the most significant indications that it represented a preference that could be dispensed with at any moment was the occasional party decision to cease the ideological debates between the various ideological currents when they appeared detrimental.[57] This is the reason that so many ideo-logues who had been doctrinaire Turkists since the beginning, and who made great contributions toward the development of a political ideology of Turkism, nevertheless possessed no political influence whatsoever, either in the party or in the Union and Progress movement.[58]

Thus, the CUP did not view Turkism as a complete break with other doctrinaire preferences, such as Islamism and Westernism.[59] Even when the Unionists had become Turkists, they still wanted to view this as simply a type of Ottomanism, and they propounded a policy of Turkification that did not entirely reject Ottomanism.'Rather, Ottomanism and Pan-Islamism were downgraded and applied only intermittently whenever occasion demanded...the top leadership was pragmatic in its approach.'[60] Changing ideologies by political decision was completely natural for them.

Enver and his colleagues envisaged the three policies being pursued simultaneously and side by side, each one being emphasized in whatever place and at whatever time it was most appropriate. Ottomanism continued to be the keynote of internal politics; Turkish nationalism, the keynote of relations with the Tatars of Russia, Pan-Islam, that of relations with the Arabs and other non-Turkish Moslems within the Empire and, elsewhere outside it.[61] The sole reason for this attitude was that, for them, everything other than keeping the Empire together was of secondary importance.

The Theoretical Framework for Turkism

The series of articles 'Turkification, Islamification, Modernization,' which Ziya Gökalp published in the Turkist journal *Türk Yurdu* (Turkish Home) in 1913, essentially argued that these different ideologies should be under-stood as essentially saying the same thing, and thus formed the necessary theoretical foundation for the CUP's pragmatism.

Let the Turkism movement cease being the opposite of Ottomanism, in truth, it is its most powerful support...There has never been a contradiction between Turkism and Islam, because one possesses the character of a nationalism, the other, of international unity...Turkism is simultaneously Islamism.[62]

In other words, any one of them could be taken out and used, depending on the situation.

In many of his writings, Gökalp took up the various problems that the Turks faced as a nation, and explained the necessary ideological, political and economic foundations for the Turkish national state. In these writings he provides us with the broad outline of the program implemented by the CUP after 1913. At the head of these theoretical efforts we find a sharp critique of the policies implemented since the Tanzimat. According to

Gökalp, the Tanzimat's greatest mistake was its desire to establish within the country the principle of universal equality, by giving non-Muslims the status of citizens. This was mistaken, and what now needed to be done was 'to return the term Ottomanism to its former meaning.'[63] In short, it was necessary to dispense with the illusion of trying to achieve Muslim–Christian equality.

These ideas were laid out in a secret communiqué concerning the goal of equality, which was sent by the CUP to its cadres. However unwillingly, attempts at living together ceased and in their place came an attempt to establish a new state on the foundations of Islam and Turkishness. In an article he wrote in 1911 for the *Yeni Hayat* journal, Gökalp claimed that 'the "super" men imagined by the German philosopher Nietzsche are the Turks. They are the new men [who appear] every century (*asır*). Therefore, new life will spring forth from Turkishness, which is the source of all of their youthfulness.'[64]

The Turks, then, had to abandon their unwillingness to possess their Turkishness and needed to look at ways to immediately do away with the negativity that this situation had created. This was because 'the notions of "state and homeland" that had been revived among the peoples of the Empire were destined to remain simply passionless, dull, colorless and meaningless concepts. Just as there could be no shared lover, there could be no shared homeland.' For Gökalp, the question was painfully clear: 'a state that was not based on a shared consciousness' could not survive. This shared consciousness is 'the ideal of nationhood' (*milli ülkü*). 'The weapon of nationalism, therefore...had to be employed among Muslims.'[65]

These efforts, which must be understood as the theoretical foundations for the creation of a national state, also possessed an economic aspect. Along with the model of the nation, whose development was influenced by the understanding of the nation found in German Romanticism, the state was likened to a living organism which needed to be an organic whole. According to Gökalp, the nation had to be seen as a 'social totality' (*içtimaî küll-i tam, tout complet*). As for the Turks' ability to achieve this political unity, it would be possible, he claimed, if they followed the German model. 'Cultural unity, economic unity and political unity' were necessary stages through which a nation had to pass. Economic unity could be achieved along with a common conscience and national consciousness. For this nation, the necessary totality could be achieved through a 'national economy.' The national economy thesis emphasized the formation of Muslim-Turkish guilds, and this necessitated a continual focus on the ethnic dimension of the economy, because the national economy could be realized through ethnic uniformity: 'The modern state emerged from the division of labor which developed in a single ethnic community.'[66] These statements must be seen as the theoretical groundwork for the eventual establishment of a homogenous national state in Anatolia: There must be a division of labor based on one ethnic group, which has shared moral values.

Turkification Put into Practice

Turkism became an official party policy in the spring of 1913.[67] It was as if the Turkist stream of the CUP 'suddenly emerged out of the smoke of war. The Turks, who had previously been unable to say 'I exist,' could now, at the end of the Balkan War, say this.'[68] Still reeling from the blow delivered by the Balkan War, the CUP, having abandoned the idea of a unity of subject peoples (*ittihad-ı anasır*), was now convinced that a thorough and extensive nationalization was necessary. In the decision taken at the 1913 party congress, the desire to grapple with the problem at its source was openly expressed as an article of the party program:

> Just as the Union and Progress Party will work to remove the financial and economic concessions and preferences (*istisnaat*) that obstruct the independence of its national economic policy, it considers the completing of the conditions for the general abolition of the capitulations as the most holy of aims.[69]

Immediately following the CUP's military coup, known in Turkish as the Babiâli Baskını (Raid on the Porte), in January 1913, the National Defense (*Müdafaa-ı Milliye*) Committee[70] was established. Later in 1913 the National Solidarity Committee (*Muzaheret-i Milliye*) was formed in order to replace it.[71] Other associations were founded with the aim of fostering national sentiments, especially among the youth, the Turkish Strength Society, Ottoman Strength Associations and Youth Associations being but a few of the more significant ones. In its program, the Turkish Strength Society stated that its goal was 'to save the Turkish race from destruction.' It added that: 'the iron first of the Turk shall once again seize hold of the world, and the world shall once again tremble before its fist.' The society's main slogan was 'Turkish strength is sufficient for every task.'[72]

One of the main targets of Turkism, which developed rapidly from this point onward, was the non-Muslim communities within the country. The non-Muslims were portrayed as responsible for the disasters that had befallen the country. The Muslim-Turkish communities on the other hand, while not asserting their own Turkishness out of a desire to keep the state together, nevertheless expended efforts to rid the Empire of the non-Muslims. 'With the visible decline of Ottoman power...there was a catastrophic change for the worse in the position of the Ottoman non-Muslims...In these circumstances, suspicion, fear [and] hatred' that developed among the Turks with the Balkan defeat 'transformed the Turkish attitude to the subject peoples.'[73] In the words of Talat Paşa, the non-Muslim subjects 'had always planned disasters against Turkey. Because of the hostilities of these local peoples, Turkey was destroyed, one province after the other...so that the Turkish Empire had shrunk almost to the point of non-existence.'[74] The idea that came to prevail among the CUP leaders was that the salvation of the Empire would not be found in efforts to bind these elements to the state. According to Talat, if Turkey were to survive with what it currently possessed, it would be necessary to save it from these foreign peoples.[75] In his memoirs, the former president of the Ottoman Chamber of Deputies, Halil Menteşe, says 'that Talat Bey proposed that the country be rid of the elements whose treacheries were apparent.'[76] This state of mind (ruh hali) 'often led to terrible oppression and brutality' against the non-Muslims.[77]

In the words of Ziya Gökalp, the first step that needed to be taken on the path of Turkification was to save 'the Turks who had lived unaware within the Ottoman state,' and whose voices had been stifled due to the policy of a unity of the subject peoples. It was necessary 'to throw off the deceitful veil [of Ottomanism] that had covered the eyes' of the Turks since the Tanzimat.[78] As a second step, it was necessary for Turkification to be spread to those communities trusted by the Empire, and they had to be integrated into a new construct along with the Muslim-Turkish communities of the Caucasus and Central Asia. The question 'Where is the homeland of the Turkish nation?' would have to be answered anew. Gökalp had as much as answered this question in 1911.[79] This new homeland was Turan, in his mind, 'an ideal (mefkûrevî) homeland that gathers in all the Turks and excludes foreigners.' Turan, he wrote, is 'the whole of all of the countries in which the Turks live, in which Turkish is spoken.'[80]

The CUP nurtured a great aim: 'This lofty goal was the unity of Islam and there were streams of Turkism directed toward uniting the Turks who dwelled outside of [the borders] of Turkey.'[81] In 1914 Gökalp formulated all of this propaganda into a political objective: to reestablish the Empire that had been lost in Europe and the Balkans in the East, among the co-racialists and co-religionists of the Turks. 'The country of the enemy shall be ruined, Turkey shall increase and become Turan.'[82] The person who most fervently defended these ideas was Enver Paşa.

> In the mind of the former Minister of War these objectives grew so large that he never tired of imagining himself the ruler of a future Ottoman state, which, by uniting the Turks and Muslims of Asia and retaking the lands in Europe that we had lost, would be established from the Adriatic Sea unto the waters of India.[83]

This then was the plan for halting the decline of an Empire.

Concrete Plans for the Homogenization of Anatolia

Although the CUP took over the government in January 1913 through a military coup, it was only on June 11, 1913 that the party achieved full control of the power of the state, when Grand Vizier Mahmut Şevket Paşa was assassinated by opposition forces. This event gave the CUP the pretext to seize the reins of power and eliminate the opposition once and for all.[84] 'In June and July, following the killing of Mahmut Şevket Paşa, the leaders of the CUP decided on the main outline for the policies they would pursue.'[85]

Thorough and comprehensive efforts encompassing all areas—economics, politics and administration—were immediately embarked on and detailed plans were drawn up for each area in order to bring to life a general policy that could be characterized as a reliance on the Turkish element inside the country and the inclusion of the Turkish-Muslim peoples of the Caucasus and Central Asia into the imperial edifice. The first priority for the CUP was to relieve themselves of the non-Muslims within this construct.

Economic Measures

Through policies that can be characterized as creating a Turkish bourgeoisie, the Muslim-Turkish elements began to employ political force to remove non-Muslims from their economic position and to replace them. Economic nationalization was both begun and directly administered by the CUP. 'Through the economic policies of the state, non-Muslim subjects and foreigners were eliminated from the market.'[86] In implementing these policies, the associations established within the economy had a special role. Communities of guilds were to be established, and small guilds, in particular, were to be organized. This organizing spread to the point that it even reached the porters (*hamallar*). Significantly, 'Christians were not to be accepted into these institutions [but rather] excluded from them.'[87]

The creation of the Committee for National Independence (*İstiklal-i Milli Cemiyeti*) on July 3, 1913 was the first indication of the future National Economy policies. Soon thereafter, a considerable number of new companies were established—the most significant of which were established by Kara Kemal—with the aim of creating a bourgeois class consisting solely of Turks.[88] The aforementioned Kemal was the government minister responsible for Provisioning (*İaşe Nazırı*), and the national economic policies were implemented with full government support. In addition to abolishing the Capitulations, which had for years been like a hump on the back of the Ottoman state, other important steps were taken during the First World War toward economic nationalization, such as 'a law concerning the use of Turkish in the communications and transactions of public institutions (*müessesât-ı nafia*) and concessionary companies (*imtiyazlı şirketler*),'[89] which was passed in 1916, and which made it obligatory that all company correspondence be done in Turkish. The organizations formed with the help of the CUP reaped enormous profits through illegal means. The party defended this, claiming that, due to the holiness of the final objective, resorting to such methods was correct. In his parliamentary defense of the 1917 budget, finance minister Mehmet Cavit Bey said the following:

> [As for] the support and protection [afforded these companies]—even if we perceive them to be unlawful as some have claimed—so great in my view is the benefit to be assured by the popular esteem felt toward the economic initiative as a result, that it may well erase this illegality.[90]

The implementation of forceful political methods, such as the seizing of the property of the Christian communities, was one of the most significant pillars of these national economic policies. Economic nationalization was carried out through policies of compulsion in the spring of 1914, in particular, and as part of the general plan described below. It has been generally accepted by Turkish researchers that Turks replaced the non-Muslims who were crushed through the use of political force. Toprak, for instance has this to say:

> During the war, political actions played a significant role in the transfer of certain fields of economic activity into the hands of the Turkish-Muslim guilds, and enterprising Muslim-Turkish entrepreneurs filled the vacuum left by the Armenian Deportations. Meanwhile, during the war against speculators, the Commission for the Prevention of Hoarding (*Men'i İhtikâr Hey'eti*) was directed especially against non-Muslims, and thereby easily eliminated the competitors of the Muslim-Turk merchants.[91]

We also know that economic motives played a particularly important role in the Armenian deportations. Here it will suffice to give the example of a report sent by the Austrian embassy in Istanbul in 1917, in order to show the relationship between the policies of economic nationalization, political compulsion and Armenian Genocide. The ambassador includes in his report some sections from the annual report sent by the Governor-General of Aleppo province, Mustafa Abdülhak, who played a crucial role in the massacre of Armenians, to the Ministry of Trade:

> It is with pleasure that I report that we have, in accordance with the government's wishes, succeeded in completely transforming the conditions here and in the district (*sanjak*) of Maraş. My province has been cleansed of Christian elements. The merchants and business owners, who two years ago were 80 percent Christian, are now 95 percent Muslim and 5 percent Christian.[92]

After this introduction, the report offers a detailed accounting in the form of a list of each and every shop or place of business that passed into the hands of reliable Muslims.

One of the most important subjects of the inquiries made in Istanbul after the war was the connection of the economic organizations established by the Unionists with the party itself and with the Armenian deportations. For example, in the trials held in the Extraordinary Court-Martial (*Divan-ı Harb-i Örfi*) after the war, the suspects were continually asked whether or not the National Defense Committee had been established by the CUP. Although the Unionists who were subjected to questioning rejected any such connection, the suspect Atıf Bey claimed that the National Defense Committee had provided financial assistance to the Special Organization.[93] In particular, the committing of great crimes throughout the war, such as speculation and corruption, by those companies founded by Kara Kemal, together with the Unionist Party's use of the monies acquired through these practices, formed the most important part of these interrogations. On May 6, 1919, the third session of the main trial against the Unionist leaders was essentially devoted to this subject. But the suspects reiterated the claim that they knew nothing about this matter.[94]

Political Steps

There was a turning point in the political actions taken in an attempt to homogenize the population of Anatolia when Enver was promoted to General (*Paşa*) and appointed Minister of War. With this step, which was taken January 4, 1914, great strides were made, especially in regard to the reorganization of the Ottoman army. The Special Organization was also established—or at least reorganized—in this period. If we can believe the information provided by Eşref Kuşçubaşı, he had a conversation with Enver Paşa in the War Ministry on February 23, 1914.[95] Painting a picture of collapse within the country, Enver claimed that the only way to escape further total collapse was to achieve a unity of the Turkish and Islamic worlds. As for the non-Muslims within the country, they had shown themselves not to be in favor of the further continuation of the state's existence. The salvation of the Ottoman state, then, was dependent on measures being taken against them.

The task of the Special Organization was to carry out 'services which the visible government forces and public security organizations would certainly be unable to accomplish.' In the words of Eşref Kuşçubaşı, 'the first task was to separate the *loyal* from the *traitors*.'[96] In this regard, they 'prepared a great plan...This plan consisted of measures that would minimize to the greatest extent possible the damage to the legacy of the past, which the Ottoman state had borne upon its shoulders as its centuries-old burden and inheritance.'[97] What was this plan? What were its contents? On this topic Kuşçubaşı provides important information. At the beginning of 1914 the Ottoman rulers determined that they were faced with two important problems: '(1) an immoderate opposition that was prepared to exploit and abuse their liberties in all manner of ways; (2) separatist, non-Turkish elements who threatened the integrity and unity of the Empire through both open and secret means. [The first problem]...was a political phenomenon that could be solved. But the second one was more difficult, a deadly illness whose cure called for grim measures.'[98]

In response to the 'deadly illness' within the non-Muslim communities, '[t]he government struggled [to take] preventive measures outside of its normal activities against the damage of a *fait accompli* within the [CUP] Central Committee and the Ministry of War. Secret meetings were convened within the Ministry of War whose main focus was [militarily] strategic points and the elimination of concentrations of non-Turks who were connected to negative foreign influences.'[99] In his own memoirs, Kuşçubaşı says that these meetings also continued to be held in May, June and August of 1914. Included in the meetings were 'reliable...worthy, self-sacrificing, patriotic elements' of the CUP in Anatolia, 'each one summoned to Istanbul by [various] means. Equally significant, perhaps, is that 'even some members of the cabinet did not possess knowledge' of these important meetings.[100]

Detailed reports were prepared as part of this planning, which can be characterized as the Turkification of Anatolia through the elimination of the Christians. As a result, the measures decided upon were put into effect in the Aegean regions long before the beginning of the war. 'The CUP was going to eliminate the Greeks, who they saw as the 'head of the boil' in Anatolia, through the implementation of both political and economic measures. Above all, it was necessary to bring down and destroy the Greek [population], which had grown economically powerful.'[101] In the minds of the CUP leaders,

> the greatest danger lay in the Aegean region...It could be said that the destruction that could be wrought on a country's independence and unity by negative, non-national elements (*gayrı milli unsurlar*) who decided to betray [it] was in full display (*geçit resmi*) in Izmir. For this reason, it was decided that the measures to be taken would be concentrated in Izmir. These measures were of three different aspects: a) general measures to be taken by the government; b) special measures taken by the military; c) measures taken by the CUP.[102]

Earlier, Kuşçubaşı had conducted an exploration of the Aegean region and in the report he submitted to Istanbul he had the following to say:

The nationalizing movement was very difficult [to create] in Izmir...Because here there were all of the consulates, of both friends and enemies, and their large cadres...The serious measures to be taken here were understood to be much more as the broad implementation of a governmental decision on a national scale than the result of local decisions. For this reason it was necessary that the implementation of the nationalizing actions be placed in the hands of resolute, forceful and pure patriots whose values were sincere.[103]

At this time the World War had not yet broken out. The CUP government, which hesitated to fully implement its program against the non-Muslim minorities within the Empire because of its fear of external pressure from Europe, organized actions such as terror, repression and robbery by means of the Special Organization, and made sure that there was no connection to the government itself. Halil Menteşe, who was cognizant of the plans that were devised, says in his memoirs that the intention was that 'the Governors-General and other officials would not appear to be officially involved; the Committee of Union and Progress' organization would run the affair.'[104] Carrying out the plan so as to appear that there had been no government decisions to that effect was made possible through the close control of high-level functionaries.

The cleansing of the Aegean region was to be performed militarily by Cafer Tayyar Bey, the head of the General Staff of the IV Army (the late general Cafer Tayyar Eğilmez), which was under the command of Pertev Paşa (Mr Pertev Demirhan); by the Governor-General of Izmir, Rahmi Bey (now deceased), who acted as the administrative commander; and by the CUP's Responsible Delegate, Mahmut Celal Bey (subsequently President of the Republic Celal Bayar.) All of the forces of the state were to be activated in accordance with the orders given by the Ministry of War and the Commander-in-Chief for the implementation of this plan.[105]

A large portion of this work fell to Kuşçubaşı:

Through a variety of means, the Greeks were caused distress, and were forced to emigrate through the pressures exercised [against them]. The armed gangs under the command of Special Organization Chief Kuşçubaşı Eşref Bey...conducted raids into the Greek villages...The Greek youths, able to bear arms, were rounded up in the name of the Labor Battalions, and forced to work on the roads, in the forests and in construction.[106]

Despite the attempts to keep these actions secret or the implementation of all these measures away from the government, the events caused another outcry in Europe, and as a result of the pressures exerted by the foreign powers—France, in particular—the Unionists were forced to halt their forced migration of the Greeks. Moreover, a committee of inquiry was even dispatched to the region under the chairmanship of Talat Paşa, and 'before embarking on the trip,' Talat was forced to take along 'a representative from each one of the foreign ambassadors in Istanbul.'[107]

On the subject of the efforts to eliminate the Christian presence from the Aegean region, the British historian Arnold Toynbee provides the following account:

> The Turkish reprisals against the West Anatolian Greeks became general in the spring of 1914. Entire Greek communities were driven from their homes by terrorism, their houses and land and often their movable property were seized, and individuals were killed in the process.[108]

Unaware of Kuşçubaşı's memoirs, Toynbee corroborates his claims, asserting that '[t]he procedure bore evidence of being systematic'.[109]

The expulsion of the Greeks from the Aegean region also continued between 1916 and 1918. The second wave of expulsions was carried out more for military reasons, but they, too, 'were carried out with great brutality.'[110] For example, the entire Greek population of Ayvalık between the ages of 12 and 80 was exiled to inner Anatolia. The wave of expulsions was organized by the German general Liman von Sanders. In his report to the Ottoman government, von Sanders reported that if the forced deportations were not carried out, he 'would be unable to assume the responsibility for achieving the security of the army.' Furthermore, he communicated that he wished to begin the deportation at the soonest possible moment upon arriving in Ayvalık, saying 'weren't they [the Ottoman army] capable of throwing these infidels into the sea?'[111] After the Armistice, an inquiry was called for in the Ottoman Chamber of Deputies in regard to the person responsible for this deportation, namely Liman von Sanders.[112]

The American ambassador to the Porte during the war years, Henry Morgenthau, drew attention to the fact that the methods used during the Armenian massacres were similar to those used throughout this entire period.

> The Turks employed the [same] methods against the Greeks that they had used against the Armenians. They took them into the Ottoman army, and [then] transferred them to the Labor Battalions…Thousands of these Greek soldiers died from cold, hunger and other deprivations, just like the Armenians…The Greeks were everywhere gathered into groups. Then, under the promised protection of the Turkish gendarmes, they were generally transported by foot to the inner regions [of Anatolia].[113]

Morgenthau says that it is not known how many persons were dispersed in this manner, but that estimates run between 200,000 and one million.[114] The Greek prime minister, Venizelos, claimed at the Paris Peace Conference that 300,000 Greeks had been annihilated, and that another 450,000 had escaped to Greece.[115]

While the Turkish historian Doğan Avcıoğlu, who cites these figures in his work, claims that 'there is no existing information in regard to a large-scale massacre of the Greeks having been carried out,'[116] we do indeed possess some information on the subject. The aforementioned Celal Bayar was brought from Bursa to Izmir and specially commissioned to direct the economic aspect of the plan of eliminating the non-Turkish elements from the Aegean region. This consisted, among other things, of finding Turks who would operate the property and workplaces that Greeks had been forced to abandon or that had been forcibly seized. Bayar reports that as a result of 'the removal of concentrations of non-Turks...who had been concentrated at strategic points' around 130,000 Greeks had been forced to emigrate to Greece from Izmir and its environs alone.[117] Halil Menteşe puts the number of Greeks driven out of the Izmir region at 200,000.[118] But these are the numbers only for the Izmir region. The number of Greeks driven out of eastern Thrace was given as 300,000–500,000 in discussions in the Chamber of Deputies in 1919.[119] Kuşçubaşı says that in 1914 alone, in the first months of the war, the number of those deported from 'the Greek-Armenian population...that had settled and concentrated in the Aegean region—and especially in the coastal areas' was 1,150,000.[120] In this manner, the entire Aegean region, and first and foremost 'Infidel Izmir, which we neither possessed nor even guarded...was purified' through a series of actions Kuşçubaşı describes generally as 'conquest operations.'[121] In a report sent by the British Intelligence Service to the French Ministry of War on June 19, 1918, the figure given for the number of Greeks expelled or killed is very close to that given by Kuşçubaşı:

> The number of persons dispatched from Thrace and Anatolia is greater than 1.5 million; half of this number were killed as a result of deprivation or murdered. The Turkish officials and officers do not refrain from declaring that Christians shall no longer be given permission to live in Turkey, and that the Greeks shall be forcibly converted to Islam.[122]

The true dimensions of the cleansing operation carried out in western Anatolia came thoroughly to light in the period following the Armistice. In particular, there were heated debates on this topic in the National Assembly in Istanbul. The matter was first raised during the Assembly's 11th session (November 4, 1918). The deputy from Aydın, Emanuel Emanuelidi Efendi, asked that the current government provide an explanation 'concerning the actions of the former government.' Emanuel Efendi, who touched on the Armenian massacres in his proposal, claimed in regard to the Greek migration that '250,000 souls from the Greek communities were expelled across the border of the Ottoman [state] and their property confiscated,' adding that another '550,000 Greeks were killed and annihilated in the coastal regions and environs of the Black Sea, Çanakkale, Marmara and Aegean islands and their property was seized and usurped.'[123]

Inquiries were made in regard to the forced migrations from Ayvalık, Edirne and Çatalca and, according to the figures reported, the number of Greeks from the Edirne and Çatalca regions whose houses and properties were plundered and who were forced to migrate to Greece was 300,000. Moreover, armed gangs had carried out massacres in the region. It was also reported that the Armenians in the region had been murdered. This series of events was described as a 'massacre blanche,' with total loss of life estimated at 500,000.[124] But instead of an inquiry being begun in regard to those who had been ordered to carry out the massacres, these persons instead became the objects of praise: 'just as the Governor-General of Edirne, Hacı Adil Bey, who had led the campaign of annihilation, was subsequently made President of the Chamber of Deputies, the Lieutenant Governor of the provincial district of Tekfurdağı (Tekirdağ), Zekeriya Bey, who had displayed extraordinary fervor in this matter when he had served in official capacity in the region, was also rewarded by being promoted to Governor-General of Edirne.'[125]

The deputy from Tekfurdağı, Dimistokli Efkalidis Efendi, said that all of these massacres had been part and parcel of the Turkification policies that the CUP government had systematically put into effect in the wake of the Balkan Wars. The thing that led to such policies was the large and concentrated Greek population. The solution that the government found to this 'was the principle of thinning out the Greek population. They saw to it that there was such a thinning and they were without any moral restraint whatsoever [in carrying this out] (Allah'tan da korkmak tabii kârları değildi). After thinning out their concentrated [population], it appeared necessary to do away with the bodies.'[126]

Efkalidis Efendi provides the following information concerning the plan that was pursued during this cleansing operation:

> The internal policy that [the CUP] wanted to put into effect was to plunder the property of the Christians with the aim of enriching the Muslims. At the same time, two different political considerations were merged. It was not merely the seizure and plundering of their property, it was the policy of thinning out the concentrations of Greeks—and it was even described as such. In the name of this policy of thinning out…the first order was [performed] by volunteer armed gangs (fedaî çeteler) created through the government's special connivance in order to throw the Greeks out of the country. After publicly plundering all of their property and goods in the villages, on the streets, they would be sent packing to Greece under the watchful eye of the police or gendarmes, who did not prevent this and sometimes even participated. Afterward they plundered the permanent and immovable property and possessions. Now and for whatever

reason, this annihilation operation began in Edirne, and, not limiting itself to Edirne, then started to be implemented in a broader manner.[127]

Efkalidis Efendi then gave several interesting explanations on the question of how this policy, 'which was given the name 'emigration' or 'deportation',' and which he himself characterized as 'the policy of devastation and annihilation,' was put into effect. According to him:

> ...it was as if branches had been formed here at that time by the political agents of Venizelos and they had all been swept away by the delusion, and it appeared as if they were unhappy with the misadministration and had chosen to go to Greece. And [after being subjected to repression and terror]...they received from these persons quittance documents (*evrakı ibraîyye*)...about their going to places unknown to them, and with their full consent and with absolute ardor.[128]

He relates that, when recourse was made to Talat Paşa regarding the events, Talat showed them telegrams containing messages along the lines of 'we are dissatisfied with Turkey; we are members of Venizelos party. We will go to Greece...why won't you give us permission?' Efkalidis's own property and possessions had been looted, despite the fact that he was a deputy in the National Assembly, and when he requested that it be returned to him, he was asked to seek information from the commission that had been established in the environs in which his property was located.[129]

An Armenian deputy, Nalbandyan Efendi, who also participated in the discussions, drew attention to the parallels between this cleansing operation and the Armenian massacres, claiming that 'the Turks can indeed be opposed to the oppressions and [criminal] actions that were carried out again and again, but the atrocities that were carried out, were done so in the name of the Turks.' The actions had been the result of the systematic policy pursued since 1913, and had been performed in the name of 'achieving Turkish domination.' Therefore, the matter at hand was one of the Turks' collective responsibility.[130] The connection between the [two events] was that they were parts of a plan. The Unionist leaders, having successfully completed the forced deportation of the Greeks, took courage from this fact: 'The Istanbul Police Chief, Bedri Bey himself, told one of his secretaries that the Turks had been very successful in driving out the Greeks, and that his administration had decided to implement this policy also against the Empire's other communities.'[131]

The Last Wave of Turkification: The Armenian Genocide

The Armenian Genocide of 1915–17 was the most important step toward the Turkification and homogenization of Anatolia. We possess powerful evidence that these operations had been centrally conceived and planned.

But we shall not get into that here. However, we can say that the pre-conditions for the establishment of the Turkish Republic were in large measure created by means of this massacre. It is significant that the leaders of the period did not even refrain from expressing this fact openly. Halil Menteşe says in a letter he wrote during his exile in Malta that '[if] we had not rid our eastern provinces of those Armenian revolutionary bands (*komitacılar*) that were collaborating with the Russians, there would have been no possibility of establishing our national state.'[132] During the first National Assembly of the new Republic in Ankara, discussions were held in which it can be seen that the Turks dare to call themselves 'murderers' for the purpose of saving the homeland:

> The question of the deportations was, as you know, an event which set the world in an uproar, and which caused us all to be perceived as murderers. Even before this was done, we knew that the Christian world would not stomach this, and would turn all their wrath and anger upon us because of it. [But] why have we attached the title of murderer to ourselves? Why have we gotten involved in such an immense and problematic cause (*dava*)? These things were done for the sole purpose of ensuring the future of our homeland, which we know is more beloved and sacred than our own lives.[133]

At present, another wave of nation building is under way in Anatolia. At the time of the first wave, Turks embraced their national identity in a violent manner that would form the foundation for the future political organization of the country. It is no exaggeration to say that the potential for the same violent embrace of their national identity exists in the Turkish nation today. For this reason, it is of particular importance that we learn from the past. It will be possible to establish Turkey's future on democratic foundations only if Turks are able to display the courage to fully confront their history.

The Armenian Genocide was largely a by-product of the First World War —as far as its successful execution is concerned. But the preconditions were already created through an ideology that aimed at transforming the troublesome heterogeneous social structure of the Ottoman Empire into a more or less homogenous one. The success with which the Ottoman Turkish leaders, namely the new Young Turk nationalists, through a combination of overt and covert-legitimate and surreptitious criminal means, managed to expel huge portions of the Greek population of western Turkey, served to embolden that leadership to proceed against the Armenian population of the Empire under cover of the exigencies and emergencies of the First World War. The Greek experiment had demon-strated the viability against all odds of a comprehensive scheme of ethnic cleansing that could allow the application of massive genocidal violence. The sequence of events described below is emblematic of the ease with

THE HOMOGENIZING AND ETHNIC CLEANSING OF ANATOLIA

which a perpetrator group can be sufficiently emboldened to proceed from a successful scheme of wholesale expulsion to a daring scheme of wholesale extermination.

NOTES

1. An earlier version of this chapter first appeared in Turkish under the title 'Hızla Türkleşiyoruz' (Our Rapid Turkification) in Nuri Bilgin, ed., *Cumhuriyet Demokrasi ve Kimlik* (Republic, Democracy and Identity) (Istanbul, 1997).
2. Quoted in Taner Timur, *Osmanlı Kimliği* [Turkish translation: Taner Timur] (Istanbul, 1986), p. 9.
3. Norbert Elias, *Studien über die Deutschen* (Frankfurt a.M., 1990), pp. 8, 165.
4. I use the term 'nation building' (*uluslaşma*) in a political sense here, referring to the creation of the political trappings of the state. For the cultural/ethnic homogenization process that so often accompanies nation building, I have opted for the neologism 'ethnification'.
5. There is a broad body of literature on the points I have taken up here, so I have not made any special attempt to cite sources. My aim is to place all these well-known debates (well-known at least in Turkey) in a long-term perspective.
6. In the late 1920s and early 1930s, with the influence of racist theories developed in Europe there were some attempts to define Turkishness in racial terms. These attempts were not successful, however, and a Turkic-Islamic synthesis became again almost the official definition of Turkishness.
7. The Welfare Party (Refah Partisi) was declared to be in violation of Turkish law and was disbanded by Turkey's Constitutional Court (January, 1997). Its successor, the Virtue Party (*Fazilet Partisi*), was also banned. A split in the Virtue Party led to the creation of two new parties. One is the Happiness Party (*Saadet Partisi*), which is still active. The other is the Justice and Development Party (AKP) which in November 2002 became the ruling party.
8. It should be noted that the Kurdish conflict of 1970–1999 was not a war between Turks and Kurds, but a war between the Turkish military and the PKK. Of course the Kurdish people suffered from the violent attacks of the Turkish security forces, but there were no direct clashes between the Turkish and Kurdish peoples as such. The National Movement (*Milliyetci Hareket Partisi, or* MHP) tried to incite Turks in certain areas against the Kurdish population, but these attempts failed. For a brief period the PKK also tried to give a racial character to the war, but soon stopped. Abdullah Öcalan, the leader of the PKK, underlined this issue in his defense and stated that he consciously avoided a policy of open war between the two peoples.
9. The legal equality of all of the Empire's nationalities (which was mostly defined according to religious affiliation) was declared in the Imperial Rescripts (*Hatt-ı Hümayun*) of 1839 and 1856 and was later confirmed in various laws. On February 19, 1869, the law of citizenship was decreed, and an important step in the transition to the principle of citizenship was achieved. But beside this principle of universal equality, permission was given to the various religious communities to organize themselves through separate laws. This allowed the two different legal systems to exist side by side, something which is referred to as the duality of the Tanzimat, and which left its mark on the entire 19th century.
10. We can observe from a decree published on July 27, 1910 that this goal had been

consciously put forward: '...the provisioning of soldiers and money are the foundations of a nation's sovereignty, its defense and good government. Those who give neither taxes nor military service do nothing for their country...' (quoted in Feroz Ahmad, *The Young Turks: The Committee of Union and Progress in Turkish Politics, 1908–1914* (Oxford, 1969), p. 84.

11. These quotes from Yusuf Akçura are found in François Georgeon, *Türk Milliyetçiliğinin Kökenleri: Yusuf Akçura (1876–1935)* (Ankara, 1986) pp. 131–2, Appendix 8.

12. Şerif Mardin, *Jön Türklerin Siyasa Fikirleri* (Istanbul, 1983), p. 118.

13. Tarik Zafer Tunaya, *Türkiye'de Siyasal Partiler* (Istanbul, 1952), p. 209.

14. Sina Akşin, *Jön Türkler ve İttihat ve Terakki* (Istanbul, 1987), p. 149.

15. *Meclisi Mebusan Zabıta T. Ceridesi, Devre; 1, İçtima Senesi 1,* vol. V, (Ankara, n.d.), pp. 26–7. It should be noted that when introduced in the chamber, the draft—and these articles in particular—was fiercely debated, with the opposition to these articles coming mainly from non-Turkish and non-Muslim deputies. In the end, the bill was passed into law by a vote of 90 to 60.

16. Bernard Lewis, *The Emergence of Modern Turkey* (Oxford, 1968), pp. 217–18.

17. Zafer Toprak, '1909 Cemiyetler Kanunu,' in *Tanzimat'tan Cuyhuriyet'e Türkiye Ansiklopedisi,* vol. I (Istanbul, 1985), p. 206.

18. The Law of Conscripting non-Muslim Communities was passed on 8 Temmuz 1325 (July 21, 1909). *Meclisi Mebusan Zabıta T. Ceridesi, Devre; 1, İçtima Senesi 1,* vol. V, (Ankara, n.d.), pp. 475–86.

19. For centuries Albania had been governed by its own laws, unconnected to the central legal system of the Ottoman Empire. Measures such as subjecting the Albanians to the imperial legal, tax, educational and military systems, and the collecting of weapons were not accepted by the local powers, who were accustomed to greater autonomy. These measures, combined with the violence and policies of terror carried out by Ottoman units in this region, made revolt inevitable. For more detailed information on the revolt, see Stanford & Ezel Shaw, *History of the Ottoman Empire and Modern Turkey,* vol. II (Cambridge, 1977), pp. 287–8; Süleyman Külçe, *Osmanlı Tarihinde Arnavutluk* (Izmir, 1944), pp. 351–419.

20. 'It was the Albanian revolt, more than any other event, which convinced the Turks that it would be impossible to conciliate different national interests and attain a unified empire.' Shaw and Shaw, p. 289.

21. Lewis, p. 218.

22. Niyazi Berkes, *Türkiye'de Çağdaşlaşma* (Istanbul, 1978), p. 393.

23. Ahmad, p. 84.

24. G. P. Gooch and Harold Temperley, *British Documents on the Origins of the War, 1898–1914,* vol. IX (London, 1933), pt. 1, Enclosure in no. 181, p. 208.

25. *Ibid,* pp. 207–8; quoted in Lewis, pp. 218–19.

26. We know that this subject had been brought up earlier as well. In an interview that Dr Nazım, a member of the CUP Central Committee, gave to a newspaper at the end of 1909, he said that the [Muslim] immigrants that would arrive from Bulgaria and Bosnia and even the Jews should be settled in Rumelia (Sina Akşin, p. 206). This indicates that the idea of settling Muslims in regions with a dense Christian population in order to achieve unity within the Empire was by no means novel at that time.

27. Archives of the French Foreign Ministry, Turkey, Nouvelle Série, vol. VII, no. 486 (November 23, 1910).

28. For instance, the report on Talat's speech found in the report sent from the Austrian consulate in Manastir on October 14, 1910, is almost word for word identical with the British report. Austrian Foreign Ministry Archives (A.A.), *Die Türkei,* no. 2, vol. 12.

29. Y. H. Bayur, *Türk İnkilabı Tarihi*, vol. II, part IV (Ankara, 1983), p. 13.
30. Tekin Alp, *Türkismus und Pantürkismus* (Weimar, 1915), pp. 4–5.
31. From the Central Committee report presented at the 1911 CUP Congress, in *Tanin*, 30 Eylül, 1327 (October 13, 1911), no. 1118.
32. *Tanin*, 30 Eylül, 1327 (October 13, 1911), no. 1116.
33. *Ibid.*
34. *Tanin*, 30 Eylül, 1327 (October 13, 1911), no. 1118.
35. *Ibid.*
36. Tunaya, p. 189.
37. A.A. Die Türkei, PA 38414. Report by Salonican consul Kral dated November 13, 1911.
38. For more on these reports, see Jacob M. Landau, *Pan-Turkism in Turkey: A Study of Irredentism* (London 1981), pp. 48–55.
39. Yves Ternon, *Tabu Armenien* (Frankfurt a.M./Berlin, 1988), p. 125. In Johannes Lepsius, *Der Todesgang des armenischen Volkes* (Potsdam, 1919), pp. 220–22, detailed information is provided concerning the decisions taken at this congress. But the information given by both Ternon and Lepsius is incorrect. Turkism, in particular, was never mentioned in any decision taken at a CUP congress.
40. Uriel Heyd, *Türk Ulusçuluğunun Temelleri* (Ankara, 1979), p. 85.
41. For Ziya Gökalp's influence on the Young Pens see the memoirs of Ali Canip Yöntem, which were serialized in the first four volumes of the history journal *Yakın Tarihimiz* (1960–61).
42. Ziya Gökalp, *Türkçülük Esasları* (Istanbul, 1978), p. 10.
43. Heyd, p. 129.
44. Ziya Gökalp, *Türkleşmek İslamlaşmak, Muasırlaşmak* (Istanbul, 1988), pp. 39–40.
45. David Kushner, *The Rise of Turkish Nationalism 1876–1908* (London, 1977), p. 5.
46. M. C. Kuntay, 'Namık Kemal', *Devrin İnsanları ve Olayları Arasında*, vol. I (Ankara, 1949), p. 186.
47. Enver Ziya Karal, *Osmanlı Tarihi*, vol. VII (Ankara, 1988), p. 296.
48. *Ibid.*, p. 293.
49. Şinasi thought that the idea of Ruling Nation being insufficiently defended was one of the main reasons for publishing the newspaper *Tercuman-ı Ahval*. Lewis, *The Emergence of Modern Turkey*, pp. 147–8.
50. For example, in the May 20, 1903 edition of the official CUP organ *Şura-yı Ümmet*, the following lines critical of England appear: 'For example, instead of aiding the Turks, who are the *ruling nation* [my emphasis] and the Muslims who make up the majority, they [the English] mistakenly throw their support and protection behind just one of the Ottoman components...' Quoted in Yusuf Hikmet Bayur, *Türk İnkilap Tarihi*, vol. II, part IV, p. 104. For similar sentiments, see Şükrü Hanioğlu, *Bir Siyasal Örgüt Olarak Osmanlı İttihad ve Terakki Cemiyeti ve Jön Türklük*, vol. I (Istanbul, 1985), p. 630n.
51. Quoted in Sina Akşin, *İttihat ve Terakki*, p. 167.
52. Yusuf Akçura, *Üç Tarz-ı Siyaset* (Ankara, 1987), p. 37. (In this edition of the work, which was published with a Foreword by Enver Ziya Karal, place is also given to replies to Akçura's article by Ali Kemal and Ahmet Ferit Tek. The sentence cited comes from Ali Kemal's response.)
53. İsmail Kara, 'Bir Milliyetçilik Tartışması', *Tarih ve Toplum*, no. 30 (Haziran, 1986), p. 57.
54. Quoted in Y. H. Bayur, vol. II, part IV, p. 314. The decision mentioned by Cavit Bey did not simply remain in the minds of the rulers, who engaged in laborious efforts to counter Arab nationalist and other separatist tendencies. Important steps were taken in the direction of decentralization in the provinces through the Temporary Law on the General

Provincial Administration (*İdare-yi Umumiye-yi Vilâyet Kanun-u Muvakkati*), proclaimed on March 26; and attempts to implement policies, such as the circular dated April 19, 1913, which allowed the use of Arabic in state offices located in areas where the language was used; and the greater place given to Arabic in education. There are even some historians who have attributed Said Halim Paşa's having been made Grand Vizier to his Arab origins. After the loss of the Balkans, the CUP was frantic not to lose the various Muslim communities of the Empire as well.

55. Celâl Bayar, *Ben de Yazdım*, vol. II (Istanbul, 1966), p. 445.

56. Hüseyin Kâzım Kadir, *Ziya Gökalp'in Tenkidi*, ed. İsmail Kara (Istanbul, 1989), p. 65.

57. In 1914 a debate between the Islamists and the Turkists was stopped by just such an order. Y. H. Bayur, vol. II, part IV, p. 421.

58. Yusuf Akçura is the best example of this. For more on the problematic relations of the CUP with Akçura, and with its ideologue Ziya Gökalp, see Georgeon, pp. 54–5, 62n.

59. Landau's assessment of the subject is accurate: '...it should be emphasized that at no time did Pan-Turkism completely replace other well-established state ideologies or *Weltanschauungen* [worldviews] within the committee; rather, Pan-Turkism simply overshadowed alternative theories for a time and provided guidelines for policy-making.' Landau, p. 45.

60. *Ibid*, p. 46.

61. Harry Luke, *The Making of Modern Turkey, from Byzantium to Angora* (London, 1936), p. 157.

62. Ziya Gökalp, *Türkleşmek*, pp. 12, 14, 44. The first article was published in the March 20, 1913 edition.

63. 'Non-Muslims are not regarded as the ruling nation; that is, they are deprived of the rights of Ottomanism...The Tanzimat attempted to include all of the Muslim and non-Muslim peoples within the concept of Ottomanism in order to satisfy the Christian elements, who, in a rapture of nationalism, had shown dissatisfaction. From then on, the non-Muslims would no longer be considered subject communities; they would no longer be subjects of the Ottomans, rather, they would be Ottomans themselves...But the Tanzimat could not have attained what it wished...The Christian elements did not accept the right to be Ottoman as a favor...' Quoted in Kazım Duru, *Ziya Gökalp* (Istanbul, 1949), pp. 61–2.

64. Quoted in Hilmi Ziya Ülken, *Türkiye'de Çağdaş Düşünce Tarihi* (Istanbul, 1992), p. 310.

65. Ziya Gökalp, *Türkleşmek...*, pp. 73, 80.

66. Ziya Gökalp expressed his views on this subject in detail in the CUP-supported journal *İktisadiyat*. For a detailed account, see Zafer Toprak, *[Türkiye'de] Milli İktisat 1908– 1918* (Ankara, 1982), pp. 17–36.

67. Bayur, vol. II, part IV, p. 410.

68. Tarık Zafer Tunaya, *Türkiye'de Siyasi Partiler*, vol. III (expanded edition) (Istanbul, 1989), p. 310.

69. Tarık Zafer Tunaya, *Türkiye'de Siyasi Partiler* (one-volume edition) (Istanbul, 1952), p. 214.

70. This committee was accepted by the Council of State as an association 'beneficial to the public' in 1914; it performed important services during the war.

71. Bayur, vol. II, ksm IV, p. 497, claims the society was established in Haziran, 1329 (June 1913), while Tunaya, (p. 293) gives the date as 20 Nisan, 1329 (May 1, 1913).

72. Kuzcuoğlu Tahsin Bey, Responsible Delegate for the Turkish Strength Society. Quoted in Zafer Toprak, 'II. Meşrutiyet Döneminde Parmiliter Gençlik Örgutleri', *Tanzimat'tan Cumhuriyet'e Türkiye Ansiklopedisi*, vol. II (Istanbul, 1985), p. 531–5.

73. Lewis, pp. 355–6.

74. Henry Morgenthau, *Secrets of the Bosphorus, Constantinople 1913–1916* (London, 1918), p. 32.
75. *Ibid.*
76. *Osmanlı Mebusan Meclisi Reisi Halil Menteşe'nin Anıları* (Istanbul, 1986), p. 165.
77. Lewis, p. 356.
78. Ziya Gökalp, *Türkleşmek,...*, pp. 40–41.
79. In that year in the journal *Genç Kalemler* he wrote: 'The homeland is not Turkey. For the Turks it is not only Turkistan. The homeland a great and eternal country, Turan.'
80. Ziya Gökalp, *Türkleşmek,...*, p. 63.
81. A. Mil, 'Umumi Harpte Teşkilatı Mahsusa' (series in Newspaper) *Vakit*, 1, 2 İkinciteşrin (November), 1933. A. Mil is a fictitious name of one of the CUP's Responsible Secretaries (*katib-i mesul*) who assisted in the task of organizing the so-called Special Organization (*Teşkilat-ı Mahsusa*) in Eastern Anatolia. His real name was Akif Cemil and this serialization was published subsequently with the same title in book form (Istanbul, 1999).
82. Tarık Zafer Tunaya, vol. III, pp. 319–20.
83. A. Mil.
84. The Unionist leaders were aware of the conspiracy against the Grand Vizier. In his memoirs, Cemal Paşa claims that he informed Şevket Paşa that a plot had been hatched against him. Cemal Paşa, *Hatıralar ve Vesikalar* (Istanbul), [n.d.], p. 59. Additionally, in a debate in the Chamber on the matter in 1914, Talat Paşa 'said that the government had been aware' of the assassination plan. Tunaya, vol. III, p. 139.
85. Bayur, vol. II, part IV, p. 314.
86. Toprak, *Türkiye,de Milli İktisat...*, pp. 21, 32.
87. Tunaya, vol. III, p. 336.
88. A detailed report on the subject of these companies and their direction was submitted at the 1916 CUP Congress. For the full text of the report, see Toprak, pp. 393.
89. *Ibid.*, pp. 79–83.
90. Quoted in Zeki Sarıhan, *Kurtuluş Savaşı Günlüğü*, vol. I (Ankara, 1984), p. 68.
91. Zafer Toprak, p. 57.
92. *HHStAPA XL 275,* Konfidenten Bericht, Nr. 47, Konstantinopel 27/2/17, A. Ohandjanian ed., *Österreich-Armenien 1872–1936, Faksimilesammlung diplomatischer Aktenstücke*, Wien 1995, vol. 7, p. 5275.
93. *Takvîm-i Vekâyı*, no. 3554, May 12, 1919.
94. *Takvîm-i Vekâyı*, no. 3547. During the interrogations by the 5th Department, formed in the Chamber of Deputies in Istanbul in November 1918, and later, in the 1926 independence Tribunal trials of the former Unionists on charges of plotting to assassinate Mustafa Kemal, the activities of Kara Kemal and his companies were the subjects most dwelt upon and explored.
95. Cemal Kutay, *Birinci Dünya Harbinde Teşkilat-ı Mahsusa ve Heyber'de Türk Cengi* (Istanbul, 1962), p. 10.
96. Cemal Kutay, *Sohbetler*, no. 10: Türkiye Nereye Gidiyor (September, 1969), p. 69.
97. Cemal Kutay, *Birinci Dünya Harbinde...*, p. 18.
98. Quoted in Celal Bayar, vol. V, p. 1573.
99. *Ibid.*
100. *Ibid.* Kuşçubaşı relates the following recollection on the matter of the meetings and prepared plans being kept secret from members of government. 'One day Talât Paşa said to me half-jokingly, half-seriously: Eşref Beyefendi...Do you not have any information that you could give us about the government organization? He whispered in my ear slowly because the others had not heard of this.' Cemal Kutay, *Birinci Dünya Harbinde...*, p. 18.

101. Nurdoğan Taçalan, *Ege'de Kurtuluş Savaşı Başlarken* (Istanbul, 1970), p. 65.
102. Celal Bayar, vol. V, p. 1574.
103. *Ibid.*, p. 1576.
104. *Halil Menteşe'nin Anıları*, p. 166.
105. Cemal Kutay, *Birinci Dünya Harbinde...*, p. 62.
106. Nurdoğan Taçalan, pp. 71–3.
107. Y. H. Bayur, vol. II, part III, p. 255.
108. Arnold Toynbee, *The Western Question in Greece and Turkey* (New York, 1970), p. 140.
109. *Ibid.*
110. *Ibid.*, p. 143.
111. Quoted in Hıfzı Erim, *Ayvalık Tarihi* (Ankara, 1968), pp. 60–2 [translation of a Greek book of the same name by Yorgo Sakkaris].
112. *Meclis-i Mebusan Zabıta Ceridesi*, Devre 3, İçitma Senesi 5, vol. I (Ankara, 1992), p. 186.
113. Morgenthau, p. 212.
114. *Ibid.*
115. Doğan Avcıoğlu, *Milli Kurtuluş Tarihi*, vol. III (Istanbul, 1986), p. 1138.
116. *Ibid.*
117. Celal Bayar, vol. V, p. 1568.
118. *Halil Menteşe'nin Anıları*, p. 166.
119. *MMZC*, pp. 285, 287.
120. Cemal Kutay, *Birinci Dünya Harbinde...*, p. 6. In Celal Bayar's memoirs, which contain detailed passages from Kuşçubaşı's memoirs, various figures are given according to the different cities. The figure given in the text is the total of those figures provided by the author. Celal Bayar, vol. V, p. 1576.
121. Celal Bayar, pp. 1577–9.
122. *A.M.G.* 7 N 1653, No: AC-23602, Confidential.
123. *MMZC*, Devre 3, İçtima Senesi 5, p. 109.
124. *Ibid.*, pp. 284–87.
125. *Ibid.*, p. 285.
126. *Ibid.*, p. 289.
127. *Ibid.*, p. 287. During his oration, Efkalidis Efendi was interrupted by Turkish deputies, who said 'that's how it had been done in Bulgaria and Greece.' In the subsequent responses, heroic speeches were given which sang the praises of Turkishness, and it was mentioned that all of the evils [committed] could not be attributed to the Turks, and that they, too, had met with oppression. The Greek deputies were accused of being apologists (*müdâfi*) for the Greek government (pp. 288, 290–94). One more piece of information should be added. These policies, which could be characterized as ethnic cleansing—the cleansing was on a religious basis—were also carried out by the Balkan governments. As a result of these massacres and forced expulsions, which were implemented as a part of the conception of the national state, hundreds of thousands of Muslims were forced to emigrate to Anatolia. Toynbee gives the figure of 413,992 for Muslims forced out during the First Balkan War (Arnold Toynbee, *The Western Question*, p. 138). One can also find ample information in regard to the mutual ethnic cleansing policies in the Balkans in the consular reports of the period. (For example, certain sections of the reports by the French Ambassador at the Porte, Bompard are quoted in Y. H. Bayur, vol. II, part III, pp. 256–60).
128. *MMZC*, p. 288.
129. *Ibid.*
130. *Ibid*, pp. 316–17.

131. Morgenthau, p. 323.
132. Y. H. Bayur, vol. II, part IV, pp. 645–55. Taken from Halil Menteşe's memoirs, which were serialized in the periodical *Cumhuriyet* (November 9, 1946).
133. From a speech made by Hasan Fehmi Bey at a secret session of the Grand National Assembly on 17 Teşrinievvel, 1336 (October 17, 1920). *TBMM Gizli Celse Zabıtaları*, vol. I (Ankara, 1985), p. 177.

5

The Decision for Genocide
in the Light of Ottoman-Turkish Documents

This chapter will focus on the brief period prior to the decision taken by the Ittihat ve Terakki (the Committee for Union and Progress, CUP) for the Armenian Genocide and on its implementation. The analysis of the specific factors that led to such a decision, and the questions of why and how it was possible are outside the scope of this chapter, but the preceding chapters discuss the ground which paved the way for such a decision.

My aim here is to show that those Turkish sources we already possess provide sufficient information to prove that what befell the Armenians in 1915 was a Genocide, and for a reconstruction of how it was organized. The question I am seeking to answer is, before and after the decision for Genocide, what kind of information do the Ottoman-Turkish sources provide on the relationship between the CUP, Teşkilat-ı Mahsusa (the Special Organization), and the Department of the Interior? For this, I will primarily use the indictments and the documents that were read during the military tribunal trials of CUP officials in Istanbul between 1919 and 1922, the testimonies of defendants and witnesses, and I will supplement them with other Turkish documents as needed.

The Reorganization of Teşkilat-ı Mahsusa

We know that there is a problematic aspect in choosing a retrospective structure for reporting on historic events during a given period. The 'turning' or 'starting' points are open to criticism for having been chosen arbitrarily. I am aware that the dates I have chosen as starting or turning points may, in another context, be not more than an interim result or some unimportant detail. The representation of events that I shall present has to be evaluated in the light of this methodological problem.

My starting point will be the secret meeting of the Central Committee of the CUP on August 2, 1914 and the decisions taken there.

During the night when general mobilization was announced (August 2), there was an important meeting at the Central Committee of the CUP, and at this meeting a far-reaching decision was taken to be acted upon in the near future. The decision aimed at founding a special organization, Teşkilât-ı Mahsusa, in order to improve the capability of movement of our armies on enemy soil, whether we would enter the general war or not.[1]

Although there is differing information on the exact day of the founding of the Special Organization, we know that following the decision of August 2, 1914, the Special Organization was organized under the command of the Department of Defense and it gained official status.[2] In the military tribunal —referred to as the Main Trial from now on—that was conducted in Istanbul against the officials of the CUP and the Special Organization,[3] the defendants stated that the Special Organization was organized within the Department of Defense, and that the decision for that was taken at the August 2 meeting of the Central Committee.[4] Accordingly, a central coordination office of the Special Organization was established within the Department of Defense. This committee included members from the Departments of Defense and Interior, and the Central Committee of the CUP. The indictment and the defendants' testimonies listed names of participants and their affiliations. According to the testimony of Atif Bey, who was one of the general coordinators of the '*teşkilat*,' the institution was comprised of at least four different units.[5]

The committee was given great authority. A network was established between various state departments, units of the army, the Central Committee of the CUP, and branches of the party in different provinces. Atif stated in his testimony, 'The Department of Defense had authorized us and we were in communication with the quartermaster corps, national security, the CUP and all federal departments and national institutions.'[6] In all the correspondence between local administrators, such as governors, branches of the CUP, and the local authorities of the Special Organization, the ciphers of the Department of the Interior were used. In the fifth session of the Main Trial, the presiding judge asked Atif Bey why the ciphers of the Department of the Interior were used by an institution under the jurisdiction of the Department of Defense and the army, but did not get a satisfactory reply.[7]

The main task of the committee was to organize the paramilitary units (*çetes*) that would carry out their activities under the command of the army. The units would conduct operations mainly in Eastern Anatolia, 'to serve the purpose of unifying Islam and promote Turkism through uniting the Turks outside the Turkish border.'[8] The activities were to be implemented in two arenas: inside and outside the country. Outside the country, the aim was to organize uprisings in Egypt, Caucasia, Iran and India. Inside the country, the activities were described in the correspondence: 'As much as there is an aim to be pursued abroad, there are, however, also persons to be liquidated at home. This is the path we are following.'[9] These statements were made by the Erzurum party secretary Hilmi in a telegram responding to Bahaettin Şakir. The '*persons*' to be liquidated in the country were the Armenians.

The gangs were established through the coordinated efforts of official institutions mentioned above. Throughout the hearings in the Main Trial, telegrams and letters between local administrators (governors and *kaimakams*), local CUP representatives, the Central Committee of the CUP in Istanbul, and the Special Organization were read. The letter of the Department of the Special Organization to the Central Committee of the CUP on forming the gangs, the letter of the Special Organization to the Governor of Izmit, and the letter of the CUP branch in Smyrna addressed directly to the Special Organization may serve as examples.[10]

The Gangs of the Special Organization

The practical task of organizing the gangs in eastern Anatolia to carry out missions in Russia and provoke that counrty to enter the war was given to Bahaettin Şakir.[11] A group of secretaries of the CUP from Istanbul were to go to the region as well, and this was to be kept utterly secret.[12] Erzurum was taken as the central base for action. To this end, a separate General HQ (headquarters) for the Special Organization was formed in Erzurum. During the fifth session of the Main Trial, a telegram from Süleyman Askeri, the first coordinator of the Special Organization, to Bahaettin Şakir was read. The telegram, addressed to the province of Erzurum, revealed that 'Riza Bey of Trabzon was appointed as a member of the HQ in Erzurum.' In a telegram to Talât Paşa in Istanbul, which was read during the same hearing, Bahaettin Şakir informed Talât about his activities as the person in charge of the HQ in Erzurum.[13] In the memoirs of Ali Ihsan Sabis, one of the army commanders in Eastern Anatolia, it is reported that Enver Paşa talked about Bahaettin Şakir as 'the head of Special Organization from the HQ.'[14]

After Bahaettin Şakir left for Erzurum, Kara Kemal, a member of the CUP Central Committee, came to the region accompanied by another delegation, among which there were some German officials. The Germans were to carry out activities in Russia in connection with Georgians. In August, Bahaettin Şakir and Kara Kemal drew up a general plan of activities in the region and, in order to protect the government and the CUP from responsibility, they founded an organization called the 'Caucasian Revolutionary Association.'

Following deliberations that lasted for a number of days...a directive was written that defined in detail how to proceed...this directive had to be kept top secret and required utmost attention for it not to fall into the hands of foreigners...it was distributed to people who were involved and the local offices of the Special Organization.[15]

One of the most important tasks of the Caucasian Revolutionary Association was 'to form gangs in and outside the country.' Therefore, the 'necessary order was sent to the surrounding regions.' In this order, it was quite openly stated that the gangs would be established under the command of the Third Army. For instance, a telegram sent to the 'Governor of Erzincan and *Kaimakam* of Bayburt, Tercan and Kigi,' indicates that 'with the permission of the commanding Paşa of the Third Army and the leadership of Dr Bahaettin Şakir...an Islamic militia troop is being set up.[16] Either officers or secretaries of the CUP were appointed to lead the gangs. A report sent to Istanbul from the Third Army noted that the local authorities were instructed to form paramilitary organizations.[17] In September 1914, the Third Army prepared a set of regulations for the para-military units formed under its command and distributed it to 'the relevant places.' The order was written to provide information for the gang leaders and to those who needed it. It was quite important to uphold the secrecy of this order.[18]

It was decided in Istanbul that the gangs would be under the command of the army. In the Main Trial, Cevat Bey explained that the voluntary units (gangs) 'carried out their duty under the army commanders.' To the question of the presiding judge whether 'the units of the Special Organiza-tion were completely bound by the orders of the army commanders,' Cevat Bey, replied 'Without a doubt, sir. They were parts of the army troops.'[19] The organizing of the gangs was not limited to the Third Army. A document dated November 17, 1330 (1914) that was read in the Second hearing of the same trial, cited an earlier communication sent to the Army Corps 1,2,3,4 and 5, Army HQ in the Izmir region, and the other army commanders about organizing paramilitary units.[20]

Three Sources for Recruitment of the Gangs

The formation of the Special Organization in the region started in the second half of August. Three important sources were used for recruitment: Kurdish tribes, convicted prisoners, and immigrants from Caucasia and the Balkans. The task of organizing the gangs in the eastern region was given to Hilmi, a CUP inspector (*müfettis*) in the Erzurum region. A letter he sent to the leader of a Kurdish tribe, contains the following: 'The time is about to come to deal with the problem we talked about in Erzincan...I want 50 brave [men] from you...I shall prepare everything for their convenience here...never mind if they are young or middle-aged men, as long as they are strong and determined and willing to sacrifice their lives for their country and nation...Upon first notice from us put them on their way... Only be prepared and keep Bahaettin Şakir Beyefendi informed. For now, I submit my wishes and kiss your eyes. My brother Bahaettin Beyefendi also sends his regards.'[21]

The release of the prisoners who were to be the second source of the Special Organization was planned in August. The secretaries of the CUP who came to the region wrote in a report: '[It is necessary] to benefit from the prisoners in Trabzon Prison, to release them from prison, to form gangs with them under the command of officers, and assign the more notorious ones gang leadership.'[22] The answer from Istanbul stated that, if necessary, the release of prisoners would be allowed.[23] But even before the answer from Istanbul arrived, the release of prisoners began. The decision for this was taken at the beginning of September by the HQ of the Special Organization in Erzurum. The center in Erzurum, through intervention with official departments, secured the release of prisoners. Then the prisoners and the Kurdish leaders were recruited as gang members.[24]

The release of prisoners that started in Eastern Anatolia was later to be conducted throughout the whole country. It created a problem within the government that prisons were emptied without any such legislation having been issued, and the ministers in question were informed of the practice only after the fact. Thereupon, the Minister of Justice enacted a special amnesty.[25] The Department of the Interior sent a message to all the regions. From a document belonging to the Bursa CUP that was read during the sixth session of the Main Trial, we understand that the relevant ministerial letter was sent on September 15.[26]

The third source of gang recruits was immigrants to Anatolia from the Balkans and Caucasia. In the Main Trial many telegrams were read to verify this. Telegrams sent by party secretary Musa Beg in Balikesir and the local CUP office in Bursa disclosed that on October 15, the Central Committee of the CUP issued a 'secret order to the regions stating that one should take advantage of the immigrants when setting up the gangs.'[27] A correspondence dated November 13 between the Special Organization and Mithat Sükrü, the Secretary General of the CUP, reveals that the gangs were established in different regions.[28] The examples of telegrams read during the fifth and sixth sessions of the Tribunal were about correspondence directed to Secretary General Mithat Sükrü who, in turn, forwarded them to the Special Organization. [29]

As we see, the gangs of the Special Organization were basically organized through Istanbul, and decisions as to where the gangs had to go were taken there. The HQ of the Special Organization and the Central Committee of the CUP did this in a coordinated manner. Locally, the formation of the gangs was the direct responsibility of the party secretaries (*katibi mesul*). In the telegram mentioned above, dated November 13 and originating from the Special Organization, it is demanded 'that the people clandestinely recruited by the party secretaries in Izmit, Bursa, Bandirma, Balikesir and other relevant regions should be summoned and moved [to Istanbul] within a week.'[30]

This kind of correspondence and the testimonies of the defendants also reveal that the gangs either got their equipment and training in Istanbul or were sent directly to the regions. The CUP party secretary of Samsun, Rüstü, provides the information that the fifth gang that was formed in his region was sent by a motorized unit to its destination on November 16.[31] The Austrian Consulate in Trabzon reported on November 8, 1914 that various gangs were being trained along the coast.[32] In the fifth session of the Main Trial, Cevat testified that a special office was set up within the Department of Defense to deal with the equipment and training of those who came to Istanbul. During the same hearing, a telegram by Ismet Inönü, who at the time was working for the Department of Defense, was read. He had written it in the name of the Minister of Defense. The telegram mentions that those responsible for the recruitment and transport of the voluntary gangs formed by the immigrants from Macedonia and Thrace were acting under the orders of the army.[33]

First Actions of the Gangs

In August, soon after the formation of the gangs, military action in the interior of Russia started. According to the principle, 'like the aim pursued abroad, there are people at home that also need to be liquidated,' not only Russian troops were attacked but Armenian villages were raided. Looting and massacres counted as normal actions of the gangs. In a report Bahaettin Şakir sent to Talât Paşa in September, he quite openly expresses the view that looting is taking place: 'I'm inspecting our organization…I am quite confident. We gained experience and destroyed the Russian troops everywhere. So far we captured more than 1,000 sheep and up to 400 cows.'[34] The actions of the gangs were not limited only to actions beyond the borders. Armenian villages in Eastern Anatolia were also subjected to looting and attacks. Some Turkish officers reported in their memoirs that they witnessed the raids, looting, and destruction of Armenian villages by the gangs which were organized by Bahaettin Şakir for deployment in Russia.[35]

The actions were not restricted to attacks against villages. Armenian intellectuals and political and religious leaders were also among the targets of attacks. One example is the action planned against the leading members of the Tashnak congress, which met in Erzurum in August 1914. The importance of this event is that Turkish and Armenian sources alike report that some leaders of the CUP, such as Bahaettin Şakir, came to Erzurum to try to persuade the Tashnaks to carry out joint actions against the Russians. However, as the information above shows, the real intention of the trip to Erzurum by Bahaettin Şakir and other leaders of the CUP, was to form the units of the Special Organization. In addition, the documents indicate that there was a plan to liquidate the Tashnak leaders. Bahaettin Şakir informs Hilmi Bey, one of those responsible for the Special Organization in Erzurum, when the Tashnak leaders will depart from Erzurum. In his answer Hilmi states, 'We have taken the necessary steps to deal with the persons whose departure date from Erzurum you informed us in a coded message...I have given the necessary instructions to seize them.'[36]

Arif Cemil, one of the responsible secretaries for this region, disclosed the contents of the telegram in his memoirs, adding that Bahaettin Şakir wanted the leaders to be captured, or even better, to be liquidated en route. But the Armenians misled them and succeeded in escaping from the gangs.[37] This example shows that the leaders of the CUP, already before the war, acted with the idea that 'there are...also persons to be liquidated at home. In the memoirs, as well as in the reports of foreigners, one can find ample information on attacks against the Armenian population inside and outside the borders of the Ottoman Empire. The reports of German officers who served in the Special Organization gangs have a special importance.[38]

It was not only the Armenians who were subjected to attacks, looting, and massacres. Even if they did not reach the same level, Muslim villages were also subjected to attacks. These irresponsible and arbitrary actions were seen by the army as a serious problem. Thus, the relationship between the army and the Special Organization in the area deteriorated. The military success of the gangs in their actions between September and December 1914 partially overshadowed this problem. The gangs occupied Ardahan and went as far as Batum. But starting in December, defeats took the place of victories. The fact that Armenian volunteers helped the Russian units contributed heavily to the defeats in Caucasia and near Van.

Making the Decision for Genocide

Following the fiasco of the Special Organization's operations in Caucasia and near Lake Van, there was another defeat at Sarikamiş. This led the leaders of the CUP to review seriously the situation. The consecutive defeats destroyed their Pan-Turanist dreams and led to the loss of territory. One of the important problems that emerged during the implementation of the plan, was the power struggle between the Special Organization and the army. Actually, the question of who was to command operations in the regions was unresolved from the very beginning. This problem grew bigger with the defeats and irresponsible actions by the gangs, who attacked Muslims, as well as Christians, without distinguishing one from the other. Arif Cemil said that 'the fact that some commanders were in disagreement with the Special Organization stemmed from the lack of official notification about the structure of this organization.'[39] The army believed that law and order in the region deteriorated because of the actions of the gangs. Erzurum's Inspector Hilmi reported in a letter he sent to Bahaettin Şakir on September 3 that near clashes arose between the guarding units of the army, augmented for security reasons, and the Special Organization.[40] The German officer in the area, Colonel Stange, reported continuous friction between the gangs and the army due to lack of discipline and the actions of the gangs.[41]

The issue was not limited to the problems created by gang members who deserted. It was observed that in some regions the gangs operating as part of the army executed Muslim villagers or shot them in groups without questioning them, only because they had appeared 'suspicious.'[42] Based on this, the army argued that the gangs had to be either abolished completely or integrated into the regular army units. The wing of the Special Organization loyal to the CUP was absolutely opposed to this. They did not want to bring the gangs under the army's command, saying 'we have struggled and strived for such a long time. Now they want to take possession of the Special Organization.[43]

Before returning to Istanbul to report on the negative situation in the region, Bahaettin Şakir attended a meeting where it was decided to release the Special Organization from control of the army, to put the gangs ('individuals and groups') directly under the control of the Erzurum HQ of the Special Organization, and to authorize them to operate autonomously. 'Drafting of the programs should be left up to the local authorities. In particular local delegations should possess the necessary devices.'[44]

Hilmi, whom Şakir had left as his second-in-command, sent telegrams to Istanbul on a daily basis demanding that 'as long as there is no order to release the Special Organization from the control of the army, there is no sense in returning to the Caucasian front.' These events occurred in February. Bahaettin Şakir most likely went to Istanbul either at the end of that month or in March.[45] The subject of discussion in Istanbul was not only the practical dimension of the relations between the army and the Special Organization; there would be basic changes in the duties of the Special Organization. '[Bahaettin Şakir] was convinced that because of the Armenians' attitude towards Turkey and the support they had given to the

Russian army, one had to be afraid of the internal enemy as much as of the enemy abroad.'[46] The doctor, who came to possess some documents on the activities of the Armenians in the region, was trying to persuade his friends in Istanbul that it was necessary to eliminate this danger.[47]

There is a high probability that the actual decision for Genocide was taken during this set of meetings in Istanbul at the end of March. The leaders of the CUP reviewed the situation in the light of the new information they had received. As a result of these discussions 'it was decided that Bahaettin Şakir Bey should stay away from the responsibilities of the Special Organization's activities concerning the enemies abroad and should deal only with the internal enemies.'[48] Arif Cemil stated: 'finally the deliberations resulted in the passage of the law on deportation.' He continued: 'By the time Dr Bahaettin Şakir returned to the Caucasian front his assignment was completely clear.'[49]

All these documents indicate that in March a clandestine decision was made against the Armenians. Bahaettin Şakir was tasked with the implementation of the decision. Ottoman-Turkish sources verify also that two decisions were taken during these deliberations, one on liquidation and one on deportation.

The Decision Was Made After Long Deliberations

There is ample evidence that the decision for a Genocide of the Armenians was made by the Central Committee of the CUP following intense discussions and deliberations. In the indictment of the Main Trial, the following information is provided: 'The massacre and liquidation of Armenians were the result of decisions by the Central Committee of the CUP.' These decisions were made as a result 'of broad and deep discussions.' In the indictment Dr Nazım is quoted as having said the following on the Armenian problem: 'The Central Committee had intense deliberations to make a decision,' and 'this undertaking would solve the Eastern Question.'[50]

In the memoirs of Celal, the Governor of Halep (Aleppo), it is reported that the same words were transmitted to him by a deputy from Konya with 'regards from a person of the Central Committee.' The deputy who transmitted these words to Celal added that 'in case he disagreed with their stance on this subject, they would do away with him.'[51] The private secretary of the Department of the Interior, Ihsan Bey, testified that when he was the *Kaimakam* of Kilis, Abdu'lahad Nuri Bey, who was sent from Dersaadet (Istanbul) to Halep, admitted to him that the aim of the deportations was liquidation. Nuri said: 'I was in touch with Talât Bey and received the orders for liquidation directly from him. Salvation of the country depends on it.' With these words Nuri tried to persuade Ihsan Bey.[52] In December 1918, in written testimony to the special Commission Investigating Sordid Affairs (established in 1918 in the Department of the Interior for investigating genocide) Vehip Paşa, the commander of the Third Army since February 1916, stated, 'The massacre and annihilation of the Armenians and the looting and plunder of their properties were the result of a decision of the Central Committee.' According to the Paşa, the atrocities

> were carried out under a program that was [specifically] determined upon and represented a definite case of premeditation... They [the atrocities] were made possible primarily through the involvement of Ittihat's representatives and provincial central bodies [of the Party], and secondarily through higher governmental officials who, abandoning their conscience and discarding the law, allowed themselves to be co-opted by the Party and issued the necessary order.[53]

The Paşa added that state officials did not take any preventive measures, even though they saw and heard of these crimes. Furthermore, they incited further killings, which was one of the most important proofs that this operation was planned.[54]

In the reports of foreign consulates and embassies, particularly those of German officers, one can find statements indicating that the order for the deportation of Armenians by the CUP leaders was a well-thought-out plan to liquidate them.[55] Clearly, the most definite statement on this subject was made by Talât Paşa to the Istanbul consul Mordtmann. Mordtmann quoted Talât in a report to Berlin: 'The subject of the matter is...the liquidation of the Armenians.'[56]

It is further possible to conclude that the decision for deportation directly aimed at liquidation when one looks at the dismissals and even killings of officials who thought that the 'deportation' should merely involve resettlement. In addition, telegrams, which clearly point to this fact, were read during various hearings in the Istanbul trials, but mostly during the Yozgat trial, where, during the ninth session (February 22, 1919) 12 telegrams were read which made clear that the deportations meant liquidation and massacre.

For instance, in a telegram sent by Mustafa, commander of the Bogazliyan gendarmes detachment, to the Deputy Commander of Ankara's Fifth Army Corps, Halil Recyai, on July 22 (August 5) 1915, it is reported that a group 'of harmful Armenians gathered from the towns and countryside were sent on to their destination.'[57] In his reply on the same day, Halil Recyai asked for the exact meaning of the word 'destination.'[58] In response, the commander of the gendarmerie stated that 'the aforementioned Armenians were massacred because they are malicious.'[59] In the same trial, a telegram of the commander of the Bogazliyan gendarmerie, Hulusi, was read on March 6, 1919, during the twelfth session. Here the same language is used. The telegram says that 'transport means destruction.'[60]

Everything Is Reorganized

In light of the deliberations and decisions of the Central Committee of the CUP, the Special Organization was reorganized. The most important decision was to keep the units outside the control of the army from that point forward. The units were to act under the command of Bahaettin Şakir. From a document that was read in the Main Trial concerning the relationship between the army and the Special Organization, we understand that the relations between them came to a standstill in early February. This document is an official order from the Department of Defense to the army commanders, dated February 3. It was handed over to the court by Cevat. It reveals that the army thereafter would stop the formation of the gangs.[61] Again, during the fifth hearing on May 14, 1919, Cevat stated that, 'on 2.10.1331 [April 1915], there were no procedures left to do by the committee.'[62] According to the testimony of Atif (another defendant), the commission for the Special Organization that was formed in the Department of Defense had been disbanded by the end of April 1915.[63]

During the fifth hearing on May 12, 1919, Riza reported that besides the Special Organization formed under the Department of Defense, there were also units of the Special Organization under the control of local administrators or the secretary of the CUP in Anatolia. These groups were formed in order to organize the deportations.[64] Similar information was provided during the sixteenth hearing of the Trabzon trial on May 5 by the commander of the garrison, Avni Paşa, who stated that under the command of the governor of Trabzon, Cemil Azmi Bey, there was a gang of the Special Organization responsible for deportation and massacre.[65] It is a well-known fact that the Armenians, who were forced to leave their homes under the order for deportation, were basically liquidated by the units of the Special Organization. What is important to us at this point is that testimonies of defendants and other documents verify what Arif Cemil reported, and that these units were reorganized, taken out of the control of the army, and put directly under the supervision of the CUP.

How Was the Genocide Organized?

Based on the documents at hand, we can roughly frame a scheme as to how the deportation and the Genocide were organized. It is very likely that the Central Committee of the CUP took the two decisions for the deportation and the Genocide concurrently. In accordance with these decisions, the Department of the Interior devised a secret scheme for deportation and sent this information to the regions through its own channels. In general the decision for genocide was delivered personally to the regions by the responsible party secretaries and implemented by the gendarmes and the gangs of the Special Organization.

From some published Turkish documents we can conclude that the secret decision for deportation was telegraphed to the regions towards the end of April by the Department of the Interior. Başkatip Ragip came to Erzurum on April 14 and left on April 26. In his memoirs he remarked, 'Because of deportations of Armenians, the destitute, pitiful and wretched state of the Armenian girls and women in the area broke our hearts.'[66] In its reports, the German consulate stated that the evacuation of villages around Erzurum started in early May. 'By May 15, all villages were evacuated.'[67] From a coded telegram sent by the Ministry of the Interior on May 9, 1915 to the governors in the eastern region, we learn that there was a previous directive to the governors of Van and Bitlis for the deportation of Armenians in the Van area upon the news of the uprising in Van. This telegram also mentions that the deportation should cover Bitlis, the south of Erzurum, around Muş and Sasun and that a similar telegram was sent to Erzurum.[68]

The Department of the Interior administered the deportation through its organs, the General Department of Security and the 'Office for the Settlement of Nomadic Tribes and Refugees.' The local organs of the Departments of the Interior (the Governor and *Kaimakams*) were responsible for the deportation at the local level. Talât Paşa became the general coordinator of the collaboration of all these institutions. While the Department of the Interior used its own channels to transmit the decision for deportation to the regions, the Central Committee of the CUP transmitted the decision for Genocide via the party secretaries. This information is given by Reşit Akif Paşa. Following the resignation of Talât Paşa in October 1918, Reşit Akif Paşa served as President of State Council in the first government after the Armistice in the cabinet of Ahmet Izzet Paşa. In the parliamentary assembly of November 21, 1918, he gave an important speech. According to Reşit Akif Paşa, the Genocide of the Armenians started with the delivery of the secret decision for deportation by the Department of the Interior to the governors.

During my tenure as your humble servant to the new cabinet, only 25–30 days old, I become cognizant of some secrets. I came across something strange in this respect. It was this official order for deportation, issued by the notorious Interior Ministry and relayed to the provinces. However, following [the issuance of] this official order, the Central Committee undertook to send an ominous circular order to all points [in the provinces], urging the expediting of the execution of the accursed mission of the brigands. Thereupon, the brigands proceeded to act and the atrocious massacres were the result.[69]

Some newspapers called this speech of the Paşa highly important and published it word for word.[70] Unfortunately Reşit Akif Paşa does not mention the date of this secret document.

We understand that there was a two-fold mechanism: (1) the official decision for deportation by the Department of the Interior, and (2) the decision for liquidation by the Central Committee. In his written testimony submitted to the military tribunal, Vehip Paşa provides very important information about the fact that the official orders for deportation were distributed through the governors and the decision for liquidation was implemented by Bahaettin Şakir. Once appointed to serve in the region in February 1916, Vehip Paşa initiated an investigation into the massacres of the Armenians who were deported from Erzurum and Trabzon. He had members of the gendarmerie, whom he believed to be responsible for the liquidation, arrested. He interrogated them personally. They told the Paşa that 'orders for the deportation of families were from Memduh Bey...who at the time was responsible in Erzincan, and the people who participated in the liquidation of the families received their orders from Dr Bahaettin Şakir Bey.'[71]

We can assume that the mechanism worked more or less in the following way. The Department of the Interior informed the governors of the official order for deportation, and the governors in turn forwarded this information to the security forces in their area, primarily to the gendarmerie. The liquidation was organized by the Central Committee of the CUP, especially through Bahaettin Şakir. The most important task in this process was carried out by party secretaries. Also, the Central Committee of the CUP decided that the army would not be involved in the plans for deportation and liquidation. This decision was forwarded to all army units. On February 11, 1919, in the seventh hearing of the Yozgat trial, Halil Recyai stated that he had received an order from the Secretary of Defense, Enver Paşa, that the army was not to interfere in the deportation of the Armenians. On March 26, during the 14th hearing, he repeated the same testimony.[72] On May 5, 1919, in the 16th hearing of the Trabzon case, the commander of the garrison, Avni Paşa, stated that he had received an order from the Department of Defense not to interfere in the duties of the governors.[73] Even though we know that in some regions the army was involved in the liquidation of its own labor battalions, in general we can say that the Genocide was committed by the gendarmerie under the order of the Department of the Interior and the gangs of the Special Organization under orders from the CUP.

The Role of the CUP Secretaries and Bahaettin Şakir

From the documents sent on September 13, 1330 (1914) by the Special Organization to the Central Committee of the CUP, we realize that the party secretaries were responsible for the formation of the gangs in the regions. In fact, during the hearings, further telegrams were read proving that the secretaries had responsibilities for organizing the gangs. The telegram stating that the responsible secretary of Samsun, Rüştü, formed the gangs required in his region serves as an example. During the same hearing, the defendants stated that the correspondence with party secretaries was not held by the Special Organization but by party secretary Mithat Şükrü.[74]

Because of the important role of party secretaries in the Genocide, an additional indictment was prepared. This indictment asserts that the party secretaries, on the one hand, showed active involvement in the CUP but, on the other hand, were also active within the government, forming a secret wing.[75] Because of their important function, the trial against the party secretaries was separated from the other cases and heard at another court. In the verdict of the respective trial, it is stated that the party secretaries were directly involved in the organization and implementation of the criminal acts of the CUP.[76]

The party secretaries were appointed as the heads of the Special Organization gang units and given wide-ranging authority. They not only carried the orders directly to the regions, but also organized and controlled the liquidation on a local level. Testimony was given to this effect in all the trials. The presiding judge in the Main Trial repeated several times that many documents indicated that the party secretaries took the order to the regions. The judge also reiterated that governors who disobeyed the party secretaries were removed from office by force. It was repeatedly mentioned by the judge that the governor of Ankara, Mazhar Bey, the governor of Kastamonu, Reşit Paşa, and the Yozgat governor (Mutassarıf), Cemal Bey, were thus relieved of their duties as demanded by the party secretaries.[77]

The dismissed governors testified to this effect. For example Mazhar Bey reported on his dismissal: 'I received the orders for the deportation of the Armenians from the Department of the Interior in Istanbul and pretended not to have understood them. As you may know, while other governors had started the deportation I did not. Atif Bey came...and gave a verbal order to massacre and liquidate the Armenians. I said, no, Atif Bey, I am a governor not a criminal; I can't do it. I shall leave this chair; you come, sit here and do it.'[78] The story of the governor of Kastamonu, Reşit, is the same. According to the verdict of the trial against the party secretaries, Governor Reşit is reported to have stated: 'I won't have blood on my hands,' and, therefore, he was dismissed on the intervention of Secretary Hasan Fehmi.[79]

We possess varied evidence that the Central Committee forwarded its decision on liquidation to the regions by special couriers. Ahmet Esat was the director of the Second Department of the Police HQ of the Department of the Interior. Following the Armistice he tried to sell protocols, allegedly taken during a meeting, concerning the Genocide of the Armenians, to some English authorities. He handed over four different documents. Two of them were in his own handwriting. According to the information provided by Esat, the messages were read to the governors and then the originals were brought back to be destroyed.[80]

The information concerning the method of transmission of the orders to the regions was confirmed during the trials in Istanbul. In almost all the trials it was reported that the orders were forwarded to the regions by special couriers (party secretaries of the CUP). During the Main Trial, the presiding judge repeatedly stated that, 'special delegates were sent to places, such as Ankara, Kastomonu, Erzincan, Yozgat, Trabzon, Sivas, etcetera, and they gave secret instructions to the governor and mutasarrıfs,' and the judge asked each defendant whether they knew anything about that.[81]

On December 12, 1918, the Mutasarrıf of Yozgat, Cemal, gave written testimony to the special 'Commission Investigating Sordid Affairs.' In his testimony he said that Necati Bey showed him an official document concerning the liquidation of the Armenians, but when he asked for the letter, it was not given to him. Thereupon Cemal said that he, Necati, had no official authority, therefore he would not implement the order. A few days later, Cemal was dismissed.[82] In the 11th hearing of the Yozgat trial (on March 5, 1919), Cemal reported that, according to Necati, this order came from the Central Committee of the CUP.[83]

In the verdict of the Bayburt trial, it is repeated that the decision for genocide was taken by the Central Committee and sent to the regions by special couriers. In this trial, the defendant, Nusret, who later was sentenced to death and executed, said that he received a secret order from Istanbul not to leave any Armenian alive. Officials who disobeyed the order would be executed.[84]

In addition to the party secretaries, Bahaettin Şakir also travelled through the eastern provinces and talked to governors and other authorities, informing them of the decision by the Central Committee.[85] In the Main Trial, the presiding judge stated that Bahaettin Şakir was appointed as the sole leader of all units of the Special Organization.[86] In addition, the judge asked the defendants whether they knew that Bahaettin Şakir Bey visited some counties in the province of Trabzon and delivered secret orders.[87] During the hearing of August 2 in the Mamüretülaziz trial, the governor of

Erzurum, Tahsin, stated that Bahaettin Şakir had two separate ciphers, one to communicate with the government and the other with the Department of Defense.[88] Telegrams that were read during various trials make it clear that Bahaettin Şakir directed the killing operations. In the Main Trial, it emerged that one important telegram read as follows: 'Are the Armenians who are being dispatched from there being liquidated? Are the troublesome people you tell us you have expelled and dispersed being exterminated, or are they just being deported? Answer explicitly…'[89] This telegram was read not only in the Main Trial, but also in others as well, such as for Mamüretülaziz and for the party secretaries and it influenced the verdicts. In the verdict of the Mamüretülaziz, it is reported that the Mutasarrrıf of Antalya, Sabur Sami Bey, received a coded telegram from Bahaettin Şakir. In this telegram Bahaettin Şakir inquired of Sami Bey about the state of the operation in Antalya, adding that in the areas of Erzurum, Van, Bitlis, Diyarbakir, Sivas and Trabzon not one single Armenian was left. All had been deported to Musul and Zor.[90]

We possess some information about situations where the order for liquidation was sent by a telegram, and it was ordered that the telegram be destroyed after reading. For instance, in the indictment of the Main Trial we learn that the Governor of Der Zor, Ali Suat, received an order to destroy the telegram after reading it.[91] In the third hearing of the Yozgat trial (on 10 February), the presiding judge read the testimony of the Kaimakam of Bogazliyan, Kemal, given to the previously mentioned special commission to investigate genocide. Kemal testified that he had received telegrams and was asked to destroy them after reading.[92] During the hearing of March 24, Kemal was reminded of his testimony given to the commission. Kemal rejected his testimony of February 10, saying that he was very tired at that time. The prosecutor objected to this statement: 'I am a member of the investigating commission and I declare the testimony to be correct. He thought about it for three to four hours before writing it down.'[93]

Besides the government officials who were dismissed, there were also some others who were killed because they refused to implement the order. The Kaimakam of Lice did not carry out the order for annihilation of the Armenians. He requested a written version of the order. He was thereupon dismissed and called to Diyarbakir. He was killed en route.[94] The memoirs of the son of the Kaimakam of Lice, Abidin Nesimi, said that the order for elimination of government officials was given by the governor of Diyarbakir, Dr. Reşit; it also cited names of other victims. The governor of Basra (Ferit), the Kaimakam of Müntefak (Bedi Nuri)…the Deputy Kaimakam of Beşiri (Sabit) and the journalist Ismail Mestan were among those who were killed.[95] The Kaimakam of Midyat was murdered by order of the governor of Diyarbakir because he opposed the massacre of Christians in his county.[96] During the hearing of May 11, 1919 in the Trabzon trial, Kenan Bey, a secretary in the Department of Justice, stated that he had gone to Samsun for investigation, where he saw the implementation of the deportation; he also reported that the *Kaimakam* of Bafra was murdered.[97]

Finally, it has to be noted that the party secretaries not only established the gangs and delivered the order for genocide to the regions, they were involved also in such activities as inciting the Moslem population to demonstrate against the Armenians, looting Armenian possessions, and enriching themselves through the process. In the trial of the party secretaries, the defendants were questioned about these activities. The verdict of the same trial emphasizes that there was evidence to conclude that the party secretaries incited the people to hold demonstrations (like Dr Mithat did in Bolu), to confiscate the houses of the Armenians, to seize their belongings, and to organize looting.[98]

Talât Paşa as General Coordinator and His Telegrams

The information shows that the overall coordination of the Genocide was taken over by Talât Paşa. German ambassador Metternich described Talât Paşa as the 'soul of the Armenian persecution.'[99] The indictment of the Main Trial includes some of the confiscated telegrams he sent to the regions. These telegrams cover such matters as removing corpses from the roads and punishing those who did not follow orders. For instance, a coded telegram, which was sent to the governors of Diyarbakir, Mamuretülaziz, Urfa and Zor on July 21, 1915, ordered that the corpses left on the roads be buried and not be thrown into streams, rivers or lakes, and that the belongings of the dead left on the road be burned. Another coded order from the governor of Mamuretülaziz to the governor of Malatya expressed disappointment because, 'there are reports that in spite of strict orders many corpses still remain on the streets. Those who procrastinate in this clean-up effort will be severely punished by the illustrious Department of the Interior.'[100] The role of Talât Paşa as the head organizer and coordinator of the Genocide is clear in the telegram of the German consul in Jerusalem. He reported on September 9, 1915 that Cemal Paşa told him that he was only responsible for the military implementation of the decrees issued by Department of the Interior. Cemal added, 'Talât Paşa decided on the extent of the deportations.'[101]

Among the secret telegrams of Talât, one he sent to the governor of Diyarbakir on July 12, 1915, is important. In the telegram, Talât reported that he had heard the news of massacres of Armenians and other Christians in the provinces and that the estimated number of persons killed was around 2,000. The telegram finishes with these words: 'To extend the disciplinary and political decisions about the Armenians to other Christians will have a bad influence on public opinion. Especially when this sort of atrocity threatens the lives of Christians indiscriminately, it should be stopped immediately.'[102] The wording of the document is very clear. People, including government officials, are being killed by order of the governor. But this is not important to Talât. Clearly, his instruction was to exempt the non-Armenian Christians from the persecution; that is, to put an end to the inclusion of the non-Armenian Christians in the liquidation process.[103]

I have restricted myself mostly to the documents that came to light during the trials against the CUP in Istanbul. These sources alone reveal sufficient material on how systematically the liquidation of a people was carried out. If we possess the moral basis to protest against mass murders and call them a crime against humanity, then we should not have the slightest doubt in calling the events of 1915–17 a Genocide. To create such a moral basis, what needs to be done is to start an open discussion among Turkish and Armenian academicians on what really happened.

It is a truism that the success of a crime, especially a capital crime such as organized mass murder, hinges on the meticulous care with which the perpetrators prepare and eventually execute the crime. Utmost secrecy, cover-ups, and deflections are part and parcel of this process of scheming. Nevertheless, it seems that for a crime of the magnitude of genocide, it is impossible to destroy or withhold completely the evidence attesting to that crime. The documents cited in this chapter give testimony to a very important aspect of the Armenian Genocide, namely, that the decision for Genocide was made by the highest strata of the leadership of the CUP.

NOTES

1. A. Mil, 'Umumi Harpte Teşkilâtı Mahsusa,' Vakit Gazetesi, Tefrika No: 1, 2 Ikincitesrin (November) 1933.
2. Further information on the Special Organization can be found in Taner Akçam, İnsan Hakları ve Ermeni Sorunu, İttihat ve Terakkiden Kurtuluş Savaşına (Ankara, 1999), pp. 161–9.
3. The trial against the officials of the CUP and the Special Organization started on 28 April 1919. There were seven hearings. When the Greeks entered Izmir, the court case was interrupted on 17 May. After the defendants were taken to Malta, the hearings did not resume. In this case, the files of members of the government first were separated and,

together with other members of the government, another court case was opened. For this trial, which started on 3 June, an additional indictment was prepared, and this trial, too, lasted over seven hearings. The verdict was jointly declared on 5 July 1919.

4. *Takvimi Vekâyi* 3543, 3547, 3549; sessions 2–4 on 4 May, 6 May and 8 May 1335, in particular the testimonies of Talât (Kücük) and Atif.

5. *Takvimi Vekâyi* 3543, 2nd session on 4 May 1335.

6. *Ibid.*

7. *Takvimi Vekâyi* 3554, 5th session on 14 May 1335 (there is a misprint; it should be 12 May).

8. A. Mil, Part no: 1.

9. A. Mil, ibid, Part no. 13, 15 November 1933.

10. The documents were read out in the 5th and 6th hearing, when the defendants rejected their relationship with the Special Organization. For other examples see *Takvimi Vekâyi* 3554, 14 May 1335 and 3557, 14 May 1335.

11. A. Mil, Part no: 2. 3 November 1933.

12. *Ibid.*

13. *Takvimi Vekâyi* 3554, 5th session, 14 May 1335.

14. Ali Ihsan Sabis, *Harp Hatiralarim, Birinci Dünya Harbi*, 2nd volume, (Istanbul 1990), p.197.

15. A. Mil, Part no: 6, 7 November 1933.

16. A. Mil, Part no: 13, 15 November 1933.

17. Askeri Tarih Belgeleri Dergisi, Year 32 (2 March 1983): 7, Document no. 1894.

18. A. Mil, Part no: 15, 17 November 1933.

19. *Takvimi Vekâyi* 3543, 2nd session, 4 May 1335.

20. *Ibid.*

21. This letter, sent with the signature of the responsible person for the CUP association in Erzurum, Hilmi, carries the date of 23 August 1330 (4 September 1914). (This document is in my private archives.)

22. A. Mil, Part no: 4, 5 November 1933.

23. *Ibid.*, Part no: 4.

24. *Ibid.*, Part no: 19.

25. During the interrogation of the Fifth Department, the Justice Minister, Ibrahim Bey, said in his testimony (p. 41) that the release of prisoners started well before the amnesty. The minutes of the parliamentary research commission that was founded in November 1918 were later published as a book with the long title of *The contents of the Fifth Department that was founded on the suggestion of the late Deputy Fuat Bey in order to bring the cabinets of Said Halim and Mehmet Talât Paşas to justice* [in front of a military court] (*Protocols of Parliament*, number 521, period 3, session 5, published by Istanbul Printing House for Parliamentary Protocols, 1334). This document will be referred to as the 5th Department. The page numbers were given by Erol Sadi Erdinc according to the transcription. Page numbers were given for each interrogated person separately.

26. *Takvimi Vekâyi* 3557, 6th session, 14 May 1335.

27. *Ibid.*

28. *Takvimi Vekâyi* 3554, 5th session, 14 May 1335. (This should be 12 May. There is a printing mistake.)

29. *Takvimi Vekâyi* 3557, 6th session, 14 May 1335.

30. *Takvimi Vekâyi* 3554, 5th session, 14 May 1335.

31. *Ibid.*

32. HHStA PA I 942, ZI 79/P, Trabzon, 8 November 1914. Artem Ohandjanian, ed., *Österreich-Armenien 1872–1936, Faksimilesammlung diplomatischer Aktenstücke*

(Wien 1995), vol. 6, pp. 4462–3.

33. *Takvimi Vekâyi* 3554, 5th session, 14 May 1335.
34. A. Mil, Part no: 15, 17 November 1933.
35. Governor of Mütekaid, Serif Köprülü, *Sarikamiş, Ihata Manevrasi ve Meydan Muhare-besi*, Istanbul 1338 (1922), p. 119 (page number according to the transcribed version of the text).
36. A. Mil, Part no. 13, 14 November 1934.
37. *Ibid.*, Part no. 15, 17 November 1933.
38. For details on this subject, see: Taner Akçam, *İnsan Hakları ve Ermeni Sorunu*, pp. 233–44.
39. A. Mil, no. 15, 17 November 1933.
40. *Ibid.*, Part no. 13, 15 November 1933.
41. W. D. Bihl, *Die Kaukasus-Politik der Mittelmaechte*, vol. I (Wien-Köln-Graz 1975), p. 74.
42. Mustafa Ragip Esatli, *Tarihinde Esrar Perdesi* (Istanbul 1975), pp. 400–2, 405. Arbitrary killings by Yakup Cemil in Çorum and Erzurum-Hasankale, annoying the army, are narrated on these pages.
43. A. Mil, Part no. 96.
44. *Ibid.*, Part no. 107.
45. At the time of B. Şakir's communication, while still in Istanbul, Artvin had not yet fallen. Using the phrase, 'not much time had passed,' Mil says that Artvin was evacuated in 23 March. That means that Bahaettin Şakir was in Istanbul at the beginning of March at the latest. *Ibid.*, Part no. 96, 8 February 1934.
46. *Ibid.*, Part no. 98, 10 February 1934.
47. 'Dr Bahaettin Şakir Bey submitted the [documents he had got hold of] to the attention of the HQ of the Committee of Unity and Progress in Istanbul and was engaged in talks on the measures that had to be taken in order to save the army from the great danger.' Ibid., Part no. 100, 12 February 1934.
48. *Ibid.*, Part no. 98, 10 February 1934.
49. *Ibid.*, Part no. 100, 12 February 1934.
50. *Takvimi Vekâyi* 3540, 1st session, main indictment, 27 April 1335.
51. 'Halep Valisi Celal'in Anilari,' *Vakit*, 12 December 1918.
52. *Takvimi Vekâyi* 3540, 1st session, indictment of the Main Trial.
53. Quoted from the written testimony of Vehip Paşa that he gave to the investigating commission on 5.12.1334 (1918). I am in possession of a copy of this testimony, which has been registered at the Armenian Patriarchate in Jerusalem under box 7, file H, no. 171–82. Apart from the Main Trial, this testimony of Vehip Paşa played a decisive part in the Trabzon and Harput trials. In the Trabzon trial the testimony was read out in 29 March 1919 and in the Harput trial a copy was included in the files.
54. *Ibid.*
55. Some examples: Henry Morgenthau, *Ambassasor Morgenthau's Story* (New York, 1919), p. 333; PA-AA/Bo.Kons., volume 170, report by Stange of 23 August 1915; and PA-AA/R 14094, report by Scheubner Richter of 4 December 1916.
56. PA-AA/Bo.Kons., volume 169. Report by Consul Mordtmann of 30 June 1915.
57. Archives of the Armenian Patriarchate in Jerusalem, box 17, file H, no: 616.
58. Archives of the Armenian Patriarchate in Jerusalem, box 21, file M, no: 511.
59. Archives of the Armenian Patriarchate in Jerusalem, box 21 file M, no: 511. On the 9th sessions see: *Renaissance, Yeni Gün, Ikdam*, 23 February 1919.
60. Archives of the Armenian Patriarchate in Jerusalem, box 21, file M, no: 506, *Renaissance*, 7 March 1919.
61. *Takvimi Vekâyi* 3543, 2nd session, 4 May 1335.

62. *Takvimi Vekâyi* 3554, 5th session, 14 May 1335.
63. *Ibid.*
64. *Ibid.*
65. *Alemdar*, 6 May 1919.
66. Main secretary Ragip Bey, Tarih-i Hayatim (Ankara, 1996), pp. 59–60.
67. J. Lepsius, *Der Todesgang des armenischen Volkes*. Bericht über das Schicksal des armenischen Volkes in der *Türkei während des Weltkrieges*, Potsdam 1919, p. 43.
68. General Directorate for the State Archives with the Prime Ministry, *Osmanli Belgelerinde Ermeniler, 1915–1920* (Ankara, 1994), pp. 28–9.
69. Meclisi Ayan Zabit Ceridesi, Period III, Içtima senesi 5, 1st volume (Ankara, 1990), p. 123.
70. *Ikdam*, 5 Kanunu evvel [December] 1918.
71. Testimony of Vehip Paşa, *ibid.*
72. *Alemdar*, 27 March 1919.
73. *Renaissance*, 6 May, Hadisat 7 May 1919. We know that a similar document was published by Andonian, referring to Talât Paşa. Aram Andonian, *Documents officiels concernant les massacres arméniens* (Paris 1920), pp. 16, 57, telegrams of Talât Paşa of 9.3.1915 and 20.2.1916.
74. *Takvimi Vekâyi* 3554, 5th session, 14 May 1335.
75. *Takvimi Vekâyi* 3586, 28 June 1914.
76. *Takvimi Vekâyi* 3772 (Trial of the secretaries in charge, copy of the verdict of 8 January 1920).
77. *Takvimi Vekâyi* 3557, 6th session, 14 May 1335.
78. Archives of the Armenian Patriarchate in Jerusalem, box 21, file M, no. 492.
79. The information can be found in *Takvimi Vekâyi* 3772, the verdict in the trial against the secretaries in charge of 8 January.
80. Great Britain, Foreign Office Archives (London and Kew: Public Records Office), 371/4172/31307, p. 396, report of 10 February 1919.
81. An example can be found in *Takvimi Vekâyi* 3549, 4th session, 8 May 1335.
82. Archives of the Armenian Patriarchate in Jerusalem, box 21, file M, no. 494.
83. *Renaissance*, 6, 7 March 1919.
84. *Tercümani Hakikat*, 5 August 1920; *Vakit*, 6 August 1920.
85. Hüseyin Cahit Yalçin, *Siyasi Anilar* (Istanbul, 1976), p. 236.
86. *Takvimi Vekâyi* 3549, 4th session, 8 May 1335.
87. Ibid.
88. *Alemdar*, 3 August 1919.
89. *Takvimi Vekâyi* 3540, 1st session, indictment of the Main Trial, 27 April 1335.
90. *Takvimi Vekâyi* 3771, 9 February 1920, verdict in the Mamüretülaziz trial.
91. *Takvimi Vekâyi* 3540, 1st session, indictment of the Main Trial, 27 April 1335.
92. *Renaissance* 11, 12 February, Ikdam 11 [February] 1919.
93. *Alemdar*, 25 March 1919.
94. Lepsius, *Der Todesgang*, p. 76.
95. Abidin Nesimi, *Yillarin Içinden,* (Istanbul: Gözlem, 1977), pp. 39–40.
96. *Die Diplomatischen Akten des Auswärigen Amtes*/Botschaft Konstantinopel (PA-AA/Bo.Kons.) volume 69, Telegram of the Consul of Musul, Holstein, of 16 July 1915.
97. *Alemdar*, 11 May 1919.
98. Takvimi Vekâyi 3772, Trial of the secretaries in charge, verdict of 8 January 1920.
99. PA/AA/R 14089, Report by Ambassador Metternich of 7 November 1915.
100. *Takvimi Vekâyi* 3540, 1st session (indictment), 27 April 1335.
101. A.A. Bonn, Bo.Kons. volume 170, telegram of Schmitt of 9 September 1915.

102. *Osmanli Belgelerinde Ermeniler*, 1915–1920, Document No: 71, pp. 68–9.

103. These events are mentioned in the report of the German consul. The information was provided by the governor of Mardin, who was in Diyarbekir at the time. Upon receiving this information, the ambassador approached Talât Paşa for information. In his own telegrams Talât uses the same expressions as in the reports. See PA-AA/Bo.Kons. volume 169, Reports by the Consul of Musul, Holstein, of 10, 15 July 1915; the French text the ambassador gave to Talât on 12 July 1915.

6

The Treaties of Sèvres and Lausanne:
An Alternative Perspective

The prevailing understanding of history in Turkey views Turkey's War of Independence essentially as a war over land and borders. Along very general lines we can characterize this understanding in the following fashion: the events of 1918–23 were a war between the Turks, who desired after the First World War to preserve their sole remaining territory, and other nationalities who wished to divide up this territory among themselves. Turks basically just wanted to preserve the lands and borders defined by the 1918 Mondros Armistice and which they later called the National Pact (*Misak-ı Milli*).[1] In contrast to this, the other nations involved, such as the Armenians, Greeks and Kurds, wanted to establish, with British support, their own national states and to partition Anatolia through an understanding with the British, French and Italians.

The two important agreements that symbolize this understanding of history are the treaties of Sèvres and Lausanne. The Treaty of Sèvres essentially decided the issue of the partition of Anatolia in favor of the non-Turkish nationalities. It is for this reason that, in the eyes of the Turks, Sèvres remains a black mark, and the Ottoman leaders who signed the agreement were sentenced to death as traitors by the resistance movement in Anatolia. As for the other peoples in Anatolia, the Armenians, Greeks and Kurds, although Sèvres did not fully meet their expectations for territory, they saw it as an unprecedented historical opportunity to resolve the issue in their favor. A similar attitude can be seen on the Turkish side with regard to the Treaty of Lausanne. That treaty guaranteed Turkish sovereignty in Anatolia, and therefore for the Turks it stands as a milestone and validation of their continued national existence. Conversely, the other nationalities see it as a great historical injustice.

I believe we can safely say that, were the opinions on Sèvres and Lausanne reversed, all of these groups would accept that all of their struggles, as reflected in the two treaties, were wars for borders and territory. As for the main debate, it revolves around the question of borders and territories from which the various sides should have withdrawn, and of who was justified, and who suffered an injustice. Doubtless, the developments were all inextricably intertwined with the question of how the territories should ultimately be divided up. But this was not the main element that determined subsequent historical developments. In short, there is an alternative, little-known history of Sèvres and Lausanne.

A portrayal of the events of 1918–23 as merely a war for territories and borders does not fully reflect the history as it was experienced. There is another dimension which is equally important and which fundamentally determined the matter of territories and borders. This was the dimension that today would be termed 'human rights.' The thing that in large measure determined the course of events in those years was the Genocide that had been perpetrated by the Ottoman government against its Christian population during the First World War. It is possible to characterize the prevailing mood among the victorious Entente powers as follows: 'the Turks'[2] organized the massacres of other peoples, above all the Armenians, during the First World War. Thus, it was necessary to punish 'the Turks' in order to rescue the other peoples (Arabs, Greeks, Armenians, etcetera) from Turkish domination. Punishing 'the Turks' had to be done in two phases. The first was done by individually trying the members of the Ottoman government and other officials, who were held to be responsible for the crimes carried out against the other religious and national communities. The second was to limit 'the Turks' to a state that would be as small and as weak as possible.

In short, the main ostensible reason for seeking to partition Anatolia among various national groups was the desire to punish 'the Turks' for the barbarities they had committed. That which determined the course of events in the period after 1918 was the perception that 'the Turks' had committed 'crimes against humanity'—in particular because of their massacres of the Armenians—and needed therefore to be punished. The Turkish War for Independence was therefore basically viewed as the result of this accusation and of the consequent desire, on the basis of it, to punish 'the Turks.' Basically, the various sides that took part in the War for Independence can be divided up according to their different views on the issue of punishment.

Conceptualizing history along the axis of human rights and punishing 'the Turks,' as it was described in that period, opens the door to exploring an entirely neglected dimension which up to now has been missing in accounts of the history of the War for Independence. Yet this dimension determined many of the developments of the period. The issue was the massacres that the Ottoman regime perpetrated against non-Muslim communities within the Empire. Although the roots of the ethnic, national and religious hostility stretched far back in Anatolian history, here the concern was, in particular, the events during the First World War. It was the approach taken by the Entente to the question of punishment that determined the character and policies of the Turkish independence movement. As I shall attempt to show here, the Turkish independence movement admitted to the occurrence of the massacres during the World War, but it adopted a very different attitude with regard to the issue of the degree of punishment. In the minds of the movement's leadership, any punishment for these crimes must be limited to trials of the Unionist (Committee of Union and Progress, CUP) leaders who had committed war crimes and massacres during the war years. Even the trials themselves were seen as judicially and politically necessary.

The prevailing approach was not to deny the massacres of the war years, or to consider them as not having taken place at all, as current Turkish histories do, but rather to accept these events openly and fully. At the time, the objection of the Turkish independence movement was not that the victorious powers wished to punish 'the Turks.' Rather, it was that they wished to do so by partitioning Anatolia. Mustafa Kemal perceived the trials against those responsible for the massacres committed during the war years as a necessary price to be paid for the recognition of the National Pact. But the Entente powers' insistence on punishing 'the Turks' as a whole through partition of the country paved the way for resistance and the War for Independence. This is the background for the consistent denial of the human rights dimension in Turkish historiography, even though the human rights issue was as critical as the history of wars over land and borders, and had at times even determined the latter.

My main assertion on this matter is that, had the Entente powers managed to separate the issues of the National Pact and the punishment of those responsible for the crimes committed during wartime, we would today be recounting a very different history. However, the Entente's plans for the partition of Anatolia formed a serious obstacle to this. The Allies preferred to divide it up among themselves in accordance with their own imperial interests, not to punish crimes committed against humanity. It could be argued that they could have punished the war criminals while recognizing the sovereign rights of the Ottomans.

The Views of the Entente Powers
Concerning the Punishment of the Turks

That the losing side in a war will be penalized can almost be taken as a given. The desire of the Entente Powers to punish 'the Turks' can be seen in this light. Four main factors played a decisive role in fostering this desire for punishment. The first was extremely personal. The fierce resistance of the Turks at Gallipoli caused the Entente immense losses in personnel, money and equipment and was at least partially responsible for the war dragging on for another two years. Against subsequent criticisms of the Sèvres Treaty, which claimed that it had made very severe judgments against the Turks, British prime minister David Lloyd George specifically referred to Gallipoli in claiming that 'the Turks' deserved this harsh judgment.[3]

The second factor was the Great Powers' long-held desire to partition the Ottoman state among themselves, which had begun to take on more concrete parameters as the 19th century progressed. These parameters began to take shape with the Congress of Vienna in 1815, in what came to be known as the 'Eastern Question,' which was nothing more, in fact, than the desire for Ottoman lands. The great number of secret agreements concluded immediately before and throughout the First World War is by now well known. The Istanbul Understanding of March–April, 1915, the London Agreement of April 26, 1915, the Sykes–Picot Agreement negotiated between May 9 and 16, 1916, the Agreement of St. Jean de Maurienne of April 17, 1917 are the most important of these deals, which defined the areas of control of the Great Powers within the region, as well as the borders of the states to be newly formed. All in all, we can identify ten different agreements, many of which differed from one another in important details.[4]

We can identify the third factor that contributed to the call to punish 'the Turks' as the 'cultural dimension.' The idea of ejecting 'the Turks' from Europe had been present to some extent in the minds of European states-men, clergy and others since the conquest of Constantinople in 1453. After the 18th century, in particular, this idea became one of the most important cultural–political weapons used by the European powers to establish their domination over the Christian areas within the Ottoman Empire. Concrete political plans were even devised for this ejection. For instance, the Russian czars, who saw themselves as successors and heirs to the Roman and Byzantine empires, continually used this cultural myth as a pretext to rescue Constantinople. After 1774 this myth became a mission and, under the name of the Grand Plan of the Eastern System, plans were devised to topple the Ottoman Empire and establish a Greek state in its place.[5]

Similar ideas were frequently expressed by Lloyd George, who received news of the Turks' entrance into the First World War on the side of the Germans with great glee, believing that this action would grant him the opportunity to settle long-overdue accounts with the Turks. According to Lloyd George, how to cast 'the Turks' out of Europe 'was a problem that had preoccupied the political life of Europe for the last 500 years.' The war and the subsequent defeat of 'the Turks' would now allow Europe the chance 'to resolve this question once and for all.' He believed that it was essential to use 'this opportunity, for which Europe has waited for some 500 years and which wouldn't come again.'[6]

The fourth reason given for the need to punish 'the Turks' was the Armenian Genocide. It should be added here that the idea that it was necessary to expel the Turks from Europe was fundamentally explained throughout the 19th century on the grounds of human rights. It was argued that a nation that had trampled on human rights needed to be cast out of civilized Europe. The words of Lloyd George are relevant here. On November 10, 1914, while explaining that the Ottomans had entered the war on the side of the Germans, he claimed 'to be most pleased that the Turks will finally be called to account for their crimes against humanity.'[7] With the claim of genocide against the Armenians, accusations against Turkey reached their zenith, and those who argued the need to expel 'the Turks' now had compelling grounds. This was because, in Balfour's words, the 'massacres in Armenia and Syria were far more horrible than the previous ones that history has recorded in these unhappy lands.'[8]

The factors that were considered grounds for punishment fell into two main groups, the first being the Great Powers' plans for a colonialist division of Anatolia, and the second, the massacres that the Ottoman government continuously carried out against its own subjects. It is true that the second group, which would today be characterized under the heading of 'human rights', provided an important opportunity for the Great Powers to obscure their colonialist goals behind the mask of 'humanitarian inter-vention.' But it is not correct to view their interventions in this regard as simply an excuse, though when the question of colonial interests and human rights are weighed, the former certainly carried more weight than the latter. It could also be argued that the imperialist interests ultimately produced a reaction in the form of a weakened level of Ottoman support for human rights. The Turkish War for Independence, then, came about against the backdrop of relationship and tension between these two factors.

On May 24, 1915, the European powers declared for the first time that the Ottoman government would be held responsible for the Armenian massacres. When the news reached Europe that a mass slaughter of the Armenians was taking place, a joint announcement was made:

> In light of these crimes, which Turkey has perpetrated against humanity and civilization, the Entente Powers openly inform the Sublime Porte that they will hold the members of the Ottoman Government and their subordinates who are involved in the massacre personally accountable for this crime.[9]

The phrase 'crimes against humanity' was employed as a legal category for the first time, and it was declared that persons who appeared guilty of such crimes would face criminal prosecution, regardless of their official positions or ranks.

In 1915, the British government made two separate announcements that 'the Turks' would be punished, and even declared that one of the most important aims of the war was the punishment of the Turks for the massacres that were committed. On December 18, 1916 the Entente, in a reply to the peace memo of US President Woodrow Wilson, declared that one of its main war objectives was 'to save the nations held captive under the bloody oppressions of the Turks.'[10] Similar words were voiced by the French foreign minister on January 10, 1917: '[t]he lofty war aims include the rescue of peoples now living under the murderous tyranny of the Turks and to uproot and cast out of Europe the Ottoman Empire, which has proven that it is, in extreme measure, foreign to Western Civilization.'[11]

What was the Concrete Understanding of Punishment?

The commander of the British forces in the Caucasus, Milne, expressed the sentiment prevalent among the allies when he said that it was 'necessary to teach the Turks a very harsh lesson.'[12] Lloyd George said that 'when the peace terms were announced, it would be seen just how much greater was the punishment faced by the Turks than their own madness, blindness and crimes...The punishments are horrible enough to sufficiently please even their greatest enemies.'[13] Lord Curzon, the British foreign secretary during that period, characterized Turkey as 'a criminal awaiting sentencing.'[14] With the Mondros Armistice, 'the bringing to freedom of the peoples who have lived a long life of captivity subjected to arbitrary rule and massacres' became the most fundamental demand of Western public opinion. Heading the 'list of abominations and crimes [committed by the Turks]...was the massacre of the Armenian and Greek populations.'[15] But what did it mean, in concrete terms, to punish the Turks? What did it mean to punish a nation for massacres?

Already in a speech he made on December 20, 1917, Lloyd George expressed very openly what he thought should be one dimension of the punishment: 'What is to be in Mesopotamia must be left until the convening of the Paris Congress. But there is one thing that will absolutely not be repeated. The bloody dictatorship of the Turks shall never be restored.'[16] The attitude on this matter became clearer after the war. A telegram sent to the Paris Peace Conference on April 3, 1919 by the Assistant High Commissioner of Istanbul, Webb, reads as follows:

In order to punish all of those persons who are guilty of the Armenian horrors, it is necessary to punish the Turks as a group. Therefore, I propose that the punishment be given on a national level through the partitioning up of the last Turkish Empire, and on a personal level by trying those high officials who are on the list in my possession, and in a manner that would serve as an example for their successors.[17]

Thus, from the Allies' point of view, two important goals had appeared that were directed at punishing 'the Turks': dividing Anatolia between various countries and peoples, and trying those who appeared guilty of war crimes and massacres. Yet, when we review the works written in Turkey on the Paris Peace Conference, we discover that only the discussions concerning the partition of Anatolia are examined. It is impossible to find any work that mentions the talks that were held on the question of how the war criminals were to be tried. Nevertheless, a commission was established at the talks that focused on this subject and this subject alone, and within it was debated the question of which legal framework could be used to try the German emperor, Kaiser Wilhelm II, members of the Ottoman government and other responsible persons, in connection with those crimes described as crimes against humanity.

For the first time ever, the issue was tied to a decision taken at a meeting held in mid-January between the five victorious powers (the USA, Britain, France, Italy and Japan), and through a proposal made there a commission to examine the matter was established on January 18, 1919. The commission, which was established as the Commission on the Responsibility of the Authors of the War and the Enforcement of Penalties, was known informally as the Commission of 15, and was entrusted with determining who was to be accused of war crimes, as well as the statutes and rulings that could be legally employed against them. The commission, which carried out its activities by separating itself into three sub-commissions, sought to resolve such problems as how to reveal publicly who was responsible for and instigated the war; how to determine how the laws and customs of war had been neglected and by whom; how to determine who was responsible for these crimes; and how the accused were to be tried.

Apart from the question of trying the German Kaiser, the problem that most occupied the commission was how the Turks who carried out the massacres could be brought to trial. The commission was able to reach a unanimous decision on the question of Germany having begun the war, as a result of its mobilization and preparations. Along with Germany, Turkey and Bulgaria were found guilty of having consciously instigated the war.[18] The concluding sentence of the relevant section states that 'The war was conducted by the Central Empires and their allies, Turkey and Bulgaria, in barbaric fashion and through illegal methods which violated established laws, customs of war and the principles of humanity.'[19]

An important section of the commission's report dealt with the public revelation of actions contrary 'to the laws and customs of war' and to 'the laws of humanity.' Among these actions, those taken during the war by the Ottoman state against its Greek and Armenian populations were listed one by one. These acts were described as 'primitive barbarism' and were said to have been planned by a terrorist system and carried through to the end. In classifying these crimes, the commission divided the actions into two categories. In the first category, which would be considered war crimes in the classical sense, were crimes perpetrated by one state against the soldiers of another state, and against another state's civilian citizens within areas that it had occupied. The second category, however, was for crimes that Germany and Turkey had perpetrated against their own citizens, in areas under their own sovereignty, in particular the massacres and similar acts that the Turks had carried out against the Armenians and Greeks. Thus, the commission had, for the first time, made a clear division between war crimes and crimes against humanity.

Despite their extensive efforts, the commission failed to reach a consensus both on the matter of which legal principles the suspects should be tried under and even on the question of what should be done in regard to the alleged war criminals. The crimes committed by the Unionists had been perpetrated against their own citizens, and no international agreement existed on this issue. At the end of the commission's deliberations on this matter, it was argued that it would be necessary to accept a new category for war crimes, for even though no international law existed that identified actions taken by a state against its own citizens as crimes, it was painfully evident that such actions were contrary 'to the laws of humanity and morality.' The commission based its decision on the Hague Convention of 1907, which stated that even in situations in which laws of war did not exist or in which clear rules had not yet been constituted, action could be taken on the basis of 'established customs that existed between civilized peoples, the laws of humanity and the demands of the public's conscience.' In this manner the decision to try 'the Turks' became dependent on the principles of humanity advanced by the Hague Convention. Additionally, the commission's report stated that 'everyone from the hostile countries who was found guilty of crimes against the laws and customs of war or against the laws of humanity, including government ministers, no matter how high their position and regardless of their rank, shall be subject to criminal prosecution.'[20]

The questions of the determination of guilt and the classification of crimes were generally not a source of division between the commission members, although on the issue of prosecution of war crimes and massacres before an international tribunal a sharp difference of opinion emerged within the commission. There was consensus on the moral imperative of indicting and prosecuting persons committing such crimes. The entire disagreement centered on the questions of whether or not to create an international tribunal, or one made up of representatives of the Entente powers, and what the authority of such a court would be.

A significant question in this debate was whether or not individuals would be held accountable for crimes committed in the name of the state. It was demanded that, in the case of Germany, the Kaiser be personally tried, and in the case of the Ottoman Empire, that the CUP leaders be tried as personally responsible for the Armenian massacres. The Laws of Nations, which were in force in 1914, contained no statute whatsoever with regard to the question of whether or not a political act performed on behalf of a state could be criminally investigated and prosecuted. What could be done was to create legal arrangements that would make it possible to undertake criminal investigations for this type of action, which was understood to be contrary to the basic principles of the laws of nations. However the rule of positive law, according to which a new law could not be applied to transgressions retroactively, effectively blocked this option. The Americans announced that they had no doubt that similar acts committed in the future would constitute a crime according to the laws of nations, and that those perpetrating these crimes should be prosecuted. In the end, the commission agreed that the path to such prosecutions was open in light of the fundamental principles of the 1907 Convention. The discussions concluded with the Americans vetoing the commission's decision.

The commission finished its report on March 29, 1919, and the matter was then examined within the highest committee, where the discussions continued until it became apparent that the entire peace talks would break down over the issue. Finally the Americans abandoned their obstinacy and on April 9, 1919, the members of the Paris Peace Conference agreed to establish an international court on the basis of a proposal prepared by President Wilson.[21] Following the American delegation's demand, it was decided that the persons were to be tried only for 'crimes committed in contravention of the laws of war' but not for crimes in the category of 'crimes against humanity.' The burden of trying such cases was given to the military courts that the Allies would establish. Wilson himself admitted that the points that had been accepted were very weak, and that the whole issue of international tribunals had been put in an impossible position.[22]

In the end, articles relating to the issue were placed in the agreements made with the relevant countries. According to these articles, the Entente powers retained the right among themselves to try war criminals in an international court. Provisions to require the surrendering to the Entente powers of both those persons accused of committing war crimes and the documents relevant to this subject were included in the various peace agreements. Articles 227–230 of the Versailles Treaty (June 28, 1919) made with Germany, and Articles 226-230 of the Sèvres Agreement (August 10, 1920) made with the Ottoman state were all concerned with the prosecution of war criminals. The articles in the Treaty of Sèvres read:

Article 226: The Turkish Government recognizes the right of the Allied Powers to bring before military tribunals persons accused of having committed acts in violation of the laws and customs of war. Such persons shall, if found guilty, be sentenced to punishments laid down by law. This provision will apply notwithstanding any proceedings or prosecution before a tribunal in Turkey or in the territory of her allies. The Turkish Government shall hand over to the Allied Powers or to such one of them as shall so request all persons accused of having committed an act in violation of the laws and customs of war, who are specified either by name or by the rank, office or employment which they held under the Turkish authorities.

Article 227: Persons guilty of criminal acts against the nationals of one of the Allied Powers shall be brought before the military tribunals of that Power. Persons guilty of criminal acts against the nationals of more than one of the Allied Powers shall be brought before military tribunals composed of members of the military tribunals of the Powers concerned. In every case the accused shall be entitled to name his own counsel.

Article 228: The Turkish Government undertakes to furnish all documents and information of every kind, the production of which may be considered necessary to ensure the full knowledge of the incriminating acts, the prosecution of offenders and the just appreciation of responsibility.

Article 230: The Turkish Government undertakes to hand over to the Allied Powers the persons whose surrender may be required by the latter as being responsible for the massacres committed during the continuance of the state of war on territory which formed part of the Turkish Empire on August 1, 1914. The Allied Powers reserve to themselves the right to designate the tribunal which shall try the persons so accused, and the Turkish Government undertakes to recognize such tribunal. In the event of the League of Nations having created in sufficient time a tribunal competent to deal with the said massacres, the Allied Powers reserve to themselves the right to bring the accused persons mentioned above before such tribunal, and the Turkish Government undertakes equally to recognize such tribunal.[23]

The idea of trying 'those accused of war crimes and massacres,' which was first expressed within the framework of 'crimes against humanity,' was never fully implemented due to the different approaches of the Entente powers to the issue. As a result, they satisfied themselves with the national courts which appeared in Leipzig and Istanbul. However, subsequent discussions on the issue did help to create the necessary legal framework for the prosecution of the Nazi leaders at Nuremberg. The relevant principles were made into international legal norms by the United Nations on December 9, 1948, by inserting them into the first section of its agreements on preventing Genocide and punishing those responsible for committing it. The whole point of the issue is that when 'human rights' are employed as a key concept in explaining historical events, the concept of crimes against humanity was used for the first time in the most clear and open manner against 'the Turks.' Additionally, the principles of holding those who had perpetrated crimes against humanity personally responsible, regardless of their position or authority, and of legally prosecuting them for such was also first raised with regard to 'the Turks.'

Attitudes toward Punishing 'the Turks'

Both the Ottoman government in Istanbul and the government established by the nationalist forces in Anatolia accepted that, using today's terminology, 'crimes against humanity' had been committed during the First World War. They referred to these crimes as 'the crimes that occurred during the Forced Deportation (*tehcir*)' and as 'the massacre (*kıtal*),' and argued for the absolute need to punish the guilty. They knew that, for them, achieving a more beneficial outcome from the Paris Peace Talks would be conditional upon the steps that 'the Turks' would take in punishing those responsible for the massacres. The commanders of the Entente forces who arrived in Istanbul in order to supervise the armistice conditions warned from the very outset that it was necessary to act swiftly and without mercy on this matter. On February 8, 1919, for instance, the French general Franchet d'Esperéy, who arranged the ceremony marking the occupation of Istanbul on his white horse, summoned the Grand Vizier, Tevfik Paşa, before him and warned him, 'If your government does not demonstrate determined action [against the previous regime], the judgment that will be given in regard to it will be grave in the extreme.'[24]

On this matter the British were even more severe. In response to various appeals made to them, they took extra care to send the message continually that 'the Turks' would be punished. On January 18, 1919, High Commissioner Calthorpe told the Ottoman foreign minister that 'His Majesty's Government is resolved on the matter of properly punishing those responsible for the Armenian massacres.'[25] Ten days later a cable was sent to London, informing the British government that 'the [Ottoman] Government...has been informed that the British statesmen have promised the civilized world that those persons connected to this affair (i.e., the massacres) shall be held personally accountable, and that His Majesty's Government is entirely resolved to fulfill its promise.'[26]

The British Occupation Forces behaved in markedly proper and cold fashion toward the Ottoman government. In the first months of the occupation, all of the Sultan's attempts to establish some sort of relations, both with the High Commissioner and with the General Staff Headquarters, were rebuffed.[27] In reply to a question by Said Molla, the founder of the Turkish–English Friendship Society, regarding 'the reason for such noticeably cold behavior toward Turkey on the part of the British High Commissioner,' an official said that this was due to the 'desire to avoid raising even the slightest doubt in the mind of a single Turk that the sentence…against Turkey…would be extremely severe.'[28]

After the armistice in October 1918 a new government was established in Istanbul drawn mostly from anti-Unionist circles. After a short period of time, however, Istanbul lost its control over Anatolia because of the increasing strength of the Turkish nationalist movement. Towards the end of 1919 there were two different powers within the Ottoman Empire. The Turkish nationalist movement, founded mostly by old CUP members, established a central organ (the Representative Committee) after a series of congresses in Erzurum (July 1919) and Sivas (September 1919); it resided later in Ankara (December 1919). The relation between the Ottoman government and the nationalist movement in Anatolia changed from time to time according to the character of the government in Istanbul. In certain periods there was strong cooperation, and at other times the tension was very high, and there was even armed conflict.

Both the Istanbul and Ankara regimes knew the attitudes of the Entente powers on the matter, and were in agreement on the need to punish those guilty of war crimes and massacres. But the main outstanding question was the extent of the punishment. Ankara and Istanbul generally agreed that any punishment must be limited to those leaders of the CUP involved and members of the government. Above all, punishment absolutely must not take the form of dividing up the sovereign territories of the Ottoman state.

Even for Grand Vizier Damad Ferid Paşa, who was perhaps the most ardent Ottoman advocate of punishment, the responsible parties were three fugitive individuals: Talat, Enver and Cemal. In truth, there are also a few secondary accomplices.' But that was it. And an entire nation could not be held accountable for 'one or two good-for-nothings (*serseri*)'. 'The innocent Turkish nation is exempt from the stain of tyranny (*şaibe-yi zülumden muarra*).'[29] Damad Ferid Paşa explained this view at the Paris Peace Talks: 'The entire guilt clearly belongs to a handful of leaders of the [Committee of] Union and Progress, who, by means of their alliance with Germany and their control of the army, terrorized everyone in Turkey other than themselves and subdued them.'[30] In a memorandum he submitted to the Council of Ten, Damad Ferid Paşa announced that he was decisively opposed to the partitioning of Turkey on account of what had occurred during the war. 'The Ottoman Government shall not accept the partitioning of the Empire or its being divided up as various mandates.'[31] The Grand Vizier's attitude was met with surprise and irritation by the Entente Powers. '[President] Wilson announced that he had not seen anything more nonsensical than this. As for Lloyd George, he characterized the memorandum as "a good joke."'[32]

In the reply they gave to the memorandum in June, the Council of Ten made it abundantly clear that 'the Turks' would not be able to save themselves as a nation from responsibility, and announced that the responsibility for the slaughter would be borne by the Turkish people as a whole. 'The Turkish people have, by murdering the Armenians without any cause, descended into a condition of guilt. Therefore, the responsibility shall be met entirely by the Turkish people.'[33] 'In the Council's written reply it rejects the idea of the innocence of the Turkish people, and expresses the view that "a nation must be valued according to the government that rules it."'[34]

Various Attitudes on the Question of War Guilt

Among the Turks a number of different attitudes appeared on the question of whether or not entry into the war constituted a crime. While the Istanbul governments of Damad Ferid Paşa and others were exploiting the idea that the CUP had, in adventurous fashion, hurled the nation into the war,[35] the nationalist movement in Ankara was adopting a sharply different attitude from this. The idea was being propounded there that entry into the war should not be considered a crime, and furthermore, that the country had been forced into the war against its will. This stance was expressed in meetings held with the Ali Rıza Paşa government, which came to power on October 2, 1919.

The government in Istanbul sent a cable to the leader of the nationalist movement, Mustafa Kemal, in Sivas and proposed certain preconditions for being able to begin discussions with the Representative Committee that was formed after the Sivas Congress of September 4–11, 1919. According to this cable, the Representative Committee would first have to make declarations along the lines of '(1) it did not have relations with [the Unionists or] Unionism, (2) that it had been wrong for the Ottoman State to enter the World War and that certain publications [should] be made against those responsible [for entering the war], through the naming of names, and they [should be] legally prosecuted and punished, (3) that the actors in all manner of offense perpetrated during the war should not be able to escape legal retribution.' It was proposed that these articles were indispensable to the country's interests, 'because their explanation and distribution would prevent certain misunderstandings, both at home and abroad.'[36]

Mustafa Kemal gave a lengthy reply to these demands, stating openly what he did not understand about war guilt. In it he argued that there should not be punishment for having entered the war; he said the nationalist movement in Anatolia rejected out of hand the idea that the country could be considered guilty for the following reason. 'It certainly would have been far more desirable not to enter the World War. But there existed no material possibility of this.' A number of reasons (the impossibility of maintaining the neutrality of the Bosphorus Straits during wartime; the lack of funds, industry, and other means necessary to maintain this neutrality, etcetera), and, in particular, the existence of plans on the part of the Entente Powers to divide up the Ottoman state, 'were among the clear evidence showing that it would have been impossible to refrain from entering the war against the Entente States.' Therefore, it was incorrect 'to interpret our entry into the war as a crime, and to imagine that a great nation would be merely a plaything for four or five persons.' In such a case, it was clear what needed to be done: 'to courageously speak the truth, and, while this great nation, which struggled heroically, is enduring the bitter fruits of defeat (*netayic-i zaruriyesi*), not to accept the interpretation of its actions as a crime, or that it should be accused and punished on this account.'[37]

In the talks held in Amasya between October 20 and 22, 1919, Ankara retreated somewhat on this matter, placing in the joint protocol that was signed the following article: 'The government does not object to interpretations as to whether or not it was appropriate to enter the war. But it is currently necessary for the country's well-being to conceal such interpretations that would find this entry [into the war] appropriate.'[38] Despite the different opinions that were found there, it should be added that Mustafa Kemal also 'argued that the group who perpetrated the administrative evils and abuses and threw the country into ruin consisted of only a small clique (*hizb-i kalil*) from among the Unionists, and that these persons should be prosecuted.'[39]

After these negotiations, elections were held, and a parliament was convened in Istanbul on January 12, 1920. Mustafa Kemal struggled to establish a faction loyal to the Anatolian government within the new Chamber of Deputies. In the draft text that he had prepared for this group, Kemal argued that prosecutions for war crimes and massacres should be limited only to members of the government then in power, saying '…we absolutely demand that legal proceedings be undertaken in regard to those cabinets which bear the responsibility for entering the war and which forcibly invalidated the Constitution.'[40]

Attitudes Regarding Those Guilty of Massacre

In regard to the question of punishing those guilty of the Armenian Genocide, the attitudes of the Ankara and Istanbul governments were the same in principle. In a reply to Istanbul during the two governments' September correspondence, it was stated that

> it is our fervent hope (*ehassi amalimiz*) to see [the exposure and punishment of those responsible for the massacres], and that in our homeland responsibility is shared by both the young and the old, and that the era of law (*kanun devri*) has begun through [a] completely impartial and fair [system of] justice' (*tamamen bitarafane ve kemali adlü hakkaniyetle*).

Beyond this, it appeared 'more appropriate and beneficial for these punishments to be revealed to both friend and foe (*yârü ağyar*) through their actual implementation, rather than their mere publication in the press as notices, something that would give rise to a good number of heated debates.'[41] What was expected, then, was not that the punishments simply be announced, but that they be carried out as well.

The issue of trying those responsible for the massacres was discussed at the Amasya talks. During the discussions five protocols—three open and signed, two secret and unsigned—were attached to the final decision. The first protocol, dated October 21, 1919, stated that 'the reawakening of the idea of Unionism, of the Union and Progress [Party] in the country, and even the witnessing of certain signs [of this] are politically detrimental ...the legal prosecution of those who perpetrated a crime (*irtikab*) by means of the Deportation (*Tehcir*) is judicially and politically necessary.'[42] The third protocol[43] dealt with the elections that were to be held, and in it an understanding was reached on the need to prevent those Unionists who were being sought in connection with the Armenian Genocide from participating in the elections. For this the Anatolian government secretly retained the right to intervene in the elections, because, in the words of Mustafa Kemal,

> it would be improper for individuals who are connected to the evil deeds of the Unionists, or persons who have been sullied by the nefarious acts of the deportation and massacre or other wicked actions that are contrary to the true interests of the nation and the country to be found among the council of deputies that will convene. All possible means may be resorted to in order to prevent such an occurrence.[44]

As we have seen, both Ankara and Istanbul believed that those who had perpetrated 'war crimes and massacres' should be prosecuted since both hoped thereby to attain a more positive outcome from the Paris Peace Talks. This fact was clearly stated in the protocols, which expressed the idea that the Entente states were hostile to the CUP, and therefore if the two governments did not take strong measures against the Unionists, it would have a negative effect on the Paris Peace Conference. This 'might well be a disaster for the country' and it was therefore necessary to prevent 'complaints and interventions from being made against us.'[45] This was the prevailing mood of the period. On January 23, 1919, certain political leaders presented a formal request to the Sultan, informing him that they saw the punishment of those guilty of war crimes and massacre as absolutely necessary (şart).[46] Meanwhile, in the press, we frequently find articles discussing 'what they think abroad.'[47]

Instead of the political division of Anatolia, what the Turks wanted was for an agreement to be made along the lines of those made with Germany and Bulgaria, whereby the existing borders of those states were not touched.[48] The Allied Powers' plans for punishment met opposition over both their intention of partitioning Anatolia, and their proposal to try the perpetrators of war crimes and massacres before an international tribunal. Any such trials, the Turks insisted, must be carried out in accordance with Ottoman Law. When the British began arresting Turkish officers in December 1918, and trying them in the courts they had set up in the occupied areas, the Ottoman government sent notes protesting the trials.[49] Even later, the government continued to insist that those accused of massacres must be tried according to Ottoman law.[50]

A similar stance was taken by the government in Ankara. In their discussions with the British on the question of returning those CUP members exiled to Malta, the Turkish government in Ankara repeated three times within a six-month period its promise that those accused of massacre would be tried on the basis of the national laws of the Ottoman state, if Britain released them to Turkey. The promise was given for the first time during Turkish foreign minister Bekir Sami's London meetings in March, 1921.[51] But in the understanding that was reached, it was decided that the trials would be administered by the British. This decision caused the Ankara government to reject the agreement. 'Our government cannot have approved and ratified such an agreement, because to ratify such an agreement would have been to ratify a manner of jurisdiction by a foreign government over actions within Turkey.'[52] It was reported to Lord Curzon on July 28 that Yusuf Kemal Tengirşenk, who had since replaced Bekir Sami as foreign minister, would not sign the London agreement 'because it was a violation of Turkey's sovereignty over its citizens.'[53]

The second promise in regard to the trials of those accused of massacres was given on June 11, 1921 by the Istanbul government's foreign minister Safa in the name of the Ankara government.

The Turkish Government in Istanbul proposes, in the name of the Turkish Nationalists, to call on the British Ambassador to release all of those held on Malta. It declares that, just as was done to the German prisoners in Germany, those [Ottomans who stand] accused must be tried by an impartial court in Ankara.[54]

The third and final promise was given directly by Refet Bele, the Interior Minister of the Ankara government, to General Harrington on September 14, 1921. As Harrington informed the Ministry of War:

I am here and at this moment receiving, in the capacity of an unofficial representative, a firm promise from the Ankara Government's Interior Minister, Refet Bele, that we shall send all of the detainees back from the port by a 15-day march, in order that they shall be tried by their own countries for the causes of which they are charged.[55]

In short, it was admitted that crimes had been committed during the war, but it was demanded that prosecution for these crimes be limited to the CUP leaders and members of the wartime Ottoman government, and that the trials be performed in accordance with the Ottoman legal system. Any sort of punishment that would entail the partition of Anatolia was sharply rejected. The main point that determined this attitude was the hope that, as a result of such trials, a more favorable outcome to the Paris Peace Talks would be attained. In other words, the National Pact would be preserved.

The first concrete steps toward trying those accused of war crimes and massacres were taken by the Istanbul government. As we observed in the Amasya Protocols, the Ankara government adopted a supportive attitude. However, when the Entente powers refused to forgo their plans to divide up Anatolia, Ankara abandoned this stance and instead adopted one openly opposed to the trials.

The Armenian Genocide
as a Handicap for the Anatolian Movement

Foremost among the problems confronting the leaders of the Turkish War for Independence was the claim that they themselves were merely the continuation of the Unionist regime that had carried out the Armenian Genocide. They were regularly accused of organizing similar massacres against the Christian population. The opponents of the Anatolian movement, in particular, spread a great deal of propaganda to this effect. Against this, explanations continued to be made throughout the entire period that the movement was not made up of Unionists, and that one of the movement's founding principles was proper treatment of the remaining Christian population. In short, proving that they were not Unionists and that there was no question of them carrying out massacres against the Christians, as the Unionists had, was one of the most important issues throughout the Turkish War for Independence, and one that determined the character of the movement and the war.

A great deal of coverage was devoted to this issue in the Western press. For example, the movement that arose in Erzurum to protect the eastern provinces was characterized as a second annihilation operation against the Armenians; it was repeatedly stated in the Western press that the Erzurum Congress had been organized 'in order to attack the Armenian Republic,' and that the Turkish army was prepared to 'root out the Armenians in the Caucasus in order to prevent the possibility of establishing an Armenian state.'[56] Literally hundreds of reports appeared in the Western press reporting that 'the Turks' had initiated a new slaughter of Christians. 'While the decisions of the Peace Conference were being announced, the Eastern Christians feared another large-scale massacre.'[57]

Another example comes from a February 1919 issue of *Journal des Débats*, which describes the situation as one in which 'the massacres, tortures and all manner of oppression against the Christian population of the villages is continuing apace...' These reports were accompanied by others that the CUP was active in Anatolia. On February 15, 1919, *Le Temps* reported that 'the Union and Progress Party is continuing its efforts in Anatolia...The aim is to liquidate the Christian land owners. A new massacre is looming.'[58] Hardly a day passed without the papers printing headlines such as 'The Tyranny of the Turks in Asia Minor,' 'Greeks killed by the Turks,' 'Tortures against the Greeks of Thrace' and 'Greek children massacred in Aydın.' The Kemalist forces were accused of 'planning to utterly uproot the Armenians' and of 'making preparations for a general massacre.'[59]

The Ankara government knew full well that its chances for success would largely depend on how it fared on these two points. By using every means at its disposal, the movement waged an extensive war of propaganda against the claims that it was preparing for new slaughters and attacks against the Christian population. In his report, General Harbord recounts that he was given assurances on precisely this subject:

> Mustafa Kemal Paşa has assured me in no uncertain terms that this national movement has no intention of assaulting and inflicting violence on the non-Muslims. Also, he said that a declaration would be published in order to dispel the fear and confusion into which the Armenian citizens have fallen, and has fulfilled his promise by publishing it.[60]

Likewise, Kemal himself repeated that this promise had been given, when he recounted the meeting with Harbord to Kazım Karabekir Paşa:

General Harbord came here yesterday with his entourage. At his request, we spoke totally confidentially for 3–4 hours...Future notes were communicated in the explanation-filled responses that were given at length to the questions asked...We are not conspiring against the Armenians, or against any of the non-Muslim communities who live within our country. On the contrary, we are completely respectful of all of their natural rights. Any reports to the contrary are the result of meddling or British delusions.[61]

As part of the agreement that was reached, a written text was given to Harbord on September 24, and in it, along with a reiteration that the movement had no connection to Unionism, the following promise was given in regard to the Christian population: 'We have no other view or sensibility than to nourish the best intentions and sincere feelings in regard to our non-Muslim citizens (Armenians, Greeks, Jews, etc.), with whom we have lived together for a very long time, and to consider them as our complete equals.'[62] Also, on the same date Mustafa Kemal made a similar promise in an interview he gave to the *USA Radio Gazette*: 'We have no plans to expand whatsoever...*We guarantee that there will be no new Turkish terror against the Armenians* [italics mine].'[63] Similar declarations, which were a type of admission of those past occurrences, were given to Turkish newspapers: 'the national organization harbors no hidden designs against the non-Muslim communities.'[64]

Due to the accumulation of reports of Armenian massacres in the Western press and to the accusations of the Armenian Patriarch in particular, the Representative Committee took a number of decisions to the effect that this was simply propaganda, and the Ankara government initiated efforts to state in the presence of both the Istanbul government and the representatives of foreign countries that these accusations were baseless. On September 16, 1919, for instance, 'a decision was taken to compose a general memorandum stating that the national organization was not against non-Muslim communities or foreigners. On the 24th another decision was taken, this time to deliver an announcement to the commissioners of the Entente states as well as to the embassies of the neutral countries stating that the national movement was not opposed to the non-Muslim communities.'[65]

But Ankara's concern was not only for propaganda. It was well aware that one bad incident could bring extremely negative results in regard to its own interests. Indeed, one of the reasons that prompted the British to occupy Istanbul on March 16, 1920, was the claim that such massacres had occurred in the Maraş region in the first two months of the year. While speaking at the Paris Peace Talks of the need to occupy Istanbul, Lord Curzon listed punishing 'the Turks' for the Maraş massacre as the most important reason for such action.[66] Because of this, almost immediately after the Entente powers' occupation of Istanbul, the subject was addressed in the Representative Committee's first circular sent to the provinces. After declaring that 'the value of the humanitarian treatment that we display toward the Christian population living in our country today is great indeed,' it announced that anyone who perpetrated evil acts against the Christians would be punished in the severest manner.[67]

In a speech he made to the Grand National Assembly one year later, Mustafa Kemal recalled the importance of this circular:

> In spite of the murderous assaults of regular and irregular Armenian forces in Cilicia and its environs, as well as beyond our eastern border, against those with whom we share religion and race, we have understood it to be an important civilized duty to safeguard from all manner of assault those innocent Armenians who peacefully reside within our country…We have informed all of our [regional government] offices of the need to protect the well-being of the Armenian population.[68]

As to the result that was to be achieved in connection with adopting such measures, Kemal boasted:

> Not a single individual from the Anatolian Armenians, who have not received the protection of any other state, has been subjected to even the simplest violation, during the days of anguish which have continued from the occupation of Istanbul until today. This is a very important point that will redden the faces of intriguing Europe, which has at every turn imputed that we were criminals and has [claimed to have a] monopoly on civilized sensibilities, and will prove the sublime level of the humane traits that our nation innately possesses.[69]

Because he was aware that this type of accusation had been made over the massacres that took place between 1915 and 1917, Mustafa Kemal adopted an attitude that was sensitive and critical in the extreme on the topic of the massacres; he used every opportunity when speaking with representatives of the Western countries to declare the need to try those accused of such crimes. While speaking with General Harbord, who had been sent by President Wilson to study the political, military and financial dimensions of a possible US mandate for the Armenians, Kemal admitted that some 800,000 Armenians had been killed. The fact that Kemal gave this figure is significant, because a commission appointed by Ottoman interior minister Mustafa Arif [Değmer] in December 1918 had grappled with the issue of publishing a figure for the Armenians killed according to ministry records. The results of the inquiry that was subsequently carried out were announced by interior minister Cemal on March 13, 1919. According to him, the number of Armenians killed during the deportations was 800,000.[70] This declaration provoked a great response.[71] Harbord said of Mustafa Kemal that 'he also condemns the slaughter of the Armenians.'[72]

According to Kemal, 'the killing and deportation of the Armenians [was] the work of a small committee that seized control of the government.'[73]

Kemal's critical talk in regard to the Armenian massacres was not only for the consumption of Western representatives. In a long speech that he gave on convoking the Assembly on April 24, he openly condemned the massacres, referring to them as a 'shameful act [fazahat] of the past,' while harshly criticizing the accusations—especially by the British—'that a calamity such as this was [still] being carried out' in Turkey.[74] A similar tone can be detected in a cable he sent to Kazım Karabekir on May 6, 1920, in which we see the importance Mustafa Kemal attached to the image of Turkey abroad. What he most feared in a war against the Armenian state was to be accused by the Western powers of 'carrying out a massacre.' He proposed delaying the campaign, which had already been planned, simply to avoid such accusations. In the aforementioned cable, he says that one 'of the most important factors turning the entire world of Christendom against us is the Armenian deeds,' and that if they were 'to destroy the Armenian government, which has been both accepted and confirmed by us, by the force of our arms,' it would be interpreted 'naturally, as a new slaughter of the Armenians.' Thus, such a military action had to be halted, because if such a thing were done 'by us' [the reaction] would be very bad.[75]

Many more examples could be given. Nevertheless, we can now draw the conclusion that the massacres perpetrated by the Unionist leaders during the First World War were one of the main issues of concern for the Anatolian national movement. Furthermore, the nationalist leaders saw accusations by the West against themselves of further massacres as a great injustice.

An Attempt at a Conclusion

If we were forced to characterize the events that transpired between 1918 and 1923 with two general theoretical concepts, these would be the questions of national sovereignty and human rights, and of interference in the sovereign rights of states that violate such rights, as well as the clear conflict between these two principles. On the one hand, both the Ankara and Istanbul governments saw themselves as heirs to the Ottoman state, and both desired a continuation of Ottoman sovereignty over the areas not occupied under the 1918 Mondros Agreement. Indeed, the National Pact was formulated as a written expression of this understanding of sovereignty. On the other hand, there were the crimes of the war years. To advocate the need to try those accused of such offenses according to international legal principles and to actually carry this out were in conflict with the principle of the sovereign rights of the state. As we know from the examples of Nazi Germany and the events in the former states of Yugoslavia, such a situation makes interference in the internal affairs of the nation-state unavoidable. The Turkish side wanted to see the trials of the accused conducted under national law. The Entente powers, on the other hand, saw the partition of Anatolia as one aspect of the punishment meted out for crimes against humanity. The Turkish War for Independence came against the background of tension between the issues of the rights of national sovereignty and that of the crimes being prosecuted by national or international courts. Over time, the issues of partitioning Anatolia between the occupational and Entente powers and trying those guilty of the massacres merged into one and the same thing.

The principal actors of the period failed to keep these two events separate. (Whether or not they actually wanted to is a different question). The Entente powers' wish to divide up Anatolia pushed them to adopt an unenthusiastic stance toward the issue of the trials. This raises an important question: if the Entente Powers had simultaneously recognized trying those accused of carrying out the massacres and the National Pact, and had proposed a recognition of the Turks' rights of national sovereignty in exchange for their consent and cooperation on the issue of trying the accused, might things have turned out differently?

It could be argued that, in the absence of a plan to partition Anatolia, and especially in light of Greece's invasion of western Asia Minor in 1919, it would have been possible to achieve a markedly different outcome in regard to prosecuting and punishing the crimes against humanity of the war years, and we would today be recounting a very different history. This is not merely a theoretical argument. There are more than enough indications that such a scenario was entirely within the realm of possibility, from the standpoint both of the Turks and of the Entente powers.

Andrew Ryan, who worked in the British High Commission, claimed that 'the Turks' were very exhausted during the period of the first armistice, and 'would have gladly welcomed a peace, regardless of the condition of most of the people.' We have separate confirmation of this assessment in a speech made in the National Assembly in Ankara on April 27, 1920 by Fevzi Paşa, who served as foreign minister in the Istanbul government, and who later joined the Anatolian movement: 'I have said to the British with all sincerity, 'You cannot achieve anything by threats...We are prepared to do anything and everything, if you recognize our right to life.'[76] It was this failure to recognize the right to life, that is, the right of sovereignty, which had spurred Fevzi Paşa to flee to Anatolia. In particular, it was the occupation of Izmir and the plans for partition that produced a hardening of previously flexible attitudes on the issue of peace. The British General Staff noted this situation:

A very great section of the population is weary of the war in the full sense of the term. But it will nevertheless be prepared to fight most bitterly in order to prevent a portion of their land being given to either Greece or Armenia...With the expansion of the areas under occupation, the rebellion will also continue apace.[77]

Within the Entente states themselves, there were circles that advocated very different policies from those implemented on the issue of the sovereign rights of the Ottoman state. More precisely stated, different views on the subject were expressed at different periods. In 1918, both Wilson and Lloyd George made statements that were mindful of the principle of the sovereignty of the Ottoman state. The twelfth of Wilson's Fourteen Points, which on January 8, 1918 he declared as the US's peace objectives, advocated the establishment of an independent Turkish state in the areas in which the Turkish population was the majority. In its subsequent efforts toward preparing for the peace talks, the US formulated its policy on Turkey as follows: 'The existence of Turkey as a separate state will continue under a Turkish government. This may be the existing government, or it may well be another government.'[78] Three days earlier, Lloyd George had said that '[the British] are not fighting in order to leave the Turks bereft of their capital, or their wealthy and famous lands, such as Asia Minor and Thrace, on which persons of the Turkish race have dwelt in great number.'[79]

Ultimately, in defiance of these words, Anatolia was divided up by partitioning it into different areas of sovereignty. On May 17, 1919, during the Peace Talks, when reminded of their statements from the previous year, both Wilson and Lloyd George said that 'they had forgotten.'[80] The partition plan was thus put into effect and on May 16, 1919, Izmir was occupied by the Greeks. The question of prosecuting those involved in the Armenian Genocide was dealt a mortal blow by this action because, in the words of the then Defense Secretary, Winston Churchill, 'righteousness has now changed sides. Justice has passed to the other camp.'[81]

The attitudes of the British High Commission and General Staff reinforce this thesis. These two institutions also argued for the need to combine the issues of partition and of punishing the perpetrators of the massacres. The High Commission, which opposed the Greek occupation of Izmir, had previously warned Paris about the decision that had been taken to occupy the city:

I am to hope that...the Hellene Kingdom shall not be spread to the Eastern shores of the Aegean Sea. This hope of ours does not derive from the lack of fervency in the sympathy that we have felt toward their aspirations to be free of the tyrannous regime of the past... but because it is believed that this action shall not serve the happiness of any one of the concerned parties...[82]

But the occupation took place despite these warnings. In his report of November 23, 1919, Admiral Sir J. de Robeck of the High Commission wrote that '[t]he Turks had to be punished, but from the point of view of...British advantage, this punishment should not have taken the form of partitioning the Ottoman provinces in which they constitute a great majority.'[83] Thus, it can be seen that in punishing 'the Turks,' the motive was not to punish those guilty of massacre and other war crimes, but to seize the opportunity to partition Anatolia. Two separate issues were merged into one. It is fair to assume that, if the Entente powers had been able to pursue a different policy on the issue of Ottoman sovereignty, the outcome could have been very different.

In the initial period, we also find on the Turkish side tendencies that would strengthen this theory. As we have seen, the dominant belief of the period was that the decision of the Entente powers with regard to the fate of the Ottoman Empire and Istanbul depended on the punishing of those involved in the massacres. Numerous examples of this attitude can be found, even outside of the Amasya Protocols. The main change in the attitude adopted by the nationalist movement toward trying those guilty of war crimes and massacres occurred after the contents of the Treaty of Sèvres became clear. In this agreement, the Entente powers essentially showed that they interpreted the punishment of 'the Turks' as the elimination of the Ottoman state's right of sovereignty. For that reason, the Entente powers included in their program the punishment of the leaders of the nationalist movement. As a result of their pressure, the court-marshal in Istanbul started trying not only those who were accused of war crimes and massacres but also important members of the Turkish nationalist movement. In April, 1920, the First Extraordinary Court Martial in Istanbul began to try the leaders of the Anatolian movement, and Mustafa Kemal foremost among them (in absentia).

Three factors changed the attitude of the nationalist movement regarding the punishment of the perpetrators of the massacres. First, as we have said, was the formulation of the Treaty of Sèvres, which became known by April 1920. The second was the sentencing to death in absentia of Mustafa Kemal and other leaders of the nationalist movement. The third was the occupation of Istanbul in March 1920. These events made it clear that the punishment of the perpetrators was not the necessary condition for hindering the partition of Anatolia. A letter written by Mustafa Kemal to Istanbul on August 20, 1920, highlights this change in attitude. In the letter, he states that, '[t]he Ottoman Government...continues to hang the children of the homeland on accusations of [having perpetrated] deportation and massacres, which now became totally senseless.'[84] Kemal meant that for the Ottoman government to punish Turks for what they had done to the

Christian minorities would make sense only if Turkey got some positive result, in terms of a better treaty to secure the Ottoman territories. In the changed circumstances, these 'senseless' death sentences should be halted. As I have labored to show here, if the Western powers had taken seriously the Turkish independence movement's demands in regard to the National Pact, and if this had been made conditional on bringing to trial those who had perpetrated crimes against humanity, we would today be faced with a very different history of the period. The merger of these two issues into one essentially condemned the issue of human rights, which had left a fundamental stamp on the Turkish War for Independence, to oblivion. If we examine the history of this period from a human rights perspective, we can conclude that a significant part of this history has been ignored not only in Turkey but generally in the historical writing on the Turkish War of Independence. The founding of the Turkish Republic was not only a matter of resistance against foreign powers; it was strongly related to the issue of crimes against humanity, and particularly, the Armenian Genocide.

The ultimate triumph of the Turkish national movement, symbolized but also celebrated through the signing of the Lausanne Treaty, made it critical for the emerging Republic of Turkey to disavow any responsibility for the First World War Armenian deportations and massacres. To institutionalize this disclaimer of responsibility, the new Republic's founders not only made a conscious offer to distance themselves from the leaders of the CUP regime that had carried out the Armenian Genocide, but also went out of their way to denigrate and even to dispute their Ottoman legacy in several respects. This attempt at disconnecting from their recent history is a phenomenon full of implications for the denial of the Armenian Genocide. Chapter 7 will deal with the dynamics of this phenomenon, insofar as it related to the formation of a Turkish syndrome of denial and its various taboo components.

NOTES

An earlier version of this chapter appeared in Hans-Lukas Kieser and Dominik J. Schaller, eds., *Der Volkermörd an den Armeniern und die Shoah* (The Armenian Genocide and the Shoah) (Zurich: Chronos Verlag, 2002).

1. The National Pact was first adopted by the nationalist forces in Anatolia at the Erzurum (July 1919) and Sivas (September 1919) Congresses. In February 1920, it was adopted by the Ottoman Parliament still meeting in Istanbul. For an English translation of the text of the pact and its statement of principles, as well as the various declarations and resolutions from which it evolved, see Stanford and Ezel Kural Shaw, *History of the Ottoman Empire and Modern Turkey*, vol. II (Cambridge, 1977), pp. 343–48.

2. In this chapter I place the term 'Turks' within quotation marks on many occasions. Although the term was used in the discussions of the time, it is clear that in explaining

historical events general terms such as this are not only wrong to use, but also incorrect from the standpoint of attempting to write a scientific history. The racialist and nationalist view attempts to homogenize the 'other' and encompass him within a single term, by bestowing the other with shared qualities. Nevertheless, it is incorrect for such general terms as 'Turks' and 'Armenians' to be used to describe collective actors when discussing historical events. On the historical stage, it is a group who undertakes joint actions as a collective that is described by its political or other characteristics. This group represents only a portion within any people or religious community of which it is a part. In history, the 'Turks,' 'Armenians' or others are not actors. Therefore, such terms— especially in regard to the actors within historical events—are both wrong and create a situation wherein racist and chauvinistic attitudes toward others are accepted. This chapter should be read with that warning in mind.

3. Gotthard Jäschke, 'Mustafa Kemal und England in neuer Sicht,' *Die Welt des Islams*, vol. XVI (1975).

4. Concerning these various agreements, see Paul C. Helmreich, *From Paris to Sèvres: The Partition of the Ottoman Empire at the Peace Conference of 1919–1920* (Columbus, 1974), pp. 3–38.

5. Akdes Nimet Kurat, *Türkiye ve Rusya* (Ankara, 1990), p. 32.

6. Gotthard Jäschke, *Kurtuluş Savaşı ile İlgili İngiliz Belgeleri* (Ankara, 1971), p. 54.

7. Gotthard Jäschke, 'Beiträge zur Geschichte des Kampfes der Türkei um ihre Unabhängigkeit,' *Die Welt des Islams* [new series], vol. V (1958): 2.

8. *Ibid.*, p. 2.

9. James F. Willis, *Prologue to Nuremberg: The Politics and Diplomacy of Punishing War Criminals of the First World War* (London, 1982), p. 2.

10. H. W. V. Temperley, ed., *History of the Peace Conference of Paris*, vol. 6 (London, 1969), p. 23.

11. Quoted in Lloyd George, *Memoirs*, vol. 2 (Boston, 1934), p. 64.

12. Milne's words, spoken on January 12, 1919, quoted in Bilal Şimşir, *Malta Sürgünleri* (Ankara, 1985), p. 15.

13. Tarik Zafer Tunaya, *Türkiye'de Siyasal Partiler, vol. II: Mütareke Dönemi* (Istanbul, 1986), p. 27.

14. Statement made July 4, 1919, in *Documents on British Foreign Policy, 1919–1936*, vol. 4, 1st Series. W. Woodsward and R. Butler, eds. (1952), p. 661.

15. *Le Temps, Journal des Débats*, November 2, 1918. Quoted in Yahya Akyüz, *Türk Kurtuluş Savaşı ve Fransız Kamuoyu, 1919–1921* (Ankara, 1988), p. 70.

16. Richard G. Hovannisian, 'The Allies and Armenia, 1915–1918', *Journal of Contemporary History*, 3 (1968): 148.

17. FO 371/4173/53351, folios 192–3.

18. The commission's report was later published several times. The information given here was taken from the relevant sections of the report. See, 'Commission on the Responsibility of the Authors of the War and on Enforcement of Penalties. Report', *American Journal of International Law*, vol. 14 (1920), pp. 95–155 (hereafter cited as simply 'Report').

19. Report, p. 115.

20. Report, p. 117.

21. Fritz Dickmann, *Die Kriegsschuldfrage auf der Friedenskonferenz von Paris, 1919* (Munich, 1964), p. 40.

22. Christopher Simpson, 'Die seinerzeitige Diskussion über die in Nürnberg zu verhandelnden Delikte,' *Strafgerichte gegen Menscheitsverbrechen*, Gerd Hankel und Gerhard Stuby, eds. (Hamburg, 1995), p. 45.

23. Seha L. Meray and Osman Olcay, *Osmanlı İmparatorluğunun Çöküş Belgeleri* (Ankara, 1977), pp. 113–14.
24. Ali Fuat Türkgeldi, *Görüp İşittiklerim* (Ankara, 1987), p. 186.
25. FO 371/4174/118337, folio 253.
26. *Ibid.*
27. Sina Akşin, *İstanbul Hükümetleri ve Millî Mücadele, vol. I: Mutlakiyete Dönüş (1918–1919)* (Istanbul, 1983), p. 146.
28. *Ibid.*, p. 24.
29. *Meclis-i Ayan Zabıt Ceridesi*, Devre 3, İçtima Senesi 5, vol. I (Ankara, 1990), p. 122.
30. Helmreich, p. 109.
31. *Ibid.*
32. *Ibid.*, p. 110.
33. Kurt Ziemke, *Die neue Türkei* (Berlin, 1930), p. 83.
34. Helmreich, p. 110.
35. After the war twelve separate governments were formed in Istanbul between October 11, 1918 and November 4, 1922. Of these, five separate governments were established by Damat Ferit Paşa between March 4, 1919 and September 30, 1919 (three governments) and between April 5, 1920 and October 17, 1920 (two governments). For a complete list of the governments of the Armistice period, see Tarik Zafer Tunaya, vol. II, p. 37.
36. Mustafa Kemal, *Nutuk, vol. I: 1919–1920* (Istanbul, 1934), p. 161.
37. *Ibid.*, p. 166.
38. Kemal, *Nutuk*, vol. III, pp. 193–4 (document no. 159).
39. *Ibid.*, p. 165.
40. Sina Akşin, *İstanbul Hükümetleri*, vol. II, p. 316.
41. Kemal, *Nutuk*, vol. III, pp. 166–7.
42. *Ibid.*, pp. 193–4 (Vesika 159).
43. In Mustafa Kemal's famous speech the document that is reported as the 'Third Protocol' (*Nutuk*, p. 194, document no. 160) actually consists of an alternative formulation proposed by Kemal for the sixth article of the First Protocol, which had been proposed by the Istanbul delegation and accepted. Akşin, (vol. II), p. 445.
44. Kemal, *Nutuk*, vol. III, p. 194 (document no. 160).
45. *Ibid.*, pp. 193–4 (document no. 159–60) .
46. Şerafettin Turan, *Türk Devrim Tarihi: 1. Kitap* (Ankara, 1991), p. 87.
47. The article in the October 10, 1918 edition of *Ati* is but one example.
48. Kemal, *Nutuk*, vol. III, p. 94 (document no. 97). From a letter sent by Kemal to the Sultan on October 2, 1920.
49. FO 371/4174/102553, note dated 25.2.19.
50. For more detailed information on the Ottoman government's attitude toward the trials, the reader may refer to my book *Armenien und der Völkermord, die Istanbuler Prozesse und türkische National Bewegung* (Hamburg, 1996).
51. FO 371/6499/E 3110, Folio 190. From the report of the meeting between Lord Curzon and Bekir Sami.
52. Kemal, *Nutuk,* vol. II, pp. 110, 239.
53. James F. Willis, p. 161.
54. FO/371/6504/E 9112, Folio 47.
55. FO/371/6504/ E 10411, Folio 130. Telegram from General Harrington to the Ministry of War.
56. *Le Temps*, July 11, 1919. Quoted in Paul Dumont, *Mustafa Kemal* (Ankara, 1993), p. 35.
57. *Daily Mail*, April, 1919. Quoted in Yahya Akyüz, p. 75.
58. *Ibid.*, p. 76.

59. Dumont, pp. 35–6.
60. 'Rauf Orbay'ın Hatıraları,' *Yakın Tarihimiz*, vol. II, pp. 179.
61. Kazım Karabekir, *İstiklal Harbimiz* (Istanbul, 1960), p. 225.
62. *Atatürk'ün Tamim Telegraf ve Beyannameleri* (Ankara, 1964), pp. 74–84. Quoted in Seçil Akgün, *General Harbord'un Anadolu Gezisi ve Ermeni Meselesine Dair Raporu* (Istanbul, 1981), p. 168.
63. Bilal Şimşir *British Documents on Atatürk (1919–1938)*, vol. I (Ankara, 1973), p. 171.
64. *Atatürk'ün Söylev ve Demeçleri*, vol. I–III (Ankara 1989), p. 4. (This is one book but each volume starts with a new page number.)
65. Bekir Sami Baykal, *Heyeti Temsiliye Kararları* (Ankara, 1974), pp. 5, 10. The adoption of similar decisions by the Representative Committee on September 24, 28, 29 and October 11, 1919 shows that the committee approached the issue with great seriousness and concern.
66. Helmreich, p. 278.
67. Mustafa Kemal, *Nutuk*, vol. I, p. 296.
68. Kazım Öztürk, *Atatürk'ün TBMM Açık ve Gizli Oturumunlardaki Konuşmaları*. Vol. II (Ankara, 1981), p. 67.
69. *Ibid.*
70. *Vakit* and *Alemdar* newspapers, 15 Mart (March), 1919.
71. *TBMM Gizli Celse Zabıtları*, vol. IV (Ankara, 1985), pp. 439–40. Cemal was later referred to as '*Artin* Cemal' (for his protection of the Armenians) and as 'that fellow' in the Grand National Assembly in Ankara, and his name was included in a list of 150 persons that were exiled, largely on the basis of his stance on this matter.
72. 'Rauf Orbay'ın Hatıraları,' *Yakın Tarihimiz*, vol. III, p. 179.
73. *Ibid.*
74. *Atatürk'ün TBMM Açık ve Gizli Oturumlarındaki Konuşmaları*, vol. I (Ankara, 1992), p. 59.
75. Kazım Karabekir, p. 707.
76. Jäschke, *Kurtuluş Savaşı*, p. 152.
77. Jäschke, *Mustafa Kemal und England*, p. 210.
78. Jäschke, 'Präsident Wilson als Schiedsrichter zwischen der Türkei und Armenien,' *Mitteilungen des Seminars für orientalische Sprachen zu Berlin (M.S. O.S.)*, 38 (1935), p. 75.
79. Jäschke, *Beiträge...*, p. 2.
80. Jäschke, 'Ein amerikanisches Mandat für die Türkei', *Die Welt des Islams*, NS VIII, (1962–63), p. 222.
81. Jäschke, *Beiträge...*, p. 6.
82. Jäschke, *Kurtuluş Savaşı*, p. 61.
83 Sina Akşin, vol. II, pp. 246–7.
84. Bilal Şimşir, p. 334. The letter was written to the first Grand Vizier of the Armistice period, Ahmet İzzet Paşa, with the aim of its contents being communicated to the British High Commission.

7

The Causes and Effects
of Making Turkish History Taboo

It is generally accepted that debates on violence against Greeks, Armenians, and Kurds are under a taboo in Turkey. In what follows, I will try to explain why discussions of the history of minority groups are taboo topics in Turkey. Hardly any scientific research has been done on this history. Some limited treatments of the issue have been published by employees of government organizations or by institutions receiving state support. The aim of these efforts is to refute what are perceived as 'slander and 'lies' against Turkey. The subject is dealt with under headings such as 'ingratitude'[1] and 'defamation' or in terms of 'the Armenian problem that is threatening our national and social existence'.[2] The logic used when answering allegations of 'genocide,' 'massacre' and 'expulsion' is invariably exculpatory. We can summarize this logic as, 'Nothing has happened, but the others are guilty.' And those studies that do exist are written in an explicitly racist manner. The Armenians are characterized as 'mean people,'[3] 'thieves,' and 'liars' who have 'no values.'[4] On the other hand, intellectuals known for taking a critical approach rarely deal with the subject. One could call this a blind spot in their work. For example, the encyclopedia *Socialism and Social Struggle in Turkey* makes no reference to this complex question.

Schoolbooks and curricula likewise include nothing on the subject. Despite a history of 600 years' cohabitation with non-Muslim people in the Ottoman Empire and the continuing cohabitation with the Kurds, there is no professional chair at any Turkish university for study of the language and culture of non-Muslim ethnic minorities and the Kurdish people. Great historical epochs and events appear not to exist, as if they have been obliterated from history and memory. We might reasonably talk of a collective effort to forget about these issues. Anyone who wants to discuss them is faced with one of two reactions. On the one hand, there is lack of interest and indifference and, on the other hand, the response is one of aggression and hostility. Here I will deal only with the second type of reaction.

Should you dare to speak about the Armenian Genocide, massacres of Greeks and their expulsion from Anatolia, the Kurdish uprisings and the terrorist methods used by the state to repress them, you risk a storm of fierce denunciation. Whoever dares to speak about these matters is aggressively attacked as a traitor, singled out for public condemnation and may even be put in prison. The refusal to take a critical stance on these questions and the aggression shown towards those who seek to open a debate on them are closely related. In this context, indifference and hostility seem to be two sides of the same coin. These phenomena indicate the existence of a national subconscious in Turkish society; a discussion of its mechanisms, which manifest themselves in language and culture, may help to illuminate the concept of a particular type of national subconscious.

Whether 'genocide,' or 'massacre,' or 'expulsion' is the appropriate term to describe these historical events, some would argue that these words are too emotive to allow an objective treatment of the problems being faced within Turkey. That it is not my point here. What I want to emphasize is that the real problem in Turkey is the absence of a culture of discussion that would enable one to talk about the issues calmly and from a certain distance. The most common reaction is either to terminate the discussion abruptly, or to justify what happened, or to put forward the counter-thesis that lays all responsibility on the minority groups. The attitude that is displayed in such works, as well as by many Turks, can be referred to as the logic of *revanchism*, that is, the logic of turning attacks and accusations made against oneself against the attacker.

It is very difficult to proceed beyond defiant apologetics to a consideration of the causes and reasons for the events. The feeling of being upset, the desire for revenge, and hatred for those thought to be responsible are overwhelming. It is impossible to put such feelings aside and talk dispassionately about what happened. The traumatic impact of personal experience mixes uneasily with historical objectivity. Any attempt to break through the wall of silence is felt to incur the most severe judgment imaginable. One would like to respond by saying 'keep cool,' 'don't be afraid,' 'nothing will happen' and it is 'not the end of the world.' It is as if reason has gone on holiday in Turkish society.

We might talk of an overriding social amnesia. Remembrance and discussion of historical events seem to have been expelled from the national consciousness. In their place, Turkish society contents itself with a fictitious reality and a comfortable self-portrait. This may be a significant factor in the absolute lack of interest alternating with extreme hostility that is the characteristic response to those who would like to alter this mental state.

The questions we must answer are these: why have such widely known issues in Turkey's recent history been turned into taboo subjects? What is the source of these emotional reactions, which have rendered impossible any calm discussion of these aspects of our history? For help in answering these questions, we must appeal to the field of psychology, because there are important similarities between the creation of taboos and the emotional reactions they often engender, on one hand, and the reactions found in neurotic persons, whom psychology identifies as pathological personalities, on the other.

On Taboos

Let's begin with the very simple question of what is a taboo. Sigmund Freud gives the following answer: 'The notion of taboo diverges into two opposite directions. For us it can on the one hand mean something "holy" or "divine," while on the other, "mysterious," "dangerous," "forbidden" and "dirty"...[In this sense] the "taboo" is something that is not to be approached.'[5] The taboo 'is a prohibition placed on the touching of an object or using it in order to extract personal advantage, or on the use of certain forbidden words, [and is] either designated in practice or through custom, or through clearly formulated laws.'[6] The history of taboos is as old as human history itself. Freud assumes it to have begun thus: taboos are the ancient prohibitions that were externally imposed on primitive human generations during an earlier era. That is to say, they are assumed to have been forcefully imposed by an earlier generation.[7]

I am interested in the connection between taboos and the inclination towards them. Freud claimed that at the 'basis of the taboo' was 'a forbidden action toward which a powerful inclination was felt in the subconscious.'[8] If we claim that it is not possible to speak openly about certain aspects of Turkish history, that certain events have been made taboo, then this would be a determinant of the first order of importance, because we can at the very least assert that in this state, the powerful desire to engage in those taboo areas still continues in Turkish society today. Yet, if those things which are claimed to have been made taboo also include violence and clear demonstrations of barbarism, it could be understood that the desire for violence still persists in this society.

Freud said he approached the issue of taboos from the aspect of exploring the subconscious portion of the individual's spiritual makeup. He claimed that if people who abided by such taboos had not already been defined by psychologists as having an 'obsessive-compulsive disorder', it would be necessary to define them as having a taboo illness. Freud added that the purpose of his work in this regard was to apply the information acquired from psychoanalytical examinations on the subject of obsessive-compulsive disorders to parallel social phenomena.[9] In other words, it would not be too far off the mark to say that a modern society that has surrounded itself with a number of prohibitions and taboos could be considered as ill or, at the very least, might be displaying similar traits to those of a sick person. If Freud's claim is correct, the present condition in Turkey could indeed be argued to be a national 'illness.' This compels us to grapple with some particular aspects of Turkish history and the reason for their being made into a taboo. The difficulties of Turkish society with its history are very complex. Generally speaking, even the mention of such topics provokes the most extreme emotional reactions, such as anger and rage. My assertion is that such emotional outbursts are not normal, and resemble a pathological condition.

The Desire to Forget History: A Defense Mechanism

The first response that comes to mind is this: turning certain historical events and a discussion of them into taboo subjects, and the emotional reaction displayed at their mention are simply a defense mechanism. The purpose of this defense mechanism is to prevent Turkish society from recalling events that are described as massacre, genocide and expulsion. The purpose is the avoidance of the negative psychological, emotional or moral consequences produced by such memories.

There are actually a wide variety of defense mechanisms that persons develop against things that are seen as threatening, or that they do not want to remember. In addition to *forgetting*, the other important defense mechanisms are *repression*, or the preventing of unwanted instinctual drives from surfacing in the conscious mind, by limiting them to the subconscious; *suppression*, or the distancing of inappropriate desires and recollections from the conscious mind; and *denial*, or the ignoring of this type of memory. In psychology, these are considered the 'primary defense mechanisms,' which emerge in situations in which the personality is not, in the true sense, fully formed. We can consider *projection* as another major defense mechanism. Projection can be defined as 'a defense mechanism in which the individual attributes to other people impulses and traits that he himself has but cannot accept. It is especially likely to occur when the person lacks insight into his own impulses and traits.' The primary defense mechanisms that Turks use regarding their history are denying those things that were experienced, marginalizing them and behaving as if they never occurred, and projecting their deeds and claiming that 'we Turks did not murder Armenians; Armenians murdered us.' As a rule, these approaches are used by persons possessing a 'damaged' past. This manner of relating to the past is a product of the illness itself.

Making the act of forgetting into a major foundation of a society is not exclusive to Turkish society. More than one hundred years ago, Ernest Renan drew attention to the fact that the act of forgetting played a very important role in the establishment of the national state, and in the creation of the nation itself. Renan accepted that this act of forgetting was an historical mistake.[10] But this act of forgetting should not be understood as always necessarily ending in failure, and as paving the way for the appearance of pathological reactions within society. There are situations in which the act of forgetting is indeed successful. As a result of the interesting findings that he made during the course of his work on so-called 'primitive' societies, Claude Lévi-Strauss rejected the distinction often made between peoples 'possessing history' and those 'not possessing history,' a distinction rather well established in Western thought. In place of this, he proposes the division between 'hot' and 'cold' societies.

The dividing line in this distinction is the manner of connection that these societies have established with their histories. Societies that we are inclined to refer to as 'primitive' and which Lévi-Strauss denoted as 'cold,' are those which have succeeded in eliminating the negative effects which these events can produce on their own psychological equilibrium and continuity. They do so by erasing those negative historical events from their collective memories by means of the institutions they have established. 'Hot' societies, on the other hand, transform history into a subject for continuous discussion and engagement, making it an engine for their own development.[11] Forgetting, or not possessing history, is not a vacuum or a lack of something. Rather, it can be seen as a benefit. Here, 'the group's shielding itself against a history that is liable to threaten its stability is perceived as attaining stability through institutionalization.'[12]

A similar thesis can be found in Freud's works. According to Freud, the ardent effort shown in banishing from one's mind an historical event, which was experienced but which the person does not wish to remember, must not always be perceived as a pathological phenomenon. Freud claims that a person who is under psychological conditions resembling the original situation that he wants to forget, cannot know how to achieve this forgetting. 'That which I do know,' he asserts, 'is that the patients who have undergone analysis with me have been unable to forget, and this has opened the door to pathological reactions as serious as hysteria, obsession, or hallucinatory psychosis.'[13] The person who is unable to muster sufficient strength to overcome the trauma of a past event, through a conscious act of thinking by the ego, prefers instead to forget it, repress the memory of it, or deny its occurrence by erasing it from the conscious mind. This opens the way to pathological reactions in a situation where conditions similar to those of the original event appear. What I am asserting here is that 'Turkish' society's reactions toward its own history share these same features and can be described as pathological. My fundamental thesis is that this attitude of Turkish society toward its history is a neurotic, pathological attitude, which can well be described as that of a hysterical personality. In other words, I am speaking of the existence of hysteria on a societal level.

Doubtless, the use of a good number of terms from individual psychology in social psychology—where their meaningful content may not be the same—is not without its problems. But the fact that, even within the framework of psychoanalysis itself, these terms are used in a variety of different senses should permit us a broad range of usage for these terms in the area of mass psychology. Likewise, it is incorrect to attempt to detach the psychological unease of societies from the psychological unease of individuals, or to attempt to claim that societies or groups possess a separate psychology from that of individuals. The societal hysteria that I mentioned above is nothing other than the cumulative shared effects of the combined mental conditions of its members. But this is not to be understood as the simultaneous shared witnessing of these individual experiences. Indeed, a collective hysteria may only manifest itself after several generations.

Hysterical-Neurotic Behavior

One of the most important indicators of hysterical neurosis is the 'emptiness of memory,'[14] or 'emptiness of recollection.' The relationship of persons suffering from this ailment regarding past events is along the lines of 'if only this had not occurred.' They are better forgotten. In this manner, history is expunged from the conscious and from the field of memory. The internal and external worlds of such persons are separate and different. In their internal worlds, these persons are affected by those things that they have personally experienced, but their external worlds are formed according to how they desire to present themselves to others. They offer an image to the outside world showing how different they are, and how much they have changed.

Because the approach toward certain past events tends to be along the lines of 'if only it hadn't been experienced,' these events are expunged from memory, and thus significant gaps emerge in a person's life story. In order to fill these inner lacunae, the subject devises a contrived history with regard to himself, and an artificial view of his current condition. Presenting oneself as changed and as being something different toward both oneself and the outside world is a characteristic of this type of behavior.

It is very difficult to say that this type of behavior is realized outside of the conscious mind. On the contrary, it is performed consciously.

Knowledge regarding one's own past remains, but it is simply not held for evaluation, or it is not paid attention to. This effort to present one's own history and one's current condition differently has as its main purpose to spare oneself from an internal psychological conflict, from a conflict with oneself. The person who performs such a psychological operation feels that he or she has been cleansed of all of his or her sins concerning the past, which has oppressed and discomforted them. They are now clean, and purged of all feelings of guilt.

The hysterical reaction is an attempt to flee from the sense of emptiness, which these persons have themselves created and in which they find themselves, by taking shelter in their artificial personality. In performing such an action, there are a variety of means to which the patient may turn: very strong or exaggerated identification of oneself with a thing (or person), resorting to excessively emotional behavior, the expunging of certain memories, or the intentional breaking off of some tie or connection.

It is generally accepted that the hysterical personality shows great success in fabricating or otherwise altering his or her life history to the extent that is wished; unpleasant matters, especially feelings of guilt, are successfully forgotten. As Nietzsche puts it, 'My memory tells me that I did this, but my honor tells me that I cannot have done any such thing and uncompromisingly resists any suggestions to the contrary. Ultimately, it is the memory which gives in.'[15] This mastery that is displayed in the severing of temporal and causal connections between events also bestows upon such persons a flexibility—and one that is not at all unpleasant— that enables them to live their lives free of any negative history or past. So that, things, or the recollection of such events, which appear as burdens in their life stories are easily discarded. But this refuse resurfaces, to some extent, due to the lack of a sense of continuity in the conscious mind. This, then, is the cause of the illness.

In hysterical neuroses it has been observed that there is no continuity of personality, or what can be described as character. These persons are caught up in a constant swirl of emotional imbalance.[16] There are great swings in the personality's confidence in itself, and in its own sense of worth, and both are very easily shattered. Such personalities are exaggeratedly sensitive, or 'thin-skinned' toward even the slightest criticism or attack. Their reactions are always laden with emotion, and are not limited to this: they even develop feelings of hatred toward those who criticize them. 'The persistent fear, in which one feels that everything may well collapse upon oneself, or that a catastrophe will occur,'[17] is a feeling that determines behaviors and modes of action.

The relationship between this personality and violence is significant. The sensitivity, often to the point of narcissistic hyper-sensitivity, is easily incited. As the hysterical behavior grows stronger, it increases the desire for violence, in order to dominate everything, and ultimately this dominates the person himself. Ever ready to be incited, he lashes out violently against his environment, so that he finally succeeds in expelling all tendencies and attempts from his environment to cross him or accuse him. In this way, the hysterical personality proves his own righteousness. This process is always the preferred response to a new calamity or disturbance, including war.

The starting point for our topic of collective hysteria 'is always any historical occurrence which has been experienced in a disturbing manner.'[18] But we are not speaking of a normal, everyday disturbance here. Rather, we mean those disturbances that create the sense among members of a society that the society itself does not possess the means to endure them, or to solve the problems created by them. Such a situation can occur in the way of a dispersion of political authority, a revolution, a military defeat or foreign occupation. On a national level hysterical phenomena can manifest themselves as a continual fear that plots are being hatched against oneself, anxiety about dispersion, occupation or partition, the conjuring up of imaginary enemies, or the perception of being mercilessly persecuted by other enemies, real or imagined.[19]

This brings us to the following question: what are the situations in which those disturbances and disruptions surpass the limits of a society's ability to tolerate or endure them? There are at least five conditions: (1) when the disturbance is entirely unexpected and is of very great magnitude; (2) when, as a result of the disturbance, there is an imbalance of suffering, when the suffering is of a level out of proportion to the situation; (3) when there is a great magnitude to the problems brought about by the disturbance; (4) when the society's character is not yet fully formed or mature; (5) when historical experiences divert a society onto the path of delusion, either by opening the way for the awakening of great hopes, or by allowing for the creation of unrealistic optimism or expectations.

The immensity of this disturbance tends to mold the way that society thinks about the occurrence into an *idée fixe*. Whether right or wrong, the result of this is seen in attempts to find 100 percent guarantees that another such catastrophe does not come about. Thoughts, feelings and actualities are inevitably bound to the neurotic conceptualization of a single action. In this petrified, frozen and paralyzed state, the resolution of actual problems, especially those related to a critical situation that was experienced, becomes impossible.

Neither individuals nor societies are far from openly admitting this situation to themselves. They take shelter behind the solution of putting on an outward show. By basically saying to themselves that they will find a solution, that they will get rid of those things that caused the problems, the causes of the problems continue to be protected and hidden away. The society that lives in this type of delusional state establishes a warped relationship with reality. In attempting to solve the problems that appear, the starting point is not the actual or the possible; rather, it is fantasies and illusions created for the sake of the future. The society that lives in this type of contradiction to reality produces clear thought patterns in order to help it explain events to itself. It struggles to find an answer to every problem that arises, an explanation for every event. The hysterical worldview suggests a totality, and is closed within itself. It can explain everything, account for everything and justify everything. Within this view, everything is in agreement with everything else. The only problem is that this world is in serious contradiction with reality.

The natural result of those shocks and the suffering that have been experienced is the desire to forget history, or to divest it of its content. In such a situation we can even say that 'societies that have lost their collective memories have lost their minds. An inability to think about the past and/or its rejection has a price: it is the loss of the ability to think.'[20]

The Reasons That Turkish Society Desires to Erase History from Its Memory

Most of the characteristics I have presented here correspond to the manner in which 'Turkish society' approaches its own history, and attempts to solve its social problems. This is the reason for the exaggerated emotional reaction displayed when reminded of its past. The new personality which Turkey claims to have, formed by erasing a segment of history from its memory, displays even more so the signs of a 'substitutional' personality, behind which it hides in order to save itself from history. If Turkey had indeed been rescued from the effects of history, if it had displayed the necessary reflexive actions to it at the conscious level, it would not have such emotional reactions. We know generally that those peoples and cultures that are able successfully to remember and confront their history can consciously and successfully leave it in the past.[21] The reason for Turkey's emotional reaction to those reminders lies in its failure, up to now, to put the necessary distance between itself and history.

The problem that confronts us now is to analyze Turkish history with this critical eye: why is Turkey's relationship to its history one of forgetting, of placing certain events into the category of things not experienced? From where does its need to ignore certain past experiences, and to fill the lacunae with fantasies and myths originate?

From social psychology we know that human collectives, much like individuals, have difficulties in integrating bad or traumatic events into their life stories. This, too, is Turkey's primary problem. Turkey's history is, at a very basic level, the history of the shocks and traumas experienced in the last hundred years. These shocks and traumas are not simply limited to the violent outbursts that have been characterized by such terms as massacre, genocide and expulsion. This history is also perceived as one of violations of honor and of humiliations, experienced in great measure against the background of continuous military defeats, losses of territory and anxiety over Turkey's continued existence as a nation. In other words, the desire to forget history doesn't simply derive from 'feelings of guilt.'

The difficulty is for Turkey to integrate this history into its life stories by thinking about events. This act of integration may be achieved by analyzing the factors behind the traumas. But up to now, Turkey has preferred to ignore these events, to erase them from its memory, out of the belief that it does not have sufficient strength to face them. The cause of failing to confront and Turkey's instinctive reaction when these unwanted dimensions of history are recalled is the fear of insecurity toward itself. Turkish society is afraid that it will again return to face conditions similar to those experienced in the past. By placing a sort of veil across the past, Turkey not only covers up its history, it also covers up the same reactions that it had in the past and its continuing potential for violence as a response to collapse and dispersion. It is thereby understood that the same potential for violence has been preserved and continues.

What must be done, then, is to retrieve that history that has not been thought about seriously, but which is not lost, and still exists in Turkish collective memory. It must be retrieved and brought into the conscious mind. Turkish society must make an historical inventory of the true nature of those shocks and traumas which gave rise to such enormous disturbances. Which of these shocks and traumas connected to our past have given birth to those feelings of guilt, from which Turkish society has tried to escape by wishing they had not occurred? What are the reasons that Turks feel themselves dishonored and humiliated? Why do they, even today, view every problem as one vital to their national existence? If Turkey cannot answer such questions, then it has no possibility of emerging from social hysteria, and new catastrophes, new traumas will be unavoidable.

What I have proposed, then, is an attempt to re-conceptualize Turkey and its history. For this to be successful in the face of forgetting, and ignoring, and repressing, it is necessary to consciously resort to active remembering. For active remembering, the place to go is society's collective memory. We know from psychology that those things which we assumed forgotten or overlooked are preserved, in all of their vitality, within our memories. In other words, 'there is no such thing as an absolute emptiness in memory.'[22] Everything that has been experienced is recorded in memory. Even if occurrences are not written about in books, if they fail to appear before us when we turn the pages, they continue to exist, as if written, in society's collective subconscious. Numerous factors, however, block those things that exist in memory from surfacing to the conscious mind. There is an inverse relationship between the writing of Turkish history and society's collective memory in Turkey. What needs to be done is to reverse this relationship, and so make the way down that long, difficult corridor of memory.

I cannot provide answers to all of the questions I have raised above. I will therefore restrict myself to conceptualizing, within a general framework, those elements which I claim dominate Turkey's attitudes toward history and the present. I call these 'hysterical neurosis,' and I believe them to be influential elements in the formation of Turkish society's pathological mindset. These are the feelings of guilt, the sense of humiliation and dishonor, and the fear of dispersion and annihilation.

The following assertion may then be made: Turkey has not yet been able to fully digest the problematic aspects associated with the transition from Empire to Republic. It is utterly unwilling to accept the political transformation from a mighty Empire straddling three continents to a Republic squeezed between two continents. Herein lies, I believe, the main problem. In short, if Turkey had indeed reconciled itself to what it has become and to where it has arrived as a result of the collapse and dissolution of the Ottoman Empire, it would not have had to create taboos with regard to its own history, nor would it display the hysterical-neurotic reactions that it does. Basically, Turkey desires to be at the highest position it believes it had in its past (at its glorious, magnificent time), and does not accept where it is today. This is the primary reason for Turkey's emotional reaction to history.

It is possible to describe this process along the following general lines. The Ottoman Empire was a great Empire which experienced a process of dissolution and partition which lasted for close to 150 years. This process of collapse was accompanied by wars, disruptions and traumas, which resulted in immense loss of life, and it awoke profound fears about the possibility of the Empire's own continued existence. In order to portray the immensity of this trauma, it is perhaps sufficient to simply recall the fact that 'Between the years 1870 and 1920, the Empire lost 85 percent of the lands it had ruled and 75 percent of its population.'[23] And just as, during this process, every attempt to halt the collapse met with failure, the collapse itself was accompanied by a continual series of humiliations and insults to Ottoman-Turkish honor at the hands of other states. Turkey has been unable, and remains unable, to come to terms with these realities.

The main reason that this series of territorial losses, insults and humiliations could not be more easily accepted is that the Ottoman ruling class was crushed under the magnificence of its own former greatness. The gap between, on the one hand, ruling an Empire which had lorded it over three continents, and on the other, sinking to abject dependency on foreign powers, is vast indeed. In all fairness, it would be hard to imagine that any nation, falling from such heights to a condition of such weakness, could make this transition easily.

> Throughout the course of human history and up until now it has been a provable fact, that the inhabitants of states..., which have lost their claim to a dominant position during the decisive wars of their age, often need a great deal of time, sometimes as much as an entire century, to fully reconcile themselves with the changing situation and the corresponding loss of self-worth.[24]

This describes Turkey's condition. Turkey's problem, however, is not only limited to merely digesting this transition from Empire to Republic. Another, equally important factor has defined and characterized this process. The more accelerated the collapse and dissolution became, the greater the hope and longing to reestablish the old Empire. This hope was obliterated by those aforementioned shocks and traumas, but, convinced that they could put a halt to this process, Turkish leaders did not refrain from massive demonstrations of barbarism, which reached their climax in the Armenian Genocide.

More specifically, the picture of the pre-Republican period is this: the slow and inevitable collapse of a great Empire; wars that were embarked on in order to halt this, but which, once entered on, were impossible to stop and which ended in defeat; humiliation and a continual loss of self-worth; laboring under the weight of a glorious past and the dreams of reviving it (the various Pan-isms), followed by their subsequent collapse; the inability to accept this, and the violent displays and massacres that followed, and which reached their peak in the mass slaughter of the Armenians.

The Turkish Republic, then, perceived itself like an end point, punctuating this long process of collapse, dishonor and fear of annihilation. The Republic is the point at which, in the words spoken by Mustafa Kemal to commander İsmet İnönü after the first Battle of İnönü, 'a halt was put to the Turk's misfortunes.'[25] The strong desire to see the Turkish Republic as a new beginning is the reason that there has still never been a full attempt to come to terms either with the transition from mighty Empire to small state, and the insults to honor experienced, or with the historically unprecedented levels of violence during this long process of decline.

This being the case, we find ourselves confronted by the following picture:

First, the fear that Turkey might be considered guilty for events in the past is a concern that pushes it to try and forget its history. 'Researchers on the subject of collective memory have pointed out a highly interesting relationship between feelings of guilt and the possession of long or short-range collective memory...It is a proven anthropological reality that the collective memory of those who feel guilty is relatively rather short.'[26] Adorno claims that there is a close parallel between the desire not to have any guilt feelings whatsoever after a great catastrophe and the desire to forget.[27] This is because the state of feeling oneself continually accused is unendurable. To remedy this, it is best to forget about it. Adorno provides a number of examples regarding the manner in which the past is taken up in such societies (for example, 'we may have done it, but so did they; the numbers aren't really that high; most of them died from disease; the fundamental responsibility belongs to the foreign powers; the other side must have done some things to provoke this response, otherwise why should so many persons have been killed or sent to their deaths there,' etcetera). Adorno says that 'there is a stupidity embedded within all of these attitudes,' adding that these explanations demonstrate that 'the problem has not been psychologically resolved,' but rather remains 'as a wound.'[28]

Second, Turkey has not yet displayed the necessary reaction to the territorial loss, insults to its honor and humiliation. It keeps it consciously suppressed. Instead, toward everything that reminds Turks of these events, they show extreme emotional reactions, such as are observed in cases of hysterical neurosis. This is because these events are not really forgotten; rather, they continue to live on in the subconscious, in collective memory. Freud, from his observations of patients, claimed that the main cause of hysterical phenomena was that those memories of past experiences that had been pushed back into the subconscious continued to exist.[29]

Due to these two factors, whereby Turkish society erases from its memories a portion of its history and revises history to conform to its present desires, it is not only content to pretend nothing happened, but at the same time, it preserves the mentality that allowed for the violent outbursts and barbarisms of that period in the first place, and thereby allows that mentality to persist. This is the cause of Turkey's profound rejection of any open discussion of violence in its history, first and foremost of which is the Armenian Genocide. Sublimation is not only negation, but rather rejuvenation in a new form. In other words, sublimation cannot prevent the representation of these impulses from continuing to exist in the subconscious.[30] In this way such impulses continue to develop undisturbed, when they are removed from any conscious interference on our parts.[31]

A powerful collective narcissism was created through ideals such as Turanism, Pan-Turkism and Pan-Islamism. But numerous military defeats left these narcissistic desires unfulfilled. This collective narcissism received some serious blows, and certain members of the society, who identified themselves with the collective, never fully came to terms with these feelings of dissatisfaction. Abandonment of earlier goals was not the result of coming to terms with the past, but rather by internalizing the dissatisfaction. In this regard, Mustafa Kemal's utterances on Turanism and Pan-Islam are highly enlightening. He neither claimed to oppose Pan-Turanism or Pan-Turkism in principle, nor did he clearly come to terms with them. Essentially, he said that these two ideologies were wrong, but the reason he gave is that the Turks had attempted to do what they were incapable of achieving. Furthermore, he explained, they had claimed things that they could not do, and he exhorted them not to make such claims.[32] This was not exactly a ringing condemnation of expansionism. Instead, such an attitude clearly leaves the door open for such an enterprise, providing that the nation is up to the task.

In other words, our current reality is that 'in the socio-psychological sense...collective narcissism is ever lying in ambush, waiting for the opportunity to reappear.'[33] And it is, above all else, intimately bound up with everything that would bring Turkey's past into harmony with the narcissistic desires of its conscious mind. But this reality is reestablished in a way in which the hardships, sufferings and barbarities of the past are not presented as they actually took place. I am not claiming here that the collective narcissism that was created before would emerge today with the same Pan-Islamic or Turanist aims as in the past. It is able to define itself in a variety of ways. For example, the manner in which present-day political elites understand the idea of the Republic is far from the fundamental meaning of it as the democratic basis for Turkish citizenship. Rather, they believe that ethnic–cultural brotherhood with other Turkish communities, or religious brotherhood, is the basis of the state. For example, the Turkmenians in northern Iraq are referred to in official language as 'our kin,' while the Kurds in Turkey are referred to as if they were not Turkish citizens, and even as a threat. Even more striking is how Turkey relates officially to its Armenian citizens compared to Azeris in Azerbaijan. Still today the Armenians are described in official publications as foreign citizens (*yabancı vatandas,*) while the Azeris are considered kin.

The result is that this chapter of Turkey's past has yet to be truly finished, and it is preserved in the subconscious, waiting for its chance to be opened anew.

Toward a Conclusion

If Turkey continues to see the 'forgetting' of the past as a precondition for both making peace with history and for living in peace today, it will not achieve peace, because the aim of forgetting is the desire to wipe the slate clean of certain experiences. This almost always means not wanting conflict, seeking peace of mind. But what this desire 'to start from scratch' or to find peace of mind fails to understand is that there is no 'scratch,' no historical 'zero point' from which to start. That which determines whether or not one adopts the alternative of starting anew or of continuing the old is not a readiness to forgive or the longing to find peace of mind. Rather, it is an understanding, one that leads to the rediscovery of events one has forgotten, that will fundamentally determine whether or not such mentalities and modes of behavior will continue to exist.

The easiest way to put a stop to this process of forgetting is to place remembering at the center of all historical writing. The concept of history is generally used in order to contemporize our collective past, whereas remembering is more often concerned with contemporizing the personal past of individuals. For this reason, we may define remembering as a type of 'personalizing' or 'privatizing' history.

> History means an exploration of the past through a collective, supra-individual subject. For this reason, it possesses a natural affinity for national, social and economic history: in short, for the subjects which refer to a collective history; on the other hand, 'remembering' corresponds to those things in the past that have been marginalized by the collective.[34]

In other words, remembering serves to bring to light the areas that have been forgotten or neglected by historical writing. 'Remembering encompasses everything in the human past which has been ignored, excluded or suppressed, and which, for this reason, is never known and acknowledged by the collective and cannot surface in the accepted public space.'[35] As I have previously suggested, we must place remembering squarely at the center of writing history. Only in this way can the gap between the official history that prevails in Turkey and the collective memories of individuals be bridged. My point of departure is the assumption that there are no insurmountable barriers between the individual and collective pasts, because individual remembrance is also a social phenomenon, and for this reason, what is being proposed is the socialization of individual memory.

The truth that we must hold to is this: thinking about the past means transforming it into a component of identity, as an instance of identification; it is a work that could be easily done by the new generations who do not have a direct responsibility for past events. In other words, this task falls upon today's generation. This is both because they possess the 'innocence' of having been 'born late'—and I use this term fully cognizant of its rather negative connotations[36]—and because we know that a collective cannot easily erase the fears and anxieties bequeathed to it by its historical experience. What I propose, however, is that, with the help of the social sciences and of psychology in particular, it is still possible to bring these anxieties down to a level at which they may be borne, and, what is more, to use them in such a way that they can be a beneficial factor for the present development of society.

Memories that are of a traumatic character and situations of past conflict must be returned to the conscious mind, and must be responded to in a conscious manner. The ability to render remembering harmless and unproblematic is directly linked to whether or not a sufficiently conscious response can be manifested toward past experiences. When getting rid of hysterical phenomena, the most important aspect of the therapy is for past events to be brought to the level of the conscious and discussed. With regard to Turkey and its history, there is a definite need to accept this as a sort of societal therapy.

The understanding of the denial syndrome through the establishment of a series of taboos is not merely a matter of psychology or social psychology. Overarching these conditions are economic–political developments associated with the planning, organization and implementation of the wartime Armenian Genocide. Indeed, as has been pointed out above, many of the operatives in the Turkish national movement were among the foremost organizers of the wartime Genocide. Chapter 8 sets out to examine the primary motivation of these accomplices, who so eagerly joined the national movement. Two factors emerge. One concerns the immense wealth these perpetrators acquired as a result of the pillage and robbery attending the Genocide. There was a fear that with the help of the victorious Entente powers some surviving Armenians might be able to reclaim these stolen riches. The other factor concerned the prosecution and punishment of these perpetrators by the courts-martial which had issued arrest warrants against some of them. Beyond these considerations was the general public aversion, if not indignation, to any identification with the crime of organized mass murder. Chapter 8 will try to differentiate the class of the actual perpetrators and the culpable associates from the rather hetero- geneous mass of the rest of 'Turkish society,' beset with problems of ignorance, apathy, reticence, etcetera.

NOTES

1. Süleyman Kocabaş, *Ermeni Meselesi Nedir ve Ne Değildir* (Istanbul, 1987), p. 9.
2. Ihsan Sakarya, *Belgelerle Ermeni Sorunu*, T.C. GenelKurmay Yayını (Publication of the General Staff) (Ankara, 1984), p. 160.
3. Enver Ziya Karal, *Osmanlı Tarihi*, vol. VIII (Ankara, 1988), p. 145.
4. Salâhi R. Sonyel, *Türk Kurtuluş Savaşı ve Dış Politika*, vol. II (Ankara, 1986), p. 36.
5. Sigmund Freud, *Totem und Tabu, Gesammelte Werke: Band IX* (Frankfurt a.M., 1972), p. 26.
6. *Ibid.,* p. 32.
7. *Ibid.*, p. 41.
8. *Ibid.*, p. 43 Freud used the term 'unconscious' in the same sense that we today use 'subconscious,' and thus, the latter term will be used throughout this chapter.
9. *Ibid.*, p. 36.
10. Translated and cited in Gary Smith, 'Arbeit und Vergessen,' in Gary Smith and Hinderk M. Emrich (eds.), *Vom Nutzen des Vergessens* (Berlin, 1996), p. 15.
11. Claude Lévi-Strauss, *Das wilde Denken* (Frankfurt a.M., 1968), pp. 270–1.
12. Alois Hahn and Herbert Willems, 'Schuld und Bekenntnis in Beichte und Therapie,' in Jörg Bergmann, Alois Hahn and Thomas Luckmann, eds, *Religion und Kultur* (Opladen, 1993), p. 310.
13. Sigmund Freud, *Gesammelte Werke, Band I: Die Abwehr-Neuropsychosen* (Frankfurt a.M., 1972), p. 62.
14. The information which follows was taken from Stavros Mentzos, *Hysterie, Zur Psychodynamik unbewusster Inszenierungen* (Munich, 1980), pp. 72–82.
15. *Ibid*, p. 160.
16. *Ibid*, p. 163.
17. *Ibid*, p. 178.
18. Istvan Bibó, *Die Deutsche Hysterie, Ursachen und Geschichte* (Frankfurt a.M. and Leipzig: 1991), p. 25.
19. *Ibid.*, p. 22.
20. Russell Jacoby, *Soziale Amnesie, Eine Kritik der konformistischen Psychologie von Adler bis Laing* (Frankfurt a.M., 1980), p. 23.
21. Eberhart Lämmert, in Gary Smith and Hinderk M. Emmerich (eds.), *Vom Nutzen des Vergessens*, p. 11.
22. Maurice Halbwachs, *Das Kollektive Gedächtnis* (Frankfurt a.M., 1991), p. 62.
23. *Tarihi Araştırmalar ve Dökümantasyon Merkezleri Kurma ve Geliştirme Vakfi, Ottoman Archives, Yıldız Collection: The Armenian Question*, vol. I (Istanbul, 1999), p. xii.
24. Norbert Elias, *Studien über die Deutschen* (Frankfurt a.M., 1990), p. 10.
25. The reality is that there was no actual battle, and therefore no actual victory. Kemal's overstatement shows the importance for the Turks of putting a stop to the process of decline.
26. Dan Diner, 'Gedächtnis und Methode, über den Holocaust in der Geschichtsschreibung,' in Hanno Loewy, ed., *Auschwitz: Geschichte, Rezeption und Wirkung* (Frankfurt a.M., 1996), p. 11.
27. Theodor W. Adorno, 'Was bedeudet: Aufarbeitung der Vergangenheit,' *Gesammelte Schriften*, vol. 10.2 (Frankfurt a.M., 1977), p. 555.
28. *Ibid.*, p. 557.
29. Sigmund Freud, *Der psychische Mechanismus hysterischer Phänomene, Gesammelte Werke Band. I* (Frankfurt a.M., 1972), pp. 88–9.
30. Sigmund Freud, *Die Verdrängung, Gesammelte Werke, Band. X* (Frankfurt a.M., 1972), p. 249.

31. *Ibid.*, p. 251.
32. For Mustafa Kemal's various speeches on this subject, see *TBMM Gizli Celse Zabıtları,* vol. II (Ankara 1985), p. 355; and Gazi Mustafa Kemal, *Nutuk, vol. II (1920–1927)* (Istanbul, 1934), p. 2.
33. Theodor W. Adorno, 'Was bedeutet: Aufarbeitung der Vergangenheit,' p. 564.
34. Frank R. Ankersmit, 'Die postmoderne "Privatisierung" der Vergangenheit,' in Herta Nagl-Docekal (ed.), *Der Sinn des Historischen, Geschichtsphilosophische Debatten* (Frankfurt a.M., 1996), p. 208.
35. *Ibid.*
36. This is an allusion to Helmut Kohl's notorious statement regarding the Holocaust debate in Germany in the 1990s.

8

The Genocide and Turkey

The question widely asked, and for which an answer is frequently sought in the West is: 'Why do the Turks deny the Armenian Genocide?' In my opinion, the manner in which this question is posed is problematic and does not fully explain the situation with which we are confronted. First of all, it is not completely clear who this denying 'Turk' is. Is the typology of the Turk that is formed in Western literature on the subject a definition used to designate a concrete group of persons, or rather, is it used in the far more negative sense of 'the other'? For example, is what is implied here by the term 'Turk' all of those persons who live in Turkey? Are we obliged to answer such questions as whether or not we must also include the Kurds, Circassians, Alevis and other groups as falling within the boundaries of this term? If not, does this not simply reproduce the prevailing hegemonic discourse that does not recognize Turkey's ethnic-cultural plurality? And more important, is it possible to equate a common attitude of these different groups relating to genocide with the notion of denial?

When we think a little more deeply about the words we use spontaneously, we see that we have, through our own perceptions, actually contributed to the creation of clichés; we have narrowed our horizons, and have, by our own devices, destroyed our own possibilities for deep analysis.

If we leave aside the abstruse concept of 'the Turk' for a moment, we can see that the attitude of denial to which we have frequently alluded is essentially a state policy. Are the terms we use to define the attitude of the Turkish state regarding the Genocide adequate to explain and clarify the attitude adopted by Turkish society[1] toward this subject? If not, would it not be more correct to say that the attitude of Turkish society cannot be explained with the terms 'rejection' and 'denial'.

Before offering any detailed answers to these questions, I would first like to mention several key points we should keep in mind. The term 'Turkish society' is more illuminating than the term 'Turk.' Second, the term 'denial' does not explain the attitude of Turkish society toward the subject of the Genocide. My assertion is, then, that any effort to consider seriously the relationship between Turkey and the Armenian Genocide cannot merely view Turkey as consisting of the state apparatus and its approach to the subject. Rather, it must also make Turkish society an important element in its analysis. If you make the society an important element of analysis, you soon see just how adequate the term 'denial' is for explaining the subject.

As we will see, the fundamental support for my assertion derives from my separation of the attitude of society from the attitude of the state. I believe that these two attitudes are of a different order, and must be considered separately. In order to understand how the Genocide is dealt with in Turkey, it is essential to make the state–society division the main element of theoretical analysis. Although I am aware of how problematic such a strict distinction can be, I believe that such a separation must nevertheless be made our point of departure. This separation is important in regard to the aforementioned questions and will provide us with some clues on how to answer them. If we start with this separation as our foundation, it will be possible to identify denial as a policy of the state, and to see those who deny the Genocide more concretely. But can we say the same thing about society?

A sentence beginning with the phrase 'the attitude of Turkish society on the subject of the Armenian Genocide,' is likely to reflect the outlook of the person doing the explaining more accurately than that of the society. This is the case because Turkish society, as such, does not in fact possess a single point of reference which we might ask in order to learn its attitude. That being the case, just how can we go about learning who this society is and what its attitude might be?

Strictly speaking, we find that we currently possess no field research from Turkey concerning how the Genocide is perceived by the various segments of Turkish society. In other words, we are confronted with a situation in which the explanation is placed in the mouth of the entity we call society, like a ventriloquist's dummy uttering the thoughts of another. I am aware of this danger, and have therefore laid out several determinants, with the knowledge that what I will say below cannot extend beyond the level of my subjective observations.

First of all, when one speaks of the attitude of Turkish society on this subject, I suggest that it be portrayed as ignorance, apathy, fatalism, reticence and silence rather than denial. I use here silence and avoidance not in the sense of a single attitude that is jointly held by all segments of society, but merely to mean not openly taking a stance toward the official state narrative.

Second, I believe that one cannot truly speak of a monolithic Turkish society, or its attitude toward the Armenian Genocide. Instead of a single Turkish society, what we have are many elements, a construct formed out of different sub-collectivities, like the different wagons of a train. But the construct formed by this collective of subgroups does not derive from a shared belief and understanding concerning their need to live together as a society. In the most optimistic of interpretations, we could perhaps say that they are joined together in a search for such shared values. But to the extent that these groups show interest in our topic, each subgroup's understanding of the Armenian Genocide is filtered through its own collective memory, and its own historical experience.

Although the manner in which the subject locates itself in the collective memory of each one of these subgroups does not suggest uniformity, it is still possible to speak of the prevalence of a general tendency in these groups, as we know from the examples of the Alevis and Kurds. The collective memories of the subgroups basically rely on the principles of oral narrative, or word-of-mouth transmission. The questions that remain to be researched are: who are these subgroups, and what are their attitudes on the subject of the Genocide?

Third, there is a difference between these subgroups' collective memories and the state's official policy of denial. With regard to the attitude adopted by society, there are also clear differences between one region and another, and between one group and another. Various attitudes can be observed, from one that claims that, 'Yes, such things happened, but the Armenians had it coming,' to an attitude best characterized by pity, sorrow and/or shame, one that essentially admits that the Armenians were annihilated. In particular, the residents of Eastern Anatolia will even today continue to relate the narratives that they heard from family members of the previous generations. As for the prevailing attitude in environments which do not possess a strong connection with the East, it is ignorance in the true sense of the word. It would be fair to say that, in addition to this ignorance, the attitude of 'I don't know about it, and don't want to get involved,' prevails widely within much of Turkey. State-sponsored education, consisting of nationalistic historiography, is the reason for this ignorance and this attitude. In recent years, this situation of not knowing and not caring has slowly begun to give way to an interest in learning what really happened.

Two different facts would seem to be more important than the attitudes about the subject that are adopted by these collective subgroups. The first is that, in fundamental contrast to the example of Germans and the Holocaust, the attitude of 'We didn't know; we weren't aware' does not appear. That is to say, in Turkey the various aspects of the subject are discussed openly in a positive or negative manner. The second fact, however, is that these discussions are undertaken in the private sphere. Even in situations in which the state's policies on the subject are known to be wrong, no one ventures to oppose them openly. The official position of the state is justified in the public sphere, but its errors are freely discussed in the private sphere. Turkish reality is that, in the public arena, the official state narrative appears to be embraced, while in private, markedly different opinions are voiced and defended. It would not be an exaggeration to say that this has led to a schizophrenic situation.

The silence of which I spoke, or the lack of openness toward the state's position, cannot be explained simply by the intensely oppressive policies of the state. Certainly, this attitude can be understood as a type of survival strategy. But I believe that there are also other causes such as indifference toward or disregard of history. I believe this ignorance and apathy toward historical events reflects a deeply entrenched attitude within Turkish society, which is fostered by Islamic thought and mysticism. This is another point that calls for further consideration and research.

In short, there is a serious gap between the writing of official histories and society's ways of privately remembering and transmitting historical memories. The situation in which Turkey now finds itself can be described as two completely separate attitudes, which have existed side by side without a problem, but which are now beginning to come up against one another. Along with developments in both the international and the national arenas, the silence within society and the private collective memories of the subgroups have begun to confront the official pronouncements of the state and its version of history. I would like to say that Turkey has experienced a process wherein the official state narrative and the narratives of society will slowly end up in confrontation with one another. More specifically, I believe that this encounter, which began earlier in other taboo spheres,[2] will acquire a new dimension through the subject of the Armenian Genocide. I would like to explain this by means of a simple model of how Turkey should be understood.

A Simple Model by Which to Understand Turkey

The Republic of Turkey has in great measure taken over the customs of the Ottoman state with regard to the administrative philosophy and mentality that were prevalent during the Ottoman period. This situation has come about as the result of one significant characteristic of Ottoman-Turkish modernization, namely that, in contrast to the Western example, Ottoman-Turkish modernization did not experience a broadening of power among the new social classes brought forth by this modernization—at least not to the extent that they came to share political power. Ottoman-Turkish modernization began from above with the state as its agent, and as a result there was a limitation on who shared power. In other words, the transition to the Republic was experienced without a fundamental transformation or expansion of the ruling classes. On the contrary, there occurred instead a narrowing of the power base.

I do not say this simply because the cadres who established the Republic were Committee of Union and Progress (CUP) members who had run the Ottoman Empire during its last years. In the broader sense, the Republic was essentially established under the leadership of the Ottoman bureaucracy, and, in particular, a military cadre. The army was the central pillar upon which the Republic was founded, and subsequently it would, in large measure, determine the norms of behavior for the Republic's political elites. This is the most important reason that the values that prevail in Turkish society today are not democratic or liberal values, but rather the values and behavioral norms of the military, such as heroism, authority, and discipline.

The Ottoman administrative tradition and Ottoman conceptions of power derived from an archaic imperial tradition. In this tradition, power draws its legitimacy solely from itself. The state is sacrosanct; the nation does not possess the state, the state possesses the nation. This philosophy treats the state as something apart from society, which counts itself as a special entity, and is organized almost in opposition to society. In the transition from the Ottoman state to the Republic, this philosophy of the state formed itself around the ideology that the state was established in order to counter threats. If we desire to understand the Republic correctly, we might well liken it to a hand brake that has been pulled. In an empire which was broken up and that faced the danger of disappearing entirely, the state apparatus became the brake against disorder and collapse. When the century-old 'sick man of Europe' psychosis is combined with: (1) the Great Powers' plans for partitioning the Ottoman Empire between them; (2) the collapse during the First World War of the plans of the Pan-Islamists and Pan-Turanists, which, it had been believed, would pull the Empire back from the brink of partition; and (3) in parallel with this, the aims of the other nations then on Anatolian soil to establish their own national states, the concept of countering threat emerges as the most important foundation of the legitimacy of the newly established Republic.

Even today, the greatest source of the state's ideological legitimacy is the argument that 'there are forces which continually seek to disperse and destroy us, and it is necessary to defend the state against this danger.' In this work and elsewhere, I call this psychosis of being under threat the 'Sèvres Syndrome,' in reference to the 1920 Treaty of Sèvres, which foresaw a dividing up of Anatolia between the Kurdish, Armenian, Greek and Turkish nations.

The leaders of the new Turkish Republic were imbued with military values and some even had military backgrounds. Their desire was to organize the Republic as a homogenous nation-state. However, it was not long before they saw that the pluralist makeup of Turkish society would create a serious obstacle to this. Thus, the understanding of the 'external threat,' which forms the founding philosophy of the Republic, dovetails with another threat, the 'internal threat.' To overcome this, however, the leaders of the Republic preferred to take the easy road. In order to safeguard their vision of the homogenous nation which was adopted and defended, social differences that threatened this idea of homogeneity were declared taboo, and the discussion of these taboo subjects was included within the scope of legally punishable crimes.

1. 'There are no classes in Turkey. All of us are one unified nation,' it is said. The 141st and 142nd Articles of the Penal Code forbid discussion of the existence of social classes.

2. 'There are no Kurds in Turkey; the Kurds are actually mountain Turks,' it is said. The 125th and 171st Articles of the Penal Code and others have been employed against those who claim that Kurds actually exist as a separate ethnicity.

3. 'In Turkey there is a secular, Western society. One is not allowed to speak of or promote Islamic values and culture,' it is said. The 163rd Article of the Penal Code was created in order to forbid the claim of a prevailing Islamic culture. Mentioning Alevism (another religious minority in Turkey) is not considered a crime according to the Penal Code. However, openly worshipping according to Alevi practice or establishing an association that includes the word Alevi etcetera, are included in this prohibition.

4. 'There is no Armenian Genocide; such a thing never happened,' it is said. For this matter there was no need to have a special article for the Penal Code, because there was virtually no one left who would claim otherwise.

5. The armed forces are the guardian for these taboo subjects. Their task is to defend and protect the Republic, which was founded upon these taboos. For this reason, it was also taboo to speak about the role of the armed forces in politics.

These taboos stand as the basic principles of the Turkish Republic, and they became state dogmas. In other words, the Turkish state was established by denying its own social reality and the existence of ethnic-religious and cultural differences in society. The different groups were seen as problems and threats to the security of the Republic.

First, in the 1920s and 1930s, the period in which the republican state was attempting to establish and stabilize itself, Kurds, Islamic groups and various social classes revolted against the aforementioned principles. Between 1920 and 1938, there were more than twenty Kurdish uprisings against the denial of their existence. By the end of the 1930s, repeated and successful government suppression had brought these revolts to an end. The second phase of the uprisings began after the Second World War, when the state decided to implement a multi-party system as a result of international pressure.

In the 1950s and especially in the 1960s, leftist movements began to rebel against the country's imposed political system. Shortly thereafter, Kurdish and Islamic groups began to resume their revolts as well; they rapidly began to play an important role in the growing and general resistance against the state. All of these groups, regardless of how openly they might have expressed their own views, were attempting to destroy the state in order to replace it with an ideal state of their own. As a result, the military, which perceived itself as the owner of the state and the guardian of the five taboos, organized four *coups d'état* as a way to forestall and suppress these revolts. The first coup took place in 1960, and has been followed by others at a rate of one per decade, in 1971, 1980 and 1997. Even though the Kurds and all of the other groups ultimately failed to destroy the state, through their efforts they did succeed in altering the political structure. It is no longer a taboo to discuss the existence of these groups; the restrictions against public discourse concerning them were lifted one by one.

Turkey's continuing attempt to join the European Union has also resulted in an ongoing struggle to lift social and cultural restrictions on the various ethnic, religious and social groups within Turkey. In addition, discussion of the role of the military in Turkish social and political life (the fifth taboo) is no longer off limits. It is therefore no coincidence that the fourth taboo—the Armenian Genocide—has become an important topic on the national and international agenda, since the other areas have become more or less publicly acknowledged. It is also apparent that the international community is using this issue as a basis to interfere in Turkish affairs, just as they did with the other issues in the past. There is, however, a significant difference between lifting the Armenian taboo and lifting the other taboos.

It must be added that the process of cracking open the door of the Armenian taboo has taken place in a healthy manner, to a degree incomparably greater than that of the other taboo areas. The social forces that were activated in order to eliminate the other taboo topics demonstrated a political attitude that basically aimed to destroy the existing state. The enemy was perceived to be the existing state, and thus the problem was to be resolved by overthrowing it. As for the Armenian taboo, however, those who broached the subject have no such design or intention; they are only advocating a change of state policy towards the Armenians and calling for an open debate on this issue as a crucial part of the democratization process. In this respect, we can see them as a grassroots movement. I have no doubt that this taboo will eventually be lifted, yet it will take some time as it is a painful subject for the Turkish state and society to deal with. The core problem is this: the state's policy with regard to the Armenian Genocide is denial, while society's attitude is to keep aloof from the issue. Society has begun very slowly to take a stance, albeit with differing accounts and tendencies. For this reason, when considering Turkey's relationship to the Armenian Genocide, we must develop a discourse that does not simply take the entity of the state as its basis, but that takes the various segments of society into consideration, as well.

Why Do 'Turks' Get So Upset When The Subject Is Brought Up?

One important question is why 'Turks' are unable to speak calmly about the Genocide when the subject is brought up. In this regard it is possible to provide some very simple answers. I am leaving aside the state-society model here, and instead I would like to limit myself simply to the level of ideological critique and to set forth several arguments.

'Unfair Accusations'

The Turks are unable to speak calmly about the subject because, as a nation, they feel confronted by a serious accusation and indictment. In nationalist discourse this sentiment is perceived as an accusation that puts into question four thousand years of glorious Turkish history, and attributes to the Turkish nation a crime of which it is not capable. My own nephew, for example, an aspiring businessman who works at a bank in New York and knows nothing about the subject, perceives the Genocide as an enormous accusation and indictment because, as he stated, 'It's a very bad feeling to be accused of being a killer. How can I admit that I'm a killer?'

There are questions that must be addressed. Is the harsh reaction of Turks caused by displeasure at being accused of something with which today's Turks have no connection? If not, are we merely confronted with the fact that the state authorities, who know full well what was done, are using nationalist discourse to manipulate successfully the understandable feelings of the Turk on the street? Third—and in my opinion, the most important question: what answer shall we give to my nephew and others like him? If he admits that great evil was done to the Armenians, and even that what occurred was Genocide, will my nephew be branded as belonging to a nation of murderers? What does it mean to be a member of a collective group that possesses this dubious honor? These questions still await answers.

Let us leave the answers for Chapter 9. What is important here is to know that we possess ample material with which to refute the claim of 'unfair accusations.' What I mean, though, is not only that the existing documented and archival material is sufficient to show that an enormous, organized crime was committed, whatever name we care to give it. The Turkish reaction that we observe is far beyond being the reaction of a person who is unfairly accused. If Turkey really believes that it is innocent, the easiest thing would be to bring forward the evidence proving its innocence. The accused should provide his own exculpatory material, translate foreign archival material into his own language, invite the accuser to an open debate, and so prove his innocence. But not only are such things not being done on the Turkish side, it is well known that those who claim that such events did indeed occur have been put on trial. There is a state ban on every debate on the Genocide, and the state controls, through its various institutions, how the debate actually takes place. Turkey's attitude resembles in a way the attitude of a person who knows he is guilty.

Beyond that, there is ample evidence that puts into serious doubt the Turkish position that the accusations are unfounded. From various public statements and publications by those involved at the time and from writers today, we know of the existence of the widespread assumption that Turks did those things. Let it suffice here for me to give but a few examples. After the resolution of the French Parliament in 2001 recognizing the Armenian Genocide, the following appeared in a Turkish newspaper:

> If anyone lived on our lands and assaulted Turkish property, lives and honor, however dishonorable (*namussuz*) and mongrelized a race (*soyukırık*), we have given them their just rewards…We think those things that our uncles and fathers did were correct, and if the same assault were to occur again, we would do what was necessary, come what may…Let world opinion know this…Too bad they didn't cut them all down, so that those who survived could not bring disaster upon us.[3]

The original cadres who founded the Republic had no aversions to openly and repeatedly expressing similar views. For example, Halil Menteşe, who was one of the well-known CUP leaders, wrote: 'If we had not rid our eastern provinces of the Armenian brigands, who collaborated with the Russians, there would have been no possibility of establishing our national state.'[4] Lengthy discussions were conducted in the first parliament of the young Republic, discussions in which Turks even dared to allow themselves to be called 'murderers' for the purpose of saving the homeland.

> You are aware that the Deportation matter was an event which has put the world in an uproar and has caused us all to be thought of as murderers. We knew even before this was carried out that the Christian world would not stand for this and

that they would direct all of their wrath and fury at us on account of it. [But] why have we attached the title of murderer to ourselves? Why have we entered into such an immense and difficult matter? These are things that were done in order to secure the future of our homeland, which we know is greater and holier than even our own lives.[5]

In scholarly works written on the subject, it is possible to find similar explanations: the well-known researcher Bilal Şimşir writes the following in regard to the Governor General (vali) of the Province of Diyarbakır, Dr Reşit, who was arrested on the charge that he had personally organized the massacre of Armenians in his province. Reşit later escaped from prison, and, upon learning that he would be captured, committed suicide:

> The Governor General is a conscious idealist...He sees the frightful revolutionary organization of the Armenians through their eyes. His thoughts are 'that if we leave this organization as it is, before long we will be hard-pressed to find a single Turk left in Anatolia.' To himself he says 'Hey, Dr. Reşit, there are two possibilities here: either the Armenians clear out the Turks, or they are cleared out by the Turks.' In 1915, when the 'Law on Deportation' was issued and the order came to deport the Armenians beyond [the borders of] Anatolia, Governor General Dr. Reşit Bey implemented this command enthusiastically in the region of Diyarbakır.[6]

Dr Reşit did this with such great enthusiasm that he began to kill not just the Armenians, but all of the Christian population within the city. Talat Paşa became disturbed by the situation and was forced to intervene, saying to Dr Reşit 'you have misunderstood the orders.'[7]

It is possible to find dozens of other, similar examples. For this reason, it would seem rather difficult to place this problem under the rubric of 'anger at being falsely accused.' The most important aspect of the 'Yes, we did it, and if necessary, we'd do it again' attitude is the absence of any sense of guilt, in particular because this situation makes it extremely difficult for the subject to be examined with concepts like 'trauma' and 'repressed memory.' This is because if a fact is made into a taboo and psychologically suppressed, it requires a moral stance in order for it to be considered a crime. Such a moral stance is what we are missing in this kind of response.

Guilt and Trauma

Another response that could be given concerning the subject is: 'We don't want to be reminded of the past, because of the great bitterness associated with what happened.' This response reflects the mental state of every collective that has experienced great traumas in its history, but which has not had the courage to confront them face to face and for this reason has preferred to either suppress or forget them. Some articles that follow this line of argument have begun to appear in the Turkish press. For example:

> Such great bitterness and sorrow lie in our past that we desire not to study them, but to forget them entirely. We simply don't have the strength to face this much grief. Because others have accused us of having caused their suffering, the claim of the Armenian Genocide incites us—we who have struggled to forget our own grief—to indignation and rebellion.[8]

The primary claim is this: the Turks also suffered greatly, especially in the Balkans and in the Caucasus. We prefer to forget this grief of ours. You should do the same thing. Come, together let us wipe the slate clean and forget about it. The first point here is of the desire for equalizing the suffering. This sentiment can be expressed with the words, 'We did it and so did they. Why is it that only those things done to the Armenians are put on the agenda, and those things done to us Turks and Muslims are not?' These claims can be read two ways:

First, we have the desire of those individuals who know what was done to the Armenians to cover up those things out of feelings of guilt. We can assert that this attitude contains an important difference from that of 'Yes, we did it. And what of it?,' particularly in regard to the feeling of guilt. The fear that they might be considered guilty for things which occurred in the past is a concern that pushes them to try and erase history.

> Researchers on the subject of collective memory have pointed out a highly interesting relationship between feelings of guilt and the possession of long- or short-range collective memory…It is a proven anthropological reality that the collective memory of those who feel guilty is relatively rather short.[9]

Theodor Adorno claims that after great catastrophes there is a strong parallel between the desire not to possess any feelings of guilt and the desire not to remember the catastrophe, to forget it and to erase it from history,[10] because the continual sense of being accused is something unbearable and therefore best forgotten. Adorno provides some examples of how the past is dealt with in such societies: they did it and so did we; the actual numbers weren't that high; many of them died of disease; the foreign powers were chiefly responsible; the others certainly must have done something, otherwise, why would so many people have been cut down or sent to their deaths. 'There is a certain stupidity embedded in all of these, which,' he says, are indications 'that these problems have not been psychologically resolved,' and that they remain 'as a wound.'[11] If one reads the official Turkish arguments and declarations regarding the Armenian Genocide, one finds word for word the same arguments. So we can assume that a deep feeling of guilt is one important reason for this kind of reaction.

The feelings of guilt are further complicated by a fear of punishment. This punishment could be realized in such ways as international censure and being forced to pay reparations. In Turkish discourse, the following argument is commonly heard: 'If we accept the Genocide, then the claim for reparations will soon follow.' It shows that the main fear is not what we should call the event, but what comes after the event.

The second reading is along the lines of avoiding those things that were indeed experienced in the past, due to their horrific nature. For this reason, confronting the grief is avoided, and an escape is sought from the negative consequences of recalling this grief. The preferred option here is to act as if nothing happened, to deny those things that were experienced. We can argue, however, that this kind of approach to history resembles the pathological attitude described in psychoanalysis as the hysterical personality and becomes a source for psychological diseases.[12] According to Freud, 'neurosis is to be compared to a traumatic illness. It comes about through the inability to deal with an emotional experience of exceptional intensity.'[13] As I argue elsewhere in this book, Turkish society suffers from this problem and the only way to healing is an open discussion of past grief.[14]

In short, even in denial discourse there are different reactions to the Armenian Genocide. These range from 'yes we did it and would do it again', to 'not only Armenians were killed by Muslims but Muslims were killed by Armenians,' to 'something happened but it is better not to talk about it.' Despite the differences, there is a common characteristic in all these reactions: to avoid any open debate about the history. The main reason seems to be the belief that these events belong to a past that does not relate to today's Turkey. With the establishment of the Turkish Republic came the creation of a new identity and the opportunity to ignore old wounds. This belief seems to me problematic.

We Do Not Want the Identity That We Have Created to Be Dissolved

By condemning history to obscurity, Turks are not content simply to be released of all its burdens. They believe they have created an entirely new Turkish national identity. For this purpose they erase all the unpleasant connections between the Armenian Genocide and today's Republic. Yet one of the key reasons for avoiding all discourse on the Genocide and the repression of the history of the Republic is precisely the connection between the two.

I dealt with this issue in detail in a previous book and do not want to delve too deeply into the matter here.[15] My central argument is that there is a continuity of the ruling elite from the Ottoman Empire to the Turkish Republic, and so there is a strong relationship between the Armenian Genocide and the foundation of the Republic. In brief, I would like to mention three aspects of this connection. First, the Turkish resistance movement in Anatolia was essentially organized by the CUP, which also organized the Genocide. It is known that the plans for this movement were already drafted during the First World War. In case of military defeat, preparations were to be made to organize a long-lasting resistance. These plans were carried out during the Armistice of 1918 and thereafter.[16]

An important point is that organizations, such as the 'Society for the Defense of the Rights of Anatolia and Rumelia' and 'Rejection of Occupation,' that were the mainstay of the forces supporting the national movement in Anatolia, were formed either directly on the order of Talaat Paşa or with the aid of the *Karakol* (police force) organization connected to Talaat and Enver. If we look at the regions in which those organizations were established and the order in which they were founded, it becomes clear that these events initially took place everywhere that a perceived Armenian or Greek danger existed. Of the first five resistance organizations that were founded after the Mudros Armistice agreement, from October 30, 1918 to the end of the year, three were directed against the Armenian and two against the Greek minorities.[17]

The local cadres of the CUP constituted the main elements among the founders of these associations. This overlap of membership was so great that when later the central organization the A-RMHC (Society for the Defense of the Rights of Anatolia and Rumelia), formed a party, it was stipulated that no one from the Freedom and Accord Party, seen as an enemy of the CUP, could become a member.[18] An important mission of the *Karakol* movement, which organized the national movement in Anatolia, was to arrange the escape to Anatolia of those CUP members who had been involved in the Armenian Genocide and who were then being sought by the British. To some extent the organization was a symbol of the nexus linking the Armenian Genocide to the resistance movement in Anatolia.

The second important connection between the Genocide and the national movement concerned the formation of a new class of wealthy men in Anatolia who had enriched themselves thanks to the Genocide. Even Turks point to the fact that the economic motive played an important role in the Armenian Genocide. An important figure in the national movement, Halide Edip, said, 'there was a strong economic [motive]...this was to end the economic supremacy of the Armenians thereby clearing the markets for the Turks and the Germans.'[19] The prominent people who had enriched themselves through the Genocide feared that the Armenians could return to avenge themselves and reclaim their goods. After all, this was part of the Allied agenda. These *nouveaux riches* were drawn even closer to the national movement on those occasions when Armenians did return with occupying forces to reclaim their goods and carry out a few acts of revenge, especially in the Çukorova (Adana) region. The newly rich thus became an integral part of the national movement. In many areas, resistance was directly organized by these elements. It was no accident that in many regions the leadership of the national resistance organizations included people whose fortunes had been made as a consequence of the Genocide of the Armenians.

Among those who had been enriched through the Genocide were some who served directly at the side of Kemal himself. Topal Osman, for example, was one who later advanced to the rank of commander of the guard battalion, (which protected the institution of the Grand National Assembly in Ankara, and the person of Mustafa Kemal); and Ali Cenani, who had been exiled to Malta, and later became the minister of commerce in the new Republic. The list can be expanded. It is not surprising, therefore, that on September 22, 1922, the national government reinstated the decree of September 1915 which confiscated the so-called 'Abandoned Goods' of the Armenians.[20] (The September 1915 decree had been repealed by the Istanbul government on January 8, 1920.) The government in Ankara knew it had to take into account the interests of those who had a share in the founding of the Republic.

The third important link between the Genocide of the Armenians and the Republic is a natural outcome of the first. The initial organizers of the national movement were people who had directly participated in the Genocide. Those who set up the first units of the National Forces in the Marmora, Aegean, and Black Sea regions and held important posts in these units were for the most part people sought by the occupation forces and the government in Istanbul for their participation in the Genocide. When Kemal began to organize the resistance in Anatolia, he received the strongest support from the CUP members, for whom there were arrest warrants on account of their role in the Genocide.[21]

Many who were sought or who were actually arrested and deported to Malta for their role in the Genocide, but fled or escaped later, received important posts in Ankara. There are many examples, but a few should suffice here. Şükrü Kaya became the interior minister and held the office of secretary-general in the Republican Peoples Party (Cumhuriyet Halk Partisi), founded by none other than Mustafa Kemal. During the deportations of the Armenians, he was director general of the Office for the Settlement of Nomadic Tribes and Refugees. This was attached to the interior ministry and was officially responsible for the implementation of the Armenian 'deportations.' For this reason Şükrü Kaya was also known as director general for Deportation (*Sevkiyat Reis-i Umumisi*). Mustafa Abdülhalik (Renda) was the governor of Bitlis and later Aleppo during the Genocide. Rössler (Germany's veteran consul at Aleppo) said of him that:

'[He] works inexorably on the annihilation of the Armenians.'[22] In an affidavit prepared by Vehip Pasha, the commandant of the Third Army during the war, the special role of Abdülhalik Renda in the Genocide is emphasized.[23] According to General Vehip's testimony, thousands of human beings were burned alive in the region around Mush, a district under the control of Mustafa Abdülhalik. This event is mentioned in German consular reports as well as by eyewitnesses.[24]

Arif Fevzi (Prinçcizade), who was a deputy from Diyarbekir during the war years, was suspect number 2743 in the warrant prepared by the British for the detainees in Malta. He had been assigned to the group implicated in the Genocide, and was to be charged as such. Subsequently he held the office of minister of public affairs from July 21, 1922 to October 27, 1923. Ali Cenani Bey, the CUP deputy for Aintep, was suspect number 2805. He had enriched himself from the spoils associated with the Genocide, and 'In the English archives...a very dirty file exists on him.'[25] He was the minister of commerce between November 22, 1924 and May 17, 1926.[26] Dr Tevfik Rüştü Aras was also one of those who held important political posts in subsequent years. During the First World War he was a member of the High Council on Health, which was responsible for the burial of Armenians.[27] Between 1925 and 1938, he served as foreign minister of the Republic of Turkey.

This list could be extended by several pages. It can be stated conclusively that Mustafa Kemal led 'the war of liberation...with Ittihatists [CUP members] who were sought for Greek and Armenian incidents and... was supported by and relied on prominent persons who carried the ghost of the Greeks and Armenians into the subculture of the resistance movement.'[28] Participation in the national war of liberation was a vital necessity, a last refuge for all members of CUP, and especially the Special Organization that masterminded the organization of the Genocide. Only two alternatives existed for them. Either they surrendered to be sentenced to hard labor or death, or they fled to Anatolia and organized the national resistance. A well-known journalist and close friend of Mustafa Kemal, Falih Rıfkı Atay, expressed this clearly:

> When the English and their allies began to demand an accounting from the Ittihatists [CUP members] and especially the murderers of the Armenians, after the end of the war everyone who had something to hide armed himself and joined a gang.[29]

I think the main reason the Turks avoid any discussion on history and make it a taboo lies in the reality of this connection between the Armenian Genocide and the foundation of the Turkish Republic. The devastation that would ensue if Turks had to now stigmatize as 'murderers and thieves' those whom they are used to regarding as 'great saviors' and 'people who created a nation from nothing,' is palpable. It seems so much simpler to deny the Genocide completely than to seize the initiative and face the obliteration of ingrained notions about the Republic and Turkish national identity.

One of the most unusual aspects of the Armenian Genocide is the inordinate survival of the conflict between the Turkish and Armenian communities, which are still quarreling and vilifying each other on the issue of that Genocide. An attempt is made in Chapter 9 to diagnose the underlying problems sustaining this conflict, at the same time offering suggestions for possible remedies, with a view to achieving new opportunities for reconciliation. A poignant aspect of this discussion is the explicit and firm recognition that the Turkish state, as it is constituted today, will for the foreseeable future remain the unyielding pillar of the denial of the Armenian Genocide. Nevertheless, Chapter 9 will propose alternatives through which the powerful inertia of this policy of denial can be confronted and eventually eroded.

NOTES

1. It should be noted here that the liberal/critical thinkers in Turkey generally prefer the phrase 'society of Turkey' over 'Turkish society' and other phrases that are not felt to reflect adequately its pluralistic construction. Here I will continue to use the latter term, but in the sense conveyed by the first.
2. This subject is explored in more detail in Chapter 1 of this book.
3. *Akit*, 12 Şubat (February), 2001.
4. Y. H. Bayur, *Türk İnkilabı Tarihi*, vol. II, part IV (Ankara 1983), pp. 654–5.
5. From the speech made by Hasan Fehmi Bey at the secret session of the Turkish Grand National Assembly on 17 Teşrinievvel 1336 (October 17, 1920), *TBMM Gizli Celse Zabıtaları*, (Ankara, 1985), vol. I, p. 177.
6. Bilal Şimşir, *Malta Sürgünleri* (Ankara, 1985), p. 47.
7. For detailed information concerning the event, see Taner Akçam, *Insan Hakları ve Ermeni Sorunu* (Ankara, 1999), pp. 25–6.
8. Gündüz Aktan, *Radikal*, 27 Eylül (September), 2000.
9. Dan Diner, 'Gedächtnis und Methode, über den Holocaust in der Geschichtsschreibung,' in Hanno Loewy, ed., *Auschwitz: Geschichte, Rezeption und Wirkung* (Frankfurt a.M., 1996), p. 11.
10. Theodor W. Adorno, 'Was bedeutet: Aufarbeitung der Vergangenheit,' *Gesammelte Schriften*, Vol. 10.2 (Frankfurt a. M., 1977), p. 555.
11. *Ibid.*, p. 557.
12. The following information was taken from: Stavros Mentzos, *Hysterie, Zur Psychodynamik unbewußter Inszenierungen*, (München, 1980), pp. 72–82.
13. Sigmund Freud, *Die Vorlesungen zur Einführung in die Psychoanalyse*, *Gesammelte Werke, Band XI* (Frankfurt a.M., 1972), p. 285.
14. See Chapter 7.
15. Taner Akçam, *Insan Hakları ve Ermeni Sorunu* (Ankara, 1999).

16. For information about such plans compare Şeref Çavuşoglu, 'Ittihat ve Terakkinin Gizli Plânı,' *Yakın Tarihimiz* 1 (1962), p. 263; Nurdoğan Taçalan, *Ege'de Kurtuluş Savaşı Başlarken* (Istanbul, 1970), pp. 165–6.

17. Baskın Oran, *Atatürk Milliyetciliği. Resmi Ideoloji Dışı Bir Inceleme* (Ankara, 1988), p. 146.

18. Mete Tuncay, *Türkeye Cumhuriyetinde Tek Parti Yönetiminin Kurulması, 1923–1931* (Ankara, 1981), p. 36.

19. Halide Edip, *Memoirs of Halide Edip* (London, 1926), p. 386.

20. Gotthard Jäschke and Erich Pritsch, *Die Turkei seit dem Weltkriege. Geschichtskalender 1918–1928* (Turkey since the World War, 1918–1928: A historical calendar) (Berlin, 1929), p. 65.

21. Doğan Avcioğlu, *Milli Kurtuluş Tarihi*, vol. 3 (Istanbul, 1986), p. 1181.

22. German Foreign Office, *Turkey*, 183, vol. 41, file A4215, report of February 9, 1916.

23. A copy of Vehip Pasha's statement of December 5, 1334 (1918) can be found in the Armenian Patriarchate Archive in Jerusalem (series 7, file H, nos. 171–81).

24. German Foreign Office, *Turkey*, 183, vol. 48, A34435, October 1, 1917. See also Vahakn N. Dadrian, 'The Naim–Andonian Documents on the World War I Destruction of Ottoman-Armenians: The Anatomy of a Genocide,' *International Journal of Middle East Studies* 18 (1986), p. 354.

25. Bilâl Şimşir, *Malta Sürgünleri* (Ankara, 1985), p. 317.

26. Nuran Dağlı and Belma Aktürk, eds., *Hükümet ve Programlar 2, 1920–1960*, vol. I (Ankara, 1988), pp. 8ff., 26, 33. Many examples of persons who were deported to Malta and escaped to find their way into Ankara's political apparatus can be found in this work and in Bilâl Şimşir.

27. Vahakn N. Dadrian, 'The Role of Turkish Physicians in the World War I Genocide of the Ottoman Armenians,' *Holocaust and Genocide Studies* 1 (1986), p. 175.

28. Doğan Avcıoğlu, vol. III, p. 1233.

29. F. R. Atay, *Çankaya, Atatürk'ün Doğumundan Ölümüne Kadar* (Istanbul, n.d.), p. 236.

9

Some Theoretical Thoughts
on the Obstacles to
Armenian–Turkish Reconciliation

In this final chapter, I should like to discuss three ideas on the subject of obstacles to Armenian-Turkish reconciliation, and make some remarks on the possibility of reconciliation between the Turkish and Armenian communities. The first point concerns thinking in collective categories, or the question of the balance of 'I' and 'We' regarding individual and group identity. The second concerns the relationship between past and present, or the problem of defining collective identity over time. The third point is related to the stereotyping and dehumanizing of one group by the other. I will try to show how all these points impede or distort Armenian–Turkish relations.

First, I make a general observation. Most people who are familiar with the Armenian Genocide issue believe that the real problem lies in the disagreement over historical events, yet this is true only to a limited extent. If the issue were only a dispute about history, then we could easily verify the facts through available information in terms of official and non-official documents; however, these documents exist in many different languages and are dispersed over many different areas. What needs to be done is very straightforward: we need to create a historical or truth commission to review these documents; we need to make these documents available to everyone; and, we need to have an open and serious discussion about their contents.

That such attempts have never been made (especially in Turkey) suggests that there are problems other than simple disagreement over historical events. We can surmise that these problems lie not in the actual historical occurrences but in the current relationship between the Turks and the Armenians. In other words, their current perceptions of each other seem more important than the past itself. However, I make no judgment here as to the origins or validity of these perceptions. My point is that Armenians and Turks have developed a certain discourse, that is, separate narratives about the past which are an important part of each collective group identity and are used only to reinforce existing national stereotypes. In this way, the perception by each party of itself and others, quite apart from the historical debate, becomes an obstacle to common understanding.

In the discussion between the two groups about the Armenian Genocide, the same arguments are constantly reiterated; each side seems interested only in scoring points against the other or in gathering evidence to confirm long-held views about the other. Instead of thinking about the ways towards an eventual solution, each side makes 'deposits' into a kind of World Bank of trauma and guilt.[1] We can also think of this process as stockpiling rhetorical weapons to be used in political debates. We can argue that the main reasons for such an attitude lie in how the parties think about the relationship between past and present, in how they construct the 'self' and 'other,' as well as in the relationship between the 'self' and 'other.'

In order to disentangle and to clarify this complex issue, I believe we need to make a clear distinction between the actual problem and the manner in which the problem is handled. Apart from the history, our current perception of each other, the language we use, in short our current rela-tions, create additional problems and exacerbate the conflict itself.

Thinking in Collective Categories:
The Terms 'Turks' and 'Armenians'

Up to now, I have been consciously using the terms 'Turks' and 'Armenians' as they are commonly used in the literature and in the debates. The debates are often presented in terms of what the 'Turkish' or 'Armenian' side thinks, says, and/or acts out. Who is this 'Turk' or 'Armenian'? Actually, at first glance, we can surmise what these terms imply. Regarding the 'Turks,' we can say that there is a certain policy which is determined to deny the historical events and we define the agent of this policy as the 'Turk.' As for the term 'Armenian,' it too is an abstract term, one that characterizes the group of people who claim that what happened in 1915 was genocide. Both terms are the abstract symbols for certain policies. However, if we closely analyze these categories as social actors, we would quickly realize that the terms 'Turk' and 'Armenian' are an ahistorical generalization: not so much a definition as a construction. As such, one can easily substitute the terms 'Turk' and 'Armenian' for any characteristic of what comprises the 'Other.' So rather than a historically defined category, we have empty constructions. Hence, the Turk is what the Armenian is not and the Armenian is what the Turk is not.

One of the reasons for using these categories is our way of thinking in collective terms. Almost every individual in both communities identifies him- or herself with their community. I argue that there is little space for being individuals in these relations. I want to show how these collective identities are shaped and operate in Armenian–Turkish relations with the help of sociological analysis of the balance of 'I' and 'We.'

In the popular imagination the individual, 'I', and the group or 'We', are distinct and separate entities that exist in some relation to one another. I believe it is incorrect to think of the individual and the group as separate and distinct. We know from sociology and psychology that such an individual never existed. 'There is no "we" identity where there is no "I" identity.'[2] Although the 'I'/'We' balance is in constant flux, the 'I' and 'We' are never completely separate. Individual identity is a balance of 'I' and 'We.'

The 'We' identity is an important part of individual identity, but its relative weight changes from individual to individual and from group to group. In oppressed groups, for example, the 'We' identity is very strong.

> The sense of self, of either an individual or a group, is intertwined with a sense of ethnicity and nationality to which an individual or a group adheres and adheres even more stubbornly when under the stress of political, economic, or military crises. The more stressed the groups feel, the more important their sense of their nationality will become to them. The more unfavorable a situation is for a group, the more its members will shun contamination with the symbols of its enemy and strive to keep intact their shared identity.[3]

However, the very nature of group affiliation complicates the 'We' and 'I' balance even further. Group identification is not like membership in an organization, from which a person can easily resign. 'It is tinged with raw and primitive effects pertaining to one's sense of self and others and to their externalizations and projections.'[4] The theoretical distinction between 'I' and 'We' that we imagine very easily cannot be made in practice. There is no neat distinction between 'individual' and 'national' identity.

One of the most important characteristics of national identity is the emotional connection. We can define this as the *like/love* relationship. But 'love of nation is never something which one experiences toward a nation which one refers to as "you".' This love is something we experience towards the group we call 'we.' It is a kind of self-love.[5] For this reason, one's image of one's own nation is at the same time a self-image. In fact, this partnership of 'I' and 'We' causes members of the same nation to identify with each other, and makes it very difficult to distance oneself from one's nation. Every criticism or accusation of a collective is perceived by its members as a personal assault.

In everyday life we can observe how complicated this relation is. When a Turk and an Armenian meet each other for the first time, they see each other as the collective representative of the other group. At the same time, the Armenian sees a murderer of his people from the past, and the Turk sees a traitorous Armenian from 1915. They usually talk in collective terms. They are no longer individuals, feeling themselves instead to be representatives of their nations; therefore, every critique from the other side is perceived not only as an assault on the group but also as an individual assault. They do not relate to one another as individuals.

Interestingly enough, this characterization of the public demeanor holds true in academia as well. Today, scholars still debate the Armenian Genocide in relation to their ethnic origin. The ethnicity of the scholar takes precedence over the subject matter almost entirely, as if there were only 'Armenian' and 'Turkish' ways of discussing the subject. Hence, we as scholars witness the strange social condition of the 'ethnification' of the language and discourse around us, as the position cannot be defined independently of the ethnic identity of the speaker. Yet the critical question remains how to separate the subject matter from the ethnicity of the speakers. I would contend that we could only do so by redefining the categories of 'we' and 'other,' and by prioritizing the position that we take over the ethnicity we think we are born into. We need to strive for the ability to observe our own nation at arm's length. My main criticism of Turkish and Armenian scholars is that they have not put enough distance between their theoretical approach and their ethnic belonging. This makes it difficult to create a common language between both societies. And this difficult task can only be accomplished by developing new epistemologies and methodologies in the social sciences.

How Do We Define Collective Identities?

In relations between the communities, how we define collective identities over time creates certain problems. In dealing with the Armenian Genocide, we connect the existing collectivities to past ones that either committed wrongs or were victimized. We create a 'pastness,' a temporal bridge between past and present.[6]

In order to do this we imagine two levels. First we identify two collective groups as perpetrator and victim in the past. Second, we construct two groups that meet each other in the present as representatives of that past. Equating the past perpetrator with its current representative, we hold the present group responsible for atoning for the past perpetrator's action. For this process to be credible, we must tacitly assume that collective identity remains stable over time. Between the past harm and the present atonement, we establish a fictive genealogy from the original perpetrator and victim to their representatives today. In constructing these lineages, we create a sense of 'sameness' between present-day collectives and their counterparts in the past.

I would argue that in current Turkish-Armenian relations the perception of 'sameness' of the present actors (Turks and Armenians) with the past determines in large part how the actors behave toward each other. I have to add that I am not discussing the problem of continuity in terms of institutions or political responsibilities; I am discussing the issue only in terms of the construction of collective identities and the perceptions of these identities. A Turk and an Armenian living today generally tend to speak to each other in terms of their history. They take on the role of historical actors and speak on behalf of them. In their interaction with each other an Armenian today tends to see a Turk and use the term 'Turk' as someone who murdered his ancestors in 1915, while a Turk tends to see and label the Armenian as a 'national traitor.' In other words, both are incapable of viewing each other on their own personal terms in the present. The question is, to what extent can we identify past perpetrator and current collective as 'the same'?

Equating the past and the present is not the only problem. Beyond treating nations or ethnic groups as static entities, we also perceive collective groups as if they are individuals. Because identifying a past perpetrator with a present group becomes increasingly difficult as time passes, we individualize the collectives. That means we ascribe personality to the collective. But this 'collective' individual must be a particular model of individual that transcends constraints of time: it is an abstract, ahistorical individual. We attribute some characteristics to the collective that we actually attribute to the individual, such as shame, honor, guilt, dignity, pride, etcetera. So we establish some groundwork for our expectation from the collectives that are in interaction with each other.

As a result of this mindset the collectives engage in a process of communicating with each other in the name of their historical ancestors. I argue that the 'sameness' between past and present identities is the dominating feature that controls almost every interaction between Armenians and Turks.

Through the operation of this mindset, we not only imagine collective actors as ahistorical abstracts, but there is a double approach to history. On the one hand, we discard history in order to link past actors to their current representatives, while on the other hand we use a particular event of history to define these groups in relation to one another.

In this way of thinking, we gloss over differences between 'I' and 'We' in the present as well as in the past. At the same time we disregard the differences between past actors and their present representatives. Individuals, collectives, past and present are all collapsed together.

One interesting result of this way of thinking reflects itself in the 'accusation' and 'guilt' problem. I would like to give some examples of how this way of thinking is a big obstacle in today's Turkish–Armenian relations. Atom Egoyan's 2002 film *Ararat* was strongly criticized in Turkey as being full of violence even if the violent scenes take up very little of the general flow of the movie. This critique indicates a major psychological problem within the Turkish community. I think the real reason why the violent scenes are perceived as so prevalent in the film, and why many Turks feel offended, is because they view these scenes as directed towards them personally. A friend of mine, whom I consider liberal-minded, wrote me the following after viewing the film with an Armenian friend.

> I was very upset by the content of the film. It had me up all night. After seeing the film...we joined some Armenian friends for drinks. For the first time that I can remember I didn't even enjoy drinking Ouzo. After a film like this, I don't care what your thoughts are, being introduced as a Turk is not easy.

After seeing the film, my friend felt that it was not the historical actors involved but rather *he* that was being accused of the cruel acts depicted. I know that generally in Turkey, this is how 'genocide accusations' are perceived. The present generation, perceiving itself accused of murder, has reverted to a position of psychological self-defense and has attempted to distance itself from such accusations.

This moral issue makes sense only if we create 'sameness' between past and present and imagine the collective as an ahistorical entity with individual characteristics. This just goes to show how little psychological distance there is between the past and present. For people in Turkey to so personally identify with the perpetrators of the Genocide in the film is an indication of where the problem lies. It is the problem of glossing over the differences between individuals and collectives, of sameness, and of equating past and present.

Again, because of this collapse of the past into the present, the representative of the victim group sees the representative of the perpetrator group as an embodiment of the past. Messages intended for the perpetrator are addressed to his current stand-in. In the case of Turkey, official denial makes the situation even worse. I regard this way of thinking as problematic. Instead, we must try to develop a discourse that regards past and present as different entities. We have to know that history is a construction. Not only is there a difference between past and present, but there is also a difference between past and history. 'History' does not equal that which was actually experienced in the past; it is a present-day construction, a narrative interpretation of the past. In other words, the only reality is today, and history ends up being a representation of present-day perceptions of the past. 'History' is not an independent fixed entity that awaits discovery. Rather, it exists only within the context of today and gains meaning only in the space it occupies in the relations between people today. Its importance lies not in what actually occurred, but in how that is perceived by people today.[7]

To sum up, discussing history actually means mostly using the past as a communication tool for discussion with each other today. We think, when we are talking with each other, that we are discussing history, but what we are actually doing, more often than not, is discussing our present. We are discussing our present-day selves, and history is simply a means for this discourse. We have to see history as having meaning only in our present context. Unless we distinguish between our past and our present, communication will remain an obstacle.

In order to overcome this impediment, Turks and Armenians should stop hiding behind historical actors when speaking to each other. It is current-day Turks and Armenians speaking to each other, not their ancestors, and it is as their present selves that they should address each other. Doing so would definitely promote better understanding between the two communities.

Constructing the 'Other'

In constructing the other as an ahistorical, abstract entity, an 'Other', each side has developed a very negative picture of the other, to which they constantly refer. There is a simple mechanism for constructing collective identities. In order to define ourselves mostly in positive terms, we define the other as our opposite. We are wiser, fairer, kinder, more capable, more attractive, and generally better than the other party. The 'other side' is deceitful, aggressive, heartless and incapable of change for the better. Such labels as 'barbaric Turks' or 'Armenian traitors' are frequent and unequivocal. Military terminology is also employed. Some Armenians speak of a 'war' with the 'Turks.' Meanwhile, in the 'enemy camp,' Turkish columnists such as Gündüz Aktan (a former ambassador to the UN and member of the Turkish–Armenian Reconciliation Committee) write of 'psychological war' and develop strategies for conducting it.

There are, of course, many reasons for constructing monolithic, stereotypical images of the other side. Social psychology offers us a general explanation for this attitude: development of the sense of self is strongly related to its separation from the identity of others for its protection and regulation.[8] 'People use and 'need' enemies as external stabilizers of their sense of identity and inner control'[9]

Beyond this general theory, we can give some particular explanations for the Armenian–Turkish case. One very important and obvious one is the denial policy of the Turkish state. Furthermore, some parties may have a vested interest in perpetuating rather than resolving the problem. In particular, nationalistic circles in both camps have formed their narratives and identities in opposition to an imagined enemy. In fact, Turkish ruling elites employ an anti-Armenian attitude to rally the Turkish public around a common national identity. If Turkey were to alter its official stand on the Genocide, its entire national history would have to be rewritten. As for some of the Armenian circles, they too benefit from the existence of an image of the Turk as barbaric and savage; they use these images to explain the Genocide as a natural outcome of the Turkish character.

In general, dehumanized images of the other side are deeply rooted in the mentality of opposing ethnic or religious groups. In addition, all parties, especially in a conflict, have a differentiated view of themselves while maintaining an undifferentiated, stereotypical view of the other. Dehumanization or stereotyping

> may be viewed as a defensive maneuver against painful or unacceptable inner emotional positions. The overwhelming feelings of shame that are the unbearable consequence of historical violation of one's sense of self may easily give rise to the process of dehumanization. Perhaps the easiest way for us to deal psychologically with the cruel attacks of another is to attribute an evil and subhuman nature to that other.[10]

Such deeply ingrained belief systems are extremely resistant to change, especially if they are reinforced by an intense victimhood psychology. Until these attitudes, feelings, behaviors, and mentality are changed, no solution is possible.

The first step in getting Turkish–Armenian relations back on track is to replace negative stereotypes with new and accurate information about each group. Transforming public consciousness is the starting point in every effort at conflict resolution.

Dialogue and Reconciliation

I take the existence of the Turkish state policy of genocide denial as a constant, unchangeable given; it is a policy that has been made consciously and will not change for a considerable period of time. The basic problem is that this policy determines how Turks and Armenians speak about the Genocide, and how they relate to each other. It is not an exaggeration to say that the existence of this policy is the epicenter for all thinking on the issue of the Genocide. Both groups are fixated on the Turkish state policy. The discourse, the language is mostly determined by the paradigm created by the policy of denial.

Without downplaying the importance and crucial character of this policy, I would argue that there is something hypocritical in this fixation. It seems to me that both Turks and Armenians, at least in critical circles, are hiding behind this policy. They are sequestering themselves in order to avoid making themselves active participants in the process of debate on the Genocide. Both societies tend to see each other through the prism of this policy of denial. The relationship between the two communities is chained to the Turkish state policy. Both societies are essentially prisoners of this paradigm. The basic question here is how they can break free from this prison, because therein lies the basic obstacle to the reconciliation.

One important consequence of such hypocrisy is the lack of self-reflection. Neither group is capable of viewing itself critically. The denial policy is the beginning and the end of every explanation for the problems we encounter in Turkish–Armenian relations, but this is not the whole story. In the knowledge that policy change is unlikely in the foreseeable future, I ask, is there any possibility of interaction between the two parties?

We have to put both societies under the microscope in order to create another paradigm, another way of intercommunicating. How can we set aside the practice of seeing each other through this paradigm and instead create a new space in which we can communicate openly with each other? It is a general rule that conflict can only be resolved through direct interaction between both communities. In order to achieve this interaction, both groups have to concentrate their energies on mobilizing their political, cultural, social, and religious resources.

A paradigm shift is necessary that includes new aspects of the conflict, aspects that have never previously been considered. We must reconceptualize the problem and put both societies at the center of our analysis. This paradigm shift should focus on the creation of a new cultural space that encompasses both societies, a space in which people from both sides have the opportunity to learn about each other. In this new sphere of communication we can set our own rules without taking into account the Turkish denial policy.

From conflict resolution theory we know that the reconciliation process embodies the four concepts of truth, mercy, justice, and peace, which lead to reconciliation.[11] Without acknowledging the truth, that is, articulating the events of the past, conflict will never be resolved. We can describe this step as a journey through history to disclose unknown facts. Yet truth alone is insufficient for reconciliation. Truth must be paired with compassion and forgiveness, which would lead to acknowledgement of past injustices and to a new beginning of relating to each other. Without compassion and forgiveness, healing and restoration would be impossible. Yet, mercy alone is insufficient, if it is not combined with justice. Justice, which in this case would mean the search for social restructuring and restitution, would heal wounds, would establish equality, and would rectify the past. Peace is the last step, and would bring respect, mutual understanding and security. The process of reconciliation is the forum in which these four factors are brought together.

The theoretical formulation of this political question is very simple: every kind of discourse, as well as the language we use, is the product of power relations. There are no 'objective' or 'impartial' terms. The words we use are a reflection of certain hegemonic relations or certain mindsets. It is not difficult to see that the existing discourse between the two communities is determined mostly by the Turkish state's policy of denial of the Armenian Genocide. For that reason, if we really want to create a new approach to Armenian–Turkish relations, we have to acknowledge that we should start by creating our own language, our own terms, which would be a product of this new mindset of being willing to reach reconciliation. For example, if we start to think about how we use the terms 'Turks' and 'Armenians,' it would be a great first step. We should avoid using abstract terms and define exactly what we mean. Do we mean the ruling elite, certain social groups, organizations, movements? If we called the subject by name and not simply a 'Turk' or 'Armenian' it would be a huge step towards creating a new language. The languages we use, the narratives that are an important part of our collective identities are products of and produce certain mindsets. We have to consider a new way of thinking. We have to create a different cultural space in which this new approach can develop. One way of doing this is to encourage direct interaction between the two communities, so that each party can develop a realistic image of the other.

NOTES

1. Johan Galtung, 'After Violence, Reconstruction, Reconciliation, and Resolution: Coping with Visible and Invisible Effects of War and Violence,' in Mohammed Abu-Nimer, ed., *Reconciliation, Justice, and Coexistence, Theory and Practice* (New York, Oxford 2001), p. 4.
2. Norbert, Elias, *Die Gesellschaft der Individuen* (Frankfurt a.M.,1987), p. 246.
3. Vamik D. Volkan, 'An Overview of Psychological Concept Pertinent to Interethnic and/or International Relationship,' in Vamik Volkan, Demetrios A. Julius, Joseph V. Montville, eds, *The Psychodynamic of International Relationships: Concept and Theories* (Lexington, Massachusetts/Toronto, 1990), p. 32.
4. Volkan, p. 36.
5. Norbert, Elias, *Studien über die Deutschen* (Frankfurt a.M., 1990), pp. 196–7.
6. My arguments here are based on some points raised by Michel-Rolph Trouillot, 'Abortive

Rituals, Historical Apologies in the Global Era,' *Interventions* 2, no. 2 (2000): 171–86.

7. Objectivity in history and the relation between the past and history is a widely debated topic. For further discussion see, Thomas L. Haskell, *Objectivity is Not Neutrality: Explanatory Schemes in History*, Baltimore and London: Johns Hopkins University Press, 1998; Keith Jenkins, *On 'What is History?' From Carr and Elton to Rorty and White* (New York, 1995); Beverly Southgate, *History: What and Why? Ancient, Modern and Postmodern Perspectives* (London and New York, 1996) and Alun Munslow, *Deconstructing History* (London and New York, 1997). For a general overview of these different approaches to history see, Christopher Kent, 'Objectivity Is Not Neutrality: Explanatory Schemes in History' (book review), *Canadian Journal of History* (December 1999), p. 385.

8. Vamik Volkan, *The Need to Have Enemies and Allies* (Northvale, New Jersey, London, 1988), p. 261.

9. Joseph V. Montville, Foreword, in Volkan, p. xi.

10. Demetrious A. Julius, 'The Genesis and Perpetuation of Aggression in International Conflicts,' in Volkan, p. 101.

11. For more information see John Paul Lederach, *Building Peace: Sustainable Reconciliation in Divided Societies* (Washington, 1997), Chapters 3 and 4.

Select Bibliography

Primary Sources:
State and National Archives, Official Documents

Armenian Patriarchate of Jerusalem Archives.
Die Diplomatischen Akten des Auswärtigen Amtes/Botschaft Konstantinopel.
French Foreign Ministry Archives. *Turkey, Nouvelle Série.*
German Foreign Ministry Archives, Die Türkei.
Gooch, G. P. and Harold Temperley, eds. *British Documents on the Origins of the War, 1898–1914*, Vol. IX. London: HMSO, 1933.
Great Britain. Foreign Office Archives. London and Kew: Public Records Office.
Meclisi Mebusan Zabıta T. Ceridesi. Devre 1, İçtima Senesi 1. Vol. V. Ankara: Türkiye Büyük Millet Meclisi, n.d.
Meclis-i Mebusan Zabıt Ceridesi. Devre 3, İçitma Senesi 5. Vol. I. Ankara, 1992.
TBMM Gizli Celse Zabıtlari. Vols II and IV. Ankara. Türkiye İş Bankası, 1985.
Woodsward, W. and R. Butler, eds. *Documents on British Foreign Policy, 1919–1936.* Vol. 4, 1st Series. London, H.M.S.O., 1952.
Zentrales Staatsarchiv Potsdam, Auswärtiges Amt, I-C, 52364, Bursa, Bd. 1.

English

Ahmad, Feroz. *The Young Turks: The Committee of Union and Progress in Turkish Politics, 1908–1914.* Oxford: Oxford University Press, 1969.
Baumeister, Roy F. *Evil: Inside Human Cruelty and Violence.* New York: W. H. Freeman and Company, 1996.
Clogg, Richard. *A Concise History of Greece.* Cambridge: Cambridge University Press, 2002.
'Commission on the Responsibility of the Authors of the War and on Enforcement of Penalties. Report.' *American Journal of International Law* 4 (1920).
Dadrian, Vahakn N. 'The Naim–Andonian Documents on the World War I Destruction of Ottoman-Armenians: The Anatomy of a Genocide.' *International Journal of Middle East Studies* 18, no. 3 (1986): 311–60.

————. 'The Role of Turkish Physicians in the World War I Genocide of the Ottoman Armenians.' *Holocaust and Genocide Studies* 1, no. 3 (1986): 169–192.

Davison, Roderic H. *Reform in the Ottoman Empire 1856–76*. Princeton: N.J., Princeton University Press, 1963.

Edip, Halide. *Memoirs of Halide Edip*. London: The Century Co., 1926.

Galtung, Johan. 'After Violence, Reconstruction, Reconciliation, and Resolution: Coping with Visible and Invisible Effects of War and Violence.' In *Reconciliation, Justice, and Coexistence, Theory and Practice*, edited by Mohammed Abu-Nimer. Lanham, Boulder, New York, Oxford: Lexington Books, 2001, pp. 3–25.

Hanioğlu, Şükrü. *The Young Turks in Opposition*. Oxford: Oxford University Press, 1995.

Haskell, Thomas L. *Objectivity Is Not Neutrality: Explanatory Schemes in History*. Baltimore and London: Johns Hopkins University Press, 1998.

Helmreich, Paul C. *From Paris to Sèvres: The Partition of the Ottoman Empire at the Peace Conference of 1919–1920*. Columbus: Ohio State University Press, 1974.

History of the Peace Conference of Paris. Vol. 6. Edited by H. W. V. Temperley. London, New York, Toronto: Oxford University Press, 1969.

Hovannisian, Richard G. 'The Allies and Armenia, 1915–1918.' *Journal of Contemporary History* 3 (1968): 145–69.

Jenkins, Keith. *On 'What is History?' From Carr and Elton to Rorty and White*. London; New York: Routledge, 1995.

Kent, Christopher. 'Objectivity Is Not Neutrality: Explanatory Schemes in History.' *Canadian Journal of History* (December 1999).

Kushner, David. *The Rise of Turkish Nationalism, 1876–1908*. London and Totowa, NJ: Cass, 1977.

Landau, Jacob M. *Pan-Turkism in Turkey: A Study of Irredentism*. London and Hamden, Conn.: Archon Books, 1981.

Lederach, John Paul. *Building Peace: Sustainable Reconciliation in Divided Societies*. Washington, D.C.: U.S. Institute of Peace Press, 1997.

Lewis, Bernard. *The Emergence of Modern Turkey*, 2nd ed., Oxford: Oxford University Press, 1967.

Lloyd George, David. *Memoirs of the Peace Conference*. Vol. 2. New Haven, Yale University Press, 1939.

Luke, Harry. *The Making of Modern Turkey, from Byzantium to Angora*. London: Macmillan 1936.

Melson, Robert. *Revolution and Genocide*. Chicago and London: University of Chicago Press, 1996.

Morgenthau, Henry. *Ambassasor Morgenthau's Story*. New York: Doubleday and Page Co., 1919.

————. *Secrets of the Bosphorus, Constantinople 1913–1916*. London: Hutchinson & Co., 1918.

Mosse, George L. *The Crisis of German Ideology*. New York: Grosset & Dunlap, 1964.

Munslow, Alun. *Deconstructing History*. London; New York: Routledge, 1997.

Ramsaur, E. E. *The Young Turks: Prelude to the Revolution of 1908*. Princeton, NJ: Princeton University Press, 1957.

Shaw, Stanford and Ezel Kural Shaw. *History of the Ottoman Empire and Modern Turkey*. Vol. II. Cambridge: Cambridge University Press, 1977.

Şimşir, Bilal. *British Documents on Atatürk (1919–1938)*. 4 volumes. Ankara: Türk Tarih Kurumu, 1973.

Southgate, Beverly. *History: What and Why? Ancient, Modern and Postmodern Perspectives*. London, New York: Routledge, 1996.

Staub, Erwin. *The Psychology of Good and Evil: Why Children, Adults, and Groups Help and Harm Others*. Cambridge: Cambridge University Press, 2003.

———. *The Roots of Evil: The Origin of Genocide and Other Group Violence*. Cambridge: Press Syndicate of the University of Cambridge, 1992.

Tarihi Araştırmalar ve Dökümantasyon Merkezleri Kurma ve Geliştirme Vakfı. *Ottoman Archives, Yıldız Collection: The Armenian Question*. Vol. I. Istanbul, 1999.

Toynbee, Arnold. *The Western Question in Greece and Turkey*. New York: Howard Fertig, 1970.

Trouillot, Michel-Rolph. 'Abortive Rituals, Historical Apologies in the Global Era.' *Interventions* 2, no. 2 (2000): 171–86.

Volkan, Vamik. 'An Overview of Psychological Concept Pertinent to Interethnic and/or International Relationship.' In *The Psychodynamic of International Relationships: Concept and Theories*, edited by Vamik Volkan, Demetrios A. Julius, Joseph V. Montville. Lexington, Massachusetts/Toronto: Lexington Books/D.C. Heath, 1990.

———. *The Need to Have Enemies and Allies*. Northvale, New Jersey and London: J. Aronson, Inc., 1988.

Willis, James F. *Prologue to Nuremberg, The Politics and Diplomacy of Punishing War Criminals of the First World War*. London: Westport, Conn.: Greenwood Press, 1982.

French

Andonian, Aram. *Documents officiels concernant les massacres arméniens*. Paris: H. Turabian, 1920.

German

Adanir, Fikret. 'Die osmanische Geschichtschreibung zur Gründung des bulgarischen Staates.' *Südosteuropa Mitteilungen* 29, No. 2 (1989).

Adorno, Theodor W. 'Was bedeutet: Aufarbeitung der Vergangenheit.' *Gesammelte Schriften*. Vol. 10.2, Frankfurt a.M.: Suhrkamp, 1977.

Akçam, Taner. *Armenien und der Völkermord, die Istanbuler Prozesse und türkische National Bewegung*. Hamburg: Hamburger Edition, 1996.

Alp, Tekin. *Türkismus und Pantürkismus*. Weimar: G. Kiepenheuer, 1915.

Ankersmit, Frank R. 'Die postmoderne, Privatisierung' der Vergangenheit.' In *Der Sinn des Historischen, Geschichtsphilosophische Debatten,* edited by Herta Nagl-Docekal. Frankfurt a.m.: Fischer-Taschenbuch-Verl., 1996.

Baker, James. *Die Türken in Europa.* Stuttgart: Levy und Müller, 1879.

Benjamin, Walter. 'Vergangenheit als Prolog.' *Mittelweg* 36 (August/Sept., 1992).

Bibó, Istvan. *Die Deutsche Hysterie, Ursachen und Geschichte.* Frankfurt a.M. and Leipzig: Insel-Verlag, 1991.

Bihl, W.D. *Die Kaukasus-Politik der Mittelmaechte.* Vol. 1. Wien-Köln-Graz: Böhlaus, 1975.

Bresnitz, Philipp Franz. *Die Christenverfolgungen in der Türkei unter d. Sultan Abdul Hamid; Aufzeichnungen n. amtl. Quellen von Bresnitz v. Sydacott.* Berlin and Leipzig: F. Luckhardt, 1896.

Dickmann, Fritz. *Die Kriegschuldfrage auf der Friedenskonferenz von Paris 1919.* Munich: Oldenbourg, 1964.

Diner, Dan. 'Gedächtnis und Methode, über den Holocaust in der Geschichts-schreibung.' In *Auschwitz: Geschichte, Rezeption und Wirkung,* edited by Hanno Loewy, Frankfurt a.M.: Campus-Ver., 1996.

————. 'Die Wahl der Perspektive. Bedarf es einer besonderen Historik des Nationalsozialismus?' In *'Vernichtungspolitik', Eine Debatte über den Zusammenhang von Sozialpolitik und Genozid im nationalsozialistischen Deutschland,* edited by Wolfgang Schneider, Hamburg: Junius Verlag, 1991, pp. 65–75.

Elias, Norbert. *Engagement und Distanzierung, Arbeiten zur Wissensoziologie.* Frankfurt: Suhrkamp, 1983.

————. *Die Gesellschaft der Individuen.* Frankfurt: Suhrkamp, 1987.

————. 'Soziologie und Psychiatrie.' In *Soziologie und Psychoanalyse,* edited by Hans Ulrich Wehler, 11–42. Stuttgart, Berlin, Köln, Mainz: Kohlhammer, 1972.

————. *Studien über die Deutschen.* Frankfurt a.M.: Suhrkamp, 1990.

————. *Über den Prozess der Zivilisation.* 2 volumes, Frankfurt a.M.: Suhrkamp, 1997.

————. *Über sich selbst.* Frankfurt a.M.: Suhrkamp, 1990.

————. *Was ist Soziologie.* Munich: Juventa Verlag, 1981.

————. 'Zur Grundlage einer Theorie sozialer Prozesse,' *Zeitschrift für Soziologie* Vol. 6, no. 2 (1977).

Elias, Norbert, and Wolf Lepenies. *Zwei Reden anlässlich der Verleihung des Theodor W. Adorno-Preises.* Frankfurt a.M.: Suhrkamp, 1977.

Freud, Sigmund. *Gesammelte Werke, Band I: Die Abwehr-Neuropsychosen.* Frankfurt a.M.: S. Fisher, 1972.

————. *Totem und Tabu, Gesammelte Werke, Band IX.* Frankfurt a.M.: S. Fisher, 1972.

————. *Die Verdrängung, Gesammelte Werke, Band X.* Frankfurt a.M.: S. Fisher, 1972.

————. *Die Vorlesungen zur Einführung in die Psychoanalyse, Gesammelte Werke, Band XI.* Frankfurt a.M.: S. Fisher, 1972.

Frey, Waldemar. *Kût-El-Amâra, Kriegsfahrten und Erinnerungsbilder aus dem Orient.* Berlin: W. Bischoff, 1932.

Geiss, Immanuel. 'Massaker in der Weltgeschichte, Ein Versuch uber Grenzen der Menschlichkeit.' In *Die Schatten der Vergangenheit, Impulse zur Historisierung des Nationalsozialismus.* Edited by Uwe Backes, Eckard Jesse, and Rainer Zitelmann, Frankfurt a.M.: Propyläen, 1990.

Hahn, Alois and Herbert Willems. 'Schuld und Bekenntnis in Beichte und Therapie.' In *Religion und Kultur,* edited by Jörg Bergmann, Alois Hahn and Thomas Luckmann. Opladen: Westdt., 1993.

Hajek, Alois. *Bulgarien unter der Türkenherrschaft.* Stuttgart: Deutsche Verlags-Anstalt, 1925.

Halbwachs, Maurice. *Das Kollektive Gedächtnis.* Frankfurt a.M.: Fischer-Taschenbuch, 1991.

'Historikerstreit,' 'Die Dokumentation der Kontroverse um die Einzigartigkeit der nationalsozialistischen Judenvernichtung.' München; Zurich: Piper, 1987.

Hostler, Charles Warren. *Türken und Sowjets.* Frankfurt a.M., Berlin: Metzner, 1960.

Jacoby, Russell. *Soziale Amnesie, Eine Kritik der konformistischen Psychologie von Adler bis Laing.* Frankfurt a.M.: Suhrkamp, 1980.

Jäschke, Gotthard. 'Ein amerikanisches Mandat für die Türkei.' *Die Welt des Islams* [new series] 8 (1962–63): 219–35.

———. 'Beiträge zur Geschichte des Kampfes der Türkei um ihre Unabhängigkeit,' *Die Welt des Islams* [new series], Vol. V (1958): 1–64.

———. 'Mustafa Kemal und England in neuer Sicht.' *Die Welt des Islams* Vol. XVI (1975): 166–228.

———. 'Präsident Wilson als Schiedsrichter zwischen der Türkei und Armenien.' *Mitteilungen des Seminars für orientalische Sprachen zu Berlin,* no. 38, (1935).

———. *Die Turanismus der Jungtürken, Zur Osmanischen Aussenpolitik im Weltkriege.* Leipzig: Suhrkamp, 1941.

Jäschke, Gotthard and Erich Pritsch. *Die Turkei seit dem Weltkriege. Geschichtskalender 1918–1928.* Berlin: Dt. Ges. f. Islamkunde, 1929.

Kampen, Wilhelm van. *Studien zur Deutschen Türkeipolitik in der Zeit Wilhelms II.* Kiel: Dissertation, 1968.

Kassner, Karl. *Bulgarien, Land und Volk.* Leipzig: Verlag von Werner Kinkhardt, 1918.

Kershaw, Ian. *Der NS Staat, Geschichtsinterpretationen und Kontroversen im Überblick.* Hamburg: Rowohlt, 1994.

Lepsius, Johannes. *Der Todesgang des armenischen Volkes.* Potsdam: Tempelverlag, 1919.

Lévi-Strauss, Claude. *Das wilde Denken.* Frankfurt a.M.: Suhrkamp, 1968.

Mandelstam, André. *Das armenische Problem im Lichte des Völker und Menschenrechte.* Berlin: G. Stilke, 1931.

Mentzos, Stavros. *Hysterie, Zur Psychodynamik unbewusster Inszenierungen.* München: Kindler, 1980.

Murad Efendi. *Türkische Skizzen.* Vol. I. Leipzig: Dürr, 1877.

Ohandjanian, Artem. *Das Verschwiegene Völkermord.* Vienna: Bölau, 1989.

———., ed. *Österreich-Armenien 1872–1936. Faksimilesammlung diplomatischer

Aktenstücke. Vol. 6. Wien: Ohandjanianverlag, 1995.

Rasch, Gustav. *Die Türken in Europa.* Prague: Skrejsovsky, 1873.

Schluchter, Wolfgang. *Max Webers Sicht des Islam.* Frankfurt a.m.: Suhrkamp Verlag, 1987.

Schneider, Wolfgang, ed. '*Vernichtungspolitik': Eine Debatte über den Zusammenhang von Sozialpolitik und Genozid im nationalsozialistischen Deutschland.* Hamburg: Junius, 1991.

Schneckener, Ulrich. *Das Recht auf Selfstbestimmung, Ethno-nationale und internationale Politik.* Hamburg: Lit, 1996.

Schwan, Gesine. *Politik und Schuld, die zerstörische Macht des Schweigens.* Frankfurt a.m.: Fischer Taschenbuch, 1999.

Simpson, Christopher. 'Die seinerzeitige Diskussion über die in Nürnberg zu verhandelnden Delikte.' In *Strafgerichte gegen Menscheitsverbrechen*, edited by Gerd Hankel und Gerhard Stuby. Hamburg: Hamburger Edition, 1995, pp. 39–73.

Smith, Gary. 'Arbeit am Vergessen.' In *Vom Nutzen des Vergessens*, edited by Gary Smith and Hinderk M. Emrich. Berlin: Akademie, 1996.

Steinitz, Ritter v. *Zwei Jahrzehnte im Nahen Orient, Aufzeichnungen des Generals der Kavallerie Baron Wlademir Giesl.* Verlag für Kulturpolitik, 1927.

Sydacoff, Bresnitz von. *Abdul Hamid und die Christenverfolgung in der Türkei.* Berlin and Leipzig: Luckhardt, 1896.

Ternon, Yves. *Tabu Armenien.* Frankfurt a.M. and Berlin: Ulstein Sachbuch, 1988.

Trotha, Thilo von. *Zur historischen Entwicklung der Balkanfrage.* Berlin: Felix, 1897.

Wiesbaden, Karl Braun. *Eine türkische Reise.* Stuttgart: Auerbach, 1876.

Ziemke, Kurt. *Die neue Türkei.* Berlin: Deutsche Verlags-Anstalt, 1930.

Turkish

Newspapers

Akit [Istanbul]

Alemdar [Istanbul]

Cumhuriyet [Istanbul]

Hadisat [Istanbul]

Ikdam [Istanbul]

Radikal [Istanbul]

Renaissance [French-language newspaper published in Istanbul].

Tanin [Istanbul]

Tercümani Hakikat [Istanbul]

Vakit [Istanbul]

Yeni Gün [Istanbul]

Books and articles

Akçam, Taner. *Türk Ulusal Kimliği ve Ermeni Sorunu,* Istanbul: Dünya Yayınları, 1991.

————. *Siyasi Kültürümüzde Zulüm ve İşkence*. Istanbul: İletişim, 1991.

————. *İnsan Hakları ve Ermeni Sorunu, İttihat ve Terakkiden Kurtuluş Savaşına*. Ankara: İmge Kitabevi, 1999.

Akçura, Yusuf. *Üç Tarz-ı Siyaset*. Ankara: Türk Tarih Kurumu Basımevi, 1987.

————. *Türkçülük*. Istanbul: Türk Kültür Yayini, 1990.

————. *Yeni Türk Devletlerinin Öncüleri: 1928*. Ankara: Kültür Bakanlığı, 1981.

Akgün, Seçil. *General Harbord'un Anadolu Gezisi ve Ermeni Meselesine Dair Raporu*. Istanbul: Tercüman, 1981.

Akşin, Sina. *İstanbul Hükümetleri ve Milli Mücadele*. Istanbul: Cem Yayinevi, 1983.

————. *Jön Türkler ve İttihat ve Terakki*. Istanbul: Remzi Kitabevi, 1987.

Akyüz, Yahya. *Türk Kurtuluş Savaşı ve Fransız Kamuoyu, 1919–1921*. Ankara: Türk Tarih Kurumu, 1988.

Alkan, A. Turan. 'Osmanlı Tarihi: Bir "İnanç Alanı!"' *Türkiye Günlüğü*, no. 11 (Summer 1990): 7–8.

Alp, Tekin. *Türk Ruhu*, Istanbul: Remzi Kitabevi, 1944.

Arsen, İlhan. *Arap Milliyetçiliği ve Türkler*. Istanbul: Remzi Kitabevi, 1987.

Askeri Tarih Belgeleri Dergisi. Year 32 (March 2, 1983): 7, Document No: 1894.

Atatürk'ün Söylev ve Demeçleri. Vol. I–III. Ankara: Türk Tarih Kurumu, 1989.

Atay, F. R. *Çankaya, Atatürk'ün Doğumundan Ölümüne Kadar*. Istanbul: Dünya Yayınları, n.d. [1958].

Avcıoğlu, Doğan. *31 Mart'ta Yabancı Parmağı*. Ankara: Bilgi Yayınevi, 1969.

————. *Milli Kurtuluş Tarihi 1838'den 1995'e*. 4 volumes. Istanbul: Tekin Yayınevi, 1981.

————. *Türklerin Tarihi*. Vol. I. Istanbul: Tekin Yayınevi, 1979.

————. *Türkiye'nin Düzeni*. Vol. I. Ankara: Tekin Yayınevi, 1987.

Aydemir, Şevket Süreyya. *Makedonya'dan Ortaasya'ya Enver Paşa*, 2 volumes. Istanbul: Remzi Kitabevi, 1981.

Ayvalık Tarihi. Translated from Greek by Hıfzı Erim. Ankara: Güney Matbaacılık ve Gazetecilik, 1968.

Başbakanlık Devlet Arşivleri Genel Müdürlügü. *Osmanli Belgelerinde Ermeniler, 1915–1920*. Ankara, 1994.

Bayar, Celal. *Ben de Yazdım*. 8 volumes. Istanbul: Baha Matbaası, 1966.

Baykal, Bekir Sami. *Heyeti Temsiliye Kararları*. Ankara: Türk Tarih Kurumu, 1974.

Bayur, Yusuf Hikmet. *Türk İnkilap Tarihi*. Vol. II, part III and IV; Vol. III, part III,. Ankara: Türk Tarih Kurumu, 1983.

Berkes, Niyazi. *Türkiye'de Çağdaşlaşma*. Istanbul: Doğu-Batı Yayınları, 1978.

Birinci, Ali. *Hürriyet ve İtilaf Fırkası*. Istanbul: Dergah Yayınları, 1990.

Bozkurt, Gülnihâl. *Alman-İngiliz Belgelerinin ve Siyasi Gelişmelerin ışığı altında Gayrimüslim Osmanlı Vatandaşlarının Hukuki Durumu (1839–1914)*. Ankara: Türk Tarih Kurumu, 1989.

Cemal Paşa. *Hatıralar ve Vesikalar*. Istanbul: Vakit, n.d.

Cevdet Paşa, A. *Maruzat*. Istanbul: Çağrı, 1980.

————. *Tarih-i Cevdet, Osmanlı Tarihi*. Vol. 1. Istanbul: Üçdal Neşriyat 1993.

————. 'Tezâkir.' *Tezâkir*. Vol. 10. Türk Tarih Kurumu, 1986.

Daloğlu, Selahattin Turgay. *Ermeni Zulmü 1915–1918*. Istanbul: Dilara Yayınları, 1983.

Dumont, Paul. *Mustafa Kemal*. Ankara: Kültür Bakanlığı, 1993.

Duru, Kazım. *Ziya Gökalp*. Istanbul: Milli Eğitim Basımevi, 1949.

Ercan, Yavuz. *Osmanlı İmparatorluğunda Bazı Sorunlar Ve Günümüze Yansımaları*. Ankara: National Ministry of Education, Directorship of Educational Policy, 2002.

Ertürk, Hüsamettin. *İki Devrin Perde Arkası*. Edited by Samih Nafız Tansu. Istanbul: Pınar Yayınevi, 1964.

Esatlı, Mustafa Ragıp. *İttihat ve Terakki Tarihinde Esrar Perdesi*. Istanbul: Hür, 1975.

Georgeon, François. *Türk Milliyetçiliğinin Kökenleri: Yusuf Akçura (1876–1935)*. Ankara: Yurt Yayınları, 1986.

Gökalp, Ziya. *Türkçülüğün Esasları*. Istanbul: İnkilap ve Aka, 1978.

————. *Türkleşmek İslamlaşmak, Muasırlaşmak*. Istanbul: Toker Yayınları, 1988.

Goloğlu, M. *Milli Mücadele Tarihi*. Vol. V: *Türkiye Cumhuriyeti 1923*. Ankara: n. p., 1971.

Hanioğlu, Şükrü. *Bir Siyasal Örgüt Olarak Osmanlı İttihad ve Terakki Cemiyeti ve Jön Türklük*. Istanbul: İletişim Yayınları, 1985.

Heyd, Uriel. *Türk Ulusçuluğunun Temelleri*. Ankara: Kültür Bakanlığı, 1979.

Hükümet ve Programlar 2, 1920–1960. Vol. I. Edited by Nuran Dağlı and Belma Aktürk. Ankara: Türkiye Büyük Millet Meclisi, 1988.

İbrahim Temo'nun. *İttihad ve Terakki Anıları*. Istanbul: Arba Yayınları, 1987.

'İttihat ve Terakki 1916 Kongre Raporu.' *Tarih ve Toplum*, no. 33 (June 1986).

Jäschke, Gotthard. *Kurtuluş Savaşı ile İlgili İngiliz Belgeleri*. Ankara: Türk Tarih Kurumu, 1971.

Kadir, Hüseyin Kâzım. *Ziya Gökalp'in Tenkidi*. Edited by İsmail Kara. Istanbul: Dergah Yayınları, 1989.

Kafé, Esther 'Rönesans Dönemi Avrupa Gezi Yazılarında Türk Miti ve Bunun Çöküşü.' *Tarih İncelemeleri Dergisi, II* (1984).

Kara, İsmail. 'Bir Milliyetçilik Tartışması.' *Tarih ve Toplum* 30 (June 1986): 48–56.

Karabekir, Kazım. *İstiklal Harbimiz*. Istanbul: Türkiye Yayınevi, 1960.

Karal, Enver Ziya. *Osmanlı Tarihi*, 9 volumes. Ankara: Türk Tarih Kurumu 1988.

Karal, Enver Ziya. 'Gülhane Hattı Hümayununda Batının Etkisi.' *Belleten*, no. 112 (October, 1964).

Kemal, Mustafa. *Nutuk*. 3 volumes. Istanbul: Devlet Matbaası, 1934.

Kocabaş, Süleyman. *Ermeni Meselesi Nedir Ne Değildir*. Istanbul: Bayrak Yayıncılık, 1987.

Koçi Bey Risalesi. Translated into modern Turkish by Zuhuri Danışman. Ankara: Milli Eğitim Basimevi, 1972.

Koloğlu, Orhan. *Abdülhamit Gerçeği*. Istanbul: Gür Yayınları, 1987.

————. 'Enver Paşa Efsanesi'nde Alman Katkısı (1908–1913).' *Tarih ve Toplum*, no. 78 (June, 1990): 14–22.

Köprülü, Serif. *Sarikamiş, Ihata Manevrasi ve Meydan Muharebesi*. Istanbul, 1338 [1922].

Küçük, Yalçın. *Aydın Üzerine Tezler*. Vol. II. Istanbul: Tekin Yayınevi, 1985.

Külçe, Süleyman. *Osmanlı Tarihinde Arnavutluk*. Izmir: Ticaret Matbaası, 1944.

Kuntay, M.C. 'Namık Kemal.' *Devrinin İnsanları ve Olayları Arasında*. Vol. I. Ankara: Milli Eğitim Bakanlığı, 1949.

Kuran, Ahmet Bedevi. *Osmanlı İmparatorluğu'nda ve Türkiye Cumhuriyeti'nde İnkilap Hareketleri*. Istanbul: Çeltüt Matbaası, 1959.

Kurat, Akdes Nimet. *Türkiye ve Rusya*. Ankara: Kültür Bakanlığı, 1990.

Kutay, Cemal. *Birinci Dünya Harbinde Teşkilat-ı Mahsusa ve Heyber'de Türk Cengi*. Istanbul: Tarih Yayınları, 1962.

———. *Sohbetler*. No. 10. *Türkiye Nereye Gidiyor*.

Levent, Ağah Sırrı. *Türk Dilinde Gelişme ve Sadeleşme Evreleri*. Ankara: Türk Dil Kurumu, 1960.

Mardin, Şerif. *Jön Türklerin Siyasi Fikirleri*. Istanbul: İletişim Yayınları, 1983.

Meram, Ali Kemal. *Türkçülük ve Türkçülük Mücadeleleri Tarihi*. Istanbul: Kültür Kitabevi, 1969.

Meray, Seha L. and Osman Olcay. *Osmanlı İmparatorluğunun Çöküş Belgeleri*. Ankara: Siyasal Bilgiler Fakültesi, 1977.

Mil, A. 'Umumi Harpte Teşkilâtı Mahsusa.' *Vakit Gazetesi*, Tefrika No: 1, 2 Ikincitesrin [November] 1933.

Muharrem, Ergin. *Türkiye'nin Bugünkü Meseleleri*. Istanbul: Güryay Matbaacılık, 1975.

Mumcu, Ahmet. *Osmanlı Devletinde Siyaseten Katl*. Ankara: Birey ve Toplum Yayınları, 1985.

Nesimi, Abidin. *Yıllarin İçinden*. Istanbul: Gözlem, 1977.

Oran, Baskın. *Atatürk Milliyetciliği. Resmi İdeoloji Dışı Bir İnceleme*. Ankara, Bilgi Yayınları, 1988.

Ortaylı, İlber. *İmparatorluğun En Uzun Yüzyılı*. Istanbul: Hil Yayınları, 1983.

———. *Tanzimattan Cumhuriyete Yerel Yönetim Geleneği*. Istanbul: Hil Yayınları, 1985.

———. *Uluslararası Mithat Paşa Semineri, Bildiriler ve Tartışmalar [Edirne, 8–10 Mayıs, 1984]*. Ankara: Türk Tarih Kurumu, 1986, pp. 227–35.

Osmanlı Mebusan Meclisi Reisi Halil Menteşe'nin Anıları. Istanbul, 1986.

Özdağ, Muzaffer. 'Osmanlı Tarih ve Edebiyatında Türk Düşmanlığı.' *Tarih ve Toplum* 65 (May 1989): 9–16.

Özkök, Ertuğrul. 'Milli eylem stratejisi belgesi.' *Hürriyet* (Haziran 24, 1999).

Öztürk, Kazım. *Atatürk'ün TBMM Açık ve Gizli Oturumlarındaki Konuşmaları*, Vol. II. Ankara: Kültür Bakanlığı, 1992.

Petrosyan. Yuriy Aşatoviç *Sovyet Gözüyle Jön Türkler*. Ankara: Bilgi Yayınevi, 1974.

Ragip Bey. *Tarih-i Hayatim*. Ankara, 1996.

Rasim, Ahmet. *Osmanlı İmparatorluğu'nun Reform Çabaları İçinde Batış Evreleri*. Istanbul: Çağdaş Yayınları, 1987.

Sabis, Ali İhsan. *Harp Hatiralarim, Birinci Dünya Harbi*. 6 volumes. Istanbul:

Nehir Yayınları, 1990.

Sakarya, Emekli Tümgeneral İhsan. *Belgelerle Ermeni Sorunu*. Ankara: T.C. Genel Kurmay ATASE Yayınları, 1984.

Sarıhan, Zeki. *Kurtuluş Savaşı Günlüğü*. Vol. I. Ankara: Öğretmen Dünyası Yayınları, 1984.

Shaw, Stanford. 'Osmanlı İmparatorluğunda Azınlıklar Sorunu.' *Tanzimattan Cumhuriyete Türkiye Ansiklopedisi*. Vol. IV. 1985, pp. 1002–6.

Şimşir, Bilal. *Malta Sürgünleri*. Ankara: Bilgi Yayınevi, 1985.

———. *Rumeli'den Türk Göçleri, Belgeler*. 3 volumes. Ankara: Türk Tarih Kurumu, 1970.

Sonyel, Salâhi. 'İngiliz Belgelerine Göre Adana'da Vuku Bulan Türk-Ermeni Olayları (Temmuz 1908–Aralık 1909).' *Belletin* 51, no. 201 (December, 1987): 1241–89.

———. *Türk Kurtuluş Savaşı ve Dış Politika*. 2 volumes. Ankara: Türk Tarih Kurumu, 1986.

Sungu, İhsan. *Tanzimat ve Yeni Osmanlılar*. Vol. I: *Tanzimat*. Istanbul: Maarif Vekaleti, 1941.

Süslü, Azmi. *Ermeniler ve 1915 Tehcir Olayı*. Van: Yüzüncü Yüzyıl Üniversitesi Rektörlüğü, 1990.

TBMM Gizli Celse Zabıtları. Vol. IV. Ankara: Türkiye İş Bankası, 1985.

Taçalan, Nurdoğan. *Ege'de Kurtuluş Savaşı Başlarken*. Istanbul: Milliyet, 1970.

Takvîm-i Vekâyı [official gazette of the Turkish Military Tribunal].

Tanin, 30 Eylül, 1327 [October 13, 1911], no. 1118.

Tanpınar, Ahmet Hamdi. *Sahnenin Dışındakiler*. Istanbul: Büyük Kitaplık, 1973.

Timur, Taner. *Osmanlı Kimliği*. Istanbul: Hil Yayınları, 1986.

———. *Osmanlı-Türk Romanında Tarih, Toplum ve Kimlik*. Istanbul: Afa, 1991.

Toprak, Zafer. '1909 Cemiyetler Kanunu.' In *Tanzimat'tan Cuyhuriyet'e Türkiye Ansiklopedisi*. Vol. I. 1985, pp. 205–9.

———. 'II. Meşrutiyet Döneminde Paramiliter Gençlik Örgutleri.' *Tanzimat'tan Cumhuriyet'e Türkiye Ansiklopedisi*. Vol. II. Istanbul, 1985, pp. 531–7.

———. *Turkiye'de 'Milli İktisat' (1908–1918)*. Ankara: Yurt Yayınları, 1982.

Tunaya, Tarık Zafer. Türkiye'de Siyasi Partiler (1859–1952). Istanbul: Doğun Karde Yayınlari, 1952.

———. *Türkiye'de Batılılaşma Hareketleri*. Istanbul: Yedigün Matbaası, 1960.

———. *Türkiye'de Siyasal Partiler*. Istanbul: Hürriyet, 1989.

Tuncay, Mete. *Türkeye Cumhuriyetinde Tek Parti Yönetiminin Kurulması, 1923–1931*. Ankara: Yurt Yayınları, 1981.

Tuncer, Hüseyin. *Türk Yurdu Üzerine Bir İnceleme*. Ankara: Kültür Bakanlığı, 1990.

Turan, Şerafettin. *Türk Devrim Tarihi*. 3 volumes. Ankara: Bilgi Yayınevi, 1991.

Türkgeldi, Ali Fuat. *Görüp İşittiklerim*. Ankara: Türk Tarih Kurumu, 1987.

Türköne, Mümtaz'er. *Siyasi İdeoloji Olarak İslamcılığın Doğuşu*. Istanbul: İletişim Yayınları, 1991.

Ülken, Hilmi Ziya. *Türkiye'de Çağdaş Düşünce Tarihi*. Istanbul: Ülken Yayınları, 1992.

Yakın Tarihimiz. 4 volumes. Türk Petrol, 1962–63.

Yalçin, Hüseyin Cahit. *Siyasi Anilar.* Istanbul: Türkiye İş Bankası, 1976.

Yetkin, Çetin. *Türk Halk Hareketleri ve Devrimleri Tarihi.* Istanbul: Onur Basımevi, 1984.

Yüzbaşı Selahettin'in Romanı, I. Kitap. Edited by İlhan Selçuk. Istanbul: Remzi Kitabevi, 1973.

Index

265

Titles of Related Interest from Zed Books

Dietrich Jung with Wolfango Piccoli
Turkey at the Crossroads
Ottoman Legacies and a Greater
Middle East
ISBN   1 85649 866 2 hb
         1 85649 867 0 pb

Adam Jones (ed.)
Genocide, War Crimes & the West
History and Complicity

ISBN   1 84277 190 6 hb
         1 84277 191 4 pb

For full details of these books and Zed's subject and general catalogues. please write to:
The Marketing Department, Zed Books, 7 Cynthia Street, London N1 9JF, UK
or email sales@zedbooks.demon.co.uk
Visit our website at http://www.zedbooks.co.uk